MINES OF THE AMERICAN WEST
Lincoln County, Nevada

First Edition – Volume NV10
April, 2022

By Ivan Herring

A Publication of the Weekend Miner

Mines of the American West – Lincoln County, Nevada
First Edition, April, 2022, Volume NV10

Developed and Produced in the United States of America

MINES, GHOST TOWN AND LEGENDS OF THE AMERICAN WEST: These books are currently available in E-Book (Kindle) format, with a number of the books also being available in print form as paperbacks. Additional Hard Copy versions will be developed if demand warrants. The books area arranged below alphabetically by State and then by County, for ease in finding a book on a desired County, in a specific State:

ARIZONA
1.) Mines of the American West - Apache County, Arizona
   a. First Edition, April, 2015
2.) Mines of the American West - Cochise County, Arizona
   a. First Edition, August, 2014
3.) Mines of the American West - Coconino County, Arizona
   a. First Edition, July, 2012
4.) Mines of the American West - Gila County, Arizona
   a. First Edition, March, 2014
5.) Mines of the American West - Graham County, Arizona
   a. First Edition, October, 2014
6.) Mines of the American West - Greenlee County, Arizona
   a. First Edition, November, 2014
7.) Mines of the American West - La Paz County, Arizona
   a. First Edition, November, 2013
8.) Mines of the American West - Maricopa County, Arizona
   a. First Edition, February, 2012
9.) Mines of the American West - Mohave County, Arizona
   a. First Edition, June, 2012
10.) Mines of the American West - Navajo County, Arizona
   a. First Edition, May, 2015
11.) Mines of the American West - Pima County, Arizona
   a. First Edition, July, 2013
12.) Mines of the American West - Pinal County, Arizona
   a. First Edition, January, 2013
13.) Mines of the American West - Santa Cruz County, Arizona
   a. First Edition, January, 2015

14.) Mines, Ghost Towns and Legends of the American West - Yavapai County, Arizona
    a.   First Edition, October, 2011
15.) Mines of the American West - Yuma County
    a.   First Edition, August, 2013

CALIFORNIA
16.) Mines of the American West – Alameda County, California
    a.   Second Edition, March, 2021 (Also available in print form)
17.) Mines of the American West – Alpine County, California
    a.   First Edition – October, 2019
18.) Mines of the American West – Amador County, California
    a.   Second Edition, March, 2021 (Also available in print form)
19.) Mines of the American West – Butte County, California
    a.   Second Edition, May, 2021 (Also available in print form)
20.) Mines of the American West, Calaveras County, California
    a.   First Edition, January, 2012
21.) Mines of the American West – Colusa County, California
    a.   First Edition, August, 2019
22.) Mines of the American West – Contra Costa County, California
    a.   First Edition, March, 2020
23.) Mines of the American West, Del Norte County
    a.   First Edition, May, 2019
24.) Mines of the American West, El Dorado County, California
    a.   Second Edition, September, 2020 (Also available in print form)
25.) Mines of the American West – Fresno County, California
    a.   First Edition, December, 2019
26.) Mines of the American West – Glenn County, California
    a.   First Edition, September, 2019
27.) Mines of the American West, Humboldt County, California
    a.   First Edition, May, 2019
28.) Mines of the American West - Imperial County, California
    a.   First Edition, September, 2016 (Also available in print form)
29.) Mines of the American West –Inyo County, California
    a.   First Edition, July, 2019
30.) Mines of the American West - Kern County, California
    a.   First Edition, September, 2017 (Also available in print form)
31.) Mines of the American West - Kings County, California
    a.   First Edition, November, 2019
32.) Mines of the American West - Lake County, California
    a.   First Edition, September, 2019
33.) Mines of the American West – Lassen County, California
    a.   First Edition, June, 2019
34.) Mines of the American West - Los Angeles County, California
    a.   First Edition, July, 2015 (Also available in print form)
35.) Mines of the American West – Madera County, California
    a.   First Edition, December, 2019
36.) Mines of the American West – Marin County, California
    a.   First Edition, March, 2020
37.) Mines of the American West – Mariposa County, California
    a.   First Edition, December, 2019
38.) Mines of the American West – Mendocino County, California
    a.   First Edition, May, 2019
39.) Mines of the American West – Merced County
    a.   First Edition, December, 2019
40.) Mines of the American West – Modoc County, California
    a.   First Edition, June, 2019

41.) Mines of the American West – Mono County, California
     a.   First Edition, October, 2019
42.) Mines of the American West – Monterey County, California
     a.   First Edition, January, 2020
43.) Mines of the American West – Napa County, California
     a.   First Edition, March, 2020
44.) Mines of the American West - Nevada County, California
     a.   First Edition, May, 2019
45.) Mines of the American West - Orange County, California
     a.   First Edition, October, 2016 (Also available in print form)
46.) Mines of the American West - Placer County, California
     a.   First Edition, April, 2019
47.) Mines of the American West – Plumas County, California
     a.   First Edition, June, 2019
48.) Mines of the American West - Riverside County, California
     a.   Second Edition, November, 2020 (Also available in print form)
49.) Mines of the American West – Sacramento County, California
     a.   First Edition, November, 2019
50.) Mines of the American West – San Benito County, California
     a.   First Edition, January, 2020
51.) Mines of the American West – San Bernardino County, California
     a.   Second Edition, February, 2020
52.) Mines of the American West - San Diego County, California
     a.   First Edition, November, 2015 (Also available in print form)
53.) Mines of the American West – San Joaquin County, California
     a.   First Edition, March, 2020
54.) Mines of the American West – San Luis Obispo County, California
     a.   First Edition, September, 2019
55.) Mines of the American West - San Mateo and San Francisco, California
     a.   First Edition, June, 2015
56.) Mines of the American West – Santa Barbara County, California
     a.   First Edition, August, 2019
57.) Mines of the American West - Santa Clara County, California
     a.   Second Edition, December, 2020 (Also available in print form)
58.) Mines of the American West – Santa Cruz County, California
     a.   First Edition, January, 2020
59.) Mines of the American West – Shasta County, California
     a.   Second Edition, October, 2020 (Also available in print form)
60.) Mines of the American West – Sierra County, California
     a.   First Edition, September, 2019
61.) Mines of the American West, Siskiyou County, California
     a.   First Edition, May, 2019
62.) Mines of the American West – Solano, Sutter and Yolo Counties, California
     a.   First Edition, November, 2019
63.) Mines of the American West – Sonoma County, California
     a.   First Edition, March, 2020
64.) Mines of the American West – Stanislaus County, California
     a.   First Edition, January, 2020
65.) Mines of the American West – Tehama County, California
     a.   First Edition, June, 2019
66.) Mines of the American West – Trinity County, California
     a.   First Edition, May, 2019
67.) Mines of the American West – Tulare County, California
     a.   First Edition, November, 2019
68.) Mines of the American West – Tuolumne County, California
     a.   First Edition, September, 2019

69.) Mines of the American West – Yuba County, California
   a.   First Edition, September, 2019
70.) Mines of the American West, Ventura County, California
   a.   First Edition, April, 2016 (also available in print form)

NEVADA
71.) Mines of the American West – Clark County, Nevada
   a.   First Edition, May, 2020
72.) Mines of the American West – Churchill County, Nevada
   a.   First Edition, August, 2020
73.) Mines of the American West – Elko County, Nevada
   a.   First Edition, August, 2021 (also available in print form)
74.) Mines of the American West – Esmeralda County, Nevada
   a.   First Edition, March, 2020
75.) Mines, Ghost Towns and Legends of the American West, Eureka County, Nevada
   a.   First Edition, September 2011
76.) Mines of the American West – Humboldt County, Nevada
   a.   First Edition, June, 2019
77.) Mines of the American West – Lander County, Nevada
   a.   First Edition, July, 2019
78.) Mines of the American West – Lincoln County
   a.   First Edition, April, 2022 (Also available in print form)
79.) Mines of the American West – Mineral County, Nevada
   a.   First Edition, April, 2020
80.) Mines, Ghost Towns and Legends of the American West, Nye County, Nevada
   a.   First Edition, September, 2011
81.) Mines of the American West – Pershing County, Nevada
   a.   First Edition, July, 2020
82.) Mines of the American West – Washoe County, Nevada
   a.   First Edition, July, 2019
83.) Mines of the American West – White Pine County, Nevada
   a.   First Edition – July, 2021 (also available in print form)

UTAH
84.) Mines of the American West - Millard County, Utah
   a.   First Edition, March, 2012

LOST MINES AND TREASURE TALES series: This series of books is based on newspaper interviews, articles and stories from as early as the 1600's to the mid-Twentieth Century timeframe. The theory was, get the earliest possible information on these "lost mine and lost treasure" stories, before time has had a chance to "massage" the facts. Based on feedback, I will try to develop this series to include a separate book for each State in the United States, or region, if I cannot find sufficient data to do individual States. Books to date, available on Amazon, include:
   1.)   Lost Mines and Treasure Tales of Oregon and Washington (also available in paperback)
      a.   First Edition, April 2019,
   2.)   Lost Mines and Treasure Tales of Idaho and Montana (also available in paperback)
      a.   First Edition, April, 2019,
   3.)   Lost Mines and Treasure Tales of the Middle Mountain States (also available in paperback)
      a.   First Edition, April, 2019,
   4.)   Lost Mines and Treasure Tales of Northern California (also available in paperback)
      a.   Third Edition, March, 2019,
   5.)   Lost Mines and Treasure Tales of Central California (also available in paperback)
      a.   Third Edition, March, 2019,
   6.)   Lost Mines and Treasure Tales of Southern California (also available in paperback)
      a.   Third Edition, March, 2019,
   7.)   Lost Mines and Treasure Tales of Eastern Arizona (also available in paperback)

a.   Second Edition, February, 2019,
8.) Lost Mines and Treasure Tales of Western Arizona (also available in paperback)
a.   Second Edition, February, 2019,
9.) Lost Mines and Treasure Tales of Colorado and New Mexico (also available in paperback)
a.   First Edition, November, 2018,
10.) Lost Mines and Treasure Tales of the Great Plains (also available in paperback)
a.   First Edition, November, 2018,
11.) Lost Mines and Treasure Tales of the Lower Mississippi (also available in paperback)
a.   Second Edition, October, 2018,
12.) Lost Mines and Treasure Tales of Oklahoma and Texas (also available in paperback)
a.   First Edition, October, 2018,
13.) Lost Mines and Treasure Tales of the Southeastern United States (also available in paperback)
a.   First Edition, June, 2018,
14.) Lost Mines and Treasure Tales of the Appalachian States (also available in paperback)
a.   First Edition, June, 2018,
15.) Lost Mines and Treasure Tales of the Middle Atlantic States (also available in paperback)
a.   Second Edition, May, 2018,
16.) Lost Mines and Treasure Tales of New England (also available in paperback)
a.   First Edition, May, 2018,
17.) Lost Mines and Treasure Tales of The Great Lakes States (also available as a paperback)
a.   Second Edition, June 2018,
18.) Lost Mines and Treasure Tales of California
a.   First Edition, May, 2015, (Out of Print)
b.   Second Edition, November , 2017, Second Edition (Also available as a paperback)
19.) Lost Mines and Treasure Tales of Arizona
a.   First Edition, January 2015
20.) Lost Mines and Treasure Tales of Western North America
a.   First Edition, January, 2014
21.) The Lost Adams Mine
a.   First Edition, January, 2014

RICHES BENEATH YOUR FEET Series: These books focus on unusual, even comical – but effective (i.e. "Prospecting With Chickens and Ducks" as *Atypical Exploration Processes*) ways of finding precious metals and stones and/or are focused on individual minerals and/or mineral groups. They are currently available in E-Book (Kindle) format. Hard Copy versions will be developed if demand warrants:
1.) Atypical Exploration Processes (Unusual ways of finding and recovering precious metals)
a.   First Edition, June, 2018 (Also available as a paperback)
2.) The Potential for Platinum Group Metals in California
a.   First Edition, January, 2012

MUSINGS FROM THE FRONTIER series: This series of books is a compilation of interesting stories that I found while doing research for the Mines, Ghost Towns and Legends of the American West. The stories reflect another, simpler time in American History and often reflect values and attitudes that society today seems to have forgotten.
1.) More Musings From the Frontier
a.   First Edition, December, 2013
2.) Musings from the Frontier
a.   First Edition, March, 2013

GOOD GUYS, BAD GUYS AND MAYBES series: This series of books is also based on newspaper interviews, articles and stories from the 1850-1920 timeframe. The theory was, get the earliest possible information on these stories, before time has had a chance to "massage" the facts. Books to date include:
1.) Roy Gardner – Train Robber, Escaped Convict, "Nice Guy"
a.   First Edition, January, 2015

JONATHAN FISHER series (Fiction): The Jonathan Fisher series depicts a US Intelligence Operative, who, under the cover of being a large international buyer of raw materials, engages in various assignments in the field of intelligence gathering. This series is intended to be "realistic" in its approach; no big car chases or extended shootouts. In the real world those invariably end with the elimination of the Agent and another "Line Out" in the books of the National Security Agency. In keeping with the directive "Every day we are not in the newspapers is a day we win", Jonathan's approach is as low-key possible, although at times he may attain unwanted notoriety. Jonathan is a "small-town boy" from a modest background who is student of history, culture and geography. A bit of a "Renaissance Man", his diverse educational background and wide range of experiences serve him well in surviving the trials he faces. As such, many of the locations are viewed from their historical and cultural as well as economic and political significance. The data targets assigned sometimes may seem a bit mundane, but in aggregate they contribute significantly to our Country's better understanding of the intent and capabilities of our enemies, friends and neutrals.

    1.) Bubble Memory
        a.   First Edition, December 7, 2015 (also available in print form)

PRACTICAL EVANGELIZATION is a deviation in subject matter from most of my other books. It was put together out of a desire to help answer the concern; "Our Church wants us to evangelize, but they don't tell us how to do it!" I have heard this comment on a regular basis, not only in my own Church and hometown, but from members of other Churches in areas I have traveled to. This book, *Practical Evangelization*, is an attempt to offer ideas that might constitute at least a partial answer to the question. Some of these ideas and approaches have been developed in our Church, some have been developed in other Churches that I have found or come in contact with, and others are ideas and approaches which are yet to be fully developed. The goal of the book is to give at least one idea, and hopefully more than one, that your Church, religious or Church-affiliated organization might be able to use in an evangelization program. In the words of one of my favorite Catholic Fathers, and great source of fatherly advice, "If you can reach just one, you have been successful".

    1.) Practical Evangelization
        a.   First Edition, June 26, 2020 (also available in print form)

DEDICATION:

This book is dedicated to all of you "weekend miners", rockhounds, metal detector enthusiasts and outdoors men and women, who find this industry and related hobbies fun and rewarding. It is also dedicated, with all my love and devotion, to my wonderful wife Ana Minerva. She has stood by me in the most difficult of times; through the stress of the corporate world, my ongoing fight with cancer, a quadruple by-pass heart operation and in raising my teen-aged daughter, as a stepdaughter. For those of you who may have been through any or all of these situations, the latter may be the most trying. She has handled all of the associated frustration and pain admirably and with great compassion, while still finding the time and strength to be a friend and partner to me. For these things I can never repay her, I can only express my appreciation.

PREFACE:

This book is part of a desire to see our country remain the wonderful place it was for me to grow up and live in; for it to remain that way long after I am gone, to the benefit of my daughter, my nieces, my nephews and all of the other young people whose future lies in a strong America. Our future generations are, and will continue to be, constantly assailed, both physically and in the media, by our country's "failings". These "failings" are usually expressed in the media by those seeking to transfer our lifestyle to themselves and by those seeking to acquire the "American Lifestyle" without having to work or sacrifice to earn it. We and our children will continue to be engaged in the "economic war" that exists between countries, each seeking to maximize the benefits of scarce resources for their own people, to the disadvantage of others.

Today, one of the great weaknesses of the United States is its reliance for survival on foreign sources of raw materials. In some, if not many cases, this reliance is 100%. This puts not only our economic survival, but our very survival as a nation, at risk. Everyone is aware (or should be by now) of the problems we had with oil and how we overcame them with "fracking". However, not everyone knows about our 100% reliance on import for Indium, critical to the production of flat-panel displays and a by-product of Zinc production; Gadolinium, used as tracing element in medicine (MRIs) and key to the new technology of magnetic refrigeration; or near-total reliance on imports of Platinum, the key element in automotive fuel cells and the politically-touted "Hydrogen-Based Economy". Much of the material upon which we have built the defense of our nation and our economic base, such as Rare Earths, now has to be imported from uncaring, if not unfriendly countries. We have these minerals in our country, possibly in great quantity, but have not been able to, or worse, chosen not to, locate and develop them as sources of supply.

It is hoped that this book will increase the interest in minerals, small-scale mining and the need our country has for the fruits of these efforts. It is further hoped that this book will be of assistance to small miners and prospectors, rockhounds and metal detector enthusiasts, and others in finding new mines and mineral deposits, while rediscovering others. And that it might help lead to a better understanding of the way our daily needs are met – "Remember if you can't grow the raw material it had to be mined".

PROLOGUE:

This book was originally developed as an attempt to consolidate as much data as possible, on a county basis, regarding mines and mineral deposits. It was not and still is not an attempt to create an "Authoritative Study" on any of the individual mines but is intended to be a tool to help the reader in making a general review of the County and identifying features and/or areas that he or she may want to investigate further.

I have added, where I could, the GPS coordinates of the mines, which has led to another benefit – a form of prospecting from your computer. Using such services allows the Reader to zoom in on a location where the mine or feature is reported to have been and see what is there and what the surrounding area is like. Using this approach, I have been able to identify mines, ghost towns, buildings and other features that are helpful in planning a physical visit. To maximize the benefit of such physical visits I have also listed many of the mines under each Mining District. This allows the Reader to improve the efficiency of each visit, by visiting not only the "targeted location", but of also having the option of including nearby mines or features in such visits.

These Reference Files, and the data contained within them, are offered for general information purposes only. Data has been obtained from US Government, primarily USGS, and other sources generally thought to be reliable. If you find errors, let me know and I will correct them in the next edition. I will admit have become increasingly concerned with the quality of the USGS data, as going back and cross-checking coordinates I have found many errors, where entries covering the same property have coordinates points up to 70 miles apart. I have tried to get an explanation from the USGS, but so far, the best I have is that "there were some issues with the data conversion". I did not find any such explanation or disclaimer in the data files, even those on line, warning that some of the data may be inaccurate. Because of this, please use the USGS data, cautiously, especially the coordinates. If you find errors and can give me the correct data based on your verified coordinates, please let me know and I will update the entry in the next edition.

The listing of a location does not indicate access to such site or that sites are freely available to the public. Do not attempt to visit any site, included in the listing or otherwise, without permission of the owner. If you get the appropriate permissions and do visit a site, included in the listing or otherwise, be sure you know the safety protocol for that site and have the appropriate skills and equipment for the activities you will undertake. When leaving a site, please clean up after yourself and return it to a "better than found condition". But, most of all, "Be careful out there", we want you back!

<u>100 Foot Incline (a.k.a. 100 Foot Inclined Shaft; Our Boys In Blue Claims; NBMG Sample Sites 1743, 1744)</u>: (37.30.46N by -114.47.10W - #3) (Gold, Copper, Silver)
Coordinates are for the ore body of this underground operation.
USGS MRDS Data Base Record 10037392, Released November 1, 1979; Updated August 1, 1984: The site of the 100 Foot Inclined Shaft is shown at 37.51275N by -114.78695W, placing it about 1 mile North of Monkey Wrench Wash, in the Delamar Mining District, in the Ferguson Mining District and in the area included on the USGS Pahroc Spring SE 24K and Caliente 100K and 250K maps. The Public Land Survey System locators are Section 14, Township 5 South, Range 64 East. This record shows Gold, Silver and Copper present, with a gangue of Quartz, and all are shown as primary commodities, even though many sources do not show any Copper present. Mineralization is hosted in Early Cambrian Quartzite with Copper heavily staining the shear zones near the top of the Prospect Mountain Quartzite. The ore deposit is described as having a prominent, resistant, Silicified Vein outcrop about 3 feet high, 7 feet in length and 2 to 3 feet wide, which is composed of Iron and Manganese-stained, Silicified Quartzite cut by a network of Quartz Veins. It is difficult to distinguish the Quartzite from the Quartz Veins as the Quartzite is Silicified and Opalized and the Quartz Vein is very finely crystalline and sugary to massive. The rib strikes North 55° West (the ore body in general strikes North 30° to 55° West) and dips from 60° Southwest to vertically. Portions of the Vein are Brecciated and indicate emplacement along a fault. The deposit is in Quartzite, but brown, "marly," recrystallized Limestone is exposed in a small prospect pit North of the shaft. Limonitic and Manganese-rich Gossan was sampled from the dump. Gossan is heavily Siliceous and "earthy" and contains some boxworks and Opaline coatings. Pink, fine-grained Quartzite contains numerous drusy Quartz-lined vugs and Siliceous Veinlets deposited within fractures with a very fine-grained, Oxidized Pyrite. The geology, in the general area of the site, is described as Limestone and Dolomite with locally-thick sequences of Shale and Siltstone. The deposit was developed by one small shaft sunk on a Southern extension of the Vein outcrop and one prospect pit 25 feet North of the shaft. There was no activity at the site when it was visited in 1983. The Land Status, Ownership Category of this occurrence is shown as "Private".
See the NBMG Sample Sites 1743, 1744 entry for more information.
USGS MRDS Data Base Record 10222263, Released November 14, 1983: The main entrance to the 100-Foot Inclined Shaft is shown at 37.51277N by -114.78694W, placing it in the Delamar Mining District and in the Ferguson Mining District. The location accuracy, of these coordinates, is shown as +/- 10 meters. The Public Land Survey System locators are the Northeast ¼ of the Northeast ¼ of the Southwest ¼ of Section 14, Township 5 South, Range 64 East. Copper (only) is shown present and is shown as a primary commodity. The geology, in the area of the main entrance, is described as Limestone and Dolomite with locally-thick sequences of Shale and Siltstone. The Land Status, Ownership Category of this underground prospect is unknown.

<u>Abe Lincoln Mine</u>: (37.55.44N by -114.29.00W - #3) (Lead, Silver, Gold, Zinc, Manganese, Iron)
Coordinates are for the main entrance to this underground, past producer.
USGS MRDS Data Base Record 10046394, Released April 1, 1984: The site of the Abe Lincoln Mine is shown at 37.92885N by -114.48417W, placing it about 1½ mile West of Pioche, in the Pioche Mining District and in the area included on the USGS Pioche 24K and Caliente 100K and 250K maps. The Public Land Survey System locators are the Southeast ¼ of Section 20, Township 1 North, Range 67 East. Lead and Silver are present and are shown as primary commodities with Gold, Zinc, Manganese and Iron secondary. Mineralization includes Anglesite, Sphalerite and various Iron minerals with a gangue of Limonite and Quartz, in a host of Chisholm Shale Formation Limestone, associated with a Late Cambrian welded Tuff. The ore body is Tubular, about 3 feet thick and lies nearly flat. The Vein occurs at the base of a 3-foot Limestone body which has been largely replaced by Manganese and Iron Oxide ore. A fault, trending North 30° West, cuts off the Vein on the East. The deposit was developed by adit tunnels. The geology, in the general area of the site, is described as Limestone and Dolomite with locally-thick sequences of Shale and Siltstone. The Land Status, Ownership Category of this past producer, discovered in 1867 and put into production in 1885, is shown as "Private".
USGS MRDS Data Base Record 10198503, Released January 12, 1994: The main entrance to the Abe Lincoln Mine is shown at 37.92886N by -114.48414W, placing it in the Pioche Mining District. The location accuracy, of these coordinates, is shown as +/- 10 meters. The Public Land Survey System locators

are the Southeast ¼ of the Northeast ¼ of the Southeast ¼ of Section 20, Township 1 North, Range 67 East. Lead is shown as present and as a primary commodity with Gold, Silver and Zinc tertiary. The geology, in the area of the main entrance, is described as Limestone and Dolomite with locally thick sequences of Shale and Siltstone. The Land Status, Ownership Category of this underground, past producer is shown as "Private".

Acme Mines: (37.54.35N by -114.24.50W - #3) (Lead, Zinc)
Coordinates are for trenching associated with this past producer.

Acoma Mining District: (Perlite)
Description of the District:
Tingley, Joseph V.; "Mining Districts of Nevada"; Nevada Bureau of Mines and Geology, Report 47, Second Edition; 1998; Page 13: The Acoma Mining District is a Perlite Mining District, primarily in Clover Valley. The District extends for about 30 miles along the Union Pacific Railroad right-of-way from the village of Eccles (37.36.55N by -114.25.54W – USGS MRDS Eccles 24K map) to Crestline, in White Pine County (37.39.49N by -114.07.34W – USGS MRDS Dow Mountain 24K). Identifying Crestline is fairly easy as the White Pine County Landfill is along the tracks there.
Mines Included in the District:

Acoma Perlite: (37.30.12N by -114.08.36W - #3) (Perlite)
Coordinates are for the ore body of this prospect.

AD Prospect (a.k.a. Ad; Ad Mine; Jerry Claims; MDM Claims; Schwartz Tunnel; Swartz Canyon Head Tactite): (38.37.32N by -114.43.40W - #3) (Tungsten, Zinc, Gold, Silver, Molybdenum, Lead, Fluorite)
Coordinates are for the man entrance to this underground, exploration prospect.
USGS MRDS Data Base Record 10246799, Released April 28, 1994: The main entrance to the AD Prospect is shown at 38.62555N by -114.72865W, placing it in the Patterson Mining District and in the area included on the USGS Mount Grafton 24K, Garrison 100K and Lund 250K maps. The location accuracy, of these coordinates, is shown as +/- 100 meters. The Public Land Survey System locators are the Northwest ¼ of Section 19, Township 9 North, Range 65 East. Tungsten is present and is shown as a primary commodity with Zinc, Gold, Silver, Lead, Copper, Molybdenum and Fluorite tertiary. The geology, in the area of the main entrance, is described as Quartzite and minor amounts of Conglomerate, Phyllitic Siltstone, Limestone and Dolomite. The Land Status, Ownership Category of this underground prospect is shown as "BLM Administrative Area".
See the Schwartz Tunnel entry for more information.

Advance (a.k.a. Advance Claim; Advance Mine; Gold Stake Claim; Old Democrat Claim):
(37.41.15N by -114.30.25W - #3) (Gold, Silver, Lead, Copper, Arsenic)
Coordinates are for the ore body of this surface-underground, past producer.
USGS MRDS Data Base Record 10037350, Released February 1, 1980; Updated August 1, 1984: The site of the Advance is shown at 37.69164N by -114.51473W, placing it about 70 miles North of Alamo, in Cobalt Canyon on a North-facing slope, in the Chief Mining District and in the area included on the USGS Chief Mountain 24K and Caliente 100K and 250K maps. The Public Land Survey System locators are Section 18, Township 3 South, Range 67 East. Gold and Silver are present and are shown as primary commodities with Lead secondary and Copper and Arsenic tertiary. Mineralization includes Beudanite [$PbFe_3(OH)_6SO_4AsO_4$], Descloizite [$(Pb.Zn)_2VO_4OH$], Mimetite [$Pb_5(AsO_4)_3Cl$] and the Iron Jarosite [$KFe_3(SO_4)_2(OH)_6$] in a host of Late Cambrian Quartzite. The ore body is a group of Tabular Veins, open to the surface, that strike from North 10° East to North 5° West, although a few strike out to North 30° East to North 30° West. The dip of these Veins, which pinch and swell, is generally 25° to 45° East. They tend to be up to 4 feet wide, up to 40 feet in length and ore deposition is controlled by the Quartzite Brecciation. The mine was developed by 2 levels, two adits, 2 winzes and several pits. Most of the ore came from the upper adit stope which extended from the upper level, 45 feet to the surface. By 1983 there were several open, South-Southwest-trending adits on the North-facing slope, one shaft and several large dumps along with the two original adits and several pits. The geology, in the general area of the site, is described as Quartzite and minor amounts of Conglomerate, Phyllitic Siltstone, Limestone and Dolomite. The Land

Status, Ownership Category of this past producer, discovered in 1892, by Henry W. Lawrence and Patrick Sheahan, is shown as "BLM Administrative Area". A 1909 record shows the Owner as Advance Mining Company.

Notes to the file contained a detailed description of the ore body. "The ore shoot, composed of several North-South Veins at a fracture intersection, is about 40 feet long, 3½ feet wide and strikes from North 30° West to North 30° East. Mineralization occurs in gouge material. At the upper adit, the host rock is orange, weathered Quartzite or Silty Sandstone which forms beds from 6 inches to 2 feet thick. These strike North 10° West and dip 35° East. The rock on the dump is a slightly laminated, vitreous gray Quartzite, which shows some Calcite and Quartzite Veining. The rocks are Silicified, recrystallized and contain some Sericite in the matrix. In general, the Quartzite is covered with abundant Iron Oxides and yellow and green Oxides of perhaps Arsenic, Lead, Iron or some other mineral. The altered Quartzite contains Iron-stained Quartz and Calcite-filled vugs. Adits line up along the North-to-Northeast-trending Vein systems which apparently follow the bedding of the host rocks. The bedding plane fractures were apparently the main structural control for Vein emplacement as not much Breccia was observed. (This appears to contradict the summarized report which indicates the Brecciated Quartzite to be the primary ore deposition control.) A group of 11 assays made in 1932 returned the following data: 0.3 to 1.9 ounces of Gold and 0.5 to 5.7 ounces of Silver per ton; 0 to 1.5% Lead, an average of 20.4% Iron, 8.6% Sulfur, 0.8% Lime and 42.5% soluble materials. A sample, labeled 125, taken in 1984, gave 7,000 Parts Per Million (PPM) Lead, 2,000PPM Strontium, 500PPM Antimony, 500PPM Boron, 300PPM Zirconium, 200PPM Barite, 200PPM Zinc, 100PPM Copper, 50PPM Bismuth, 50PPM Molybdenum, and 15PPM Silver."

USGS MRDS Data Base Record 10222650, Released January 12, 1994: The main entrance to the Advance Mine is shown at 37.69027N by -114.52084W, placing it in the Chief Mining District. The location accuracy, of these coordinates, is shown as +/- 10 meters. The Public Land Survey System locators are the Center of the Northeast ¼ of Section 18, Township 3 South, Range 67 East. Gold is present and is shown as a primary commodity with Silver, Lead and Copper tertiary. The geology, in the area of the main entrance, is described as Quartzite and minor amounts of Conglomerate, Phyllitic Siltstone, Limestone and Dolomite. The Land Status, Ownership Category of this surface-underground, past producer is shown as "Private". Mineral Rights are held through "Patented, Located Claims". A 1936 Record shows the Owner-Operator as the Caliente Cobalt Mining Company of Nevada.
See the Gold Stake Claim and the Old Democrat Claim entries for more information.

Agricultural Minerals Plant: (37.54.11N by -114.28.22W - #3) (Stone)
Coordinates are for an ore body and processing plant.

Alamo Services Pit and Mill: (37.32.30N by -115.08.54W - #3) (Sand & Gravel)
Coordinates are for the deposit area of this surface past producer.

Alliance Mine: (37.56.13N by -114.29.12W - #3)
Coordinates are for the ore body of this underground, past producer.
See the Chisholm entry for more information.

Alps (a.k.a. Alps Mine; Alps Shaft): (37.55.08N by -114.25.50W - #3) (Gold, Silver, Lead, Zinc, Copper, Antimony)
Coordinates are for the ore body of this underground, past producer.
USGS MRDS Data Base Record 10037328, Released October 1, 1979; Updated September 1, 1984; Updated February 1, 1993: The site of the Alps Mine, one of the oldest mines in the District, is shown at 37.91579N by -114.43001W, placing it about 1½ miles South of Pioche on Caliente Road, just North of the Wide Awake Mine, in the Pioche Mining District, in the Ely Mining District and in the area included on the USGS Pioche 24K and Caliente 100K and 250K maps. The Public Land Survey System locators are Section 26, Township 1 North, Range 67 East. Gold, Silver, Lead, Zinc, Copper and Antimony are present and are shown as primary commodities. Mineralization includes an unusually high Gold content for Pioche ore, running up to 4 ounces per ton, and Galena with a gangue of Quartz, Pyrite and Jarosite. This Polymetallic Vein Deposit (USGS Model Code 85) is hosted in Granite and Quartzite of the Yuba Dike/Prospect Mountain Quartzite Formation, associated with Early Cambrian Shale. The ore body is described as a Tabular Vein striking North 80° East, dipping 70° South, up to 7 feet thick and controlled by faulting and Brecciation, which appears to have occurred due to an extension of the Yuba Dike intersecting

with a cross-fissure. The ore occurs in a fissure Vein and the Brecciated Zones of Lead Carbonate in a Quartz Gangue, which is usually white. The main Vein is 1 to 4 feet thick and, at depth, terminates against the Shale. The host rocks are white to grey, banded Quartzite which dips Southwest up to 40° and Phyllitic Shales. The Granite Porphyry, Yuba Dike, which is about 40 feet wide in the area, dips 70° South. The mine was developed by a 300-foot, 2-compartment shaft, with crosscuts at the 150, 200 and 300-foot levels. All production was from above the 300-foot level, as the Vein terminated in the Shale at that depth. However, with further exploration, the downward extension of the Vein may be discovered as the Vein had been dislocated by movement along the contact between the Shale and Quartzite. The development also included 3 other, shallower shafts, surface cuts, trenches and small open pits. Stopes also followed the North 30° West Rangefront Fault. The geology, in the general area of the site, is described as Quartzite and minor amounts of Conglomerate, Phyllitic Siltstone, Limestone and Dolomite. Discovered in 1870 and put into production in 1871, the Land Status, Ownership Category of this past producer is shown as "Private". A 1932 record shows the Owner as Alps Mining Company. The Alps Mining Company also owned the old Floral Mill; however, at the time of the review in 1983 there was no activity at the mill. There was indication, however, that the tailings had been milled recently and one of the shallower shafts was being used as a landfill.

USGS MRDS Data Base Record 10173595, Released November 14, 1983: The main entrance to the Alps Shaft is shown at 37.91826N by -114.43114W, placing it in the Pioche Mining District. The location accuracy, of these coordinates, is shown as +/- 10 meters. The Public Land Survey System locators are the Western ½ of the Southwest ¼ of the Northwest ¼ of Section 26, Township 1 North, Range 67 East. Silver is present and is shown as a primary commodity with Lead tertiary. The geology, in the area of the main entrance is described as Quartzite and minor amounts of Conglomerate, Phyllitic Siltstone, Limestone and Dolomite. The Land Status, Ownership Category of this underground, past producer is shown as "BLM Administrative District".

Annual Mining Review and Stock Ledger, 1876, San Francisco, Published by Verdenal, Harrison, Murphy & Company; Page 35: "The mine has been prospected to the third level during the last year with good success, the bullion extracted more than paying the expenses incurred in this detection. The amount of bullion extracted up to May, 1876, was $210,574.10, of which $102,574.40 was shipped from May, 1875, to February, 1876, inclusive. The amount of $37,500 has been distributed in dividends.

The Company has a fifteen-stamp, dry-crushing mill, with rock breaker, self-feeders, assay works; a complete mill, second to none in the State, is working to 90 per cent and above of pulp assay. The machinery alone cost $35,000. The Company has employed twenty men constantly and their payroll now amounts to nearly $6,000 per month."

Andies Mine (a.k.a. Mayday and Shendell Claims; MDDS 1-15 Claims; NBMG Sample Site 1467; Wm and Uc Fractions): (37.33.35N by -115.44.31W - #3) (Mercury, Barite)
Coordinates are for the ore body of this surface-underground, past producer.

USGS MRDS Data Base Record 10040521, Released December 1, 1975; Updated August 1, 1984: The site of the Andes Mine is shown as 37.56024N by -115.74698W, placing it about 18 miles Southwest of Tem Piute, in the Don Dale Mining District, in the Tempiute Mining District and in the area included on the USGS Tempiute Mountain South 24K, Timpahute Range 100K and Caliente 250K maps. The Public Land Survey System locators are Sections 25 & 36, Township 4 South, Range 55 East. (An old 1960 estimate of the Public Land Survey System locators, made when the area was unsurveyed, was Section 4, Township 5 South, Range 56 East.) Mercury is present and is shown as a primary commodity with Silver, Zirconium and Barite tertiary. This Hot-Spring Mercury Deposit (Model No. 177) is hosted in Rhyolite. The grade of Mercury found is directly proportional to the degree of fracturing and alteration. A few sampled assayed gave 15 to 40 pounds of Mercury per ton of ore, with the best values being found just above the Limestone base rock. The average ore grade was about 2 to 3 pounds of Mercury per ton of ore. The Nevada Bureau of Mines and Geology (NBMG) Sample 1467 assayed 20% Iron, .15% Barium, 200 parts per million (ppm) Zirconium and 7 ppm Silver. Gangue materials include Quartz, Calcite, Pyrite, Limonite, Jarosite and Gypsum. The ore body is described as Irregular, nearly flat-lying, striking Northerly, by predominantly Northeast, covered by about 40 feet of overburden, about 45 feet thick, 100 feet wide, 300 feet long and controlled by fractures. The general description of the geology is welded and non-welded Silicic, Ash-flow Tuffs; however, it is further noted that these highly fractured Volcanics are underlain by a Limestone formation, resulting in nearly, flat-lying beds containing high-grade Stringers assaying up to 30 pounds of Mercury per ton. It is believed that this could be a significant deposit, if fully developed. The Land Status,

Ownership Category of this producer (as of the date of the record), which was discovered in 1919 by C. A. Anderson and put into production in 1955, is shown as "BLM Administrative Area". A 1977 record shows the Owner as Don and Carol Williams, St. George, Utah.

USGS MRDS Data Base Record 10222362, Released November 14, 1983: The pit area of the Andes Mine is shown at 37.56076N by -115.74667W, placing it in the Don Dale Mining District. The location accuracy, of these coordinates, is shown as +/- 10 meters. The Public Land Survey System locators are the Western ½ of the Northeast ¼ of the Northwest ¼ of Section 4, Township 5 South, Range 56 East. It is noted that other references show Section 36, Township 4 South, Range 55 East and the Topographical Map Reference point is Section 36, Township 5 South, Range 56 East, making things a little more than confusing. Mercury is shown as present and as a primary commodity. The geology, in the pit area is described as welded and non-welded Silicic, Ash-flow Tuffs. The Land Status, Ownership Category of this surface-underground, past producer is shown as "BLM Administrative Area".

Andrews and Steever: (37.54.45N by -114.25.55W - #3) (Manganese, Zinc)
Coordinates are for the ore body of this past producer.

Antique Prospect (a.k.a. NBMG Sample Site 580): (37.6258N by -114.69W – USS MRDS) (Gold, Silver)
USGS MRDS Data Base Record 10046491, Released May 1, 1984: The site of the Antique Prospect is shown at 37.6258N by -114.68973W, placing it in the Delamar Mining District and in the area included on the USGS Caliente NW 24K and Caliente 100K and 250K maps. The Public Land Survey System locators are Section 3, Township 4 South, Range 65 East. Gold and Silver, with a gangue of Quartz, in a host of Highland Peak Limestone, associated with Late Cambrian to Pliocene Tuff, is present and both are shown as primary commodities. The ore body includes Pods of barren white Quartz along a structure which trends North 20° West and dips 60° Southwest in mottled grey Limestone. The deposit was developed by an old inclined shaft and a number of small cuts. Red-brown Tuff crops out 15 feet West of the old shaft, which is believed to have been sunk on the poorly-exposed, Tuff-Limestone contact. The geology, in the general area of the site, is described as Andesite and related rocks of intermediate composition. The Land Status, Ownership Category of this occurrence is shown as "BLM Administrative Area". A note to file indicates a location notice dated 1966 was found nearby.
USGS MRDS Data Base Record 10222418, Released January 25, 1994: The main entrance to the Antique Prospect is shown at 37.62577N by -114.68944W, placing it in the Delamar Mining District and the Ferguson Mining District. The location accuracy, of these coordinates, is shown as +/- 100 meters. This record shows Gold present and as a primary commodity with Silver tertiary. The ore body is described as a Tabular Fissure Vein of Hydrothermal origin. The geology, in the area of the main entrance, is described as Andesite and related rocks of intermediate composition. The Land Status, Ownership Category of this underground prospect is shown as "BLM Administrative Area".

Apex/Apex Claim: (37.55.24N by -114.26.23W - #3)
Coordinates are for the ore body of this underground, past producer.
See the Salt Lake Pioche Mining Company Mines entry for more information.

Apex Claim (a.k.a. Flagstaff): (37.28.20N by -114.46.35W - #3) (Gold, Manganese, Iron, Barite)
See the Flagstaff entry for more information.

April Fool (a.k.a. April Fool Mine; Goldcup; NBMG Sample Site 1751 and 1752; Swifter Claims): (37.27.45N by -114.45.30W - #3) (Gold, Silver, Copper, Bismuth, Antimony)
Coordinates are for the ore body of this underground, past producer.
USGS MRDS Data Base Record 10037386, Released November 1, 1979; Updated August 1, 1984: The site of the April Fool Mine is shown at 37.46247N by -114.76556W, placing it on a ridge Northeast of Delamar, in the Delmar Mining District, in the Ferguson Mining District and in the area included on the USGS Delamar 24K, Clover Mountains 100K and Caliente 250K maps. The Public Land Survey System locators are Section 1, Township 6 South, Range 64 East. Gold and Silver are present and are shown as primary commodities with Copper, Antimony and Bismuth tertiary. Mineralization includes Tetrahedrite, with a gangue of Pyrite, Barite and Quartz, in a host of Prospect Mountain Quartzite, associated with Basalt and Early Cambrian Rhyolite. The ore body is described as a Tabular Vein, offset by a Rhyolite dike,

which strikes North 32° East, dips 80° West, is up to 20 feet thick and 700 feet wide and is traceable for a distance of about 3,000 feet. A second description of the ore body is found in the notes, and this one varies significantly from the above description. It reads; "The ore body is a Fissure Vein, whose main ore shoots are less than 10 feet wide, and is divided into lenses by intersecting gouge seams, continuing for a length of 1,500 feet. The Vein contains masses of Breccia with Cherty Quartz cement and Veinlets of crustified and banded "Comb Quartz". The April Fool Vein is mineralized to a variable extent for a length of 3,000 feet at a depth of 700 feet. It is roughly parallel to, and 500 to 700 feet East, of the Delamar Vein. The controls for the ore emplacement are shown as Quartzite Breccia in the Fissure Zone.

A third detailed description of the deposit was also found in the notes. As it is somewhat more detailed than the others, I have included it in its entirety. "The Vein, which is offset by a late Rhyolite dike, is parallel to the Delamar Vein. The ore is Silicified Quartzite Breccia and Veinlets of Comb Quartz. This conspicuous Silicified rib outcrops boldly along the ridge crest adjacent to the workings. The raise above the adit explores the Vein and exposes a 2 to 3-foot-wide zone which is Iron-stained and shows sub-parallel sets of Quartz Veins which cut highly Siliceous Quartzite Breccia. On close examination, the Vein outcrop consists of an Iron-stained, Quartzite Breccia cemented with Jaspery Silica or more massive, vitreous cockade or "Comb Quartz". Some wider, massive, late-stage Quartz Veins crosscut Breccia parallel to the Vein outcrop. The upper workings are a fairly continuous line of shafts and stopes, often inclined to the West along the dip of the Vein. The Vein outcrops boldly adjacent to and West of the workings and continues upslope for several hundred feet. The sampled stope trends North 10° to 20° East and dips 75° Northwest along the Vein. At the South end of the stope, the Vein outcrop consists of pink, angular Quartzite fragments cemented by Comb or drusy Quartz. Prismatic Quartz encrusts vugs as do fine-grained crystals of late-stage Jarosite. Dark bands in the Quartz are very fine-grained Sulfides, of which the only recognizable material is Pyrite. Iron and Manganese Oxides are common. Part of the Vein consists of shattered Quartzite and Malachite is deposited along fine fracture surfaces in the Quartzite and also in the Vein Material. Several samples of Quartz Vein outcrop and the dump contains coarse clots of Tetrahedrite, most of which is Oxidized to Copper Oxides, and abundant Oxidized and Unoxidized Pyrite.

The workings were described in a 1937 report as being four levels in the Goldcup Tunnel. In 1983 there was one adit which trended North 35° West and then turned Northeast 15 feet beyond the portal. Stopes and shafts continued for several hundred feet up and down the slope from this adit, along the Vein structure. At the level of the adit are the remains of track and an old stone cabin. There are many drill roads estimated to be from 5 to 10 years old at the time of the review. The production from the April Fool Mine ranks it second in the Delamar Mining District.

The geology, in the general area of the site, is described as Quartzite and minor amounts of Conglomerate, Phyllitic Siltstone, Limestone and Dolomite. Discovered and put into production in 1892 by Frank Wilson and D. A. Reeves, the Land Status, Ownership Category of this past producer is shown as "Private".

History: A short history of the mine was found in the notes: "Captain Delamar purchased a part interest in the mine in 1893. In 1897 it was equipped with a 10-stamp mill. In 1899 the mine employed 35 men, at which time there was extensive mine exploration being undertaken. The April Fool was among the mines consolidated under the Bamberger-Delamar Mines Company in 1902. In 1931 the Horn Brothers of Delamar were doing a little mining and development work and shipping a little ore. In 1932 and 1933 the McGuffie and Gentry Lease on the April Fool produced considerable shipping ore. A 1983 examination indicated backhoe trenching of dumps and sorting of material near the workings done 1 or 2 years before."

USGS MRDS Data Base Record 10222321, Released January 19, 1994: The main entrance to the April Fool Mine is shown at 37.45937N by -114.76664W, placing it in the Delamar Mining District and in the Ferguson Mining District. The location accuracy, of these coordinates, is shown as +/- 10 meters. The Public Land Survey System locators are the Northwest ¼ of the Southwest ¼ of the Northeast ¼ of Section 1, Township 6 South, Range 64 East. Gold is present and is shown as a primary commodity with Silver, Copper, Antimony and Bismuth tertiary. The geology, in the area of the main entrance is described as Quartzite and minor amounts of Conglomerate, Phyllitic Siltstone, Limestone and Dolomite. The Land Status, Ownership Category of this underground, past producer is shown as "Private". Mineral Rights are held through "Patented, Located Claims".

See NBMG Sample Site 1751 and 1752 entry for more information on the grade of material in the April Fool. See the Bamberger Delamar Gold Mining Company entry for more information.

April Fool Spring Trench (a.k.a. NBMG Sample Site 3001): (37.53326N by -115.739W – USGS MRDS) (Gold)

USGS MRDS Data Base Record 10198477, Released January 26, 1994: Trenching associated with the April Fool Spring Trench is shown at 37.53326N by -115.73897W, placing it in Don Dale Mining District and in the area included on the USGS Tempiute Mountain South 24K, Timpahute Range 100K and Caliente 250K maps. The location accuracy, of these coordinates, is shown as /- 500 meters. The Public Land Survey System locators are shown as Section 4, Township 5 North, Range 55+ East. The ore body is described as a Fissure Vein. The geology, in the area of the trenching, is described as Quartzite and minor amounts of Conglomerate, Phyllitic Siltstone, Limestone and Dolomite. The Land Status, Ownership Category of this surface prospect is shown as "BLM Administrative Area".

Arcane Mining Company Property (a.k.a. Susan Duster Lode): (37.92302N by -114.454W – USGS MRDS) (Lead, Zinc, Silver, Gold)
USGS MRDS Data Base Record 10046396, Released May 1, 1984: The site of the Arcane Mining Company Property, consisting of 5 Claims adjoining the Ohio-Kentucky and Amalgamated Pioche is shown at 37.92302N by -114.45417W, placing it in the Pioche Mining District and in the area included on the USGS Pioche 24K and Caliente 100K and 250K maps. The location accuracy, of these coordinates, is shown as +/- 100 meters. The Public Land Survey System locators are the Northwest ¼ of the Northeast ¼ of Section 27, Township 1 North, Range 67 East. Lead, Zinc, Silver and Gold, are present in a host of Late Cambrian, Prospect Mountain Quartzite and all are shown as primary commodities. The ore body is described as Tabular, dipping 45° South. In 1922, ore from the adjacent property, on the same (Susan Duster) Lode assayed 7% Lead, 20% Zinc and 20 ounces of Silver and $2.50 in Gold (about 3.75 grams at then-current prices) per ton. Although idle in 1922 when reviewed, the company had plans to sink a vertical, double-compartment shaft to the 650 foot level, at which depth they hoped to cut the Susan Duster Lode. This shaft was to be 200 feet away from the Arcane-Ohio-Kentucky line. The Ohio-Kentucky had followed the Susan Duster Lode to the property line and had to stop. A total of about 1,200 feet of underground work was completed over time. The geology, in the general area of the site, is described as Limestone and Dolomite with locally-thick sequences of Shale and Siltstone. The Land Status, Ownership Category of this occurrence is shown as "Private". A 1922 record shows the Owner as Arcane Mining Company of Pioche, Nevada.
USGS MRDS Data Base Record 10246588, Released January 25, 1994: The main entrance to the Arcane Mining Company Property is shown at 37.92306N by -114.45414W. The location accuracy, of these coordinates, is shown as +/- 100 meters. This record shows Lead present and as a primary commodity, with Zinc, Silver and Gold tertiary. The ore body is described as a Tabular Fissure Vein of Hydrothermal origin. The geology, in the area of the main entrance, is described as Limestone and Dolomite with locally-thick sequences of Shale and Siltstone. The Land Status, Ownership Category of this underground prospect is shown as "Private". The Mineral Rights are held through "Patented, Located Claims".

Arrowhead: (37.07.07N by -115.34.58W - #3) (Copper, Lead, Silver)
Coordinates are for an ore body.

Atlanta Gold Property (a.k.a. Atlanta Mine & Mill): (38.46605N by -114.323W – USGS MRDS) (Silver, Gold)
USGS MRDS Data Base Record 10246480, Released May 22, 1997: The main entrance to the Atlanta Gold Property is shown at 38.46605N by -114.32274W, placing it in the Carlin Trend Mining District and in the area included on the USGS Atlanta 24K, Wilson Creek Range 100K and Lund 250K maps. This property includes the past-producing Atlanta Mine & Mill. In 1997, Golden Chief Resources plans to explore to a distance of one mile South and Southeast of the original Atlanta Pit. The location accuracy, of these coordinates, is shown as +/- 1,000 meters. The Public Land Survey System locators are Section 14, Township 7 North, Range 28 East. Gold and Silver are present and are shown as primary commodities. The geology, in the area of the main entrance, is described as Limestone, Dolomite, Shale and Quartzite. The Land Status, Ownership Category of this open pit, and Hydromet Leach plant is shown as "BLM Administrative Area". Mineral Rights are held through "Located Claims". A 1997 record shows the Owner-Operator as Golden Chief Resources of Canada.

Atlanta Mine (a.k.a. Atlanta Home; Atlanta Nos. 1-3; Atlanta Strip No. 1;Belle; Hillside; Pactolion Fraction; Sparrow Hawk; Standard Slag Mine): (38.46578N by -114.323W – USGS MRDS) (Gold, Silver, Uranium)

USGS MRDS Data Base Record 10080425, Released July 1, 1981; Updated January 1, 1985, Updated November 6, 1992; Updated September 1, 1994: The site of the Atlanta Mine is shown at 38.46578N by -114.32251W, placing it about 50 miles Northeast of Pioche, ½ mile East of Atlanta, in the Atlanta Mining District, in the Silver Park Mining District, in the Silver Springs Mining District and in the area included on the USGS Atlanta 24K, Wilson Creek Range 100K and Lund 250K maps. The Public Land Survey System locators are the Southwest ¼ of the Southwest ¼ of Section 24, Township 7 North, Range 68 East. Gold is present and is shown as a primary commodity with Silver and Uranium tertiary. Mineralization of this Hot Spring Gold-Silver Deposit includes Gold with a gangue of Quartz, Pyrite, Limonite, Jasper, Alunite, Chert and Clay, in a host of Eureka Quartzite, associated with Pliocene Rhyolite. The ore body is described as "Pipe-like", striking North 30° West, dipping 40° Southwest, about 330 feet wide, 300 feet long and the ore deposition controlled by the Silicified Breccia Zone. The geology, in the general area of the site, is described as Limestone, Dolomite, Shale and Quartzite. The Land Status, Ownership Category of this surface-underground, past producer is shown as "Private". A 1983 record shows the Owner-Operator as the Standard Slag Company, Ernie Charter, Manager, P. O. Box 97, Pioche, Nevada 89043.

USGS MRDS Data Base Record 10310401, Released December 1, 2006; Updated and Edited September 1, 2007: The site of the Atlanta Mine is shown at 38.46578N by -114.32251W, placing it in the North end of the Wilson Creek Range. This record shows the Public Land Survey System locators as Section 14, Township 7 North, Range 68 East. Gold is present and is shown as a primary commodity with Silver secondary and Manganese, Iron and Uranium tertiary. Mineralization of this Hot Spring Gold-Silver Deposit includes Gold with a gangue of Quartz, Pyrite, Limonite, Jasper, Alunite, Chert and Clay, in a host of Early Ordovician, Tank Hill Limestone; Middle-to-Late Ordovician, Eureka Quartzite; Oligocene Ash-flow Tuff and Rhyolite; and, Tertiary, Rhyolitic Volcanic Breccia; associated with Oligocene Escalante Desert Formation Rhyolite, Rhyolitic Tuff, Rhyodacite and Andesite. The mineralization of the mine was structurally controlled and associated with caldera collapse features; locally, the Gold is found in faults and Breccia in a pipe-like formation. The primary underground workings were two shafts, drifts, with a raise and a winze and crosscuts. South on the main shaft was the open pit operation, which produced most of the early Gold. The geology, in the general area of the site, is described as Limestone, Dolomite, Shale and Quartzite. The Land Status, Ownership Category of this surface-underground, past producer is shown as a combination of "Private" and "BLM Administrative Area". Discovered in 1869 and first put in to production in 1870, the mine produced intermittently from 1871 to 1878, from 1906 to 1915, from 1934 to 1938, in 1948, from 1953 to 1955 and finally from 1966 to 1985. A 2001 record shows the Owner-Operator as Golden Chief Resources, Incorporated.

<u>Detailed Geologic Description of the Property</u>: The following is from a note to the file. "Mineralization occurs in Silicified Breccia and Jasperoid, adjacent to a low-angle, normal fault separating Oligocene Ash-flow Tuffs and Ordovician Carbonate rocks. Potential exists for Disseminated mineralization in fractured Ash-flow Tuffs and deep Jasperoid in Carbonate rocks beneath the Atlanta open pit. Prominent, Irregular Jasperoid bodies, Pods and Lenses, commonly accompanied by either Iron or Manganese Oxides, occur along the Atlanta ore zone that dips about 45° Southwest. In places, Breccia Pipes and fault zones in the Dolomite overlying the Eureka Quartzite are extensively Silicified into Druzy Quartz and Brecciated, greenish-gray Jasperoid. Commonly these Brecciated, mineralized zones carry sub-microscopic Gold, Silver minerals and minor amounts of Uranium. The ore deposit contains Brecciated fragments of Limestone, Quartzite, Volcanic rocks and Jasperoid, cemented by Quartz. Gold is sub-microscopic. The Atlanta Mine is situated near the intersection of two caldera systems. The older, Indian Peak caldera, is bounded by a fault zone that dips 70° to vertically into the caldera and is exposed in the Atlanta open-pit Gold mine. The caldera-bounding fault is a one-to-six-meter-wide Breccia zone associated with Tuff dikes that has accumulated over 500 meters of substance of the caldera floor. South of the mine area, the Indian Peak Caldera margin is constrained by exposures of Paleozoic, Sedimentary rocks outside the caldera and thick collapse Breccias containing large blocks of Paleozoic rocks, which thin into the caldera. The Indian Peak Caldera margin is truncated by the Ryan Spring Caldera near the center of the District. The fault zone that bounds the Indian Peak Caldera locally contains ore-grade Gold, Silver and Uranium mineralization, within Silicified Breccias. Silica-Pyrite mineralization is localized along the caldera-bounding fault zone and near Tuff dikes within the Atlanta Mine. Ore occurred in a Hematite-rich Silicified Breccia of Limestone and Tertiary Volcanic rocks, along a North-South-trending caldera rim.

<u>Production History of the Mine</u>: Notes to file detail some of the production history of the mine. Between 1870 and 1985 the Atlanta Mine has at least 100,000 ounces of recorded Gold production. Most of this came from the open pit mine brought back into production by the Standard Slag Company, in a joint

venture with Bob Cat Properties, Incorporated, in late 1974, with commercial production beginning the following year and continuing into the mid-to-late 1980s and production is estimated as being at least 120,000 ounces of Gold. A Cyanide plant, which was part of the original workings, was expanded from 300 tons per day to around 570 tons per day by 1982. In 1983 the mine was listed as an active open pit mine, employing 45 persons. In 1996, Golden Chief Resources planned to drill 8 holes on the Atlanta Gold property. These were to test what was thought to be an area of potential Gold mineralization which ran from the old pit to the South and Southeast. In August of 2000, Franc-Or Resources Corporation announced that the Cordilleran Nevada Syndicate, of which it held 40%, signed a lease agreement on the ground adjoining its Atlanta Claim Block. The lease would add 183 Unpatented Claims to the Cordilleran property, bring its total to 447 Unpatented Claims. This would not include the 26 Unpatented and 13 Patented Claims which cover the existing pit, dumps and milling facilities. In 2001 the property was shown to be Owned by Golden Chief Resources, Incorporated. Current Inferred, plus Drill-Indicated Resources, are about 460,000 ounces of Gold and 3,900,000 ounces of Silver using a cut-off grade of 0.02 ounces of Gold per ton (about 0.625 grams). Golden Chief reported Measured Reserves of 300,000 ounces of Gold and 3,000,000 ounces of Silver.

Atlanta Mine & Mill (a.k.a. Atlanta; Atlanta Gold Property; Atlanta Home; Atlanta Strip; Belle; Hillsdale; Pactolion Fraction; Sparrow Hawk): (38.27.57N by -114.19.18W - #3) (Silver, Gold) Coordinates are for the ore body of a surface-underground, temporarily shut down (as of 1996) operation. *USGS MRDS Data Base Record 10198373, Released May 22, 1997*: The plant area of the Atlanta Mine & Mill is shown at 38.33326N by -114.36754W, placing it in the Carlin Trend and in the area included on the USGS Trail Canyon 24K, Wilson Creek Range 100K and Lund 250K maps. The Public Land Survey System locators are the Southwest ¼ of Section 14, Township 7 North, Range 68 East. Gold and Silver are present and are shown as primary commodities. Mineralization, in addition to the Gold and Silver, includes Oxy-Hydrous Manganese, Hematite, Limonite, Jasper, Barite, Quartz and Clay. The ore body strikes North 5° East, dips 45° West, and is about 650 feet wide by about 825 feet long. The ore body is in two parts; ore disseminated in a Tabular deposit, while a second is of the Breccia fill type. The ore body is described as carrying sub-microscopic Gold and Uranium in a Breccia Zone of Limestone of the Ely Springs formation, Quartz Porphyry, Eureka Quartzite, Jasperoid and Volcanic rocks, thought to be Tertiary Ignimbrite. The Breccia is cemented by Quartz. The ore zone is intruded by the Quartz Porphyry and is bounded by 2 high-angle, West-dipping, normal faults. The Tertiary Volcanic Ignimbrites form the hanging wall, with Ely Springs Dolomite the footwall. Portions of the Jasperoid are ore, with much of the Quartz Porphyry being "near ore" or low-grade ore. The precipitation Lech plant (Heap-leach, Merrill-Crowe) processed the ore from this surface-underground operation starting around 1980 although the deposit was discovered as early as 1906. Production, between May, 1975 and May of 1982, was about 12,000 Kilograms of Silver from 860,000 tons of ore. The estimated annual production was estimated at 400 Kilograms of Gold and 2,000 kilograms of Silver. The original Atlanta Pit operation was closed in 1985. A 1996 study, showed 4,082,331 tons of Demonstrated Resources with a cut-off grade of 2.743 grams per Metric Tonne Gold and 58.857 Grams per Metric Tonne Silver. Bobcat Properties, Incorporated, of Florida, the Owners of the operation, planned an exploration program in the spring of 1996. Bobcat sold to Golden Chief Resources, Incorporated, of Canada, in 1997, which had plans to explore to a distance of one mile to the South and Southeast of the original pit, which places the exploration effort in the area of Atlanta Peak and its Eastern slope.
USGS MRDS Data Base Record 10246480, Released May 22, 1997: The main entrance of the Atlanta Gold Property plant is shown at 38.46605N by -114.32274W, placing it in the Carlin Trend. The location accuracy, of these coordinates, is shown as +/- 1,000 meters. Gold and Silver are shown present and both as primary commodities. The geology, in the area of the main entrance, is described as Limestone, Dolomite, Shale and Quartzite. The Land Status, Ownership Category of this plant and surface-underground operation is shown as "BLM Administrative Area". A 1997 record shows the 100% Owner-Operator as Golden Chief Resources, Incorporated, of Canada.
Comment: On April 16, 2022, I did an Internet search for Golden Chief Resources, Incorporated, as a Canadian company, and could find nothing. I also went into SEDAR and searched there, with no results. I was attempting to get a contact at Golden Chief to inquire about the current status of the property and if the Demonstrated Resources shown in the 1996 report were accurate. In reviewing the site, using a satellite mapping program, I could find no activity at the site or in the immediate vicinity, although a number of buildings and some old equipment on the property could be seen.

See the Atlanta Gold Property entry for more information.

Atlanta Mining District (a.k.a. Indian Valley Mining District; Silver Park Mining District; Silver Peak Mining District; Silver Springs Mining District): (Gold, Silver, Copper, Lead, Tungsten, Vanadium, Manganese, Uranium)
Description of the District:
Tingley, Joseph V.; "Mining Districts of Nevada"; Nevada Bureau of Mines and Geology, Report 47, Second Edition; 1998; Page 22: Discovered and organized in 1869, The Atlanta Mining District is located at the Northern tip of the Wilson Creek Range. In 1871, A. F. White, in the *"Report of the Mineralogist of the State of Nevada for the Years 1869 and 1870",* referred to the District as Silver Peak, and located it in a low range of mountains about 35 miles Southeast of the Patterson Mining District. However, by 1873, the name Silver Park was being used for the area. In 1881, M. Angel, in his *History of Nevada,* gave the location of the Silver Park Mining District as the Southeastern corner of White Pine County, which was incorrect and created considerable confusion. Angel further described a Silver Springs Mining District as being in the "Northeastern corner of the County, in the Snake Range Mountains", which was probably the area of the modern Atlanta Mining District, if the County being referred to was Lincoln. In 1869, the *Territorial Enterprise* cited an Indian Valley Mining District, which was located about 20 miles East of the Patterson Mining District, which was likely in the area of the modern Atlanta Mining District. Around 1907 the Atlanta Camp was established at the site of a number of Gold discoveries, about 2 miles East of the area of Silver Park (38.27.20N by -114.21.13W – USGS Atlanta map). After the establishment of the Atlanta Camp, the area began to be identified with it as the Atlanta Mining District.
Mines Included in the District:
      Bradshaw (Gold, Silver, Copper, Uranium)
      Hulse Mine (Uranium, Silver, Gold, Copper, Lead, Arsenic)
      Silver Park (Silver, Gold, Copper, Lead, Zinc, Antimony, Uranium)
      Solo Joker (Gold, Silver, Barite)

Axis Vein (a.k.a. NBMG Sample Site 3053): (37.53746N by -115.781W – USGS MRDS) (Silver, Gold)
USGS MRDS Data Base Record 10295174, Released January 26, 1994: The pit area of the Axis Vein is shown at 37.53746N by -115.78117W, placing it in the Don Dale Mining District and in the area included on the USGS White Blotch Springs SE 24K, Timpahute Range 100K and Caliente 250K maps. The location accuracy, of these coordinates, is shown as +/- 500 meters. The Public Land Survey System locators are Section 6, Township 5 South, Range 55[+] East. Silver is present and is shown as a primary commodity with Gold tertiary. The geology, in the area of the pit, is described as Quartzite and minor amounts of Conglomerate, Phyllitic Siltstone, Limestone and Dolomite. The ore body is described as a Tabular Fissure Vein of Hydrothermal origin. The Land Status, Ownership Category of this surface prospect is shown as "BLM Administrative Area".

Aztec: (37.38.40N by -114.13.05W - #3) (Copper)
Coordinates are for the ore body of this underground operation.

B. W. Claims (a.k.a. NBMG Sample Sites 3026 and 3027): (37.49356N by -115.738W – USGS MRDS) (Gold)
USGS MRDS Data Base Record 10198208, Released January 26, 1994: The pit area of the B. W. Claims is shown at 37.49356N by -115.73757W, placing it in the Groom Mining District and in the area included on the USGS Groom Range 24K, Pahranagat Range 100K and Caliente 250K maps. The location accuracy, of these coordinates, is shown as +/- 500 meters. The Public Land Survey System locators are Section 21, Township 5 South, Range 55[+] East. Gold is present in this Stratiform, Contact Metasomatic Deposit and is shown as a primary commodity. The geology in the pit area is shown as Limestone and Dolomite with locally-thick sequences of Shale and Siltstone. The Land Status, Ownership Category of this surface prospect is shown as "Military Reservation".

Bamberger Delamar Gold Mining Company (a.k.a. Bamberger Gold Mining Company; April Fool Mine; Delamar Mine; Magnolia Mine; Rose and Pleides Group of Claims): (37.46219N by -114.769W – USGS MRDS) (Gold, Silver)

USGS MRDS Data Base Record 10046493, Released January 1, 1984: The site of the Bamberger Delamar Gold Mining Company is shown at 37.46219N by -114.7689W, placing it in the Delamar Mining District, in the Ferguson Mining District and in the area included on the USGS Delamar 24K, Clover Mountains 100K and Caliente 250K maps. The location accuracy, of these coordinates, is shown as +/- 100 meters. The Public Land Survey System locators are Sections 25 & 26, Township 5 South, Range 64 East and Section 1, Township 6 South, Range 64 East. Gold, in a host of Quartzite, associated with Plutonic rock, is present and is shown as a primary commodity with Silver secondary. The ore body is related to a system of North-South fault zones and East-West cross-dikes, and is about 30 feet thick and traceable for about 15,885 feet. The consolidation of the groups covered 1,600 acres along the Vein, for a distance about 3 miles. Ore shoots were found in the gouge material. The geology, in the general area of the site, is described as Quartzite and minor amounts of Conglomerate, Phyllitic Siltstone, Limestone and Dolomite. The Land Status, Ownership Category of this occurrence is shown as "Private". A 1909 record shows the Owner as the Bamberger-Delamar Mining Company.

History: Some history of the mine was found in the notes to file. "In 1902, the Delamar properties were optioned to Jacob E. and Simon Bamberger. The mill was remodeled and Chilean mills were installed and both mine and mill were electrically equipped. The new mill started in May, 1903, and in 1904 about 300 tons per day of free milling ore were treated as well as about 200 tons per day of Sulfide ore was treated. In 1906 the Hog Pen inclined shaft had reached Level 13 and the mill was treating 350 tons per day as well as 300 tons per day at the tailings plant. In 1907, underground workings totaled 35 miles and a glory hole was started in 1908 in the area around the main ore body. A series of adits, about 500 feet apart, from top to bottom, were run. In 1909 the mine closed and most of the mining equipment was sold in 1910. Minor production, in 1911, 1912 and 1913, was derived from a clean-up of the mill by lessees. Another clean up took place in 1926.

USGS MRDS Data Base Record 10246895, Released January 26, 1994: The main entrance to the Bamberger Gold Mining Company is shown at 37.46217N by -114.76894W, placing it in the Delamar Mining District and in the Ferguson Mining District. The location accuracy, of these coordinates, is shown as +/- 100 meters. This record shows Gold present and as a primary commodity with Silver tertiary. The geology, in the area of the main entrance, is described as Quartzite and minor amounts of Conglomerate, Phyllitic Siltstone, Limestone and Dolomite. The Land Status, Ownership Category of this surface-underground, past producer is shown as "Private".

Barium Prospect: (36.57.15N by -114.17.45W - #3) (Barite, Iron)
Coordinates are for the ore body.

Bay State Mining and Leasing Company (a.k.a. Ida May): (38.05.54N by -114.36.57W - #3) (Silver, Lead, Gold, Copper, Zinc)
See the Ida May entry for more information.

Bertha (a.k.a. Ida May): (38.05.54N by -114.36.57W - #3) (Silver, Lead, Gold, Copper, Zinc)
See the Ida May entry for more information.

Big Buck Claim (a.k.a. Little Buck Claim; Snowflake Mine): (37.90107N by -114.058W – USGS MRDS) Gold, Silver)
USGS MRDS Data Base Record 10246553, Released January 19, 1994: The main entrance to the Big Buck Claim is shown at 37.90107N by -114.05802W, placing it in the Eagle Valley Mining District and in the area included on the USGS Deer Lodge Canyon 24K and Caliente 100K and 250K maps. The location accuracy, of these coordinates, is shown as +/- 10 meters. The Public Land Survey System locators are the Northeast ¼ of the Northeast ¼ of the Southwest ¼ of Section 32, Township 1 North, Range 71 East. Gold is present and is shown as a primary commodity with Silver tertiary. The geology, in the area of the main entrance, is shown as Andesite and related rocks of intermediate composition. The Land Status, Ownership Category of this surface-underground, past producer is unknown.

Big Buck Mine (a.k.a. NBMG Sample Site 1721; On Winner No. 2 Patented Claim; Snowflake Group): (37.54.11N by -114.03.32W - #3) (Silver, Gold, Lead, Copper)
Coordinates are for the main entrance to this underground, past producer.

USGS MRDS Data Base Record 10046445, Released February 1, 1984: The site of the Big Buck Mine is shown at 37.90303N by -114.05999W, placing it in Midnight Wash just below its head, in the Eagle Valley Mining District, in the Gold Springs Mining District and in the area included on the USGS Deer Lodge Canyon 24K and Caliente 100K and 250K maps. The Public Land Survey System locators are the Northwest ¼ of Section 32, Township 1 North, Range 71 East. Gold and Silver, with a gangue of Quartz, Calcite, Pyrite and Limonite, are present and are shown as primary commodities with Lead and Copper secondary. Mineralization is hosted in Andesite and Latite in this Tabular ore body about 20 feet thick, controlled by the shear zone. The ore body was developed by several shafts and stopes and a number of adits. There are six or seven levels of closely-spaced drill roads on the North side of Buck Mountain, just above the workings. The main shaft had 3 levels; at 30, 50 and 100 feet; some of which were stoped to the surface. It is believed that there was some type of an exploration program at the site in 1980 or 1981. The geology, in the general area of the site, is described as Andesite and related rocks of intermediate composition. The Land Status, Ownership Category of this past producer is shown as "Private".

USGS MRDS Data Base Record 10246786, Released January 12, 1994: The main entrance to the Big Buck Mine is shown at 37.90277N by -114.05942W, placing it in the Eagle Valley Mining District. The location accuracy, of these coordinates, is shown as +/- 10 meters. Gold is present and is shown as a primary commodity with Silver tertiary. The geology, in the area of the main entrance, is described as Andesite and related rocks of intermediate composition. The Land Status, Ownership Category of this underground, past producer is unknown.

Big Buck Prospect: (38.24.15N by -114.19.15W - #3) (Gold, Silver)
Coordinates are for trenching associated with this exploration prospect.

Big Fissure Claims (a.k.a. Cave Valley Mine 002): (38.38.39N by -114.47.49W - #3) (Lead, Silver, Copper, Zinc, Gold, Vanadium, Arsenic, Clay)
See the Cave Valley Mine 002 entry for more information.

Big Red Prospect (a.k.a. NBMG Sample Site 3052): (37.53386N by -115.781W – USGS MRDS) (Gold, Silver)
USGS MRDS Data Base Record 10246533, Released January 26, 1994: The main entrance to the Big Red Prospect is shown at 37.53386N by -115.78117W, placing it in the Don Dale Mining District and in the area included on the USGS White Bloch Springs SE 24K, Timpahute Range 100K and Caliente 250K maps. The location accuracy, of these coordinates, is shown as +/- 500 meters. The Public Land Survey System locators are Section 6, Township 5 South, Range 55⁺ East. Gold is present and is shown as a primary commodity with Silver tertiary. The ore body is a Tabular Vein in a shear zone. The geology in the area of the main entrance, is described as welded and non-welded Silicic Ash-flow tuffs. The Land Status, Ownership Category of this surface-underground prospect is shown as "BLM Administrative Area".

Big Red Prospect Northwest (a.k.a. NBMG Sample Site 3050): (37.53466N by -115.784W – USGS MRDS) (Gold, Silver)
USGS MRDS Data Base Record 10295316, Released January 26, 1994: The pit area of the Big Red Prospect Northwest is shown at 37.53466N by -115.78367W, placing it in the Don Dale Mining District and in the area included on the USGS White Blotch Springs SE 24K, Timpahute Range 100K and Caliente 250K maps. The location accuracy, of these coordinates, is shown as +/- 500 meters. The Public Land Survey System locators are Section 6, Township 5 South, Range 55⁺ East. Gold is present and is shown as a primary commodity with Silver tertiary. The ore body is described as a Tabular Fissure Vein of Hydrothermal origin. The geology, in the pit area, is described as welded and non-welded Silicic Ash-flow Tuff. The Land Status, Ownership Category of this surface prospect is shown as "BLM Administrative Area".

Big Red Prospect West (NBMG Sample Site 3051): (37.53326N by -115.782W – USGS MRDS) (Silver, Gold)
USGS MRDS Data Base Record 10125291, Released January 26, 1994: The main entrance to the Big Red Prospect West is shown at 37.53326N by -115.78227W, placing it in the Don Dale Mining District and in the area included on the USGS White Blotch Springs SE 24K, Timpahute Range 100K and Caliente 250K maps. The location accuracy, of these coordinates, is shown as +/- 500 meters. The Public Land Survey

System locators are Section 6, Township 5 South, Range 55⁺ East. Silver is present and is shown as a primary commodity with Gold tertiary. The ore body is described as a Tabular Breccia Fill of Hydrothermal origin. The geology, in the area of the main entrance, is described as welded and non-welded Silicic Ash-flow Tuff. The Land Status, Ownership Category of this surface prospect is shown as "BLM Administrative Area".

Bill Nye Mine (a.k.a. Golden Rule; Helen Group): (37.56.43N by -114.04.17W - #3) (Gold, Silver)
Coordinates are for the ore body of this underground, past producer.
USGS MRDS Data Base Record 10198058, Released January 12, 1994: The main entrance to the Bill Nye Mine is shown at 37.94576N by -114.07163W, placing it in the Eagle Valley Mining District and in the area included on the USGS Deer Lodge Canyon 24K and Caliente 100K and 250K maps. The location accuracy, of these coordinates, is shown as +/- 1,000 meters. The Public Land Survey System locators are Section 18, Township 1 North, Range 71 East. Gold is present and is shown as a primary commodity with Silver tertiary. The geology, in the area of the main entrance, is described as Andesite and related rocks of intermediate composition. Discovered in 1941, the Land Status, Ownership Category of this underground, past producer is unknown.

Black Metal: (37.19.55N by -115.46.02W - #3) (Zinc, Lead, Copper)
Coordinates are for the main entrance to this underground, past producer.

Black Metal Mine 001 (a.k.a. Day Mine; Gusset Patch Claims): (38.09635N by -114.596W – USGS MRDS) (Silver, Manganese, Iron, Gold, Lead, Copper, Bismuth, Coal)
USGS MRDS Data Base Record 10047169, Released January 1, 1985: The site of the Black Metal Mine is shown at 38.09635N by -114.59612W, placing it in the Bristol-Jackrabbit Mining District and in the area included on the USGS Bristol Range SE 24K, Wilson Creek Range 100K and Lund 250K maps. The Day shaft, from where the coordinates were taken, is about 2,000 feet South of the Jackrabbit incline. The projected (from the East) Public Land Survey System locators are Section 29, Township 3 North, Range 66 East. Silver, Manganese and Iron are present and are shown as primary commodities with Gold, Copper, Lead and Bismuth secondary and Coal tertiary. Mineralization of this Polymetallic Replacement Deposit (USGS Model Code #19a) includes Cerargyrite, Psilomelane, Pyrolusite, Wad and Galena in a host of Late Cambrian, Highland Peak Limestone. The ore body is composed or Irregular Lenses, striking generally North 65° East and dipping nearly vertically and an ore Pipe which strikes North 25° East. The ore body is about 20 feet thick, about 50 feet wide and traceable for a length of about 600 feet. The deposit is located at the intersection of a prominent North-South fissure with a North 70° East, Tempest-type fissure. The mine produced an Iron-Manganese-Calcium Oxide flux for the early smelters in the region; with the silver being recovered as a by-product. In 1926 about 1,900 tons of Manganese ore was also shipped which contained about 15% to 20% Manganese, 0.8% Lead and about 3 ounces of Silver per ton. In 1927 an estimate of the Base Metal in the ore body was made which showed 0.8% Lead and 0.3% Copper. The development included the 1,200-foot-deep Day shaft, which was nearly vertical with working levels about every 75 feet. At the 300-foot level, the shaft made a connection to a surface tunnel and at the 900-foot level a drift was run (either from or to) the bottom of the Jack Rabbit inclined shaft. Stopes ran from the surface, to as deep as the 900-foot level. The mine was operated between 1911 and 1912 by the Day-Bristol Consolidated Mining Company. In 1913 it became idle, but was reopened and operated from 1919 to 1927; and then, is confirmed to have been idle from 1927 to 1941. Much of the ore was taken from the "A" Bed Stope between the 200 and 400-foot levels which followed a Limestone bed, that varied in thickness from 1 to 20 feet, struck North 65° West and dipped 15° North, for about 600 feet. The largest ore bodies were stoped from the surface to about the 300-foot level and between the 400- and 900-foot levels. Lower ore bodies occur along a North 45° East fissure which dips Southeast from the 4ᵗʰ to the 6ᵗʰ level. Below the 6ᵗʰ level, this fissure turns to dip 50° Northwest. The primary ore system consists of a vertical Pipe from which "ore beds" extend out laterally on at least 3 horizons, known as the "A", "B" and "C" beds, into the gently-dipping Limestone that encloses the Pipe. The exterior areas are higher in Manganese and lower in Lead and Silver with the best Lead-Silver ore occurring in the center of the Pipe. The ore Pipe occurs along a Vein, striking North 25° East, which consists of a 25-foot-thick belt of Brecciated, angular Limestone country rock enclosed in coarse white Calcite. The thickness of the Vein varies, bulging where it crosses certain beds. The geology, in the general area of the site, is described as Limestone and Dolomite with

locally-thick sequences of Shale and Siltstone. The Land Status, Ownership Category of this past producer is shown as "Private".
See the Bristol-Jackrabbit Mines entry for more information.

Black Prince (a.k.a. Black Prince Group; Black Prince Mine; NBMG Sample Site 1436): (37.55.27N by -114.31.56W - #3) (Silver, Gold, Lead, Zinc, Manganese)
Coordinates are for the main entrance to this underground, past producer.
USGS MRDS Data Base Record 10103585, Released January 1, 1980, Updated September 1, 1984: The site of the Black Prince Mine is shown at 37.93079N by -114.53278W, placing it 4 to 8 miles West of Pioche, ½ mile Southeast of the Wheeler Ranch, in the Highland Mining District and in the area included on the USGS Highland Peak 24K and Caliente 100K and 250K maps. The Public Land Survey System locators are Section 25, Township 1 North, Range 66 East. Silver and Gold are present and are shown as primary commodities with Lead, Zinc and Manganese secondary. Mineralization of this Replacement Manganese Deposit (USGS Model Code 19b) includes Wad and Pyrolusite, which carries Gold and Silver values, with a gangue of Calcite, Quartz and Pyrite, in a host of Highland Peak Limestone associated with Late Cambrian Granite. The ore body is Tabular, strikes Northeast, dips 51° Southeast and can be traced for about 7,000 feet on the surface in the thrust plate of the Mendha and Highland Peak Formations. An altered Granite Porphyry dike parallels the fissure footwall. The dike and the Limestone on the footwall are also mineralized. The ore is up to 35 feet thick with increasing values at depth in the main working inclined shaft, which was sunk at about a 60° angle, trending 55° Southeast along the thrust. Also included in the development are a number of small pits along the length of the Vein. The Black Prince Fissure is filled with altered, Manganese-stained ore, Hematite-stained Quartz nodules, Oxidized Pyrite, Pyrolusite and slightly magnetic nodules of Wad, some carrying crystalline Calcite Veinlets. Opaline Silica coats fracture surfaces and fills vugs. A minor shear zone is exposed in the shaft. The Limestone on the dump is pink banded, the bands possibly being Rhodochrosite, with crystalline Calcite Veinlets and nodules of platy Calcite which cement the Breccia. In 1981, 15 shallow-angle drill holes were completed; 12 of these intersected the Black Prince Vein. The drill-hole data indicated an average thickness of 12.4 feet, which contained an average of 3.4 ounces of Silver per ton. The Vein is relatively continuous along the strike in this area for a distance of about 2,600 feet.
In 1983 the area was flagged, staked and drilled but no production was made. In 1983 Altera Resources and Frejonley Mining acquired 104 Unpatented Lode Claims of the Black Prince property for $5.6 million. The probable ore Reserves are within 300 feet of the surface. An early report estimated 40,000 tons of ore grading about 1 gram of Gold and 8 ounces of Silver per ton. A 1983 study indicated 287,000 Metric Tonnes of ore with a grade of 121.413 grams (about 3.9 ounces) of Silver per ton. (Note: The report did not indicate if this was an average or a cut-off grade.)
The surface geology, in the general area of the site, is described as Alluvial deposits. The Land Status, Ownership Category of this past producer is shown as "Private". An undated record shows the Owner as Black Prince Mining Company, J. B. Wheeler – President and Director, Box B, Pioche, Nevada. A 1983 record shows the Operator as Altera Resources and Frejonley Mining.
USGS MRDS Data Base Record 10295421, Released January 19, 1994: The main entrance to the Black Prince Mine is shown at 37.92416N by -114.53304W, placing it in the Highland Mining District. The location accuracy, of these coordinates, is shown as +/- 10 meters. The Public Land Survey System locators are the Northern ½ of the Northern ½ of the Northwest ¼ of Section 25, Township 1 North, Range 66 East. This record shows Gold, Silver, Lead, Zinc and Manganese all present, but only at tertiary levels. Mineralization of this 10 hectare deposit is shown to include Psilomelane, Pyrolusite and Wad. The geology, in the area of the main entrance, is described as Limestone and Dolomite with locally thick sequences of Shale and Siltstone. The Land Status, Ownership Category of this underground, past producer, placed into production in 1952, is shown as "BLM Administrative Area". Mineral Rights are held through "Patented, Located Claims".
See the NBMG Sample Site 1436 entry for more information.

Black Shaft (a.k.a. Bristol-Jackrabbit Mines): (38.08107N by -114.617W – USGS MRDS) (Silver, Copper, Lead, Zinc, Gold, Manganese)
See the Bristol-Jackrabbit Mine entry for more information.

<u>Blind Mountain Mining District (a.k.a. Bristol Mining District)</u>: (Silver, Copper, Lead, Zinc, Gold, Manganese, Montmorillonite)
Description of the District:
Tingley, Joseph V.; "Mining Districts of Nevada"; Nevada Bureau of Mines and Geology, Report 47, Second Edition; 1998; Page 38: Tingley shows the Blind Mountain Mining District as an alternate name for the Bristol Mining District. This likely originates from the fact that Blind Mountain Spring is in the Southern part of, and the Southern boundary of the Bristol Mining District.
Mines Included in the District.

<u>Blue Bell (a.k.a. Blue Bell Mine; NBMG Sample Site 1389; Roeder Claims)</u>: (37.57.48N by -114.34.41W - #3) (Gold, Silver, Lead, Zinc)
Coordinates are for the ore body of this underground, exploration prospect.
USGS MRDS Data Base Record 10046459, Released December 1, 1984: The site of the Blue Bell Mine is shown at 37.96329N by -114.57862W, placing it in the Highland Mining District and in the area included on the USGS Highland Peak 24K and Caliente 100K and 250K maps. The Public Land Survey System locators are Section 9, Township 1 North, Range 66 East. Gold and Silver are present in the Polymetallic Replacement Deposit (USGS Model Code 19a) and are shown as primary commodities, with Lead and Zinc tertiary. Mineralization includes Galena, Anglesite and Sphalerite, with a gangue of Quartz, Calcite Pyrite and Jarosite in a host of Late Cambrian Limestone. The ore body strikes North 85° West, dips steeply Southwest, is up to 5 feet thick and is controlled by the fault zone and the contained Brecciation. It includes scattered Oxidized grains of Pyrite over the surfaces of the partings in the Limestone, the beds of which are horizontal to each other and slightly dipping, having an East-West strike. The Limestone host is also "rippled" and contains fossil hash. The fault Breccia Limestone is cemented with grainy crystalline Calcite and Quartz which carries fine-grained Galena, inter-grown with Sphalerite, altering to Anglesite, or other green alteration material and Pyrite "ghosts". The fault zone is Hydrothermally altered to Siliceous Gossan and heavily stained with Iron-Manganese Oxides. Near the fault the Limestone is unevenly Silicified. Fracture surfaces in the Gossan and Limestone are coated with Opaline Silica and a very fine-grained Calcite. Cavities are lined with drusy Quartz. Boxworks in the Gossan are coated with Limonite and very fine-grained, inter-grown Jarosite. The mine was developed by a 20-foot adit and surface cuts down the slope following the fault. There was no activity at the site, however, during the 1983 review. The geology, in the general area of the site, is described as Limestone and Dolomite with locally-thick sequences of Shale and Siltstone. The Land Status, Ownership Category of this occurrence, discovered in 1870, is shown as "Private".
See the NBMG Sample Site 1389 entry for more information.

<u>Blue Bell Prospect (a.k.a. NBMG Sample Site 1770; Piute Group; Steele)</u>: (39.00.28N by -115.42.05W - #3) (Fluorite, Gold)
Coordinates are for the claim area of this exploration prospect.
USGS MRDS Data Base Record 10046525, Released August 1, 1983; Updated January 1, 1985: The site of the Blue Bell Prospect is shown at 38.03828N by -115.7317W, placing it about 750 feet up the canyon or wash from National Forest Road 415, in the Quinn Canyon Mining District and in the area included on the USGS Badger Gulch 24K, Quinn Canyon Range 100K and Lund 250K maps. The location accuracy, of these coordinates, is shown as +/- 500 meters. The Public Land Survey System locators are the Northwest ¼ of Section 29, Township 2 North, Range 56 East. Fluorite is present and is shown as a primary commodity with Gold tertiary. Mineralization is found with a gangue of Quartz, Calcite and Chlorite in a host of Volcanic rock and associated with Pliocene Quartz Latite. The primary Fluorite ore averaged about 20% CaF_2. The ore body, or bodies, is/are in the form of Pods which strike East-West and North-South, dip from 70° West to 80° West to Vertically, is/are about 40 feet wide and 150 feet long. Development included various pits and trenches along an East-West-trending bench on the North side of a very steep cliff. Weathering has left a Fluorspar ridge up to 60 feet high. Within a 150-foot by 40-foot zone, 2 to 3-foot Veins and Veinlets are found. The workings have exposed a pod of highly-Brecciated, strongly-Silicified, vuggy Vein material containing green-purple Fluorspar. The Vein is within a highly Silicified crystal-lithic Breccia which forms bold outcrops and cliffs on the West side of the drainage. The property may have shipped a small amount in the past; however, no activity was observed at the time of the examination in 1984. The geology, in the general area of the site, is described as welded and non-welded Silicic Ash-flow

Tuffs. The Land Status, Ownership Category of this past producer, discovered in 1952 by Joe & Milt Steele and Bert Murphy, is shown as "National Forest".

USGS MRDS Data Base Record 10271290, Released November 14, 1983: The pit area of the Blue Bell Prospect is shown at 38.03055N by -115.71557W, placing it in the Quinn Canyon Mining District. The location accuracy, of these coordinates, is shown as +/- 10 meters. The Public Land Survey System locators are the Northern ½ of Section 29, Township 2 North, Range 56 East. Fluorite is present and is shown as a primary commodity. The geology, in the pit area, is described as welded and non-welded Silicic Ash-flow Tuffs. The Land Status, Ownership Category of this surface prospect is unknown.

See the NBMG Sample Site 1770 record for more information.

Comment: It was noted in the notes to file that the last ½ mile of the access road to the mine is very steep.

Blue Bird Claim/Bluebird (a.k.a. Gypsy and Helen): (37.57.03N by -114.04.35W - #3) (Gold, Silver, Copper)

See the Gypsy and Helen entry for more information.

Blue Bird Mine 001 (a.k.a. Ella Claim; Hulse Claim; Hulse Mine; Lucky Dog Claim; Minnie Claim): (38.27.19N by -114.19.58W - #3) (Gold, Silver, Uranium)

Coordinates are for the ore body of this underground, past producer.

USGS MRDS Data Base Record 10173497, Released January 19, 1994: The main entrance to the Blue Bird Mine is shown at 38.45525N by -114.33364W, placing it in the area included on the USGS Atlanta 24K, Wilson Creek Range 100K and Lund 250K maps. The location accuracy, of these coordinates, is shown as +/- 10 meters. The Public Land Survey System locators are the Northwest ¼ of Section 22, Township 7 North, Range 68 East. Gold is present and is shown as a primary commodity with Silver and Uranium tertiary. The geology, in the area of the main entrance, is described as welded and non-welded Silicic Ash-flow Tuffs. The Land Status, Ownership Category of this underground, past producer is shown as "BLM Administrative Area".

See the Hulse Mine entry for more information.

Blue Bird Mine 002: (37.56.43N by -114.04.17W - #3)

Coordinates are for the ore body of this underground, past producer.

Blue Eagle (a.k.a. Chisholm): (37.56.02N by -114.29.08W - #3) (Lead, Silver, Gold)

See the Chisholm entry for more information.

Blue Jay Claims (a.k.a. Jumbo): (37.27.18N by -114.45.30W - #3) (Gold, Silver, Zinc, Lead, Copper, Barite)

See the Jumbo entry for more information.

Blue Mary Claim North Extension (a.k.a. North Extension of Blue Mary Claim): (37.69327N by -114.522W – USGS MRDS) (Gold)

USGS MRDS Data Base Record 10046440, Released January 1, 1984: The site of the North Extension of the Blue Mary Claim is shown at 37.6933N by -114.52223W, placing it on a hill Northeast of the Old Democrat Claim, in the Caliente Mining District, the Chief Mining District and in the area included on the USGS Chief Mountain 24K and Caliente 100K and 250K maps. The Public Land Survey System locators are Section 18, Township 3 South, Range 67 East. Gold, in a host of Late Cambrian Quartzite, is present and is shown as a primary commodity. The ore body, which is described as Tabular, strikes Northwest and dips 80° Southwest to vertically. The only development was a couple of small pits. The geology, in the general area of the site, is described as Quartzite and minor amounts of Conglomerate, Phyllitic Siltstone, Limestone and Dolomite. The Land Status, Ownership Category of this occurrence is shown as "BLM Administrative Area".

USGS MRDS Data Base Record 10222303, Released January 26, 1994: The pit area of the Blue Mary Claim North Extension is shown at 37.69327N by -114.52224W, placing it in the Chief Mining District. The location accuracy, of these coordinates, is shown as +/- 100 meters. The ore body is described as a Tabular, Fissure Vein of Hydrothermal origin. The geology, in the pit area, is described as Quartzite and minor amounts of Conglomerate, Phyllitic Siltstone, Limestone and Dolomite. The Land Status, Ownership Category of this surface prospect is shown as "BLM Administrative Area".

Blue Nose Peak:
See the Crystal Mercury entry for more information.

Blue Ridge: (37.48.10N by -114.07.26W - #3) (Perlite)
Coordinates are for an ore body.

Blue Rock Placer Claims Area: (38.09.02N by -114.21.30W - #3) (Perlite)
Coordinates are for the pit area of this surface, exploration prospect.

Blue Streak Prospect (a.k.a. NBMG Sample Site 3049): (37.53826N by -115.778W – USGS MRDS)
(Gold, Silver)
USGS MRDS Data Base Record 10246438, Released January 26, 1994: The pit area of the Blue Streak
Prospect is shown at 37.53826N by -115.77777W, placing it in the Don Dale Mining District and in the
area included on the USGS White Blotch Springs SE 24K, Timpahute Range 100K and Caliente 250K
maps. The location accuracy, of these coordinates, is shown as +/- 500 meters. The Public Land Survey
System locators are Section 6, Township 5 South, Range 55+ East. Gold is present and is shown as a
primary commodity with Silver tertiary. The ore body is described as a Tabular Fissure Vein of
Hydrothermal origin. The geology, in the pit area, is described as Quartzite and minor amounts of
Conglomerate, Phyllitic Siltstone, Limestone and Dolomite. The Land Status, Ownership Category of this
surface prospect is shown as "BLM Administrative Area".

Bluebird Mine (a.k.a. Blue Bird Mine; Gypsy and Helen Groups): (37.94606N by -114.072W – USGS
MRDS) (Silver, Gold)
USGS MRDS Data Base Record 10149710, Released January 12, 1994: The main entrance to the Bluebird
Mine is shown at 37.94606N by -114.07193W, placing it in the Eagle Valley Mining District and in the
area included on the USGS Deer Lodge Canyon 24K and Caliente 100K and 250K maps. The location
accuracy, of these coordinates, is shown as +/- 1,000 meters. The Public Land Survey System locators are
Section 18, Township 1 North, Range 71 East. Silver is present and is shown as a primary commodity with
Gold tertiary. The geology, in the area of the main entrance, is described as Andesite and related rocks of
intermediate composition. The Land Status, Ownership Category of this underground, past producer is
unknown.
See the Gypsy and Helen Group and White Horse Mine entries for more information.

Bobcat Prospect: (37.22.09N by -114.30.53W - #3) (Silver, Zinc, Lead)
Coordinates are for the main entrance to this surface-underground, exploration prospect.

Boomerang Mining District (a.k.a. Pahranagat Mining District): (Silver, Lead, Copper, Manganese)
Description of the District:
*Tingley, Joseph V.; "Mining Districts of Nevada"; Nevada Bureau of Mines and Geology, Report 47,
Second Edition; 1998; Page 166*: A final alternate name for the Pahranagat Mining District, which has
come up in history, is the Boomerang Mining District. This came from an article in the September 15,
1902, *Nevada Miner*, that mentioned a Boomerang Mining District in the area of Crescent Spring. This
would have put it, by default, in the area later reverting to the Pahranagat Mining District.
See the Pahranagat Mining District entry for more information.
Mines Included in the District: (Include only those specifically referencing the Boomerang Mining
District.)

Boss Claim (a.k.a. Flagstaff): (37.28.20N by -114.46.35W - #3) (Gold, Manganese, Iron, Barite)
See the Flagstaff entry for more information.

Boston-Pioche: (3.55.21N by -114.26.43W - #3) (Silver, Lead, Zinc, Copper, Antimony, Arsenic)
Coordinates are for the ore body of this underground, past producer.

Bowery Vein (a.k.a. Salt Lake Pioche Mining Company Mines): (37.92306N by -114.437W – USGS
MRDS) (Gold, Silver, Lead, Zinc, Copper)

See the Salt Lake Pioche Mining Company Mines entry for more information.

Boyd Alunite Deposit: (37.27.50N by -114.34.07W - #3) (Aluminum)
Coordinates are for the main entrance to this underground, past producer.

Boyd Mining District: (Alunite, Clay)
Description of the District:
Tingley, Joseph V.; "Mining Districts of Nevada"; Nevada Bureau of Mines and Geology, Report 47,
Second Edition; 1998; Page 38: The Boyd Mining District is located in Rainbow Canyon, about 14 miles
South of Caliente.
Mines Included in the District: (Include only those specifically referencing the Boyd Mining District.)

Bradshaw (a.k.a. Bradshaw Mine): (38.26.35N by -114.18.34W - #3) (Gold, Silver, Copper, Uranium)
Coordinates are for the ore body of this surface-underground, past producer.
USGS MRDS Data Base Record 10037369, Released February 1, 1980; Updated January 1, 1985: The site
of the Bradshaw Mine is shown at 38.44856N by -114.3114W, placing it about 1½ miles Southeast of
Atlanta, in the Atlanta Mining District, in the Silver Park Mining District, in the Silver Springs Mining
District and in the area included on the USGS Atlanta 24K, Wilson Creek Range 100K and Lund 250K
maps. The projected Public Land Survey System locators, as the area is unsurveyed, are Section 26,
Township 7 North, Range 68 East. Gold and Silver are present and are shown as primary commodities with
Copper and Uranium tertiary. Mineralization includes Argentite with a gangue of Quartz and Goethite in a
host of Dolomite and Late Ordovician Limestone. The ore body is described generally as Tabular to
Irregular Lenses, striking North 45° to 60° West and dipping 50° Northeast. The ore was found in two zones
of red Jasperoid; a Western zone 500 feet long and 150 feet wide; and, an Eastern zone, which was smaller
and made up of narrow stringers striking North 60° West. The crevices carry Oxidized Silver minerals. The
mine was developed by a large open pit and an inclined shaft in the Western zone. There was an adit with
about 150 feet of underground workings. One of the drifts is perpendicular to the fault zone (crosscut?) and
2 other drifts parallel the fault zone. The workings penetrate a large Silicified outcrop on the Bradshaw
Fault Zone. The area of Silicified rock dips about 35° Northeast and is elongated Northwest to Southeast,
parallel to the fault zone. The rock is similar to that in the Atlanta Mine except that it has fewer open
spaces. Breccia fragments appear to be completely Silicified Carbonate rock. The deepest portions of the
mine penetrate Carbonate beds which have been Silicified intact, with only minor Brecciation. No Sulfide
minerals were found; however, the Limonite present in the open spaces has probably been derived from the
Oxidation of Pyrite. Sampling done by the Standard Slag Company indicates widespread Gold and Silver
mineralization present at the Bradshaw Mine. Invisible Uranium minerals are present, but a radiometric
survey of the mine dump in 1978 indicates anomalous radioactivity. The geology, in the general area of the
site, is described as Limestone, Dolomite, Shale and Quartzite. The Land Status, Ownership Category of
this occurrence is shown as "BLM Administrative Area".
USGS MRDS Data Base Record 10173792, Released January 19, 1994: The main entrance to the
Bradshaw Mine is shown at 38.44435N by -114.30224W, placing it in the Atlanta Mining District. The
location accuracy, of these coordinates, is shown as +/- 500 meters. The Public Land Survey System
locators are Section 26, Township 7 North, Range 68 East. This record shows Silver present and as a
primary commodity with Gold tertiary. The geology, in the area of the main entrance, is described as
Limestone, Dolomite, Shale and Quartzite. The Land Status, Ownership Category of this surface-
underground, past producer is shown as "BLM Administrative Area".

Bradshaw Mining District (a.k.a. Viola Mining District): (Silver, Gold, Lead, Zinc, Copper, Manganese,
Fluorspar)
Description of the District:
Tingley, Joseph V.; "Mining Districts of Nevada"; Nevada Bureau of Mines and Geology, Report 47,
Second Edition; 1998; Page 239: In 1995, Walter R. Averett, in his book *Through the Rainbow Canyon*,
described a Mining District, which he called the Bradshaw, which he indicated was discovered in 1928 and
was located it about 19 miles Northeast of Carp. What he identified would have been in the Eastern part of
the modern Viola Mining District.
See the Viola Mining District entry for more information.
Mines Included in the District: (Include only those specifically referencing the Bradshaw Mining District.)

Bristol City (a.k.a. Bristol; Bristol Well) –Ghost Town: (38.04.48N by -114.37.10W – USGS Bristol Range SE)
Bristol City, is a ghost town on the property of Kerr-McGee. Numerous buildings remain; however, any visit must be approved and scheduled through Kerr-McGee.
USGS MRDS Data Base Record 10310377, Released January 1, 2005; Updated September 1, 2007: The discovery of the Bristol deposits probably dates pre-1870, about the time that the Pioche deposits were discovered a few miles to the East. Prior to 1872 the town of Bristol Well or Bristol City sprang up on the Western flank of the Bristol Range, below the mines.

Bristol Mining District (a.k.a. Bristol-Jackrabbit Mining District; Blind Mountain Mining District; Jack Rabbit Mining District; Jackrabbit Mining District): (Silver, Copper, Lead, Zinc, Gold, Manganese, Montmorillonite)
Description of the District:
Tingley, Joseph V.; "Mining Districts of Nevada"; Nevada Bureau of Mines and Geology, Report 47, Second Edition; 1998; Page 38: The Bristol Mining District is located in the Northern Bristol Range about 15 miles North of Pioche. The Historic Blind Mountain Mining District (of 1871) covered the Southern part of the present Bristol Mining District. The Bristol Mining District originally only included the area around the mines on the Western slope of the Bristol Range; the Jackrabbit Mining District includes the area on the East side of the Bristol Range. The modern Bristol Mining District includes both the old Bristol Mining District and the Jackrabbit Mining District areas and extends from the West Range, North of Bristol Pass, South to Blind Mountain Spring, in the Southern Bristol Range.
USGS MRDS Data Base Record 10310377, Released January 1, 2005; Updated September 1, 2007: Four main Veins account for the bulk of the production in the Bristol Mining District: the May Day, the Tempest, the Gypsy-National and the Lead-Zinc Veins. The ore bodies occur along fracture zones, in Brecciated areas and in intersecting fissures. The main fissure system (the May Day) runs East and West and dips about 45° East. The Tempest runs about North 80° East and dips 70° Southeast. The Gypsy-National fissure system strikes Northeast and dips 70° to 85° East. The Lead-Zinc Vein strikes Northwest with a vertical dip. At the intersections of these features, Oxidized ore occurs in large Brecciated zones. Sulfide ore is rare, but occurs sometimes as nodules with Galena cores encased in Cerussite, coated by Carbonate with a film of Copper Oxide. Bedding contacts and flat bedding thrusts often localize ore disposition. Ore bodies are very Irregular in size and shape. The ore is very soft. Some of the larger ore bodies developed at intersections of the May Day and Tempest fissures. Stoping was almost continuous from the May Day collar to the 1,000 level of the Snyder Shaft. Several strongly Brecciated zones near faults carry high-grade Copper and Lead ore with Silver. At the Black Metal Mine, the ore system consists of a vertical pipe from which replacement ore bodies extend out laterally at 3 horizons into the gently-dipping Limestones that enclose the pipe. The pipe is localized by Brecciation at structural intersections. Lead-Silver ore occurred in the center of the pipe with exterior zones progressively higher in Manganese and lower in Lead and Silver.
Total production of the District is estimated at between $2 million and $6 million (period values). The Bristol Mines were sporadically productive from the 1870s to 1940, producing, at various times, Silver. Lead, Copper, Manganese, Gold and Zinc. There was no doubt much more production then officially recorded for the Bristol-Jackrabbit Mines. Production from 1881 to 1940 was 252,553 tons of ore valued at $2,541,774. Between 1924 and 1955 the Bristol Mine alone produced 4,433,800 ounces of Silver, 22,722,100 pounds of Copper, 35,943,800 pounds of Lead and 40,570,800 pounds of Zinc. Production for the period 1940 through 1941 and 1945 through 1947 was 45,620 tons of ore, which contained 391 ounces of Gold, 652,478 ounces of Silver, 2,910,521 pounds of Copper and 3,604,264 pounds of Lead. The remaining reserves of the Vein system deposit are unknown.
Mines Included in the District:
       Detroit Mine (Silver, Copper, Lead, Zinc, Gold)
       Fairview 002 (Lead, Silver, Gold)
       Fortuna Mine (Lead, Zinc, Copper, Silver, Gold)
       Hillside (Copper, Silver, Gold, Lead, Zinc, Manganese, Iron)
       Silver Horn (Silver, Lead, Gold, Nickel)

Bristol Silver Mines (a.k.a. Bristol Silver; Bristol Silver Mine; Gypsy Shaft; May Day Shaft; Snyder Shaft): (38.04.55N by -114.36.45W - #3) (Silver, Lead, Zinc, Copper, Gold, Manganese)
Coordinates are for the claim area of this surface-underground, past producer.
USGS MRDS Data Base Record 10104125, Released January 1, 1985: The site of the Bristol Silver Mine is shown at 38.08107N by -114.61695W, placing it in the Bristol-Jackrabbit Mining District and in the area included on the USGS Bristol Range SE 24K, Wilson Creek Range 100K and Lund 250K maps. These coordinates are for the Snyder Shaft, whose workings are connected to the May Day Shaft (400 feet North) and the Gypsy Shaft (100 feet to the Southwest). The projected (from the East) Public Land Survey System locators are Section 31, Township 3 North, Range 66 East. Silver, Copper, Lead and Zinc are present and are shown as primary commodities with Gold and Manganese Secondary. Mineralization of this Polymetallic Replacement Deposit (USGS Model Code 19a) includes Cuprite, Melaconite, Chrysocolla, Malachite, Native Lead, Galena, Plumbojarosite and Sphalerite, with a gangue of Quartz, Calcite, Limonite, Hematite and Pyrite, in a host of Lyndon Limestone associated with Diabase and Plutonic rock. The ore body is described as Irregular to Tabular, about 60 feet thick and about 2,000 feet long. The ore body strike and dip is different in two of the connected shafts. In the Gypsy Shaft the strike is North 60° to 10° West, with a dip 0f 80° to the East. The May Day strikes North 60° East and dips 43° South. The ore body was developed by about almost 10,600 feet of underground workings which attained a maximum depth of about 1,785 feet. In July, 1926, the mine was producing about 800 tons of ore per month. The geology, in the general area of the site, is described as Limestone and Dolomite with locally thick sequences of Shale and Siltstone. The shale is generally found below 1,700 feet in depth. The Land Status, Ownership Category of this past producer, which first produced in 1878, is shown as "Private". A record from the 1920s shows the Owner as the Bristol Silver Mines Company.
History: The mine was Owned and Operated by the Day-Bristol Mining Company in the early 1900s, who built the aerial tram in 1914. The Bristol Silver Mines Company was organized in 1919. The new company immediately purchased the Jackrabbit-Pioche narrow gauge railroad. Electric power was supplied to the mine by gasoline generators until 1926, then by diesel generators until 1937 when electric power from the Boulder Pioche powerline was obtained. This enabled a production of approximately 3,000 tons per day. The Bristol Silver Mining Company owned most of the property in the District for some time, but this record treats only the main Snyder-Gypsy-May Day workings. In 1942 the property consisted of 638 acres of Patented land and 1,222 acres of Unpatented land.
USGS MRDS Data Base Record 10222278, Released October 18, 1996: The main entrance to the Bristol Silver Mines is shown at 38.08186N by -114.61694W and in the Bristol-Jackrabbit Mining District. The location accuracy, of these coordinates, is shown as +/- 10 meters. This record shows Lead present and as a primary commodity with Silver, Gold, Copper, Zinc and Manganese tertiary. The ore body/bodies is/are described as being Irregular Replacements and Breccia-filled, Fissure Veins. It is about 300 feet thick, 30 feet wide and 250 feet long. The geology, in the area of the main entrance, is described as Limestone and Dolomite with locally-thick sequences of Shale and Siltstone. Discovered in 1868 and put into production in 1871, the Land Status, Ownership Category of this surface-underground, past producer is shown as "Private". Mineral Rights are held through "Patented Located Claims". A 1976 record shows the 100% Owner as Kerr-McGee Corporation.
See the Bristol-Jackrabbit Mines entry for more information.

Bristol Well Deposit: (38.05.17N by -114.42.36W - #3) (Montmorillonite)
Coordinates are for the main entrance to this surface-underground operation.

Bristol-Jackrabbit Mines (a.k.a. Black Metals Mine; Black Shaft; Bristol Silver; Bristol Silver Mines; Detroit; Gypsy Vein; Hillside; Home Run; Iron; Jackrabbit; May Day; National; Snyder Shaft; Tempest; Vesuvius): (38.08107N by -114.617W – USGS MRDS) (Silver, Copper, Lead, Zinc, Gold, Manganese)
USGS MRDS Data Base Record 10310377, Released January 1, 2005; Updated September 1, 2007: The site of the Bristol-Jackrabbit Mines is shown at 38.08107N by -114.61695W, placing them about 8 miles Northwest of Pioche and in the area included on the USGS Bristol Range SE 24K, Wilson Creek Range 100K and Lund 250K maps. The Bristol-Jackrabbit Mines are scattered over a few square miles in the North end of the Bristol Range, Northwest of Pioche. The Jackrabbit Mines were on the Eastern side of the Range; the Bristol Mines are just over the crest of the Range, a few miles to the West. In 1914 an aerial tram was built between the two mines and they operated as one. Many of the Bristol Mines are also

connected by underground workings, such as May Day, Gypsy (Gypsy Vein) and Snyder (Snyder Shaft). The mines are located on both sides of the Bristol Range, with the larger, more productive mines on the West. Silver, Copper, Lead and Zinc are present and are shown as primary commodities with Gold and Manganese secondary. Mineralization includes Silver Chloride, Cuprite, Tenorite, Chrysocolla, Azurite, secondary Copper minerals, Galena, Plumbojarosite, Lead Carbonate, Sphalerite, Smithsonite, Secondary Zinc minerals and Manganese Oxides with a gangue of Quartz-Clay gouge, Limonite and Hematite, with abundant Pyrite below 1,700 feet. This Polymetallic Replacement Deposit (USGS Model Code 19a) is hosted in Early Cambrian to Middle Cambrian Pioche Shale and Middle Cambrian Chisholm Shale, Lyndon Limestone, Highland Peak Limestone and is associated with Tertiary Porphyry dikes, Diabase and Lamprophyre. The ore body is described as Irregular to Tabular with the ore deposition having been controlled by both structure and lithology. The best ore occurs in Carbonate host rocks at fracture intersections, particularly along the May Day Fault which strikes North 65° East and dips 45° Southeast. The primary host rock is the Limestone, both massive and thin-bedded, with shale below 1,700 feet.
The Bristol Mines were developed through underground workings, which included the May Day shaft, tunnel and crosscut; the Snyder Shaft, sunk at a 70° South incline to 1,780 feet in the 1940's; and, the vertical Gypsy Shaft. Major stopes were the Dave Fox stope, Bingham Canyon stope, Cave stope and Perry stope. A 2-mile aerial tramway was built from the main workings, on the West crest of the Bristol Range, to the railroad terminus at Jackrabbit, on the East flank of the Range.
The geology, in the general area of the site, is described as Limestone and Dolomite with locally thick sequences of Shale and Siltstone. The Land Status, Ownership Category of this underground, past producer is shown as "Private". A 2004 record shows the Owner-Operator as Kerr-McGee/Bristol Silver Mines Company.
See the Bristol Mining District entry for more information.

Bristol-Jackrabbit Mining District (a.k.a. Bristol Mining District): (Silver, Lead, Gold, Copper, Zinc, Nickel, Tungsten, Iron)
Description of the District:
Tingley, Joseph V.; "Mining Districts of Nevada"; Nevada Bureau of Mines and Geology, Report 47, Second Edition; 1998; Page 38: The Bristol Mining District is located in the Northern Bristol Range about 15 miles North of Pioche. The Historic Blind Mountain Mining District (of 1871) covered the Southern part of the present Bristol Mining District. The Bristol Mining District originally only included the area around the mines on the Western slope of the Bristol Range; the Jackrabbit Mining District includes the area on the East side of the Bristol Range. The modern Bristol Mining District includes both the old Bristol Mining District and the Jackrabbit Mining District areas and extends from the West Range, North of Bristol Pass, South to Blind Mountain Spring, in the Southern Bristol Range.
See the Bristol Mining District entry for more information.
Mines Included in the District:
      Black Metal Mine 001 (Silver, Manganese, Iron, Gold, Lead, Copper, Bismuth, Coal)
      Ida May (Silver, Lead, Gold, Copper, Zinc)
      O. S. L. Mine (Silver, Copper, Lead, Zinc, Tungsten, Iron)
      Silver Horn (Silver, Lead, Gold, Nickel)
      Tempest Mine (Gold, Silver, Copper, Bismuth, Iron, Lead)
      Vesuvius Mine (Silver, Gold, Lead, Zinc, Copper, Iron)
      Woodbutcher (Gold, Silver, Lead, Copper)

Bruce: (36.56.55N by -114.20.45W - #3) (Clay)
Coordinates are for the ore body of this surface-underground prospect.

Bruno Prospect: (38.02.29W by -115.50.55W - #3)
Coordinates are for trenching.
Google Earth Review: I thought the coordinates might put the Bruno Prospect in Nye County; however upon review, it is about 2,900 feet south of the Lincoln County-Nye County border, in Lincoln County, and about 500 feet West of the boundary of the Humboldt National Forest. The nearest road is a trail that branches off to the West from the National Forest Development Road NF-415.

Bruson: (36.55.13N by -114.17.58W - #3) (Tungsten)
Coordinates are for the ore body of this surface, exploration prospect.

Bruson Prospect (a.k.a. MacBruson Claims): (36.96165N by -114.292W – USGS MRDS)
(Molybdenum, Tungsten, Gold, Silver)
See the MacBruson Claims entry for more information.

Buckeye-Pennsylvania Prospect: (36.52.11N by -114.21.00W - #3) (Gypsum)
Coordinates are for trenching associated with this surface, exploration prospect.

Buckhorn Prospect: (37.08.55N by -114.16.15W - #3) (Clay)
Coordinates are for the ore body of this past producer and current prospect.

Bull Hill Mine (a.k.a. Bull Hill Group; Bull Hill Shaft; Florence Prospect): (37.55.04N by -114.03.29W - #3) (Silver, Gold, Fluorite)
Coordinates are for trenching associated with this underground, past producer.
USGS MRDS Data Base Record 10046447, Released February 1, 1984: The site of the Bull Hill Shaft is shown at 37.91775N by -114.05915W, placing it in the Eagle Valley Mining District, in the Fay Mining District and in the area included on the Deer Lodge Canyon 24K and Caliente 100K and 250K maps. The Public Land Survey System locators are the Northwest ¼ of Section 29, Township 7 North, Range 71 East. Silver, Gold and Fluorite, in a host of Rhyolite, are present and all are shown as primary commodities. The Fluorite is both purple and green; however, the purple color is prevalent. Six assays of the ore were run and gave the following results; Gold, from 0.02 ounce to 0.43 ounce per ton and Silver from 0.2 ounce to 2.6 ounces per ton. The ore body is described as a Tabular Vein, which strikes North 20° East, dips steeply West and is up to 3 feet thick. The Vein splits into two, 1-foot-wide Stringers at the bottom of the 30-foot, development shaft. Metals are mainly associated with the Hematite-rich gangue material. The geology, in the general area of the site, is described as welded and non-welded Silicic Ash-flow Tuffs. The Land Status, Ownership Category of this occurrence is unknown.
USGS MRDS Data Base Record 10270989, Released January 12, 1994: The main entrance to the Bull Hill Mine is shown at 37.91807N by -114.05892W. The location accuracy, of these coordinates, is shown as +/- 10 meters. The Public Land Survey System locators are the Northwest ¼ of Section 29, Township 1 North, Range 71 East. This record shows Silver present and as a primary commodity with Gold and Fluorite tertiary. The geology, in the area of the main entrance, is described as welded and non-welded Silicic Ash-flow Tuffs. The Land Status, Ownership Category of this underground, past producer is shown as "BLM Administrative Area".
See the Florence Prospect entry for more information.

Bumagin Shaft/Bumagin Claim: (37.92386N by -114.434W – USGS MRDS) (Gold, Silver, Zinc, Lead, Copper)
USGS MRDS Data Base Record 10295149, Released January 12, 1994: The main entrance to the Bunagin Shaft is shown at 37.92368N by -114.43394W, placing it in the Pioche Mining District and in the area included on the USGS Pioche 24K and Caliente 100K and 250K maps. The location accuracy, of these coordinates, is shown as +/- 10 Meters. The Public Land Survey System locators are the Northeast ¼ of the Northwest ¼ of the Northeast ¼ of Section 26, Township 1 North, Range 67 East. Gold is present and is shown as a primary commodity with Silver, Zinc, Lead and Copper tertiary. The geology, in the area of the main entrance, is described as Quartzite and minor amounts of Conglomerate, Phyllitic Siltstone, Limestone and Dolomite. The Land Status, Ownership Category of this underground prospect is shown as "Private". Mineral Rights are held through "Patented, Located Claims". A 1944 record shows the Owner-Operator as the Salt Lake Pioche Mining Company of Nevada.
See the Salt Lake Pioche Mining Company Mines entry for more information.

Burke Mine: (37.55.34N by -114.26.47W - #3) (Silver, Lead, Zinc)
Coordinates are for the main entrance to this underground operation.

C-M Alunite Property: (37.21.19N by -114.10.05W - #3)
Coordinates are for the ore body of this prospect.

<u>Caliente (a.k.a. Culverwell's Ranch) (town)</u>:
Nevada Historical Marker #55; On U.S. Highway 93 in Caliente, Nevada: "Caliente was first settled as a ranch, furnishing hay for the mining camps of Pioche and Delmar. In 1901, the famous Harriman-Clark right-of-way battle was ended when rancher Charles Culverwell, with the aid of a broad-gauge shotgun, allowed one railroad grade to be built through his lush meadows. Harriman and Clark had been battling eleven years building side-by-side grades, ignoring court orders and federal marshals.
The population boom began with an influx of railroad workers, most of them immigrants from Austria, Japan, and the Ottoman Empire. A tent city was settled in August 1903.
With the completion of the Los Angeles, San Pedro, and Salt Lake Railroad in 1905, Caliente became a division point. In 1906-07, the Caliente and Pioche Railroad (now the Union Pacific) was built between Pioche and the main line at Caliente. The large Mission revival style depot was built in 1923, serving as a civic center, as well as a hotel."

Caliente: (37.37.00N by -114.31.35W - #3) (Zeolites)
Coordinates are for an ore body.

<u>Caliente Cobalt Mining Company (a.k.a. Advance; Contact; Gold Stake; Old Democrat; Republic Mines)</u>: (37.43.06N by -114.33.00W - #3) (Gold, Silver, Lead, Copper)
Coordinates are for the ore body of this past producer.
USGS MRDS Data Base Record 10046437, Released January 1, 1984: The site of the Caliente Cobalt Mining Company is shown at 37.68914N by -114.52278W, placing it in the Caliente Mining District, in the Chief Mining District and in the area included on the USGS Chief Mountain 24K and Caliente 100K and 250K maps. The Caliente Cobalt Mining Company took over the 3 Patented Claims and a large part of the Mining District in 1931, acquiring a total of 35 Claims. The location accuracy, of these coordinates, is shown as +/- 500 meters. The Public Land Survey System locators are Sections 7 & 8 and 18, Township 3 South, Range 67 East. Gold and Silver are present and are shown as primary commodities with Lead and Copper secondary. The ore body is described as Tabular and in 1937 a new vertical shaft was being sunk on it to extract the deeper ores. A total of 76 tons of ore had been mined and shipped in 1934, and another 189 tons were mined and shipped in 1935. Three men were employed at the time and about 250 feet of development work had been completed. The geology, in the general area of the site, is described as Quartzite and minor amounts of Conglomerate, Phyllitic Siltstone, Limestone and Dolomite. The Land Status, Ownership Category of this occurrence is described as "Private". A record from the 1930s shows the Owner as the Caliente Cobalt Mining Company – Messrs. Burt and Mathews, Principals.
See the Old Democrat entry for more information.

<u>Caliente Mining District (a.k.a. Chief Mining District)</u>: (Gold, Silver, Lead, Copper, Vanadium)
Description of the District:
Tingley, Joseph V.; "Mining Districts of Nevada"; Nevada Bureau of Mines and Geology, Report 47, Second Edition; 1998; Page 54: Discovered and established in 1870, the Chief Mining District covers the Southeastern tip of the Chief Range, about 8 miles North of Caliente. The proximity of the town of Caliente is likely the origin of the reference to the Caliente Mining District.
See the Chief Mining District entry for more information:
Mines Included in the District:
        Blue Mary Claim North Extension (Gold)
        Caliente Prospects (Gold, Silver, Copper)

<u>Caliente Prospects (a.k.a. Jumbo Pit; NBMG Sample Sites 1494 & 1495; Pennsylvania Mine)</u>:
(37.61691N by -114.52W – USGS MRDS) (Gold, Silver, Copper)
USGS MRDS Data Base Record 10046436, Released July 1, 1984: The site of the Caliente Prospects is shown at 37.61691N by -114.52W, placing it immediately North of the main part of the town of Caliente, but still within the City Limits, in the Caliente Mining District and in the area included on the USGS Caliente 24K, 100K and 250K maps. The Public Land Survey System locators are Section 7, Township 4 South, Range 67 East. Gold and Silver, with a gangue of Quartz and Jarosite, in a host of Andesite, are present and are shown as primary commodities. The ore body is described as Tabular with a main shear striking North 20° East with an intersecting shear striking North 10° West, and about 4 feet thick. Quartz

Veins and Stockworks occur along shear zones in Propylitized and Argillized Andesite. The mining effort appears to have been focused in the area where the main shear zone was intersected by the North 10° West vertical shear. The rock at the intersection and along both structures is laced with narrow Quartz Veinlets. These Veinlets have a North 20° East trend, but dip 10° to 15° Southeast. The mined ore zone contained a 3 to 4 foot-wide Brecciated Quartz Vein with Iron Oxides and Manganese spots along it. The Vein has drusy Quartz crystals filling vugs with some Jarosite on the fracture surfaces. The rock on the point surrounding the old workings is bleached and silicified near the shear zone, with bleaching decreasing as you move away from the main structure. The deposit has been developed by several adits, a shaft, open stopes and some surface cuts. There was no activity at the site when visited in 1984. The geology, in the general area of the site is described as Andesite and related rocks of intermediate composition. The Land Status, Ownership Category of this occurrence is shown as "Private".

USGS MRDS Data Base Record 10246536, Released May 29, 1997: The main entrance to the Caliente Prospects is shown at 37.61687N by -114.52003W, placing it in the Caliente Mining District. The location accuracy, of these coordinates, is shown as +/- 10 meters. This record shows Gold, Silver and Copper present and all are shown as primary commodities. The shafts and adits of the workings are all filled and inaccessible. Royal Standard Minerals, Incorporated, started exploration at the site in the Summer of 1996. The property, as currently defined, consists of 48 Lode Claims controlling the Pennsylvania Quartz Vein system. The old Pennsylvania Mine site is also located on the property, as is the partially-developed Jumbo Pit. Exploration and development were still underway when the area was checked in May of 1997. Prior exploration programs have identified a potential open-pit Resource of 700,000 tons grading 0.039 ounces per ton in the central core area. Early Gold and Silver production is also expected from the Jumbo Pit area once it is expanded and cleaned out. The former Heap Leach pad and pile is expected to also contribute Resources, albeit minimal; estimated at 50,000 to 60,000 tons at 0.03 ounces of Gold and 0.8 ounces per ton of Silver or 1,500 to 1,800 ounces of Gold and 40,000 to 48,000 ounces of Silver. The geology, in the area of the main entrance, is described as Andesite and related rocks of intermediate composition. The Land Status, Ownership Category of this surface-underground, prospect, discovered in 1994, is shown as "Private". Mineral Rights are held through "Patented, Located Claims". A 1996 record shows the Owner-Operator as Royal Standard Minerals, Incorporated of Virginia.
See the Pennsylvania Mine entry for more information.

California-Pioche Shaft (a.k.a. NBMG Sample Site 1425): (37.92107N by -114.456W – USGS MRDS) (Gold, Silver, Lead, Copper, Antimony, Manganese, Barite)
USGS MRDS Data Base Record 10046400, Released April 1, 1984: the site of the California-Pioche Shaft is shown at 37.92107N by -114.4564W, placing it in the Pioche Mining District and in the area included on the USGS Pioche 24K and Caliente 100K and 250K maps. The Public Land Survey System locators are Section 27, Township 1, Range 67 East. Gold and Silver are present and are shown as primary commodities with Lead secondary and Copper, Antimony, Manganese and Barite tertiary. Mineralization includes Galena, Chalcopyrite and Barite with a gangue of Calcite, Pyrite and Mica in a host of Lyndon Limestone of the Pioche Shale Formation. The ore body was developed by a single shaft with a foundation and head frame along with surface scrapings and development roads. The workings were along the faulted contact between Cambrian Pioche Shale and Lyndon Limestone. Here the Limestone is cut by numerous Calcite Stringers and Pods, with grains and fresh Pyrite interspersed in the Limestone, as evidenced by samples on the dump. The geology, in the general area of the site, is described as Limestone and Dolomite with locally-thick sequences of Shale and Siltstone. The Land Status, Ownership Category of this past producer is shown as "Private".
USGS MRDS Data Base Record 10125414, Released January 26, 1994: The main entrance to the California-Pioche Shaft is shown at 37.92106N by -114.45644W, placing it in the Pioche Mining District. The location accuracy, of these coordinates, is shown as +/- 100 meters. This record shows Gold present and as a primary commodity with Lead, Silver and Manganese tertiary. The ore body is described as a Tabular Fissure Vein of Hydrothermal origin. The geology, in the area of the main entrance, is described as Limestone and Dolomite with locally-thick sequences of Shale and Siltstone. The Land Status, Ownership Category of this underground prospect is shown as "Private". Mineral Rights are held through "Patented, Located Claims".
See the NBMG Sample Site 1425 entry for more information.

Carp (Ghost Town): (37.06.43N by -114.29.34W – USGS GNIS)

Carp is a Ghost Town in Lincoln County, located about 35 miles South of Caliente, along County Road 4230, on the Meadow Valley Wash, which empties into Lake Mead. Originally a small Union Pacific Railroad station under the name of Cliffdale, it received a U. S. Post Office in June of 1918, but the charter was shortly, thereafter rescinded, and the Post Office was not officially established until December, 1925. In June of 1921, the name Cliffdale was changed to Carp, after a railroad agent serving the town. In the summer of 1974 the Post Office, and all of its rural branches, closed. Today there is not much there, other than a railroad siding and the remains of an old water reservoir.

Carp Mine: (37.12.47N by -114.17.13W - #3) (Fluorite)
Coordinates are for the ore body of this surface, past producer.

Carp Mining District (a.k.a. Viola Mining District): (Silver, Gold, Lead, Zinc, Copper, Manganese, Fluorspar)
Description of the District:
Tingley, Joseph V.; "Mining Districts of Nevada"; Nevada Bureau of Mines and Geology, Report 47, Second Edition; 1998; Page 239: The Carp Mining District was shown by Tingley as an alternate name for the Viola Mining District, likely referencing the town of Carp (37.06.43N by -114.29.34W), which is now a ghost town.
See the Viola Mining District entry for more information.
Mines Included in the District:

Caselton 001 (a.k.a. Caselton Mine; Combined Metals Reduction No. 2; Raymond and Ely):
(37.55.05N by -114.29.10W - #3) (Zinc, Silver, Lead, Gold, Manganese, Iron)
Coordinates are for the main entrance to this underground, past producer.
USGS MRDS Data Base Record 10222350, Released July 20, 1988: The main entrance to the Caselton Mine is shown at 37.91916N by -114.48274W, placing about 0.6 miles South of Pioche, in the Pioche Mining District and in the area included on the USGS Pioche 24K and Caliente 100K and 250K maps. The location accuracy, of these coordinates, is shown as +/- 10 meters. The Public Land Survey System locators are the Northwest ¼ of the Southwest ¼ of the Northwest ¼ of Section 28, Township 1 North, Range 67 East. Zinc is present and is shown as a primary commodity with Gold, Silver and Lead secondary and Manganese and Iron tertiary. Mineralization includes Sphalerite, Galena and Siderite. The mine consists of a number of ore bodies, a combination of Tabular Replacements and Fissure Vein Deposits of Hydrothermal origin. The Replacement deposits occur in the Limestone Member of the Pioche Shale Formation. The upper, younger Limestone contains Oxidized ore. The Mine has not produced since 1958 and there has been no activity at the mine in the recent past. The geology, in the area of the main entrance, is described as Alluvial deposits. The Land Status, Ownership Category of this underground deposit, discovered in 1864 and put into production that year, and the flotation and beneficiation mill, is shown as a combination of "Patented, Located Claims" and "Private Leases". A 1979 record shows the Owner as Kerr-McGee Corporation of Oklahoma City, Oklahoma.
In 1985 an analysis of the mine was being made and the costs of operating the underground rail system were included as Operating costs. The plan proposed a dewatering and then a Room & Pillar approach to the underground development. The plans appeared focused on the remaining large bodies of Oxide ore as there was no formal plan for the Sulfide ore, which is believed to have been mostly exhausted.

Caselton 002 (a.k.a. Caselton Shaft; Combined Metals Reduction No. 2; St. Patrick Zinc-Lead-Silver Mine): (37.55.06N by -114.29.01W - #3) (Zinc, Silver, Lead, Gold, Manganese, Iron)
Coordinates are for the main entrance to this underground, past producer.
USGS MRDS Data Base Record 10037330, Released October 1, 1979; Updated September 1, 1984: The site of the Caselton Shaft is shown at 37.92107N by -114.46501W, placing it on the West edge of the town of Pioche, in the Pioche Mining District and in the area included on the USGS Pioche 24K and Caliente 100K and 250K maps. The location accuracy, of these coordinates, is shown as +/- 500 meters. The Public Land Survey System locators are Sections 27 & 28, Township 1 North, Range 67 East. Zinc, Lead and Silver are present and all are shown as primary commodities with Manganese secondary. Mineralization of this Polymetallic Replacement Deposit includes Sphalerite, Galena, Pyrargyrite (Ag_3SbS_3) and Proustite (Ag_3AsS_3), with a gangue of Pyrite, in a host of Limestone and Shale and associated with Granite. A quick review indicated Pyrite to be about 60% of the ore, Sphalerite up to 22% and Galena less than 15%. The

ore body Strikes North 30º East, dips 20º Northwest and ranges from 4 to 40 feet thick, averaging about 6 feet. Replacement occurs only where the steeply-dipping Greenwood fissure, intersects the Limestone member. The Shale is very Sandy. The ore bed was mined for over 10,000 feet along an East-West channel which was 100 to 1,800 feet wide. Surface mining channels paralleled the main Vein system. The ore was mined in blocks between the 300 and 1,400-foot levels. Drifting on the 1,200-foot level connected with drifting from the Combined Metals No. 1 Shaft. The ore body terminates against the Frontal fault, the hanging wall of which was explored to a depth of 2,500 feet by an exploration shaft without positive results. The exploration shaft did not penetrate the Tertiary Volcanic rocks. The mine reached a total depth of about 1,400 feet and underground workings totaled about 10,000 feet.

In the 1940s the mine was operating on electricity from the relatively new Boulder Dan, which opened in 1936 and became known as Hoover Dam in 1947, after the name was changed by Congress to honor President Hoover, who had been in the Office when the bills for the construction of the dam and power infrastructure had been passed. By 1953 the bulk of the Sulfide ore had been exhausted and the company spent about a year in an attempt to develop a commercial Manganese mine at the site. That failed and the Company then rehabilitated the mine and worked to extract the remaining Sulfide ore reserves. In 1955, until sometime in 1957 when metal prices fell significantly, they were able to produce up to 10,000 tons per month, and turn a profit. After the drop in prices the Caselton mine was placed on care and maintenance. In 1975 the St. Patrick Mining Company worked the shaft for water to run the Caselton Mill. A similar type of operation occurred in 1976 and 1977 by Bunker Hill Mining Company, which employed 7 people. In 1980, Kerr-McGee Corporation employed 25 people in underground rehabilitation of the mine. The Sulfide reserved are believed to have been exhausted, but large quantities of low-grade, proto-ore remains in the upper levels of the West end of the mine.

The geology, in the general area of the mine, is described as Limestone and Dolomite with locally-thick sequences of Shale and Siltstone. The Land Status, Ownership Category of this past producer is shown as "Private". An undated record shows the Owner as the Amalgamated Pioche Mines and Smelter Corporation and Kerr-McGee Corporation, M. T. Worley, General Manager.

Caselton Mill: (37.55.09N by -114.29.04W - #3) (Silver, Zinc, Lead)
Coordinates are for a past-producing, processing plant.
USGS MRDS Data Base Record 10198669, Released January 21, 1994: The plant area of the Caselton Mill is shown at 37.91806N by -114.48474W, placing it in the Pioche Mining District and in the area included on the USGS Pioche 24K and Caliente 100K and 250K maps. The location accuracy, of these coordinates, is shown as +/- 10 meters. The Public Land Survey System locators are the Southeast ¼ of the Southeast ¼ of the Northeast ¼ of Section 29, Township 1 North, Range 67 East. Silver is present and is shown as a primary commodity with Zinc and Lead tertiary. The geology, in the plant area, is described as Alluvial deposits. The Land Status, Ownership Category of this past producing, processing plant is shown as "Private". A 1976 record shows the Owner-Operator as the Bunker Hill Company of Idaho.
USGS MRDS Data Base Record 10222350, Released July 20, 1988: The Caselton Mill is owned by Combined Metals Reduction and is leased to the Bunker Hill Company.

Cave Valley 001: (38.38.18N by -114.48.55W - #3) (Silver, Copper, Lead, Uranium)
Coordinates are for an ore body.
See the Eagle Rock entry for more information.

Cave Valley Mine 002 (a.k.a. Big Fissure Claims; Great Western Claims; Hidden Fissure Group; NBMG Sample Sites 815-817 and 818a and 818b; Original Cave Group; Subterranean Group):
(38.38.39N by -114.47.49W - #3) (Lead, Silver, Copper, Zinc, Gold, Vanadium, Arsenic, Clay)
Coordinates are for the main entrance to this underground, past producer.
USGS MRDS Data Base Record 10045919, Released March 1, 1982; Updated February 1, 1985: The site of the Cave Valley Mine is shown at 38.64356N by -114.79613W, placing it about 50 miles South of Ely and 45 miles North of Pioche, on a hill on the East side of Cave Valley, North of Cottonwood Canyon, in the Cave Valley Mining District, in the Patterson/Patterson Pass Mining District, and in the area included on the USGS Parker Station 24K, Garrison 100K and Lund 250K maps. The Public Land Survey System locators are Sections 9 & 16, Township 9 North, Range 64 East. Silver, Lead and Copper are present and are shown as primary commodities with Gold, Zinc and Vanadium secondary and Clay and Arsenic tertiary. Mineralization includes Cerargyrite, Galena and Native Lead and Copper, with a gangue of Quartz,

Pyrite and Limonite, in a host of the Pole Canyon Limestone member of the Pioche Shale and Late Cambrian Shale. The ore body is described as being in the form of Lenses, striking North-Northwest, dipping 80° West-Southwest, up to 5 feet wide and 120 feet deep and exposed at the surface. Five North-trending fissures are exposed in the mine area. A 1 to 5-foot wide Vein and small bedded replacements in or near the lower Limestone in the Pioche Shale contains Lead, Silver and Copper mineralization. Uranium minerals were reported in 1930, but this appears to have been discounted in 1931 when none were found, but instead a yellow Lead-Zinc Vanadate called Mottramite, or by its old names Cuprodescloizite and/or Psittascinite, was discovered which was apparently confused with Carnotite. The mine was developed by several shallow prospect pits, a few shafts, none more than 20 feet deep, one 120-foot deep shaft and 2 Northwest-striking adits. The geology, in the general area of the site, is described as Limestone and Dolomite with locally-thick sequences of Shale and Siltstone. The Land Status, Ownership Category of this past producer, discovered in 1921 by J. C. Clark and J. C. Riordan, is shown as "Private". A 1969 record shows the Owner as Will and Eva Hendrix.
Pioche Record (The); January 21, 1921; "Around the Mines"; Page 3; Column 1: "Salt Lake men have undertaken the development of oil lands in Cave Valley, Lincoln County (Nevada), about 60 miles South of Ely, says the Tonopah Times. The agreement gives the Salt Lake men a lease on 1,000 acres and a company is to be formed."
See the Eagle Rock entry for more information.

Cave Valley Mining District (a.k.a. Cave Mining District; Patterson Mining District): (Gold, Silver, Lead, Copper, Vanadium)
Description of the District:
Tingley, Joseph V.; "Mining Districts of Nevada"; Nevada Bureau of Mines and Geology, Report 47, Second Edition; 1998; Page 51: Discovered and organized in 1869, as the Cave Mining District, the Cave Valley Mining District covers the area around Cave Spring and the Northern end of Cave Valley. The current Cave Valley Mining District includes an area of low hills running Southwest from the Schell Creek Range, about 8 miles Northwest from Patterson Pass. The Cave Valley Mining District is often included with the Patterson Mining District, which borders it on the East.
Mines Included in the District:
        Cave Valley Mine 002 (Lead, Silver, Copper, Zinc, Gold, Vanadium, Arsenic, Clay)
        Cinch Mine (Tungsten, Gold, Silver)
        Pip (Tungsten, Gold, Silver)
        Schwartz Tunnel (Tungsten, Zinc, Gold, Silver, Molybdenum, Lead, Fluorite)

Cedar Mining District (a.k.a. Delamar Mining District): (Gold, Silver, Copper, Lead, Perlite)
Description of the District:
Tingley, Joseph V.; "Mining Districts of Nevada"; Nevada Bureau of Mines and Geology, Report 47, Second Edition; 1998; Page 66 & 67: In his 1872 work *Preliminary Report Concerning Explorations and Surveys Principally in Nevada and Arizona*, G. M. Wheeler included the area of the current Delamar Mining District in a large Cedar Mining District, described as being located on the "Western side of the Bennett Spring Mountains". This would have been West of Meadow Valley Wash and Southwest of Clover Valley.
See the Delamar Mining District entry for more information.
Mines Included in the District:

Cedar Wash Prospects: (32.27.20N by -114.48.15W - #3) (Silver, Copper)
Coordinates are for the ore body of this surface operation.

Centennial Shaft: (37.54.00N by 14.28.04W - #3) (Lead, Silver, Manganese, Zinc, Copper, Gold)
Coordinates are for the main entrance to this underground, past producer.
USGS MRDS Data Base Record 10305626, Released January 12, 1994: The main entrance to the Centennial Shaft is shown at 37.89996N by -114.46864W, placing it in the Pioche Mining District and in the area included on the USGS Pioche 24K and Caliente 100K maps. The location accuracy, of these coordinates, is shown as +/- 10 meters. The Public Land Survey System locators are the Southwest ¼ of the Northeast ¼ of the Southeast ¼ of Section 33, Township 1 North, Range 67 East. Lead is present and is shown as a primary commodity with Gold, Silver and Copper tertiary. The geology, in the area of the main

entrance, is described as Alluvial deposits. The Land Status, Ownership Category of this underground, past producer is shown as "Private".

Centennial-Pioche:
See Prince Consolidated, *Goodwin's Weekly, November 23, 1912* article for more information.

Charley Ross Mine (a.k.a. Mountain View Group; NBMG Sample Site 1722): (37.54.56N by -114.03.19W - #3) (Gold, Silver)
Coordinates are for the main entrance to this underground, past producer.
USGS MRDS Data Base Record 10111460, Released February 1, 1984: The site of the Charley Ross Mine is shown at 37.90719N by -114.5638W, placing it about 1,000 feet Northeast of the Little Buck Shaft, in the Eagle Valley Mining District, in the Gold Springs Mining District and in the area included on the USGS Deer Lodge Canyon 24K and Caliente 100K and 250K maps. The Public Land Survey System locators are the Northwest ¼ of Section 32, Township 1 North, Range 71 East. Gold and Silver, with a gangue of Quartz, Calcite, Limonite, Hematite and Clay, are present in this Epithermal, Comstock-type Vein Deposit, hosted in Rhyolite, and both are shown as primary commodities. The ore body is described as Tabular, striking North 30° to 35° East, dips from vertical to 72° Northwest, is about 1 foot thick, up to 40 feet wide and 400 feet long. Some of the rocks are thoroughly Silicified and show Veinlets and clots of vitreous, grey Silica. There are also a few samples of altered Tuffaceous material, consisting of punky, Kaolin-type rocks. The main working is an inclined shaft covered by a collapsed structure and an adjacent cabin. A West-trending adit was crosscut 400 feet South of the adit to intersect the Southern extension of the Vein. The shaft was 175 feet deep and inclined at a 72° angle. It had 2 working levels, at 60 and 80 feet. At 60 feet the workings go 40 feet Northeast and 50 feet Southwest from the shaft. The 80-foot level has a 45-foot drift to the Southwest along the Vein, and the Vein has been stoped up about 10 feet above the back of the drift. At the time of the examination, in 1983, there was no activity at the mine. The geology, in the general area of the site, is described as Andesite and related rocks of intermediate composition. The Land Status, Ownership Category of this past producer is unknown.
USGS MRDS Data Base Record 10149150, Released January 12, 1994: The main entrance to the Charley Ross Mine is shown at 37.90687N by -114.05642W, placing it in the Eagle Valley Mining District. The location accuracy, of these coordinates, is shown as +/- 10 meters. This record shows Gold present and as a primary commodity with Silver tertiary. The geology, in the area of the main entrance, is described as Andesite and related rocks of intermediate composition. The Land Status, Ownership Category of this underground, past producer is unknown.
See the Mountain View Group entry for more information.

Cherokee 1-12: (37.15.57N by -114.21.16W - #3) (Silver)
Coordinates are for the main entrance to this underground, exploration prospect.
USGS MRDS Data Base Record 10270720, Released September 21, 1991: The main entrance to the Cherokee 1-12 is shown at 37.26578N by -114.35523W, placing it in the in the Viola/Pittsburg/Cherokee Mining District(s) and in the area included on the USGS Garden Spring 24K, Clover Mountains 100K and Caliente 250K maps. The location accuracy, of these coordinates, is shown as +/- 10 meters. The Public Land Survey System locators are the Northwest ¼ of Section 11, Township 8 South, Range 68 East. Silver is present and is shown as a primary commodity. The geology, in the area of the main entrance, is described as Andesite and related rocks of intermediate composition. The Land Status, Ownership Category of this underground prospect is shown as "BLM Administrative Area". Mineral Rights are held through "Located Claims".

Cherokee Mine (a.k.a. Columbia Claim, Shamrock Claim, Viola Claim, Viola No. 1 Claim):
(37.16.00N by -114.23.05W - #3) (Silver, Lead, Zinc, Gold, Copper, Barite)
Coordinates are for the main entrance to this underground, past producer.
USGS MRDS Data Base Record 10037034; Released February 1, 1980; Updated December 1, 1984: The site of the Cherokee Mine is shown at 32.2658 by -114.38555, placing it Northwest of Tule Desert, about 8 to 11 miles East of Meadow Valley Wash, in the Viola/Pittsburg/Cherokee Mining District and in the area included on the USGS Leith 24K, Clover Mountains 100K and Caliente 250K maps. The Public Land Survey System locators are Section 9, Township 8 South, Range 68 East. Silver and Copper; as Chrysocolla, Malachite and Tetrahedrite; are present and are shown as a primary commodities. Lead as

Galena, and Zinc are shown as secondary commodities with and Barite at tertiary levels. Mineralization is hosted in Limestone and associated with Pliocene to Permian Volcanic rock. The geology, in the general area of the site is described as Cherty Limestone and sparse Dolomite, Shale and Sandstone. The ore body is a tabular Quartz Vein, 10 to 40 feet thick, which can be traced for two miles, that strikes North 45° to 50° West and dips 60° to 70° East or 55° Southwest. Ore minerals line the fracture areas, with a high-grade streak 3 to 12 inches wide and total ore width of 16 to 20 feet. This underground, past producer was discovered around 1885 by an unnamed Cherokee Indian and produced until 1951. In the early days a carload shipped graded 1,400 ounces of Silver to the ton. When the mine shut down, in 1951, the ore graded 5% Copper and 24 ounces of Silver to the ton. Total workings included the Cherokee and Viola Shafts, 200 and 163 feet deep, respectively; which had connecting stopes along the strike of the Vein. The full description of the Vein was given as follows; "Vein consists of massive to coarsely crystalline white Quartz, which carries clots of Tetrahedrite, Malachite and Chrysocolla, with minor amounts of Galena, Pyrite and Iron-Manganese Oxides. Some dark, finely crystalline, Sulfide-laden lenses also occur in portions of the Vein. Tetrahedrite is abundant in the middle and lower sections of the Vein and ripped up clasts of Limestone country rock are common in the lower portion of the exposure. In places the Vein contains concentric or undulating bands of white, crystalline Calcite. Alternating bands of Quartz and Calcite are about 0.25 to 0.50 inches wide, each. Calcite is also deposited along fractures in the Quartz Veins which parallel the Vein Strike. Green Oxides are common and may be derived from Lead or Silver Chloride. Medium Gray, crystalline Limestones of the Permian Kaibab Formation outcrop on the Southwest side of the Vein. The Limestones are cut by Calcite Veins and Veinlets.
USGS MRDS Data Base Record 10295529; Released September 25, 1991: The main entrance to the Cherokee Mine is shown at 37.26667 by -114.38553, placing it between two trails and just North of two tailings piles. The location accuracy of these coordinates is shown as +/- 10 meters. This record shows Silver present and as a primary commodity with Gold and Copper tertiary. The geology, in the area of the main entrance, is described as Cherty Limestone and sparse Dolomite, Shale and Sandstone. Mineral rights are patented. The Land Status, Ownership Category is "Private".

Cherokee Mining District (a.k.a. Viola Mining District): (Silver, Gold, Lead, Zinc, Copper, Manganese, Fluorspar)
Description of the District:
Tingley, Joseph V.; "Mining Districts of Nevada"; Nevada Bureau of Mines and Geology, Report 47, Second Edition; 1998; Page 239: The Cherokee Mining District was shown by Tingley as an alternate name for the Viola Mining District, likely referencing the Cherokee Mine(s) in the District.
See the Viola Mining District entry for more information.
Mines Included in the District:

Chicago/Illinois/Wisconsin Claims (a.k.a. Hanus Claims; NBMG Sample Sites 3055-3057):
(37.39326N by -115.798W – USGS MRDS) (Gold, Silver)
USGS MRDS Data Base Record 10173976, Released January 26, 1994: The main entrance to the Chicago/ Illinois/Wisconsin Claims is shown at 37.39326N by -115.79837W, placing it in the Groom Mining District and in the area included on the USGS Cattle Spring 24K, Pahranagat Range 100K and Caliente 250K maps. The location accuracy, of these coordinates, is shown as +/- 500 meters. The Public Land Survey System locators are Sections 24 & 25, Township 6 South, Range 55 East. Gold is present and is shown as a primary commodity with Silver tertiary. Mineralization of this Tabular, Fissure Vein of Hydrothermal origin includes Galena and Pyrite. The geology, in the area of the main entrance, is described as Quartzite and minor amounts of Conglomerate, Phyllitic Siltstone, Limestone and Dolomite. The Land Status, Ownership Category of this surface-underground prospect is shown as "Military Reservation". A 1933 record shows the Owner as Charles P. Hanus.

Chief (a.k.a. Gold Chief): (37.41.57N by -114.30.00W - #3) (Gold, Silver, Zinc, Lead, Copper, Manganese, Barite, Iron, Arsenic)
See the Gold Chief entry for more information.

Chief Mining District (Caliente Mining District; Cobalt Mining District; Panaca Mining District):
(Gold, Silver, Lead, Copper, Vanadium)
Description of the District:

Tingley, Joseph V.; "Mining Districts of Nevada"; Nevada Bureau of Mines and Geology, Report 47, Second Edition; 1998; Page 54: Discovered and established in 1870,the Chief Mining District covers the Southeastern tip of the Chief Range, about 8 miles North of Caliente. This is not a large Mining District, being located primarily in the Northwest ¼ of Township 3 South, Range 67 East. In his 1962 *Directory of Southern Nevada Place Names,* W. R. Averett indicated the Cobalt Mining District and the Panaca Mining District as alternate names for the Chief Mining District, although where these names came from was not indicated.

Mines Included in the District:

        Advance (Gold, Silver, Lead, Copper, Arsenic)
        Blue Mary Claim North Extension (Gold)
        Contact (Gold, Silver, Iron, Arsenic)
        Gold Chief (Gold, Silver, Zinc, Lead, Copper, Manganese, Barite, Iron, Arsenic)
        Gold Stake Mine (Gold, Silver, Lead, Arsenic)
        Gold Stake Tunnel (Gold, Silver, Lead, Arsenic)
        NBMG Sample Site 126 (Gold, Silver, Lead, Arsenic)
        Old Democrat (Gold, Silver, Zinc, Lead, Copper, Manganese, Cadmium, Uranium, Iron, Arsenic, Zirconium)
        Republic (Lead, Gold, Silver, Zinc, Copper, Vanadium)
        Soa Lode Claims (Lead, Gold, Silver, Arsenic, Barite)

Chinaman Diggings: (38.05.34N by -114.37.21W - #3)
Coordinates are for the main entrance to this underground, operation.

Chisholm (a.k.a. Chisholm Mine; Alliance; Blue Eagle; Old Times; Whale): (37.56.02N by -114.29.08W - #3) (Lead, Silver, Gold)
Coordinates are for the main entrance to this underground, past producer.
USGS MRDS Data Base Record 10037329, Released October 1, 1979; Updated September 1, 1984: The site of the Chisholm Mine is shown at 37.93357N by -114.48612W, placing it West of Mount Ely, about 2 miles West of Pioche, in the Pioche Mining District and in the area included on the USGS Pioche 24K and Caliente 100K and 250K maps. Lead, Silver and Gold are present and all are shown as primary commodities. Mineralization includes Galena in a host of Late Cambrian, Chisholm Shale. The ore body is a bedding Vein, less than 2 feet thick and controlled by the bedding plane. This may be an extension of the Half Moon Vein. A 1938 analysis of the ore indicated Gold at about 14 grams per ton, Silver at about 12 ounces per ton and Lead at 13%. The geology, in the general area of the site, is described as Limestone and Dolomite with locally-thick sequences of Shale and Siltstone. The Land Status Ownership Category of this past producer is shown as "Private".
USGS MRDS Data Base Record 10295598, Released January 19, 1994: The main entrance to the Chisolm Mine is shown at 37.93386N by -114.48614W, placing it in the Pioche Mining District. The location accuracy, of these coordinates, is shown as +/- 10 meters. The Public Land Survey System locators are the Northeast ¼ of the Southeast ¼ of the Northeast ¼ of Section 20, Township 1 North, Range 67 East. Lead is present and is shown as a primary commodity with Gold, Silver and Copper tertiary. The geology, in the area of the main entrance, is described as Limestone and Dolomite with locally-thick sequences of Shale and Siltstone. The Land Status Ownership Category of this underground, past producer is unknown.

Cinch Mine (a.k.a. Cinch Claim; Fred Claim; Murphy; Pip; Walker): (38.35.58N by -114.41.29W - #3) (Tungsten, Gold, Silver)
Coordinates are for the main entrance to this underground, past producer.
USGS MRDS Data Base Record 10100744, Released March 1, 1982; Updated February 1, 1985: The site of the Cinch Claim is shown at 38.59939N by -114.69307W, placing it about 50 miles South of Ely, about 45 miles North of Pioche, on the East flank of the Schell Creek Range, near Patterson Pass, on a small hill, in the Cave Valley Mining District, in the Patterson/Patterson Pass Mining District and in the area included on the USGS Milk Ranch Spring 24K, Garrison 100K and Lund 250K maps. The Public Land Survey System locators are Sections 32 & 33, Township 9 North, Range 65 East. Tungsten, as Scheelite and Powellite, with a gangue of Quartz, Calcite and Iron, in a host of Pale Canyon Limestone and associated with Late Cambrian to Pliocene, Aphanitic, Volcanic rock, and is shown as a primary commodity with Copper secondary. The Scheelite is disseminated within the Quartz Veins. The deposit occurs on the upper

plate of a probable thrust fault. Several East-West fractures crosscut the Brecciated zone. There is a possible intrusive at a depth of 450 feet. The Breccia Zone consists of Siliceous Limestone fragments cemented in a Silica-Iron-Oxide matrix. The fault is a possible decollement (see note) along which Cambrian Sedimentary rocks were emplaced over Tertiary Volcanic rocks. The ore body is described as Pods and being Tabular to Irregular, open to the surface, about 3 feet wide and about 400 feet long. One section strikes North 45° East and dips 25° Southeast and a second strikes North 58° West and dips from 10° to 60° East. The mine was developed by several trenches, a number of adits with stopes, open cuts, pits, old ore chutes and a number of on-site buildings. Total production is about 750 MTUs of Tungsten, worth (period values) about $19,000. In 1981 Union Carbide was sampling and mapping the area. Drilling was taking place Northeast of the main workings on a low hill. The geology, in the general area of the site, is described as Limestone and Dolomite with locally-thick sequences of Shale and Siltstone. The Land Status, Ownership Category of this producer, which was discovered in 1941 by Owen Walker, and put into production the following year, is shown as "BLM Administrative Area". An undated record shows the Owner as Union Carbide.

Notes: A decollement is a gliding plane between two rock masses. It is sometimes referred to as a basal detachment fault.

USGS MRDS Data Base Record 10271233, Released June 14, 1993: The main entrance to the Cinch Mine is shown at 38.59935N by -114.69225W, placing it in the Patterson Mining District. The location accuracy, of these coordinates, is shown as +/- 100 meters. This record shows the Public Land Survey System locators as Section 33 (only), Township 9 North, Range 65 East. Tungsten is present and is shown as a primary commodity with Gold and Silver tertiary. The deposits occur in Brecciated zones and Veins. The Scheelite is extremely fine-grained and nearly all of it is in the fragments of Vein Quartz. Because of this fine-grained nature, whole pieces of the Quartz will fluoresce when exposed to ultra-violet light, even though the total WO_3 content may not be high. The Breccia zone contains large pods of coarse, crystalline, white Calcite, 2 to 3 feet across. Several small East-West fractures cut the zone at an angle. Tungsten occurs in the Quartz gangue as well as in the other gangue material. The geology, in the area of the main entrance, is described as Limestone and Dolomite with locally-thick sequences of Shale and Siltstone. The Land Status, Ownership Category of this underground, past producer is shown as "BLM Administrative Area".

Cinnabar Group (a.k.a. Cinnabar; Cinnabar No. 1; Kyle Group; Kyle Siding Prospect; Tinledge Claims): (37.3158N by -114.484W – USGS MRDS) (Mercury, Manganese)
USGS MRDS Data Base Record 10046391, Released April 1, 1984: The site of the Cinnabar Group is shown at 37.3158N by -114.48389W, placing it about 20 miles South of Caliente, about 0.4 mile North 70° East from the Kyle Station on the Union Pacific Rail Road, in the Viola Mining District and in the area included on the Leith 24K, Clover Mountains 100K and Caliente 250K maps. The Public Land Survey System locators are the Northwest ¼ of Section 27, Township 7 South, Range 67 East. Mercury, as Cinnabar in a host of Volcanic rock, and Manganese are present and are shown as primary commodities. A note here indicated that Cinnabar occurred with Manganese minerals in Veinlets in the Volcanic rock, however, exploration failed to find mineable ore. The geology, in the general area of the site, is described as Andesite and related rocks of intermediate composition. Discovered by James and Bill Bradshaw in 1968, the Land Status, Ownership Category of this occurrence is shown as "BLM Administrative Area". See the Kyle Siding Prospect entry for more information.

Cinnamon Bear Mining District (a.k.a. Little Mountain Mining District): (Copper, Molybdenum, Silver)
Description of the District:
Tingley, Joseph V.; "Mining Districts of Nevada"; Nevada Bureau of Mines and Geology, Report 47, Second Edition; 1998; Page 137: In the April 13, 1873 issue of the *Territorial Enterprise* an article described an area, referred to as the Cinnamon Bear Mining District, that was about 20 miles Southeast of Pioche, and may have been in the area of what is today the Little Mountain Mining District.
Mines Included in the District:

Coalition Mines Company (a.k.a. Old Democrat): (37.41.36N by -114.31.45W - #3) (Gold, Silver, Zinc, Lead, Copper, Manganese, Cadmium, Uranium, Iron, Arsenic, Zirconium)
See the Old Democrat entry for more information.

Cobalt Mining District (a.k.a. Chief Mining District): (Gold, Silver, Lead, Copper, Vanadium)
Description of the District:
Tingley, Joseph V.; "Mining Districts of Nevada"; Nevada Bureau of Mines and Geology, Report 47, Second Edition; 1998; Page 54: In his 1962 *Directory of Southern Nevada Place Names,* W. R. Averett indicated the Cobalt Mining District and the Panaca Mining District as alternate names for the Chief Mining District, although where these names came from was not indicated.
See the Chief Mining District entry for more information:
Mines Included in the District:

Columbia Claim:
See the Cherokee Mine entry for more information.

Combined Metals: (38.05.40N by -114.42.43W - #3) (Clay)
Coordinates are for an ore body.

Combined Metals No. 1 Mine (a.k.a. No. 1 Mine): (37.92466N by -114.455W – USGS MRDS) (Silver, Zinc, Lead, Gold)
USGS MRDS Data Base Record 10270978, Released January 21, 1994: The main entrance to the Combined Metals No. 1 Mine is shown at 37.92466N by -114.45474W, placing it in the Pioche Mining District and in the area included on the USGS Pioche 24K and Caliente 100K and 250K maps. The location accuracy, of these coordinates, is shown as +/- 100 meters. The Public Land Survey System locators are the Southwest ¼ of the Southwest ¼ of the Southeast ¼ of Section 22, Township 1 North, Range 67 East. Silver is present and is shown as a primary commodity with Lead, Zinc and Gold tertiary. The geology in the area of the main entrance is described as Limestone and Dolomite with locally-thick sequences of Shale and Siltstone. The Land Status, Ownership Category of this underground, past producer is unknown.

Combined Metals Perlite: (38.10.30N by -114.15.33W - #3)
Coordinates are for the ore body of this surface, past producer.

Comet (a.k.a. Comet Mine; Comet Coalition; Silver Comet Mines; Tungsten Comet Mines):
(37.53.25N by -114.36.47W - #3) (Lead, Zinc, Tungsten, Silver, Gold, Copper, Manganese, Barite)
Coordinates are for the ore body of this underground, past producer.
USGS MRDS Data Base Record 10072156, Released February 1, 1980; Updated August 1, 1984: The site of the Comet Mine is shown at 37.89052N by -114.61334W, placing it about 10 miles West of Pioche, on the West side of the Highland Range, in the Comet Mining District and in the area included on the USGS Highland Peak 24K and Caliente 100K and 250K maps. The Public Land Survey System locators are Sections 5 & 6, Township 1 South, Range 66 East. Tungsten, Lead and Zinc are present, in this Polymetallic Vein Deposit (USGS Model Code 22c), and are shown as primary commodities with Gold, Silver and Copper secondary and Manganese and Barite tertiary. It is noted that Wolframite occurs in places as heavy Aggregates of coarse tubular crystals. Mineralization includes Scheelite, Wolframite, Galena, Plumbojarosite, Sphalerite, Argentite, Chalcopyrite, Bornite, Chalcocite, Malachite, Chrysocolla and Pyrolusite along with a gangue of Quartz, Pyrite, Limonite and Specularite, in a host of Shale and Late Cambrian Quartzite. The ore body is described as Irregular to Tabular, striking North 50° to 65° East and dipping steeply to the Northwest. Four Quartz Veins crop out discontinuously for about 1,400 feet. The largest ranges from 1 foot to 15 feet thick, but where mined averaged about 6 feet.
The Sulfide ore averages between 0.05 and 0.2 ounces of Gold and from 5 to 10 ounces of Silver per ton, along with 2% to 4% Lead and 8% to15% Zinc. The ore in 1932 assayed about $4 a ton in Gold (about 6 grams) and 5.8 ounces of Silver per ton, with 2.8% Lead, and 0.32% WO₃. The average grade of the ore in the Unoxidized portions of the Vein ran about 0.3% Tungsten, 15% Zinc, 4% Lead, 0.5% Copper and 0.2 ounces of Gold (about 6 grams) and about 10 ounces of Silver to the ton.
Sample 1440 contained greater than 2% Lead, greater than 1% Zinc, 2.0% Copper, 5,000 parts per million (PPM) Barite, 1,000PPM Arsenic, 700PPM Antimony, 500PPM Manganese, 200PPM Cadmium, 200PPM Tin, 200PPM Strontium, 100PPM Silver and 50PPM Bismuth.
The geology, in the general area of the site, is described as Quartzite with minor amounts of Conglomerate, Phyllitic Siltstone, Limestone and Dolomite. The Land Status, Ownership Category of this past producer,

discovered in 1906 and put into production in 1924, is shown as "Private". A 1932 record shows the Owner as Comet Mines Company.

USGS MRDS Data Base Record 10197953, Released January 19, 1994: The main entrance to the Comet Mine is shown at 37.89026N by -114.61334W, placing it in the Comet Mining District. The location accuracy, of these coordinates, is shown as +/- 10 meters. The Public Land Survey System locators are the Northeast ¼ of Section 5, Township 1 South, Range 66 East. Lead is present and is shown as a primary commodity with Silver, Gold, Tungsten, Copper, Lead and Zinc tertiary. The geology, in the area of the main entrance, is described as Quartzite with minor amounts of Conglomerate, Phyllitic Siltstone, Limestone and Dolomite. The Land Status, Ownership Category of this underground, past producer is shown as "BLM Administrative Area".

Comet Mining District: (Gold, Silver, Lead, Zinc, Copper, Tungsten)
Description of the District:
Tingley, Joseph V.; "Mining Districts of Nevada"; Nevada Bureau of Mines and Geology, Report 47, Second Edition; 1998; Page 58: Discovered in 1882, the Comet Mining District is situated on Comet Mountain, primarily on the Southwestern side between the summit and the area along Comet Road. Comet Mountain is on the Western side of the Southern Highland Range, just Northwest of the KLNR-FM and KBZB-FM broadcast towers.
Mines Included in the District:
     Comet (Lead, Zinc, Tungsten, Silver, Gold, Copper, Manganese, Barite)

Conception No. 1 Claim (a.k.a. Groom Mine): (37.20.45N by -115.46.03W - #3) (Silver, Lead, Zinc, Copper, Gold, Barite)
See the Groom entry for more information.

Confidence Mine (a.k.a. NBMG Sample Site 1499): (38.11552N by -114.054W – USGS MRDS) (Gold, Silver)
USGS MRDS Data Base Record 10046539, Released June 1, 1984: The site of the Confidence Mine is shown at 38.11552N by -114.05361W, placing it in the Eagle Valley Mining District, the Fay Mining District, the Gold Springs Mining District, the Stateline Mining District and in the area included on the USGS Rice Mountain 24K, Wilson Creek Range 100K and Lund 250K maps. The Public Land Survey System locators are Section 17, Township 3 North, Range 71 East. Gold and Silver ore, with a gangue of Quartz, Calcite, Jarosite and Clay, in a host of Rhyolite, are present in this Comstock, Epithermal Vein Deposit (USGS Model Code 25c), and both are shown as primary commodities. The ore body is described as Tabular, striking North 80° West, dipping 65° Northeast, about 5 feet thick, 400 feet long and controlled by a Brecciated shear zone. The Quartz Vein, along the shear zone, is moderately Kaolinized Rhyolite Tuff. The Vein is only a few inches wide within the 4-foot to 5-foot Brecciated zone. The Brecciated wall rock is Iron-Oxide-stained and some Manganese Oxide is found in the Quartz. The Vein is vuggy and contains Quartz, white Adularia and Quartz pseudomorphs after Adularia. Needle-like Quartz crystals coat the vugs. Exposures in the upper, or Southern, cuts show a purplish Rhyolite Breccia, streaky in appearance, in the Southwest wall of a 2-foot-wide Chalcedonic Quartz-cemented Breccia, which has about 2 feet of soft, Kaolinized, Iron-Oxide-stained rubble on the Northeast wall. Both Calcite and Jarosite are present in this area of the Vein. The mine was developed by numerous cuts and adits for about 400 feet along the strike; however, these were mostly caved when visited in 1984, and no activity at the site was observed at that time. Along the extension of the strike, into the State of Utah, there appeared to be activity. The geology, in the general area of the site, is described as welded and non-welded Silicic, ash-flow Tuffs. The Land Status, Ownership Category of this occurrence is shown as "BLM Administrative Area".

Contact (a.k.a. Contact Tunnel): (37.41.17N by -114.31.43W - #3) (Gold, Silver, Iron, Arsenic)
Coordinates are for the ore body of this surface-underground operation.
USGS MRDS Data Base Record 10037351, Released February 1, 1980; Updated August 1, 1984: The site of the Contact is estimated at 37.69386N by -114.5239W, placing it about 70 miles North of Alamo, in the Chief Mining District and in the area included on the USGS Chief Mountain 24K and Caliente 100K and 250K maps. The Public Land Survey System locators are the Northeast ¼ of Section 18, Township 3 South, Range 67 East. Gold and Silver, in a host of Carbonate and Late Cambrian Quartzite, are present and are shown as primary commodities with Lead, Zinc, Iron and Arsenic tertiary. The ore body consists of two

Tabular Veins, the Contact Vein and the Burnt Vein. The Contact Vein strikes North 7° West along the fault between the Quartzite and Carbonates. The Carbonates contain lenses of Iron Oxides. The Burnt Vein strikes North 45° West and dips 65° Southwest in the Quartzite and Lenses of soft, red, Iron Oxide occur periodically in and around the Vein. The sample from the Contact adit consisted of dark brown, Jasper-Gossan and Silicified (believed to be recrystallized) Quartzite from the dump. In the area of the shafts, the dominant rock is a fine-to-medium-grained, tan-purple, Quartzite, Dolomite or Limestone, altered to a punky mixture of Iron Oxides and Clay, which is also exposed along portions of the surface cuts. These cuts, or trenches, follow a highly Iron-stained Breccia zone, 10 feet to 20 feet wide, which strikes North 45° East and dips steeply Southeast. The zone contains brown and red, Siliceous or Jaspery, Iron-rich pods and Veins of grey Calcite. Limestone and Quartzite are juxtaposed by thrusting at this site, as in other parts of the District, but here the units are also juxtaposed along several high-angle structures. Some bright red-orange Oxides coat the Quartzite fault Breccia, cemented by Iron and Silica, which is found in the trench. The Vein was explored by the Contact adit and a number of shafts that follow a fault zone, which undulates, but generally strikes North-South. The ore consisted of Iron-stained, Brecciated Quartzite cemented with coarse-grained Calcite. The Contact Adit/Contact Vein samples assayed about 0.02 ounces of Gold (about 0.6 gram) and 2 ounces of Silver per ton and about 53% Iron. The Burnt Vein assayed at about 0.41 ounces of Gold (about 12.75 grams) per ton. The sample tagged Numbers 127 contained over 20% Iron, 1,000 Parts per million (PPM) Zinc, 1,000PPM Lead, 200PPM Manganese, 200PPM Zirconium, 200PPM Barite, 200PPM Arsenic, 50PPM Copper, 50PPM Vanadium and 2PPM Silver. The sample tagged 128 contained over 20% Iron, 1,000PPM Zinc, 1,000PPM Arsenic, 200PPM Manganese, 200PPM Vanadium, 200PPM Zirconium, 150PPM Barite, 100PPM Copper and 10PPM Silver.

In 1936 the workings consisted of a number of tunnels, a 175-foot-long main adit which is partially a crosscut and partially a drift, two now-inaccessible shafts and several pits. When visited in 1983 the South-trending Contact Adit was caved and the shafts North of the adit had been trenched. There was no activity at the time of the 1983 examination, but it appeared the trenching was less than 10 years old.

The geology, in the general area of the site, is described as Quartzite and minor amounts of Conglomerate, Phyllitic Siltstone, Limestone and Dolomite. The Land Status, Ownership Category of this past producer is shown as "BLM Administrative Area".

USGS MRDS Data Base Record 10222720, Released January 19, 1994: The main entrance to the Contact Tunnel is shown at 37.69167N by -114.52024W, placing it in the Chief Mining District. The location accuracy, of these coordinates, is shown as +/- 1,000 meters. This record shows Gold present and as a primary commodity with Silver and Iron tertiary. The geology, in the area of the main entrance, is described as Quartzite and minor amounts of Conglomerate, Phyllitic Siltstone, Limestone and Dolomite. The Land Status, Ownership Category of this underground prospect is shown as "BLM Administrative Area".

Copper Occurrence 001: (38.18.14N by -114.46.12W - #3) (Copper)
Coordinates are for the ore body of an underground operation.

Copper Occurrences 002: (37.38.18N by -114.19.31W - #3) (Copper)
Coordinates are for the main entrance to this underground, exploration prospect.

Cotinno Tunnel (a.k.a. Cotino Tunnel): (37.55.52N by -114.27.28W - #3)
Coordinates are for an ore body.

Cougar Prospect: (37.18.40N by -114.12.31W - #3) (Fluorite)
Coordinates are for the claim area of this exploration prospect.

Crescent 001: (37.36.50N by -115.25.42W - #3) (Gold, Silver, Lead)
Coordinates are for the ore body of this past producer.
USGS MRDS Data Base Record 10047248, Released February 1, 1980: The site of the Crescent Mine is shown at 37.62329N by -115.42586W, placing it the Pahranagat Mining District and in the area included on the USGS Crescent Spring 24K, Timpahute Range 100K and Caliente 250K maps. The Public Land Survey System locators are Sections 11 & 12, Township 4 South, Range 58 East. Silver and Lead, as Galena, with a gangue of Calcite and Quartz, in a host of Late Permian Limestone, are present and are shown as primary commodities with Zinc, Antimony and Copper tertiary. The ore body of this fissure Vein

strikes Northeast and dips 75° Southeast. In 1867 the milling ore was paying about $80 a ton. In 1868 a lot of 50 tons yielded $1,920 in Silver. By July, 1868, the Alameda and Crescent Mining Company had produced $20,000 (period values) worth of bullion. The geology, in the area of the ore body, is described as Limestone, Dolomite, Shale and Quartzite. The Land Status, Ownership Category of this past producer, which first produced in 1867, is shown as "BLM Administrative Area".

USGS MRDS Data Base Record 10246788, Released June 17, 1993: The ore body of the Crescent Mine is shown at 37.62329N by -115.42586W, placing it the Pahranagat Mining District. The location accuracy, of these coordinates, is shown as +/- 1,000 meters. The Public Land Survey System locators are Section 11 (or possibly 12), Township 4 South, Range 58 East. Gold is present and is shown as a primary commodity with Silver and Lead tertiary. The geology, in the area of the ore body, is described as Limestone, Dolomite, Shale and Quartzite. The Land Status, Ownership Category of this past producer is shown as "BLM Administrative Area".

Crescent Mine 002: (38.05.09N by -114.36.17W - #3) (Silver, Manganese, Lead, Gold, Copper)
Coordinates are for the ore body of this past producer.
USGS MRDS Data Base Record 10173973, Released January 18, 1994: The main entrance to the Crescent Mine is shown at 38.08576N by -114.60554W, placing it in the area included on the USGS Bristol Range SE 24K, Wilson Creek Range 100K and Lund 250K maps. The location accuracy, of these coordinates, is shown as +/- 10 meters. The Public Land Survey System locators are the Southwest ¼ of Section 29, Township 3 North, Range 66 East. Silver is present and is shown as a primary commodity with Lead, Gold, Copper and Manganese tertiary. The geology, in the area of the main entrance, is described as Limestone and Dolomite with locally-thick sequences of Shale and Siltstone. The Land Status, Ownership Category of this underground, past producer is shown as "Private".

Crystal-Bluenose:
See the Crystal Mercury entry for more information.

Crystal Mercury (a.k.a. Blue Nose Peak, Crystal –Bluenose, Larson): (37.14.00N by -114.19.10W - #3) (Mercury, Gold, Silver)
Coordinates are for the main entrance to this underground, past producer.
USGS MRDS Data Base Record 10125333; Released September 25, 1991: The main entrance to the Crystal Mercury is shown at 37.23498 by -114.31252, placing it in the area included on the USGS Blue Nose Peak 24K, Clover Mountains 100K and Caliente 250K maps. The location accuracy of these coordinates is shown as +/- 10 meters. The Public Land Survey System locators are Section 19, Township 8 South, Range 69 East. Mercury is present and is shown as a primary commodity with Gold and Silver tertiary. The geology, in the area of the main entrance of this underground, past producer, is described as Limestone with minor amounts of Dolomite and Shale. Mineral rights are held as located claims. The Land Status, Ownership Category is "BLM Administrative Area".

Crescent Mining District (a.k.a. Pahranagat Mining District): (Silver, Lead, Copper, Manganese)
Description of the District:
Tingley, Joseph V.; "Mining Districts of Nevada"; Nevada Bureau of Mines and Geology, Report 47, Second Edition; 1998; Page 166: In 1871 there was also a Crescent Spring Mining District around Crescent Spring, which had been cut out of the Pahranagat Mining District. The Crescent Spring District only lasted a short time and was reabsorbed into the Pahranagat Mining District.
See the Pahranagat Mining District entry for more information.
Mines Included in the District:

Culverwell 001: (37.28.37N by -114.44.52W - #3) (Manganese)
Coordinates are for the ore body of this surface-underground, development deposit.

Culverwell 002 (a.k.a. NBMG Sample Site 1707; Tom Johnson Property; Upper and Lower Independence Adits): (37.25.29N by -114.30.00W - #3) (Silver, Copper, Tungsten, Gold, Iron)
Coordinates are for the ore body of this surface, past producer.
USGS MRDS Data Base Record 10046479, Released March 1, 1984: The site of the Culverwell Adit is shown at 37.40747N by -114.47027W, placing it Pennsylvania Mining District and in the area included on

the USGS Ella Mountain 24K, Clover Mountains 100K and Caliente 250K maps. The general Public Land Survey System locators are Township 6 South, Range 67 East. Copper, Gold, Silver and Tungsten are present and are shown as primary commodities with Iron secondary. Mineralization of this Copper Skarn Deposit (USGS Model Code 18b) includes Chalcopyrite and Magnetite, with a gangue of Pyrite, Calcite, Epidote and Chloride, in a host of Limestone associated with Volcanics and Late Cambrian to Pliocene Diorite. The ore body is s series of Lenses, Veins and Pods striking North 60° West and dipping 70° Northeast along the Igneous contact, which appears to be the emplacement control for the deposit. The mine was developed by an inclined shaft along an Iron-stained, Silicified, Gossan replacement zone. The mineralized rock on the dump is reddish-black, very dense and composed mostly of Magnetite. Magnetite also occurs in Calcite-Veined Tactite and as a replacement in pods in the Limestone. Sample 1707 is of replaced Limestone collected from a bulldozer trench below the adit. The rock is banded, very dense, and contains Lenses and Veins of Calcite and Oxidized Pods and crystals of Magnetite, Copper Oxides, Pyrite and Chalcopyrite. The sample was lamped and only two, very fine, specks of Scheelite were found. The rocks exposed in the bulldozed trench consisted of a sequence of white, medium-coarsely-crystalline Marble, Epidote-Monzonite-Diorite intrusive rock and banded, light and dark green Tactite. The contact of the intrusive with the Limestone is not well exposed, but orientation is believed to be Northeast-Southwest. The rock is weathered, and is a Chlorite-altered intrusive, which outcrops at the bottom of the trenching just Northwest of the adit. The rock has Iron-stained fractures and carries a small amount of Oxidized Pyrite. The South 30° East-trending adit was recently demolished by trenching and scraping in the drainage area, the work having been done since 1978. There are the remains of a track near the portal. When visited in 1983 there was no activity at the site. The geology, in the general area of the site, is described as welded and non-welded, Ash-flow Tuffs. The Land Status, Ownership Category of this occurrence is shown as "BLM Administrative Area".

USGS MRDS Data Base Record 10271371, Released January 26, 1994: The main entrance to the Culverwell Adit is shown at 37.40747N by -114.47023W, placing it in the Pennsylvania Mining District. The location accuracy, of these coordinates, is shown as +/- 100 meters. The Public Land Survey System locators are Section 22, Township 6 South, Range 67 East. Copper is present and is shown as a primary commodity with Gold, Silver and Tungsten tertiary. Mineralization of this Lenticular, Contact Metasomatic, Replacement Deposit includes Chalcopyrite, Scheelite and Magnetite. The geology in the area of the main entrance is described as welded and non-welded Silicic Ash-flow Tuffs. The Land Status, Ownership Category of this underground prospect is shown as "BLM Administrative Area".

Culverwell Manganese Prospect 003: (37.16.18N by -114.09.57W - #3) (Iron, Manganese) Coordinates are for the main entrance to this surface-underground, exploration prospect.

Culverwell Mine 004 (a.k.a. Culverwell; Del Claims; History Repeats Claims; NBMG Sample Locations 1756 & 1757): (37.47719N by -114.746W – USGS MRDS) (Gold, Silver, Copper, Zinc, Bismuth)
USGS MRDS Data Base Record 10037387, Released November 1, 1979; Updated August 1, 1984: The site of the Culverwell Mine is shown at 37.47719N by -114.74584W, placing it about 1.7 miles East of the Magnolia Mine, in the Delmar Mining District, in the Ferguson Mining District and in the area included on the USGS Slidy Mountain 24K, Clover Mountains 100K and Caliente 250K maps. The Public Land Survey System locators are Section 31, Township 5 South, Range 65 East. Mineralization of this Comstock-type, Epithermal Vein Deposit, which is hosted in Quartzite and associated with an early Cambrian, Plutonic rock, includes Gold with a gangue of Pyrite, Sericite and Chlorite. A bulk sample of 5 tons of ore contained 1.44 Troy Ounces of Gold and 2.31 Troy Ounces of Silver. See the NBMG Sample Locations 1756 & 1757 entry for those assays. The ore is found in 2 converging, Tabular Veins, striking South 40° East and South 50° East. The width of the main Vein is about 2 feet, dipping 74° to 88° Southwest. The Vein material is leached near the surface and contains Quartz with Iron and Manganese Oxides. Some specimens of visible "Wire Gold" on Quartz were obtained. The Veins are explored by a short tunnel and several pits. A winze was noted in the tunnel as well as a 60-foot crosscut trending South 16° West. There was also a drift, on the Vein for 53 feet trending South 50° to 62° East. An open cut is connected to a drift by a raise. In 1983 there were several South-trending adits, mostly open with large dumps. There was one caved shaft and adit above and Southwest of the upper, sampled adit. The road to the workings had been recently graded, using a bulldozer blade. When visited in 1983, the cabin below the workings looked "lived in". Much of the

dump material has been sorted and there is a generator and mining equipment on the property. The mine is believed to be worked intermittently, on a small scale.

The geology, in the general area of the site, is described as Quartzite and minor amounts of Conglomerate, Phyllitic Siltstone, Limestone and Dolomite. The mine was discovered by John E. and Alvin Ferguson, two farmers from Pahranagat Valley, in 1932 and went into production in 1933. The Land Status, Ownership Category of this producer is shown as "Private".

USGS MRDS Data Base Record 10173648, Released January 12, 1994: The site of the Culverwell Mine is shown at 37.47807N by -114.74584W, placing it in the Delamar Mining District, and in the Ferguson Mining District. The location accuracy, of these coordinates, is shown as +/- 10 meters. The Public Land Survey System locators are Section 30, Township 5 South, Range 65 East. Gold is present and is shown as a primary commodity with Silver, Zinc, Bismuth and Copper tertiary.

Culverwell Mine 005 (a.k.a. Culverwell Prospect; Culverwell-Johnson Property; Johnson; Johnson Mine; NBMG Sample Site 1706; T. C. Johnson Claims; Tom and Jerry Mine): (37.41775N by -114.475W – USGS MRDS) (Gold, Silver, Copper, Tungsten, Lead)

USGS MRDS Data Base Record 10037383, Released February 1, 1980; Updated December 1, 1984: The site of the Culverwell Prospect is shown at 37.41775N by -114.47527W, placing it in the Pennsylvania Mining District and in the area included on the USGS Ella Mountain 24K, Clover Mountains 100K and Caliente 250K maps. The Public Land Survey System locators are Section 16, Township 6 South, Range 67 East. Gold and Silver are present and are shown as primary commodities with Copper and Tungsten tertiary. Mineralization included Chalcopyrite and Malachite, with a gangue of Quartz and Pyrite, in a host of Quartzite, Mudstone and Prospect Mountain Quartzite Formation Limestone, associated with Late Cambrian Diorite. The ore body is a North-South striking, flat Vein, likely the Southern extension of the Pennsylvanian Vein, controlled by fractures, the steep fault zone and the Igneous contact. Here the Limestone is altered; either Siliciated to a light green or to a dense, dark brown Tactite; or bleached and recrystallized to a white, crystalline Marble. The rocks are cut by irregular, Iron-stained Veins. Silicification suggests that the rocks are locally intruded by dikes or other intrusive bodies referenced on local geological maps, but no such intrusives were recorded as having been observed at the time of the review; in fact there was no activity at the site at the time of the review in 1983. The deposit had been explored by Kennecott and Homestake in the 1960s and by Western Ventures and Cordilleran Exploration from 1969 to 1971. It was determined that the deposit could be mined by open pit methods and about 16 carloads of Gold ore were taken out. The geology, in the general area of the site, is described as welded and non-welded Silicic Ash-flow Tuffs. The Land Status, Ownership Category of this past producer is shown as "BLM Administrative Area".

See NBMG Sample Site 1706 record for more information.

USGS MRDS Data Base Record 10222656, Released January 12, 1994: The pit area of the Culverwell Mine is shown at 37.41217N by -114.47393W, placing it in the Pennsylvania Mining District. The location accuracy, of these coordinates, is shown as +/- 10 meters. This record shows the Public Land Survey System locators as Section 22, Township 6 South, Range 67 East. Gold is present and is shown as a primary commodity with Silver, Copper and Lead tertiary. The geology, in the pit area, is described as welded and non-welded Silicic Ash-flow Tuffs. The Land Status, Ownership Category of this surface-underground, producer and leach plant, discovered in 1871, is shown as "BLM Administrative Area". A 1987 record shows the Owner-Operator as the Fisher Watt Mining Company of Nevada.

Culverwell Prospect 006: (37.13.41N by -114.18.57W - #3) (Manganese)
Coordinates are for the main entrance to this underground, exploration prospect.

Culverwell's Ranch:
See the Caliente (town) entry for more information

Culverwell-Johnson Property (a.k.a. Culverwell Mine 005): 37.41775N by -114.475W – USGS MRDS) (Gold, Silver, Copper, Tungsten, Lead)
See the Culverwell Mine 005 entry for more information.

CV Claims: (38.00.58N by -115.07.07W - #3) (Silver)
Coordinates are for the ore body of this underground, exploration prospect.

D and D Prospect: (36.50.20N by -114.51.31W - #3) (Silver)
Coordinates are for the claim area of this surface prospect.

Daly East (a.k.a. Daily East; NBMG Sample Site 1416): (37.55.05N by -114.26.08W - #3) (Gold, Silver,
Arsenic)
Coordinates are for trenching associated with this surface, past producer.
USGS MRDS Data Base Record 10037393, Released October 1, 1979; Updated August 1, 1984: The site of
the Daly East is shown at 37.91802N by -114.4364W, placing it 1 mile Southeast of Pioche, along Caliente
Road, in the Pioche Mining District and in the area included on the USGS Pioche 24K and Caliente 100K
and 250K maps. The Public Land Survey System locators are Section 26, Township 1 North, Range 67
East. Gold, Silver and Arsenic are present and are shown as primary commodities. Mineralization includes
Gold and Limonite with a gangue of Hematite, Jarosite and Quartz, in a host of Late Cambrian Prospect
Mountain Quartzite. The ore body is a Quartz Vein containing Gold ore, ranging from 1 to 4½ feet wide,
striking North 60° West, dipping 60° Southwest to vertically and controlled by a fault zone. The Quartz
Vein fills the fault, with massive euhedral crystals filling open spaces. Crystalline Jarosite is plentiful and
present. The Gold is probably found mostly in the Oxidized Pyrite of the Quartz Vein which is shattered
and stained by the Limonite. Some botryoidal Hematite occurs along with Gossan. Siliceous beds are
shattered; almost Brecciated, and contain substantial Manganese staining. Grey areas in the Quartzite
suggest the presence of finely disseminated Sulfides. Fine-grained Pyrite appears to be disseminated in the
Quartzite adjacent to the Quartz Vein. The deposit was developed by the currently-dangerous Daly East
Shaft and numerous surface cuts. There are also the remains of an old hoist, at the shaft. A total of 12
carloads of ore were reported shipped in 1934 & 1935. The Land Status, Ownership Category of this past
producer is shown as "Private".
USGS MRDS Data Base Record 10271249, Released November 14, 1983: The main entrance to the Daly
East is shown at 37.91806N by -114.43664W, placing it in the Pioche Mining District. The location
accuracy, of these coordinates, is shown as +/- 10 meters. The Public Land Survey System locators are the
Southwest ¼ of the Southwest ¼ of the Northeast ¼ of Section 26, Township 1 North, Range 67 East. Gold
is present and is shown as a primary commodity with Silver tertiary. The geology, in the area of the main
entrance, is described as Quartzite with minor amounts of Conglomerate, Phyllitic Siltstone, Limestone and
Dolomite. Discovered in 1934, the Land Status, Ownership Category of this underground, past producer, is
shown as "Private".

Dave Mathews Lead: (37.55.40N by -114.38.12W - #3) (Lead)
Coordinates are for an ore body.

Davidson Shaft: (37.89996N by -114.471W – USGS MRDS) (Silver, Lead, Zinc, Gold, Manganese)
USGS MRDS Data Base Record 10046403, Released May 1, 1984: The site of the Davidson Shaft is shown
at 37.89996N by -114.4714W, placing it in the Pioche Mining District, just East of the Virginia Louise
Mine and in the area included on the USGS Pioche 24K and Caliente 100K and 250K maps. The Public
Land Survey System locators are the Southeast ¼ of Section 33, Township 1 North, Range 67 East. Silver
and Lead are present and are shown as a primary commodities with Zinc, Gold and Manganese secondary.
Mineralization includes Galena in a host of Limestone, Shale and Late Cambrian, Highland Peak Quartzite.
Ore deposition was controlled by favorable lithology and fractures. The Davidson Mine was mined for a
time, through open cuts and drifts by the Virginia-Louise Mining Company. The geology, in the general
area of the site, is described as Alluvial deposits. The Land Status, Ownership Category of this past
producer is unknown.

Davis Claims: (38.02.54N by -115.43.55W - #3) (Fluorite, Manganese, Calcium, Silica)
Coordinates are for trenching associated with this surface, exploration prospect.

Day Mine (a.k.a. Black Metal Mine 001): (38.09635N by -114.596W – USGS MRDS) (Silver,
Manganese, Iron, Gold, Lead, Copper, Bismuth, Coal)
See the Black Metal Mine 001 entry for more information.

<u>**Deer Lodge Canyon Shaft (a.k.a. NBMG Sample Site 1708)**</u>: (37.92276N by -114.093W – USGS MRDS) (Gold, Copper)
USGS MRDS Data Base Record 10125193, Released January 27, 1994: The main entrance to the Deer Lodge Canyon Shaft is shown at 37.92276N by -114.09273W, placing it in the Eagle Valley Mining District and in the area included on the USGS Deer Lodge Canyon 24K and Caliente 100K and 250K maps. The location accuracy, of these coordinates, is shown as +/- 100 meters. The Public Land Survey System locators are the Northeast ¼ of the Northwest ¼ of Section 25, Township 1 North, Range 70 East. Gold is present and is shown as a primary commodity with Copper tertiary. Mineralization includes Pyrite and Hydrated Iron Oxides, Feldspar and Sanidine (a high-temperature form of Potassium Feldspar), along with Quartz and Clay. The ore body is a Tabular Fissure Vein of Hydrothermal origin. The geology, in the general area of the main entrance, is described as Alluvial deposits. The Land Status, Ownership Category of this underground prospect is shown as "Private".

<u>**Deer Lodge Mining District (a.k.a. Eagle Valley Mining District)**</u>: (Gold, Silver, Lead, Uranium, Pearlite)
Description of the District:
Tingley, Joseph V.; "Mining Districts of Nevada"; Nevada Bureau of Mines and Geology, Report 47, Second Edition; 1998; Page 79: The Eagle Valley Mining District lies along the Nevada-Utah Border and is made up of a number of small, scattered mining areas in the Mahogany Mountains. These include the Deer Lodge Mining District, North of Deer Canyon, in the Gold Bug Mountain area.
See the Eagle Valley Mining District entry for more information.
Mines Included in the District:
      Iris84 09 (Gold, Silver, Copper)

<u>Deer Trail</u>: (37.00.20N by -114.25.10W - #3) (Manganese)
Coordinates are for an ore body.

<u>**Delamar Mining District (a.k.a. Cedar Mining District; Ferguson Mining District)**</u>:
Description of the District:
Tingley, Joseph V.; "Mining Districts of Nevada"; Nevada Bureau of Mines and Geology, Report 47, Second Edition; 1998; Pages 66 & 67: In his 1872 work *Preliminary Report Concerning Explorations and Surveys Principally in Nevada and Arizona*, G. M. Wheeler included the area of the current Delamar Mining District in a large Cedar Mining District, described as being located on the "Western side of the Bennett Spring Mountains". This would be West of Meadow Valley Wash and Southwest of Clover Valley. What would be the current Delamar Mining District was discovered in 1891 and originally named Ferguson. The major town was Delamar and this became the name associated with the District starting in the mid-1930s. While the Delamar Mining District extends almost to Rainbow Canyon on the East, and to the upper portion of Taylor Mine Canyon, the majority of it is on the Western slopes of the Bennett Spring Mountains between Cedar Wash and Monkey Wrench Wash.
USGS MRDS Data Base Record 10037387, Released November 1, 1979; Updated August 1, 1984: The first discovery in the District was made in Monkey Wrench Wash. There was some surface exploration done in the area in the early 1980s.
USGS MRDS Data Base Record 10310400, Released January 1, 2005; Updated and Edited September 1, 2007: The dominant structural feature in the region is the Caliente Caldera Complex; an East-elongated, 50 by 22 mile complex of inset calderas in Nevada and Utah. It spans a period of at least 10 million years, from 13 to 23 million years ago, an unusually long period of activity for a caldera complex. It is bounded on the North and South by transverse zones, which are East-striking, late Mesozoic to Cenozoic structures that cross the Great Basin and accommodate different types and rates of crustal extension to the North and South. The Caliente Complex was highly extended along transverse zones and faults that were synchronous with caldera magmatism. One of these is the Timpahute Transverse Zone, along the Northern side of the Caliente Caldera Complex.
The faults and magma of the Caliente area belong to two episodes; first, the middle Cenozoic, pre-Basin-Range episode of Calc-Alkaline magmatism and Northeast and Northwest-striking, oblique-slip faults, followed by the Basin-Range episode of bimodal magmatism and North-striking faults. Gold deposits that surround the caldera complex are interpreted to represent Leaching; transport and deposition of metals by ground water moving through the transverse zones and heated to boiling by inter-caldera magmas. The

46

Delamar Gold District is situated on the Southwestern side of the caldera complex, where these processes took place. In addition to the high-grade, underground Vein targets on the Western half of the Delamar properties, Beta geologists have defined two areas of strong Hydrothermal alteration associated with anomalous Gold, Silver and trace element concentrations on the Eastern side of the properties. The mineralization is exposed in a 1,000-foot-wide zone of faulting, which can be traced for about 4,000 feet on the surface. This shear zone is the outer ring fracture zone of the Delamar Volcanic Caldera formed along the Western edge of the collapse structure. The exploration target of the Ring Fracture Zone is a disseminated Gold deposit amenable to open pit development. Rocks in the mine area consist of a thick section of tilted and faulted Cambrian Quartzite. Sediments are tilted 35° to the Southeast although the Volcanics show less tilting. Tertiary Basalt dikes and sills and post ore Lamprophyre dikes are present. Tertiary, East-West-trending Rhyolite dikes appear to be post-ore deposition. The major deposits in the District are found in the oldest rocks, the Early Cambrian, Prospect Mountain Quartzite. Other deposits are in the Volcanic Breccia, often intruded by Rhyolite dikes (such as at the Magnolia Mine) and in a number of the Limestone units.

The Delamar Mining District has produced an estimated 650,000 ounces of Gold since discovered in 1892 by James McFadden, D. A. Meikel and John Prutscher. In 1900 it was Nevada's largest producer of Gold, with the Delamar Mine being the main producer in the District.

History: The first ore in the Delamar Mining District was found by a group of Italian miners, headed by John Vietti working a lease. The Lucky Bar Claim was located by John Roeder and the Goldcup Claim by Joe Conway, John Roeder and Cap Garden. Captain DeLaMar purchased the Claims in 1893 and initiated an active development of the deposits, making the Delamar Mining District the biggest Gold producer in Nevada from 1895 to 1900. The Delamar Mines were shut down in 1909, although they were operated intermittently by the Bambergers until 1932. In 1931 the Caliente Cyaniding Company was preparing to treat tailings from the Delamar mill. The Jack Berry lease on the Lucky Bar or Hog Pen Claim produced a considerable amount of shipping ore. Beginning in 1982 the District saw renewed exploration through a series of joint ventures. Some of the names included were Phelps Dodge Mining Company, Homestake Mining, FMC Gold Company, Hanna Mining and Aur Resources. Exploration was focused on the old Delamar Mine and in the newer Easter Project about five miles East-Northeast of the Delamar Mine. On the Easter Project more than 100 drill holes were made and Homestake estimated a Resource of 4 million tons of ore grading 0.056 ounces of Gold (about 1.75 grams) per ton, based on results from 25 of their drill holes. Fischer-Watt Corporation explored the property in 2001. In 2003 Beta Materials initiated a drill project about 5 miles Northeast of the old Easter or Eastern Taylor Mine. Beta then located 135 claims covering 2,789.8 acres, or about 4.36 square miles, on the Western flank of the Delamar Caldera in the Delamar Mining District. The Beta Claims included extensions of former producing Veins, including the Delamar, Magnolia, Jumbo and the April Fool. In addition to the high-grade underground Vein targets on the Western half of the Delamar properties, the Beta geologists defined two areas of strong Hydrothermal alteration associated with anomalous Gold, Silver and trace element concentrations, on the Eastern side of the properties. This mineralization is exposed in a North-trending, 1,000-foot-wide zone of faulting, which can be traced for over 4,000 feet on the surface. This shear zone is the outer ring of the Delamar Volcanic Caldera formed along the Western edge of the collapse structure. The exploration target on the Ring Fracture Zone is a disseminated Gold deposit amenable to open pit operations, similar to those at Round Mountain. In 2004 the Beta geologists undertook geological mapping, rock chip sampling and completed two soil sample grids totaling slightly under 200 acres. This defined several geochemical anomalies which are associated with strong Hydrothermal alteration and Quartz-Adularia Veining. Beta was scheduled to conduct detailed sampling and mapping on the anomalous areas and evaluate the potential for drill targets in and along the mineralized zone in 2005.

USGS MRDS Data Base Record 60001660: The Delamar Mining District-Nevada is located around 37.45857N by -114.76774W, placing it in the area included on the USGS Delamar 24K, Clover Mountains 100K and Caliente 250K maps. Gold and Silver are present and are shown as primary commodities with Manganese and Iron tertiary. Ore deposition in the District was controlled by Brecciated shears in the Quartzite and Rhyolite dikes in the overlying Volcanic Breccia. This past-producing District was discovered in 1891 by the brothers John and Alvin Ferguson and went into production the following year. Mines Included in the District:

      100 Foot Incline (Gold, Silver, Copper)
      April Fool (Gold, Silver, Copper, Bismuth, Antimony)
      Bamberger Delamar Gold Mining Company (Gold, Silver)

Delamar 001 (Gold, Silver, Lead, Copper)
Delamar Prospect 002 (Gold, Silver, Copper, Iron)
Delamar Wash Workings (Gold, Silver, Lead, Copper)
Denton Summit Workings (Tungsten, Gold, Silver)
Easter 001 (Gold, Lead, Silver, Copper)
Flagstaff (Gold, Manganese, Iron, Barite)
Goldcup Claim
Jumbo (Gold, Silver, Lead, Zinc, Copper, Barite)
Lucky Bar Claim
Magnolia Mine (Gold, Silver, Copper, Lead, Zinc, Bismuth, Arsenic)
Monkey Wrench Wash Diggings (Gold, Copper, Iron)
NBMG Sample Site 1746 (Gold, Silver, Zinc, Lead, Copper, Manganese, Barite)
NBMG Sample Site 1748 (Gold, Silver, Iron)
NBMG Sample Site 1753 (Gold, Silver, Copper, Lead, Antimony)
Taylor Mine (Gold, Silver, Iron)
Vevada Vein (Gold, Silver, Lead)
Unnamed Adit Near the April Fool Mine 008 (Gold, Silver, Lead, Copper, Arsenic)
Unnamed Shaft 068 (Gold, Silver, Zinc, Lead, Copper, Manganese, Barite)
Unnamed Shaft 070 (Gold, Silver, Iron)

Delmar 001 (a.k.a. Delemar Mine; Delamar Wash Workings; Gold Cup; Hog Pen; Jim Crow; Lucky Bar; Monitor; Monitor No. 2 Claims; NBMG Sample Sites 1749 & 1750): (37.27.24N by -114.46.10W - #3) (Gold, Silver, Lead, Copper)
Coordinates are for the main entrance to this underground, past producer.
USGS MRDS Data Base Record 10072155; Released November 1, 1979; Updated August 1, 1984: The site of the Delamar Mine is shown at 37.45969N by -114.76667W, placing it on a ridge above the town, in the Delamar Mining District, in the Ferguson Mining District and in the area included on the USGS Delamar 24K, Clover Mountains 100K and Caliente 250K maps. The Public Land Survey System locators are Section 1, Township 6 South, Range 64 East. Gold and Silver are present and are shown as primary commodities with Copper tertiary. Mineralization of this Epithermal Vein Deposit (USGS Model Code 25c) includes Free Gold, Tetrahedrite, Chalcopyrite, Bornite, Chalcocite, Malachite and Chrysocolla, with a gangue of Pyrite and Quartz. The ore body, which strikes North 18° East and dips76° to 82° (with depth), is hosted in Prospect Mountain Quartzite, associated with Basalt and Early Cambrian Rhyolite and controlled by Brecciation, due to faulting, and black dikes. Ore is found in the Delamar or Monitor Vein, which extends 2,700 feet and includes 5 main ore shoots.
USGS MRDS Data Base Record 10295663, Released November 5, 1996: Buildings associated with the Delamar Mine are shown at 37.45667N by -114.77024W, placing it in the Delamar Mining District and in the Ferguson Mining District. The location accuracy, of these coordinates, is shown as +/- 1,000 meters. The Public Land Survey System locators are the Southern ½ of the Southeast ¼ of the Northwest ¼ of Section 1, Township 6 South, Range 64 East. This record shows Gold present and as a primary commodity with Silver, Copper and Lead tertiary. The geology, in the area of the buildings is described as Quartzite and minor amounts of Conglomerate, Phyllitic Siltstone, Limestone and Dolomite. The Land Status, Ownership Category of this underground, past producer is shown as "Private".

Delmar Prospect 002 (a.k.a. Gold Cup Claim; Hog Pen Claim; Jim Crow Claim; Lucky Bar Claim; Monitor Claim; Monitor No. 2 Claim): (37.28.07N by -114.42.57W - #3) (Gold, Silver, Copper, Iron)
Coordinates are for the ore body of this prospect.
USGS MRDS Data Base Record 10310400, Released January 1, 2005; Updated and Edited September 1, 2007: The Delamar Mine is shown at 37.45969N by -114.76667, placing it about 115 miles Northeast of Las Vegas, about 18 miles Southwest of Caliente, on the West flank of the Delamar Mountains, on a ridge above the town of Delamar, in the Delamar Mining District, in the Ferguson Mining District and in the area included on the USGS Delamar 24K, Clover Mountains 100K and Caliente 250K maps. The Public Land Survey System locators are Section 1, Township 6 South, Range 64 East. Gold and Silver are present in this Comstock-type, Epithermal Vein deposit and are shown as primary commodities with Copper and Iron tertiary. Ore minerals include Gold, Tetrahedrite, Chalcopyrite, Bornite, Chalcocite, Malachite and Chrysocolla with a gangue of Quartz and Pyrite, in a host of Volcanic Breccia, Limestone and Early

Cambrian to Neoproterozoic Prospect Mountain Quartzite, associated with Tertiary Rhyolite and Basalt and the Miocene, Caliente Caldera Complex. The dominant structural feature of the region is the Caliente Caldera Complex, an East-elongated, 50 by 22 mile complex of inset calderas in Nevada and Utah. The complex was built up over an estimated 10 million years of activity, which is considered to be an unusually long period of time for such an activity.

Ore is found in the Delamar or Monitor Vein which has a strike length of 2,700 feet and is composed of 5 ore shoots, each of which has a variable thickness ranging up to 300 feet. The material in the ore shoots varies widely as to grade, with the best material coming from above level 10. The ore is primarily Breccia cemented by Chalcedony Quartz with similar mineralization being found in Veins and along bedding planes and fractures. Most of the ore was Oxidized and had a reddish or greenish tint. Only the Hog Pen shoot contained Free Gold. The ore reserves identified by Homestake and World Wide Minerals in the 1980s are in a 1,600 foot long by 40-foot to 90-foot wide segment of the Main Vein; a part of a 7,000-foot-long mineralized structure. The Delamar ore bodies included Epithermal Veins in Sedimentary rocks as well as bedding replacement ores in Limestone. Gold values ranged up to several ounces per ton in some of the Veins, but the majority of the Gold produced came from an underground, block-cave operation called the Delamar Glory Hole containing milling grade ore. The Glory Hole orebody was located at the intersection between North-trending Gold-bearing Veins and East-West-trending faults that were intruded by Volcanic dikes radial to the Delamar Caldera. Beta Minerals' Claims cover an area that is relatively untested. Similar structural intersections are buried under recent Sediments to the North and East of the former producing areas of the Delamar Mine.

Through 1933 the Delamar Mine had a total production (period values) of $12,854,600. This production included 217,000 ounces of Gold and 420,000 ounces of Silver. In 1988 the remaining Reserves were estimated at 200,000 tons of ore grading 0.079 ounces (about 2.5 grams) of Gold per ton. Most of the old workings are now inaccessible. Originally the mine had 16 levels of underground workings and the large Delamar Glory Hole. Geology, in the general area of the site, is described as Quartzite and Minor amounts of Conglomerate, Phyllitic Siltstone, Limestone and Dolomite. The Land Status, Ownership Category of this Surface-Underground producer is shown as "Private". A 2005 record shows the Owner-Operator as Beta Minerals.

<u>Delamar Wash Workings (a.k.a. Delamar 001; NBMG Sample Site 1755)</u>: (37.27.24N by -114.46.10W - #3) (Gold, Silver, Lead, Copper)

USGS MRDS Data Base Record 10046495; Released January 1, 1984: The site of the Delamar Wash Workings is shown at 37.46025N by -114.78667W, placing it in Delamar Wash, in the Delamar Mining District and in the area included on the USGS Delamar 24K, Clover Mountains 100K and Caliente 250K maps. The Public Land Survey System locators are the Northeast ¼ of the Northwest ¼ of Section 2, Township 6 South, Range 64 East. Gold and Silver, with a gangue of Quartz, Pyrite and Limonite, in a host of Late Cambrian, Prospect Mountain Quartzite, are present and are shown as primary commodities. The adit begins in an alluvial slope of Prospect Mountain Quartzite, covered by rubble. The material on the dump includes rounded Alluvial boulders, Quartzite pebbles and some mined chunks, composed of altered Quartzite. The altered Quartzite on the dump is recrystallized and contains Quartz Veining. The host rocks and the Veins contain clots, vugs and fracture coatings of Limonite and Manganese Oxides. Sampled Quartzite is Brecciated and replaced by sugary or comb Quartz. The Quartz carries Oxidized Pyrite and specks of a dark mineral, probably a Silver, Manganese or other Sulfides. Some Jasper-Gossan is also found. The workings do not appear to have been extensive and are mostly caved, so exploration of them could not be done. The one that could be sampled was an open adit trending North 10° West. It is thought the shafts may have been for old Placer workings. There was no activity at the time of the examination in 1983. The geology, in the general area of the site, is described as Quartzite and minor amounts of Conglomerate, Phyllitic Siltstone, Limestone and Dolomite. The Land Status, Ownership Category of this occurrence is shown as "BLM Administrative Area".

See the Delamar 001 and NBMG Sample Site 1755 entries for more information.

<u>Delmar Zinc 003</u>: (37.30.00N by -114.47.12W – #3) (Zinc, Lead, Silver, Manganese, Copper, Vanadium, Strontium, Iron, Barite)

Coordinates are for the ore body of this underground, development deposit.

Delmar-Mackie Perlite Mine: (37.33.02N by -115.01.00W - #3) (Perlite)
Coordinate are for the ore body of this underground producer (as of 1996).

Delta B Claims (a.k.a. Fortuna and Helen Claims): (37.93607N by -114.087W – USGS MRDS) (Gold, Silver, Lead)
See the Fortuna and Helen Claims entry for more information.

Demijohn (a.k.a. Demijon; Pioche Demijon): (37.55.52N by -114.29.38W - #3) (Lead, Silver, Manganese, Gold)
Coordinates are for the ore body of this past producer.
USGS MRDS Data Base Record 10046404, Released December 1, 1982: The site of the 9 Claims of the Demijohn Mine, 7 of which are Patented, is shown at 37.93079N by -114.49528W, placing it in the Pioche Mining District and in the area included on the USGS Pioche 24K and Caliente 100K and 250K maps. The location accuracy, of these coordinates, is shown as +/- 500 meters. The Public Land Survey System locators are Section 20, Township 1 North, Range 67 East. Silver and Lead are present and are shown as primary commodities with Gold and Manganese secondary. The USGS shows the ore body as a Vein striking North 80° West, dipping 70° South and up to 4 feet thick. However, in a note to file by Weed, the ore is described as "making into" Limestone from the hanging wall of a fissure, which is about 40 feet wide, the ore depth varying from 1 to 2 feet. The main Vein, crossing the property has a North 5° strike (East or West is not designated, but East appears to have been assumed) and dips to the East. It is noted that the ore deposition is not "persistent". In 1918 it was noted that the deposit was developed by a 300-foot shaft, drifts, crosscuts and winzes to the 500-foot level. In that year the Operator was planning to initiate Diamond drilling from the bottom of the mine, the 500-foot level, to test the ore zone along the Yuba Dike, at a greater depth than had been developed. The results of this drilling were not found in the file; however, it is known that the Company shut down in 1922, so it is likely that the results were not good. Most of the production occurred prior to 1907, with a small quantity high-grade ore being found in 1909 on the 125-foot level. In 1915 there were 10 men working on exploration and development, during which operation a small amount of ore was recovered. The geology, in the general area of the site, is described as Alluvial deposits. The Land Status, Ownership Category of this past producer is shown as "Private".
USGS MRDS Data Base Record 10149464, Released January 12, 1994: The main entrance to the Demijohn Mine is shown at 37.93076N by -114.49474W, placing it in the Pioche Mining District. The location accuracy, of these coordinates, is shown as +/- 10 meters. The Public Land Survey System locators are the Northern ½ of the Northeast ¼ of the Southwest ¼ of Section 20, Township 1 North, Range 67 East. Silver and Lead are present and are shown as primary commodities with Gold and Copper tertiary. The geology, in the area of the main entrance, is described as Alluvial deposits. The Land Status, Ownership Category of this underground, past producer is unknown.

Denton Summit Workings (a.k.a. NBMG Sample Site 1758): (37.47691N by -114.716W – USGS MRDS) (Tungsten, Gold, Silver)
USGS MRDS Data Base Record 10046496, Released February 1, 1984: The site of the Denton Summit Workings is shown at 37.47691N by -114.71556W, placing it about 0.2 miles due South of Denton Summit, in the Delamar Mining District and in an unsurveyed area included on the USGS Slidy Mountain 24K, Clover Mountains 100K and Caliente 250K maps. The projected (from the East) Public Land Survey System locators are Section 33, Township 5 South, Range 65 East. Tungsten, as Scheelite, and Gold and Silver are present and all are shown as primary commodities. Mineralization is hosted in Pioche Quartzite and associated with Late Cambrian Rhyolite. The dump rocks show fine, Siliceous Veining and minute clots of partially Oxidized Pyrite. Above and Northeast of the adit, Micaceous, brown Shales outcrop along the slope, below a Sandy-Limey horizon which is an altered, light green, fine-grained, banded Calc-Silicate and contains abundant Epidote and Calcite. The Calc-Silicate horizon extends to the drill road located about 30 feet above the adit. The rocks on the drill road are Micaceous brown and green Shales. Some of the Shales are Limy and show Silification effects. The Mica in the Shales is recrystallized due to thermal Metamorphism. The Shales and the Limy Mudstones form 1 to 6-inch beds which strike North 65° East and dip 30° Southeast. However, attitudes on the bedding changes due to small, North-Northwest-striking faults observed in the road cut and a larger East-West fault mapped in the area in 1937. A large Rhyolite dike is located about ¼ of a mile West of the sampled outcrop. A few minute flakes of Scheelite were observed when the Calc-Silicate sample was lamped. Workings include one caved adit and a small dump. The drill

road, lying above the adit, has drill holes spaced approximately every 20 feet. There was no activity at the time of the review in 1983, but the drilling was estimated to have occurred sometime between 1978 and 1980. The geology, in the general area of the site, is described as Limestone and Dolomite with locally-thick sequences of Shale and Siltstone. The Land Status, Ownership Category of this occurrence is shown as "BLM Administrative Area".

USGS MRDS Data Base Record 10173935, Released January 26, 1994: The main entrance to the Denton Summit Workings is shown at 37.47687N by -114.71554W, placing it in the Delamar Mining District, and in the Ferguson Mining District. The location accuracy, of these coordinates, is shown as +/- 100 meters. The Public Land Survey System locators, shown in this record, are Section 28, Township 5 South, Range 65 East. Tungsten is present and is shown as a primary commodity with Gold tertiary. Scheelite is present in this Tabular, Stratiform, Contact Metasomatic deposit. The geology, in the area of the main entrance, is described as Limestone and Dolomite with locally-thick sequences of Shale and Siltstone. The Land Status, Ownership Category of this underground prospect is shown as "BLM Administrative Area".
See the NBMG Sample Site 1758 entry for more information.

Detroit Mine: (38.05.20N by -114.37.12W - #3) (Silver, Copper, Lead, Zinc, Gold)
Coordinates are for the main entrance to this underground operation.
USGS MRDS Data Base Record 10047170, Released January 1, 1985: The site of the Detroit Mine or Detroit Claim, which was part of the Bristol Silver Mines Company Property in 1924, is shown at 38.08885N by -114.62084W, placing it about 0.6 Mile, North 20° West of the Snyder Shaft of the Bristol Mine, in the Bristol-Jackrabbit Mining District and in the area included on the USGS Bristol Range Southeast 24K, Wilson Creek Range 100K and Lund 250K maps. This is in an unsurveyed area, located about 450 feet from the Iron Mine. The projected (from the East) Public Land Survey System locators are Section 30, Township 3 North, Range 66 East. Silver and Copper are present and are shown as primary commodities with Gold, Zinc and Lead secondary. Mineralization of this Tabular, Polymetallic Replacement Deposit (USGS Model No. 19a) includes Galena in a host of Late Cambrian Limestone and is controlled by the Iron Fissure. Development includes an inclined shaft 450 feet deep and a few shallow surface cuts located about 50 feet South of the shaft. The mine was worked under a lease in 1924 which included the Iron Mine; however, the ore from the Detroit Claim contained more Zinc than the ore from the Iron Mine, even though both worked the Iron Fissure. The geology, in the general area of the site, is described as Limestone, Dolomite, Shale and Quartzite. The Land Status, Ownership Category of this past producer is shown as "Private".
See the Bristol-Jackrabbit Mine entry for more information.

Devlin: (38.01.14N by -114.15.00W - #3) (Silver)
Coordinates are for an ore body.

Devlin Prospect: (38.36.54N by -114.45.14W - #3) (Tungsten, Zinc, Lead, Copper, Bismuth, Antimony)
Coordinates are for the main entrance to this surface-underground, exploration prospect.
See the Eagle Rock entry for more information.

Diamond C Group (a.k.a. Diamond C; Diamond C Nos. 2-4; Diamond C No. 6 Claims): (38.14163N by -114.669W – USGS MRDS) (Silver, Gold)
USGS MRDS Data Base Record 10047171, Released January 1, 1985: The site of the Diamond C is estimated to be in the area of 38.14163N by -114.66917W, placing it about 3 miles Southeast of Silverhorn and in the area included on the USGS Fairview Peak 24K, Wilson Creek Range 100K and Lund 250K maps. The location accuracy, of these coordinates, is shown as +/- 2,000 meters. The projected (from the North) Public Land Survey System locators are Section 10, Township 3 North, Range 65 East. Silver and Gold, in a host of Late Cambrian Limestone, are present and are shown as primary commodities. The ore body is described as a Tabular, hard Siliceous Outcrop, about 15 feet wide and traceable for a distance of about 500 feet, or almost the entire length of the Claim. A 1921 reference shows this property as a raw prospect. The geology, in the general area of the site, is described as Dolomite, Limestone and minor amounts of Sandstone and Quartzite. The Land Status, Ownership Category of this occurrence is shown as "BLM Administrative Area". A 1921 record shows the Owners as C. W. and Mrs. Peer.

<u>Don Dale Mine (a.k.a. Blue Bird Claims; NBMG Sample Sites 1468 & 1469)</u>: (37.31.40N by -
115.44.31W - #3) (Lead, Silver, Copper, Gold)
Coordinates are for the ore body of this underground, past producer.
USGS MRDS Data Base Record 10037343, Released February 1, 1980; Updated August 1, 1984: The site
of the Don Dale Mine (there appears to be a typo in the name shown on the USGS record – it shows Don
Daleminemine) is shown at 37.5369N by -115.73309W, placing it 2 miles South of the Andes Mine, in the
Don Dale Mining District and on the USGS Tempiute Mountain South 24K, Timpahute Range 100K and
Caliente 250K maps. The Public Land Survey System locators, which must be considered approximations,
as the area was unsurveyed at the time, are Section 34, Township 4 South, Range 55 East. Silver, Lead and
Copper are present and are shown as primary commodities. Mineralization includes Galena, Tetrahedrite,
Native Copper, Chalcopyrite and Malachite with a gangue of Quartz and Pyrite. The mine follows a North
65° East-trending Vein. Ore minerals are confined to the Vein and to a set of North-South cross-fractures.
Some disseminated Copper Carbonates (Malachite) are found in the Quartz Monzonite Porphyry. The last
10 feet of the 120-foot adit is cut into Quartz Monzonite. The geology, in the general area of the site, is
described as welded and non-welded Silicic Ash-flow Tuffs. The Land Status, Ownership Category of this
past producer is shown as "BLM Administrative Area". The Don Dale Mining District was organized in
1945, but as this mine was discovered before that time; it was first shown as being in the Tempiute Mining
District.
USGS MRDS Data Base Record 10046488, Released January 1, 1983: The site of the Don Dale Mine is
shown at 37.55052N by -115.77309W, placing it in the Don Dale Mining District and in the area included
on the USGS White Blotch Springs Southeast 24K, Timpahute 100K and Caliente 250K maps. The Public
Land Survey System locators are Section 34, Township 4 South, Range 55 East. Silver, Lead and Copper,
hosted in Prospect Mountain Shale and Quartzite, associated with Rhyolite and Late Cambrian Monzonite,
are present and are shown as primary commodities with Gold secondary. Mineralization of this
Polymetallic Vein Deposit (USGS Model Number 22c) includes Galena, Tetrahedrite, Native Copper,
Chalcopyrite, and Malachite with a gangue of Quartz and Pyrite. The ore body is Tabular and controlled by
the contact of the Porphyry with the Prospect Mountain Shale. The Vein contains Oxides of Lead, Silver
and Copper in a gangue of Quartz. Ore materials are also found in a set of North-South, cross-fractures that
dip 40° to 60° East. An ore shoot at the intersection of the Vein and a fracture was mined to a depth of 40
feet. The mine was developed by a 120-foot adit, which cuts Quartz Monzonite Porphyry and follows a 3-
foot-wide Hornfelsic zone, adjacent to the Quartz Porphyry intrusive, which contains disseminated Copper
Carbonates. Both the intrusive and Shale units are highly altered. Mineralization, in this area, was confined
to the intrusive. About 50 yards West of the main adit a minor surface cut was sampled. Surface scraping
revealed a Quartz Vein cutting Quartzite. Very fine-grained Pyrite, Chalcopyrite, Galena and Tetrahedrite
were in the Quartzite and the Vein on a disseminated basis. The surrounding rocks were highly fractured
and Iron-stained. The sacchroidal (sugary) Quartz Vein is estimated to be up to 8 feet wide, vuggy and
lined with euhedral Quartz crystals at the adit. Very fine sprays of Malachite were observed coating
exposed rock surfaces and filling fine fractures in the Porphyry. Ore on the dump was slightly Gossan-like,
and included Shale and Quartzite Breccia. In 1983 there were several areas of surface cuts, prospect pits
and bulldozer cuts along the Eastern and Western-facing slopes of the canyon which may have been past
assessment work. There was no activity at the site when reviewed in 1983 and the last claim notice was
dated 1964. The geology, in the general area of the site, is described as Quartzite and minor amounts of
Conglomerate, Phyllitic Siltstone, Limestone and Dolomite. The Land Status, Ownership Category of this
past producer is shown as "BLM Administrative Area".
USGS MRDS Data Base Record 10174153, Released January 12, 1994: The main entrance to the Don Dale
Mine is shown at 37.65416N by -115.73697W, placing it in the area included on the USGS Tempiute
Mountain North 24K, Timpahute Range 100K and Caliente 250K maps, placing it on the North end of the
Timpahute Range and on the East side of an area of rugged topography. The location accuracy, of these
coordinates, is shown as +/- 1,000 meters. The Public Land Survey System locators are Section 1,
Township 5 South, Range 55 East. Lead is present and is shown as a primary commodity with Silver, Gold,
Copper and Zinc tertiary. The geology, in the area of the main entrance, is described as Alluvial deposits.
The Land Status, Ownership Category of this underground, past producer is shown as "BLM
Administrative Area". A 1945 record shows the 50/50 Owners as D. F. Andrews and Dale Edwards, both of
Nevada.

<u>Don Dale Mining District (a.k.a. Tempahute Mining District)</u>: (Gold, Silver, Copper, Lead, Mercury, Zirconium, Barite)
Description of the District:
Tingley, Joseph V.; "Mining Districts of Nevada"; Nevada Bureau of Mines and Geology, Report 47, Second Edition; 1998; Page 76: The Don Dale Mining District, organized in 1945, includes the Northern end of the Groom Range, South of Highway 375, between the Groom Mining District and Coyote Summit (37.34.17N by -115.40.02W – USGS Tempiute Mountain South 24K map). In his 1872 work *Preliminary Report Concerning Explorations and Surveys Principally in Nevada and Arizona*, G. M. Wheeler included the area as the Southwestern part of a large Tempahute Mining District. Today the Northeastern part of the old Tempahute Mining District is the modern Tem Piute Mining District.
Mines Included in the District.

        Andies Mine (Mercury, Silver, Zirconium, Barite)
        April Fool Spring Trench (Gold)
        Big Red Prospect (Gold, Silver)
        Big Red Prospect Northwest (Gold, Silver)
        Big Red Prospect West (Silver, Gold)
        Blue Streak Prospect (Gold, Silver)
        Don Dale Mine (Lead, Silver, Copper, Gold)
        Gold Prospect 007 (Gold)
        Outcrop North of Radar Site (Gold)
        Ridge Vein (Gold)
        Sidewinder Prospect (Gold, Silver)

<u>Dorothy Claim</u>: (37.48.20N by -114.22.33W - #3) (Uranium)
Coordinates are for an ore body.

<u>E and F Mine (a.k.a. Ida May)</u>: (38.05.54N by -114.36.57W - #3) (Silver, Lead, Gold, Copper, Zinc)
See the Ida May entry for more information. It was operated as the E and F Mine in the early 1900s, and consisted of a series of adits and shafts, up to 100 feet in depth, which intersected the fissures.

<u>Eagle Rock (a.k.a. Eagle Rock Claims; Devlin Prospect; NBMG Sample Sites 814W & 8145; Prince Group of Claims)</u>: (38.37.00N by -114.38.25W - #3) (Antimony, Lead, Zinc, Copper, Tungsten, Silver, Manganese, Iron, Gold)
Coordinates are for an ore body.
USGS MRDS Data Base Record 10045922, Released March 1, 1982; Updated February 1, 1985: The site of the Eagle Rock Mine is shown at 38.61467N by -114.75446W. placing it about 50 miles North of Pioche, 45 miles South of Ely, on the West flank of the Schell Creek Range, in Cave Valley, about 2 miles North of where Patterson Pass exits into Cave Valley, in the Patterson/Patterson Pass Mining District, in the Cave Valley Mining District and in the area included on the USGS Shingle Pass Southeast 24K, Garrison 100K and Lund 250K maps. The Public Land Survey System locators are the Northeast ¼ of Section 26, Township 9 North, Range 64 East. Copper, Tungsten, Antimony, Lead and Zinc are present and are shown as primary commodities with Silver, Manganese and Iron secondary and Gold tertiary. Mineralization of this Tungsten Vein deposit (USGS Model Code 15a) includes Wolframite [(Fe,Mn)WO4], Bindhemimite ($Pb_2Sb_2O_6O$) and Galena, with a gangue of Quartz, Calcite, Pyrite and Limonite, in a host of Limestone, Shale and Late Cambrian, Prospect Mountain Quartzite. This mineralization occurs in 2 Quartz Veins; one of which is Iron Oxide-stained and contains massive to bladed, fine to coarse-grained Wolframite. The second Vein contains massive Quartz with Wolframite and Base Metal Sulfides present. Further description indicates that Wolframite, and possibly some Scheelite occur as scattered, small crystals with Limonite and Manganese Oxides in the seams and vugs of the 2 Tabular Quartz Veins, which are about 800 feet apart, from 2 to 3 feet thick and traceable through surface cuts and outcrops for about 500 feet along the strike of North 50° East and dip of 45° to 65° Northwest. Assays taken by the US Bureau of Mines in the early 1960s showed 1.5% Copper, from 0.3% to 0.77% Tungsten, Silver at "several ounces per ton", trace Gold and 0.15% combined Antimony, Lead, Zinc and Bismuth. The deposit was developed by an adit, surface cuts and pits along the strike and 2 old shacks. The geology, in the general area of the site, is described as Alluvial deposits. The Land Status, Ownership

Category of this occurrence, discovered in 1927 by John C. Clark and Francis Riordan, is shown as "BLM Administrative Area".
See NBMG Sample Sites 814W and 8145 entry for more information.

Eagle Valley Mining District (a.k.a. Deer Lodge Mining District; Fay Mining District; Gold Springs Mining District; Klondike Mining District; Pike's Diggings Mining District; Stateline Mining District): (Gold, Silver, Lead, Antimony, Uranium, Fluorite, Pearlite)
Description of the District:
Tingley, Joseph V.; "Mining Districts of Nevada"; Nevada Bureau of Mines and Geology, Report 47, Second Edition; 1998; Page 79: The Eagle Valley Mining District lies along the Nevada-Utah Border and is made up of a number of small, scattered mining areas in the Mahogany Mountains. These include the Deer Lodge Mining District North of Deer Canyon, in the Gold Bug Mountain area; The Fay Mining District which lies South of Deer Lodge Canyon and North of Buck Mountain; The Gold Springs mining area, lying mostly in Utah, East of Buck Mountain; and, the Stateline mining area, also mostly in Utah, which is about 5 miles North of Deer Lodge Canyon. In W. R. Averett's 1962 work, *Directory of Southern Nevada Place Names*, he described a mining district named Klondike, located near the historical village of Fay (37.54.29N by -114.04.12W – USGS Deer Lodge Canyon 24K map), which supposedly operated for a short time. Also near Fay was the Pike's Diggings Mining District, which was in operation from 1898 to about 1905.
Mines Included in the District:
        Big Buck Claim (Gold, Silver)
        Big Buck Mine (Silver, Gold, Lead, Copper)
        Bill Nye Mine (Gold, Silver)
        Bluebird Mine (Silver, Gold)
        Bull Hill Mine (Silver, Gold, Fluorite)
        Confidence Mine (Gold, Silver)
        Deer Lodge Canyon Shaft (Gold, Copper)
        Fortuna and Helen Claims (Gold, Silver, Lead)
        Gold Springs Wash Adit (Gold)
        Gypsy & Helen (Gold, Silver, Copper)
        Iris84 09 (Gold, Silver, Copper)
        Keno Claims (Gold, Silver, Barite)
        NBMG Sample Site 1500 (Gold, Silver)
        NBMG Sample Site 1710 (Gold, Silver, Fluorite, Bartie)
        NBMG Sample Site 1711 (Gold, Silver, Fluorite, Barite)
        NBMG Sample Site 1712 (Gold, Silver)
        NBMG Sample Site 1720 (Gold, Silver, Copper, Iron)
        NBMG Sample Site 1723 (Gold, Silver)
        Pope Mine (Gold, Silver, Lead, Copper, Antimony, Fluorite)
        Prince Divide (Gold, Silver)
        Red Eagle Mine (Gold, Silver)
        Silver Star Mine (Silver, Gold)
        Snowflake Mine 002 (Gold, Silver, Copper, Iron)
        Tempa Mine (Gold, Silver)
        Thor Mine (Gold, Silver, Lead, Copper)
        Unnamed Adit 003 (Gold, Silver)
        Unnamed Adit 005 (Gold, Silver)
        Unnamed Shaft 066 (Gold, Silver, Fluorite, Barite)
        Unnamed Shaft 067 (Gold, Silver, Fluorite, Barite)
        Unnamed Shaft 073 (Gold, Silver)
        Unnamed Shaft 075 (Gold, Silver)
        Utah Spur Mine (Silver, Gold, Fluorite) (Utah & Nevada)
        Uvada Tunnel (Gold, Silver)
        White Horse Mine (Gold, Silver)

<u>East Prince Shaft (a.k.a. Eastern Prince Shaft)</u>: (37.54.14N by -114.28.07W - #3) (Manganese, Iron, Silver, Gold, Zinc, Lead)
Coordinates are for the main entrance to this underground operation.

East Section 34 Prospect (a.k.a. NBMG Sample Site 1470): (37.55556N by -115.773W – USGS MRDS) (Gold, Silver, Copper, Manganese)
USGS MRDS Data Base Record 10246403, Released January 27, 1994: Trenching associated with the East Section 34 Prospect is shown at 37.55556N by -115.77257W, placing it in the Don Dale Mining District and in the area included on the USGS White Blotch Springs 24K, Timpahute Range 100K and Caliente 250K maps. The location accuracy, of these coordinates, is shown as +/- 100 meters. The Public Land Survey System locators are Section 34, Township 4 South, Range 55 East. Gold is present and is shown as a primary commodity with Silver, Copper and Manganese tertiary. Mineralization of this Hydrothermal, Tabular Fissure Vein deposit includes Malachite, Oxy-Hydrous Manganese minerals, Hematite, Pyrite and Quartz. The geology, in the area of the trenching, is described as Quartzite and minor amounts of Phyllitic Siltstone, Conglomerate, Limestone and Dolomite. The Land Status, Ownership Category of this surface prospect is shown as "Military Reservation".
See the NBMG Sample Site 1470 entry for more information.

East Side No. 1 and No. 2 Claims (a.k.a. Groom Mine): (37.20.45N by -115.46.03W - #3) (Silver, Lead, Zinc, Copper, Gold, Barite)
See the Groom entry for more information.

Easter 001 (a.k.a. Easter Mine; Easter Project; NBMG Sample Site 579; Pioche-Xray Mining and Milling Company Property; Taylor Mine): (37.25.40N by -114.36.20W - #3) (Gold, Lead, Silver, Copper)
Coordinates are for the ore body of this past producer.
USGS MRDS Data Base Record 10125211, Released January 12, 1994: The main entrance to the Easter is shown at 37.51277N by -114.63224W, placing it in the Delamar Mining District, in the Ferguson Mining District and in the area included on the USGS Chokecherry Mountain 24K and Caliente 100K and 250K maps. The location accuracy, of these coordinates, is shown as +/- 10 meters. The Public Land Survey System locators are Section 18, Township 8 South, Range 66 East. Gold is present and is shown as a primary commodity with Silver, Lead and Copper tertiary. The geology, in the area of the main entrance, is described as welded and non-welded Silicic Ash-flow Tuffs. The Land Status, Ownership Category of this underground past producer is shown as "BLM Administrative Area".
USGS MRDS Data Base Record 10310470, Released January 1, 2005; Updated and Edited September 1, 2007: The site of the Easter Project is shown at 37.51275N by -114.63306W, placing it on the East side of the Delamar Mountains, about 10 air miles Southwest of Caliente, in the Delamar Mining District and in the Ferguson Mining District. This record shows Gold and Silver present and as primary commodities with Manganese, Mercury and Iron tertiary. Mineralization of this Comstock-Type, Epithermal Vein deposit includes Gold, Cinnabar and Iron and Manganese Oxides, with a gangue of Adularia and Quartz, in a host of Miocene Rhyolite of the Caliente Caldron Complex and Tertiary Andesite. The Tabular ore body is controlled by a Brecciated shear zone along a normal fault, which curves from Northwest to nearly East-West. The property was developed by a shaft, several adits, prospect pits and stopes on one area of the Vein structure. More recent drill collars and drill cores were present at the time of the examination in 1984, from drilling done within the last 10 years. In 1912, the property was reported to have 3 tunnels; 130, 48 and 25 feet long. Adits shown on the topo map are all driven perpendicular to the Vein and all cross-cut the structure. The shaft was sunk down-dip on the Vein. The water level is just a few feet below the adit level. The stream flows along the North side of the Vein and the sloping Vein surface forms the steep Southern wall of the canyon here.
The size of the mine workings suggests that there was significant historic production, much of which is unrecorded and unknown. In 1933, 38 tons of ore was mined yielding 0.95 ounces of Gold and 3.95 ounces of Silver per ton. Drilling in 1994 on the main Vein defined Gold ore reserves of 1.5 million tons grading 0.069 ounces (about 2 grams) of Gold per ton. These are open-pit reserves delineated to an average depth of only 200 feet. The geology, in the general area of the site, is described as welded and non-welded Silicic Ash-flow Tuffs. The Land Status, Ownership Category of this past producer, discovered in 1912 and in

production from 1912 through the mid-1930s, is shown as "BLM Administrative Area". A 2005 record shows the Owner-Operator as Beta Minerals.

A more complete description of the ore body was found in the notes; it reads as follows: "Brecciated, re-cemented Vein Quartz occurs along a fault zone cutting Silicified Rhyolite. The wall rock is laced with banded Chalcedonic Quartz. Wall rock adjacent to the structure is green from Propylitic alteration. Within the Vein, Silicified Breccia fragments are embedded in a matrix of Chalcedonic Quartz with open spaces coated with needle-like Quartz crystals. Sole lamellar Quartz, after Calcite, is present. Some Quartz may have replaced the original Adularia crystals. There are traces of Iron and Manganese Oxides in the Vein material. The 10 to 15-foot-thick Silicified Breccia zone is exposed for about 1,000 feet along strike. An Iron-Oxide-stained zone in the immediate footwall of the structure has been stoped in one area. The richest ore was found in the farthest East portions of the Vein system. The Easter Property mineralization is an Epithermal Quartz-Adularia Vein Stockwork system within the Tertiary Volcanics of the Caliente Caldera Complex of Southeastern Nevada. The Easter Vein has been traced on the surface for a strike length of 6,450 feet and drill-tested to a depth of 1,740 feet. The main mineralized zone is Lens shaped in plain view, 50 to 125 feet wide in the center of the deposit, pitching to 20 to 25 feet wide to the East and West. The core of the deposit rises as a hillside above the surrounding country, allowing for surface mining with little or no waste stripping required. Gold mineralization is associated with Silicification in the form of Stockworks, Fissure-filling Veins and Silicified Volcanics. The highest grades, ranging up to ½ ounce per ton in Gold, are in the immediate hanging wall of the Vein. There is an extensive Opaline sinter and Argillically-altered, bedded Tuff sequence of the Eastern side of the property. Bedded hot-springs-pool Opalite, containing Cinnabar, indicates a once-active geothermal system with the potential for additional precious metal mineralization at depth."

Also found in the notes was a history of the mine, which is presented here in its entirety; "The property was covered by 4 full Claims in 1912, which ran along the strike of the Vein for 6,750 feet. J. W. Taylor was the principal Owner in 1912, and Mr. E. C. D. Marriage in 1933. Phil Dolan was the lessee in 1933 through 1935. The property has been the focus of renewed exploration activity by joint ventures since 1982; including work by Homestake, FMC Gold Company, Hanna Mining, Aur Resources and Phelps Dodge Mining Company. A total of 104 drill holes have been completed on the prospect; both core and reverse circulation holes. Homestake Mining Company made a Resource estimate, in 1988, of 4 million tons at 0.056 ounces of Gold per ton at a 0.02 ounce per ton cutoff, based upon 25 drill holes. In 1995, it was reported that five holes of a phase three drilling program had been completed at the Easter Gold Property by World Wide Minerals Limited. All the holes intersected the previously-identified mineralized zone. The drill program was to continue for at least 18 holes, totaling 6,000 feet. Phases 1 and 2, conducted in 1994 on the Main Vein, defined Gold ore reserves of 1.5 million tons grading 0.069 ounces per ton Gold. These open pit reserves delineated to an average depth of only 200 feet. Geophysical surveys have revealed that the Main Vein persists at least 400 feet to the West, and several strong targets were encountered. Beta Minerals acquired the Easter Gold Exploration Project in 2003. In August 2004, Beta Minerals announced completion of and assay results from their drilling program on the Easter Property. Twelve core holes, totaling 4,857 feet, were drilled during June and July to test the Gold mineralization along a strike length of 2,840 feet within the 6,500 foot-long zone, and tested mineralization to a depth of 851 vertical feet. A total of 451 samples were submitted for Gold assay. This drilling confirmed the down-dip continuity of the mineralization and expanded the Resource but did not produce the spectacular results that had been anticipated."

See the NBMG Sample Site 579 and the Taylor Mine entries for more information.

<u>Easter 002</u>: (38.22.57N by -114.21.57W - #3) (Lead)
Coordinates are for an ore body.

Eastern Mine: 37.59.30N by -114.22.15W - #3) (Gold, Silver)
Coordinates are for the ore body of this underground, past producer.
USGS MRDS Data Base Record 10125456, Released January 12, 1994: The main entrance to the Eastern Mine is shown at 37.43777N by -114.74194W. The location accuracy, of these coordinates, is shown as +/- 10 meters. The Public Land Survey System locators are Section 8, Township 6 South, Range 65 East. Gold is present and is shown as a primary commodity with Silver tertiary. The geology, in the area of the main entrance, is described as Limestone and Dolomite with locally-thick sequences of Shale and Siltstone. The

Land Status, Ownership Category of this underground, past producer is shown as "BLM Administrative Area".

Eastern Prince (a.k.a. Eastern Prince Shaft): (Manganese, Iron, Silver, Gold, Lead, Zinc)
USGS MRDS Data Base Record 10046406, Released May 1, 1984: The site of the Eastern Prince Shaft is shown at 37.90357N by -114.46945W, placing it in the Pioche Mining District and in the area included on the USGS Pioche 24K and Caliente 100K and 250K maps. This property consists of 8 Claims, believed to be extensions of the ore body of the adjoining Prince Consolidated, which contains low-grade, Iron-Manganese deposits which carry a little Silver, Lead, Zinc and Gold. The Public Land Survey System locators are Section 33, Township 1 North, Range 67 East. Manganese and Iron, in a host of Pliocene Rhyolite, are present and are shown as primary commodities with Lead, Silver, Zinc and Gold tertiary. The geology, in the general area of the site, is described as Alluvial deposits. The Land Status, Ownership Category of this occurrence is shown as "Private".
See Prince Consolidated, *Goodwin's Weekly, November 23, 1912* article for more information.

Eccles Perlite Deposit: (37.36.46N by -114.25.01W - #3) (Perlite)
Coordinates are for an ore body.

Elgin, South No. 1-2-3 Claims: (37.54.59N by -114.04.16W - #3)
Coordinates are for the ore body of this underground, past producer.

Ella Claim (a.k.a. Blue Bird Mine 001; Hulse Mine): (38.45523N by -114.334W – USGS MRDS)
(Uranium, Silver, Gold, Copper, Lead, Arsenic)
See the Blue Bird Mine 001 and the Hulse Mine entries for more information.

Ely Mining District (a.k.a. Ely Springs Mining District; Lone Mountain Mining District; Pioche Mining District): (Gold, Silver, Lead, Zinc, Copper, Antimony, Zirconium, Mercury, Barite)
Description of the District:
Tingley, Joseph V.; "Mining Districts of Nevada"; Nevada Bureau of Mines and Geology, Report 47, Second Edition; 1998; Page 86: The Ely Springs Mining District is located about 13 miles West of Pioche, on the West side of the Ely Springs Mountain Range. Much of the confusion surrounding the Lone Mountain Mining District stemmed from the fact that in 1912, J. M. Hill, in his *The Mining Districts of the Western United States*, referred to the area of the Ely Mining District as the Lone Mountain Mining District. This confusion was compounded in 1932 when C. Stoddard, in his *Metal and Non-Metal Occurrences in Nevada*, also referred to the area as the Lone Mountain Mining District; likely relying on the prior Hill publication.
Tingley, Joseph V.; "Mining Districts of Nevada"; Nevada Bureau of Mines and Geology, Report 47, Second Edition; 1998; Page 174: Discovered in 1863 and organized in 1864, the Pioche Mining District is oriented around the Pioche Hills. When established, the Pioche Mining District was called the Meadow Valley Mining District, but the name was changed to the Ely Mining District in 1868. The Highland area to the West is sometimes included in the Pioche Mining District, leading to it being referred to as the Highland Mining District at times.
Mines Included in the District:
  Alps (Gold, Silver, Lead, Zinc, Copper, Antimony)
  American Flag
  Andes (Mercury, Silver, Zirconium, Barite)
  Chief of the Hill
  Havana
  Mazeppa (Lead, Silver)
  North Star
  Parian
  Peavine
  Portsmouth
  Raymond and Ely Extension (Gold, Silver, Lead)
  Raymond Extension
  Silver Peak

Tara Claims (Gold, Silver, Lead, Manganese)
Washington and Creole

Ely Valley Mine (a.k.a. Ely Valley Mines; NBMG Sample Sites 1429 & 1430): (37.56.54N by -114.29.31W - #3) (Zinc, Manganese, Silver, Gold, Lead, Copper, Tungsten)
Coordinates are for the main entrance to this underground, past producer.
USGS MRDS Data Base Record 10037332, Released October 1, 1979; Updated December 1, 1984: The site of the Ely Valley Mines is shown at 37.9469N by -114.49306W, placing them about 2 miles North of Pioche, in the Pioche Mining District and in the area included on the USGS Pioche 24K and Caliente 100K and 250K maps. The Public Land Survey System locators are Section 17, Township 1 North, Range 67 East. Zinc and Manganese are present and are shown as primary commodities with Gold, Silver, Copper and Lead secondary and Tungsten tertiary. Mineralization of this Polymetallic Replacement deposit (USGS Model Code 19a) includes Sphalerite, Chrysocolla and Galena with a gangue of Quartz, Muscovite, Pyrite, Limonite and Hematite, in a host of Pioche Shale and Lyndon Limestone, associated with Late Cambrian, Prospect Mountain Quartzite. The ore is found in a block between 2 parallel faults. The ore body strikes North 75° West, dips vertically, is from 20 to 50 feet thick, about 400 feet wide and about 1,400 feet long. It consists of a porous, cavernous mass of Siliceous Manganiferous Limonitic ore, formed by replacement of a Brecciated Limestone. The fault separates the Lyndon Limestone from the Prospect Mountain Quartzite, with a dip slip of 1,700 feet. Hornblendite-Biotite intrusive rock is observed in the float. The dump rock was heavily Iron and Manganese stained and made up of Silicified Limestone and Shale with crystalline Pyrite replacing Limestone and cementing fault Breccia. Inter-grown crystalline Calcite and Quartz also act as Breccia cements. Jarosite crystals coat the fracture surfaces. Abundant Pyrolusite and Wad occur with the ore and some of the ore is magnetic. Oxidized material occurs with about 15% Manganese and $5/ton (period values) Silver and Gold replacing higher Limestone beds in the Pioche Shale and Lyndon Limestone. The mine contains 3 working levels; at 123, 268 and 428 feet. From the 268-foot level a winze was sunk vertically 300 feet, starting on the Vein. At the bottom, a crosscut was being driven Southwest to intersect the Quartzite contact. At the 200-foot level the Vein is Quartzose, consisting largely of milk-white Quartz. After passing into the underlying Pioche Shale, it pinches to a few inches but remains Quartzose. At the time of the examination, in 1983, there was no activity at the site; however the site had been drilled, assessment work kept up and the gates locked. The property appeared to be intermittently active. A 1922 assay of the ore showed the following results; about 10% Zinc and 1% Lead. A second assay, looking for precious metals showed 0.325 ounces per ton Gold (about 10 grams) and 3.05 ounces per ton Silver. After the Caselton mill was constructed in 1941, Ely Valley Mines began work to reach the rich Sulfide ore that had been disclosed by drill samples. Exhaustion of this Sulfide ore resulted in the closing down of full-time operations in 1951. The geology, in the general area of the site, is described as Quartzite and minor amounts of Conglomerate, Phyllitic Siltstone, Limestone and Dolomite. The Land Status, Ownership Category of this producer is shown as "Private". A 1932 record shows the Owner as Pioche Mines Company.
Notes: It was noted in the record that: "Favorable ground, which contains the offset portion of the ore body, in the hanging wall of the frontal fault, has not been adequately explored, as of 1970."
USGS MRDS Data Base Record 10174138, Released February 27, 1984: The main entrance to the Ely Valley Mine is shown at 37.94826N by -114.49304W, placing it in the Pioche Mining District. The location accuracy, of these coordinates, is shown as +/- 10 meters. The Public Land Survey System locators are the Northeast ¼ of the Southeast ¼ of the Northwest ¼ of Section 17, Township 1 North, Range 67 East. Zinc is present and is shown as a primary commodity with Gold, Silver, Lead, Manganese and Copper tertiary. This record shows the ore body as having a North 90° East strike, a 20° North dip, being about 115 feet thick, 400 feet wide and 1,400 feet long. (Note: The strike and dip vary significantly from the earlier record.) Most of the ore comes from the Combined Metals Limestone Member of the Pioche Shale, although the Susan Duster Limestone bed has some massive Sulfides also. The geology, in the area of the main entrance, is described as Quartzite and minor amounts of Conglomerate, Phyllitic Siltstone, Limestone and Dolomite. Discovered in 1907 and put into production in 1927, the Land Status, Ownership Category of this underground, past producer is shown as "Private". A 1963 record shows the 99% Owner-Operator as Ely Valley Mines of Nevada.
See the NBMG Sample Sites 1429 & 1430 entry for more information.

Emerald Prospect: (38.00.23N by -115.43.20W - #3) (Fluorite)
Coordinates are for the claim area of this exploration prospect.

Emerson Mill: (37.38.28N by -115.37.49W - #3)
Coordinates are for the main entrance to this past-producing, processing plant.

Emerson Mine: (37.38.28N by -115.37.49W - #3) (Tungsten)
Coordinates are for the ore body of this surface-underground, past producer.
See the New Tempiute Mine entry for more information.

Fairview 001: (38.10.45N by -114.41.29W - #3) (Lead, Silver)
Coordinates are for the ore body of this past producer.

Fairview 002 (a.k.a. Fairview; Nevada Lead; Robinson Mine): (38.10.00N by -114.38.14W - #3) (Lead, Silver, Gold)
Coordinates are for the ore body of this underground, past producer.
USGS MRDS Data Base Record 10026262, Released February 1, 1980; Updated February 1, 1985: The site of the Fairview Mine is shown at 38.15552N by -114.63834W, placing it about 25 miles Northwest of Pioche, in the Bristol-Jackrabbit Mining District, in the Fairview Mining District, in the Silverhorn Mining District and in the area included on the USGS Fairview Peak 24K, Wilson Creek Range 100K and Lund 250K maps. The Public Land Survey System locators are Section 1, Township 3 North, Range 65 East and Section 36, Township 4 North, Range 65 East. Lead, as Galena in a host of Late Devonian Dolomite, is present and is shown as a primary commodity with Silver secondary. The ore from the surface to about 14 feet in depth ran as high as 20% Lead. After many years as a major producer of Lead, Silver and Zinc, the mine closed in 1958. The ore body is described as a Tabular, Quartz Vein in altered and sheared Dolomite, striking North-South to Northeast, dipping about 55° East, about 14 feet thick and exposed at the surface. The deposit is made up of multiple ore deposition types. These include bedded replacement deposits in the Cambrian, Devonian and Mississippian Dolomite, Limestone and Hornfels at intersections with the fissures; replacement pipes crosscutting the bedding of the Mississippian Limestone lying under the Shale; and, fissure filling with the replacement of Breccia along fissures in the Limestone and Mississippian Quartzite. Igneous rocks present consist of small stocks, dikes and sills of Monzonite, Monzonite Porphyry and Rhyolite; all of which are from the Tertiary, likely Miocene period. Only assessment work was done on the property until 1922, when D. C. Robinson undertook its development. The early work focused heavily on the near-surface, Oxidized ore. This included a 52° inclined shaft with levels at 193 and 420 feet. There are also a couple of vertical shafts nearby having depths of 50 and 75 feet. The geology, in the general area of the site, is described as Dolomite, Limestone and minor amounts of Sandstone and Quartzite. The Land Status, Ownership Category of this occurrence is shown as "Private". A 1932 record shows the Operator as D. C. Robinson, with the Owner as the Ellis Estate of Salt Lake City, Utah.
USGS MRDS Data Base Record 10197980; Released January 21, 1994: The main entrance to the Fairview Mine is shown at 38.15416N by -114.64144W, placing it in the Fairview Mining District. The location accuracy, of these coordinates, is shown as +/- 10 meters. The Public Land Survey System locators are Section 1, Township 3 North, Range 65 East. Lead is present and is shown as a primary commodity, with Silver, Gold and Copper tertiary. The geology, in the area of the main entrance, is described as Alluvial deposits. The Land Status, Ownership Category of this underground, past producer is shown as "BLM Administrative Area".

Fairview Mining District (a.k.a. Silverhorn Mining District): (Silver, Lead, Zinc, Gold, Nickel, Perlite)
Description of the District:
Tingley, Joseph V.; "Mining Districts of Nevada"; Nevada Bureau of Mines and Geology, Report 47, Second Edition; 1998; Page 212: The Silverhorn Mining District, discovered in 1882, is located on the Southeast side of the Fairview Range, Northwest of Bristol Pass. The Eastern part of the District, on the Southeast side of the Range, is sometimes referred to as the Fairview Mining District.
See the Silverhorn Mining District entry for more information.
USGS MRDS Data Base Record 10026262, February 1, 1980; Updated February 1, 1985: The Fairview Mining District has produced Lead and Silver most of the time since 1870, with peaks in production

coming in 1915 to 1920, the late 1930s and 1940. Lows in production were experienced during the Great Depression; from 1929 to 1932. Zinc production began in the District around 1910.
Mines Included in the District:
>Fairview 002 (Lead, Silver, Gold)

Farnsworth-Jones: (36.58.20N by -114.17.33W - #3) (Manganese)
Coordinates are for the ore body of this past producer.

Fay Mining District (a.k.a. Eagle Valley Mining District): (Gold, Silver, Lead, Copper, Iron, Uranium, Fluorite, Pearlite, Barite)
Description of the District:
Tingley, Joseph V.; "Mining Districts of Nevada"; Nevada Bureau of Mines and Geology, Report 47, Second Edition; 1998; Page 79: The Eagle Valley Mining District lies along the Nevada-Utah Border and is made up of a number of small, scattered mining areas in the Mahogany Mountains. These include the Fay Mining District which lies South of Deer Lodge Canyon and North of Buck Mountain, named for the town of Fay (37.54.29N by -114.04.12W – USGS Deer Lodge Canyon 24K map).
See the Eagle Valley Mining District entry for more information.
Mines Included in the District:
>Bull Hill Mine (Silver, Gold, Fluorite)
>Confidence Mine (Gold, Silver)
>Iris84 09 (Gold, Silver, Copper)
>Keno Claims (Gold, Silver, Barite)
>NBMG Sample Site 1500 (Gold, Silver)
>NBMG Sample Site 1710 (Gold, Silver, Fluorite, Barite)
>NBMG Sample Site 1711 (Gold, Silver, Fluorite, Barite)
>Snowflake Mine 002 (Gold, Silver, Copper, Iron)
>Tempa Mine (Gold, Silver)

Ferguson Mining District (a.k.a. Delamar Mining District): (Gold, Silver, Copper, Lead, Tungsten, Bismuth, Antimony, Manganese, Iron, Arsenic, Perlite, Barite)
Description of the District:
Tingley, Joseph V.; "Mining Districts of Nevada"; Nevada Bureau of Mines and Geology, Report 47, Second Edition; 1998; Page 66 & 67: What would become the current Delamar Mining District was discovered in 1891 and originally named Ferguson. The major town was Delamar and this became the name associated with the District starting in the mid-1930s.
See the Delamar Mining District entry for more information.
Mines Included in the District:
>100 Foot Incline (Gold, Silver, Copper)
>April Fool (Gold, Silver, Copper, Bismuth, Antimony)
>Bamberger Delamar Gold Mining Company (Gold, Silver)
>Delamar 001 (Gold, Silver, Lead, Copper)
>Delamar Prospect 002 (Gold, Silver, Copper, Iron)
>Denton Summit Workings (Tungsten, Gold Silver)
>Easter 001 (Gold, Lead, Silver, Copper)
>Flagstaff (Gold, Manganese, Iron, Barite)
>Jumbo (Gold, Silver, Lead, Zinc, Copper, Barite)
>Magnolia Mine (Gold, Silver, Copper, Lead, Zinc, Bismuth, Arsenic)
>Monkey Wrench Wash Diggings (Gold, Copper, Iron)
>Nevada Vein (Gold, Silver, Lead)
>Unnamed Adit Near the April Fool Mine 008 (Gold, Silver, Lead, Copper, Arsenic)
>Unnamed Shaft 068 (Gold, Silver, Zinc, Lead, Copper, Manganese, Barite)

Financier Claim (a.k.a. Salt Lake Pioche Mining Company Mines): (37.92306N by -114.437W – USGS MRDS) (Gold, Silver, Lead, Zinc, Copper)
See the Salt Lake Pioche Mining Company Mines entry for more information.

Flagstaff (a.k.a. Flagstaff No. 2 Claim; Flagstaff Tunnel; Apex Claim; Boss Claim; June; June Claim): (37.28.20N by -114.46.35W - #3) (Gold, Manganese, Iron, Barite)
Coordinates are for the ore body of this underground operation.
USGS MRDS Data Base Record 10098365, Released November 1, 1979; Updated August 1, 1984: The site of the Flagstaff Tunnel is shown at 37.45247N by -114.76751W, placing it about 1,800 feet Southwest of Delamar, in the Delamar Mining District, in the Ferguson Mining District and in the area included on the USGS Delamar 24K, Clover Mountains 100K and Caliente 250K maps. The Public Land Survey System locators are Section 1, Township 6 South, Range 64 East. Gold is present and is shown as a primary commodity with Iron and Barite tertiary. Mineralization includes Pyrite and Barite, with a gangue of Calcite, in a host of Quartzite associated with Early Cambrian to Pliocene Plutonic rock. Ore is found in Breccia Veins cemented by cherry Quartz and in Veins and Veinlets of vuggy, "comb" Quartz, along two directions of North-Northwest and East-Northeast fractures. The main zone is North 70° East with many fractures trending North 20° to 30° West and dipping 65° to 80° North and West. The workings underlie a group of overlapping Patented Claims – the Apex, June, Flagstaff, No. 2 and Boss. An adit connects with a shaft about 350 feet from the portal, which comprise the base workings. Drifts, crosscuts and raises are run from the base workings. The amount of production is unknown, but the amount of underground workings, at least 1,600 feet, which includes a number of stopes, would indicate at least some level of production took place. The geology, in the general area of the site, is described as Quartzite and minor amounts of Conglomerate, Phyllitic Siltstone, Limestone and Dolomite. The Land Status, Ownership Category of this past producer is shown as "Private".
USGS MRDS Data Base Record 10173725, Released January 12, 1994: The main entrance to the Flagstaff No. 2 Claim is shown at 37.45217N by -114.76834W, placing it in the Delamar Mining District and in the Ferguson Mining District. The location accuracy, of these coordinates, is shown as +/- 10 meters. The Public Land Survey System locators are the Northeast ¼ of the Southeast ¼ of the Southwest ¼ of Section 1, Township 6 South, Range 64 East. Gold is present and is shown as a primary commodity with Iron and Manganese tertiary. The geology, in the area of the main entrance, is described as Quartzite and minor amounts of Conglomerate, Phyllitic Siltstone, Limestone and Dolomite. The Land Status, Ownership Category of this underground prospect is shown as ""Private", with Mineral Rights being held through "Patented Claims".

Florence (a.k.a. Florence Mine; Lady No. 1 Claim; NBMG Sample Site 1566): (37.58.51N by -114.35.44W - #3) (Silver, Lead, Gold, Copper)
Coordinates are for the ore body of this underground, past producer.
USGS MRDS Data Base Record 10046458, Released June 1, 1984: The site of the Florence Mine is shown at 37.98163N by -114.59612W, placing it in the Highland Mining District and in the area included on the USGS Highland Peak 24K and Caliente 100K and 250K maps. The Public Land Survey System locators are Section 5, Township 1 North, Range 66 East. Silver and Lead are present and are shown as primary commodities. Mineralization includes Anglesite and Galena, with a gangue of Quartz and Calcite, in a host of Late Cambrian, Highland Peak Dolomite. The mine was developed along a North 10° to 50° East, Vertical Fracture zone in Limestone. The Quartz-Calcite Vein that developed along the zone contains clots of red-brown and yellow-brown Gossan. The Gossan areas, with Jasperoid, are 2 to 6-feet wide and randomly spaced along the structure. White Quartz-Gossan contains clots of Galena rimmed with Anglesite. The ore zones appear to have been shoots and chimneys which formed within the major North 10° to 50° East structure. All are nearly vertical and controlled by the fracture zone. The Limestone host is moderately bleached near the mineralized structures. Development included two shafts, an adit containing a winze and open cuts and stopes upslope and to the Northeast. The geology, in the general area of the site, is described as Limestone and Dolomite with locally-thick sequences of Shale and Siltstone. The Land Status, Ownership Category of this occurrence is shown as "Private".
USGS MRDS Data Base Record 10246831, Released January 19, 1994: The ore body of the Florence Mine is shown at 37.98076N by -114.59644W, placing it in the Highland Mining District. The location accuracy, of these coordinates, is shown as +/- 10 meters. The Public Land Survey System locators are the Northwest ¼ of the Northeast ¼ of the Northeast ¼ of Section 5, Township 1 North, Range 66 East. Silver is present and is shown as a primary commodity with Gold and Copper tertiary. The geology, in the area of the ore body, is described as Limestone and Dolomite with locally-thick sequences of Shale and Siltstone. The Land Status, Ownership Category of this underground, past producer, is shown as "BLM Administrative Area".

Florence Prospect (a.k.a. Florence Claims; Florence No. 2 and Florence No. 1 Claims; Bull Hill Mine): (37.55.04N by -114.03.29W - #3) (Silver, Gold, Fluorite)
USGS MRDS Data Base Record 10098666, Released November 1, 1982: The site of Florence Claims (4 claims plus a fraction) is shown at 37.93023N by -115.59837W, placing it about 100 miles South of Ely, 60 miles West of Pioche, in the Freiberg Mining District and in the area included on the USGS Worthington Peak 24K, Timpahute Range 100K and Caliente 250K maps. The mine is described as being in an unsurveyed area, about a mile East of Workington Peak, about 12 miles South of the Roadside Mine and 18 miles Southeast of the Dresser Mine on Badger Creek. Gold and Silver are present and are shown as primary commodities with Lead and Copper secondary. In this Tabular to Irregular deposit, Copper and Lead ore, with a gangue of Calcite, are found in a host of Limestone associated with Basalt and Late Ordovician to Pliocene Rhyolite. Workings include an inclined shaft, with levels at 45 and 106 feet, a vertical shaft, an adit and several open cuts. When reviewed, there were several buildings at the site, which included a 10-ton Lead-Silver smelter. The geology, in the general area of the site, is described as Limestone, Dolomite, Shale and Quartzite. The Land Status, Ownership Category of this past producer is shown as "BLM Administrative Area". Undated records show the Owners as Charles Briscoe, W. L. Leland, G. A. Young and T. Young; and, the Operator as W. C. Murray, through an option. See the Bull Hill Mine entry for more information.

Fluorite Basin Prospect: (37.13.30N by -114.21.05W - #3) (Fluorite)
Coordinates are for the claim area of this exploration prospect.

Fluorine Mining District:
Description of the District:
Tingley, Joseph V.; "Mining Districts of Nevada"; Nevada Bureau of Mines and Geology, Report 47, Second Edition; 1998; Page 92: The Fluorine Mining District was organized near Pioche around 1909, but little is known about it, including its exact location or the minerals mined.
Mines Included in the District:

Forlorn Hope: (37.55.01N by -114.35.56W - #3) (Lead, Copper, Silver, Zinc)
Coordinates are for the ore body of this underground operation.

Fortuna and Helen Claims (a.k.a. Delta B Claims; NBMG Sample Site 1725): (37.93607N by -114.087W – USGS MRDS) (Gold, Silver, Lead)
USGS MRDS Data Base Record 10046541, Released February 1, 1984: The site of the Fortuna and Helen Claims is shown at 37.93607N by -114.08666W, placing it in the Eagle Valley Mining District and in the area included on the USGS Deer Lodge Canyon 24K and Caliente 100K and 250K maps. The Public Land Survey System locators are Section 24, Township 1 North, Range 70 East. Gold and Silver are present and are shown as primary commodities with Lead tertiary. Mineralization of this Comstock-type, Epithermal Vein deposit, is found along with a gangue of Quartz, Calcite, Siderite and other Iron minerals, in a host of Andesite and Rhyolite. The ore body, which is controlled by a Brecciated zone, is described as Tabular, striking North 20° East, dipping 50° to 60° Northwest and being about 20 feet thick. The deposit is on a narrow ridge underlain by a resistant rib of Quartz and Calcite Vein material, Quartz and Calcite Vein Breccia and Brecciated and Veined Volcanic rock. The Vein is quite resistant and Siliceous. Black and White Calcite and Siderite dominate the Vein composition in the lower portion with the Silica increasing towards the top. The top of the exposed outcrop has a "rubbly, Bull Quartz" or massive texture appearance. The lower contact, where the Vein was explored, would have been in the caved portion of the shaft. That contact appears to be Brecciated and contains fragments of Argillized/Kaolinized Andesite. Much of the Vein is composed of "sugary" to massive white Quartz. Pods and Veinlets of brown Siderite and white Calcite are common. Some portions of the Veins are Brecciated, and what is considered the Vein may be, in fact, just a part of the larger zone of Brecciation. Some of the Quartz Vein material in the area is Brecciated and re-cemented by Silica. Vuggy, "cocks comb" Quartz Veins, about an inch wide, crosscut fragments contained in the Volcanic Breccia which has, in places, been cemented by Chalcedonic Quartz. The fragments in the Breccia are Andesite, and to a lesser extent, Rhyolite. Several old workings are in the area but are now obliterated by recent bulldozing of the ridge area. The workings examined, at the time of the review were two North 70° W trending, inclined shafts; one of which was caved, the other open. Surface

exploration of the area, which included trenching and scraping, is believed to have occurred in the spring of summer of 1983, prior to the review. Evidence was found of geochemical sampling of the Vein outcrop. Other exploration, possibly a drill hole area, was also identified. The geology, in the general area of the site, is described as Andesite and related rocks of intermediate composition. The Land Status, Ownership Category of this past producer is shown as "BLM Administrative Area".

USGS MRDS Data Base Record 10149695, Released January 26, 1994: The main entrance to the Fortuna and Helen Claims is shown at 37.93606N by -114.08663W, placing it in the Eagle Valley Mining District. The location accuracy, of these coordinates, is shown as +/- 100 meters. The Public Land Survey System locators are Section 24, Township 1 North, Range 70 East. Gold is present and is shown as a primary commodity with Silver and Lead tertiary. Mineralization of this Hydrothermal-origin, Breccia-filled, Tabular, Fissure Vein deposit is found with a gangue of Quartz, Calcite, Pyrite and Siderite. The geology, in the area of the main entrance, is described as Andesite and related rocks of intermediate composition. The Land Status, Ownership Category of this underground prospect is shown as "BLM Administrative Area".

Fortuna Mine: (38.06.14N by -114.36.35W - #3) (Lead, Zinc, Copper, Silver, Gold)
Coordinates are for the main entrance to this underground, past producer.

USGS MRDS Data Base Record 10037331, Released October 1, 1979; Updated February 1, 1985: The site of the Fortuna Mine is shown at 38.11163N by -114.60334W, placing it about 1 mile Northwest of Jackrabbit, in the Bristol-Jackrabbit Mining District and in the area included on the USGS Bristol Range Southeast 24K, Wilson Creek Range 100K and Lund 250K maps. The area is unsurveyed so the Public Land Survey System locators are projected from the East and estimated to be Sections 19 & 20, Township 3 North, Range 66 East. Lead and Zinc are present and are shown as primary commodities with Silver and Copper secondary. Mineralization, including Galena, Calamine, Hydrozincite and various Copper ores, is hosted in Late Cambrian Dolomite. The ore body is a Tabular Vein, striking North 75° West, dipping 40° West and controlled by faults and fractures. The ore Vein is marked by a well-defined footwall that is polished and scored with grooves. Above the footwall the Dolomite is a crushed Breccia with lean mineralization. The ore on the dump contained Hydrozincite and Calamine. Development included a 40-foot long inclined shaft, dipping 58° West, with a drift at the bottom. The geology, in the general area of the site, is described as Alluvial deposits. The Land Status, Ownership Category of this occurrence is shown as "Private".

USGS MRDS Data Base Record 10149272, Released January 21, 1994: The main entrance to the Fortuna Mine is shown at 38.10386N by -114.61054W, placing it in the Jackrabbit Mining District. The location accuracy, of these coordinates, is shown as +/- 10 meters. The Public Land Survey System locators are the Western ½ of Section 20, Township 3 North, Range 66 East. Lead is present and is shown as a primary commodity with Silver, Zinc, Copper and Gold tertiary. The geology, in the area of the main entrance, is shown as Limestone and Dolomite with locally-thick sequences of Shale and Siltstone. The Land Status, Ownership Category of this underground, past producer is unknown.

Fred Claim (a.k.a. Cinch Mine): (38.35.58N by -114.41.29W - #3) (Tungsten, Gold, Silver)
See the Cinch Mine entry for more information.

Frederick: (37.54.59N by -114.04.16W - #3) (Lead, Silver)
Coordinates are for the ore body of this underground, past producer.

Free Perlite Deposit: (38.03.57N by -114.16.53W - #3) (Perlite)
Coordinates are for the ore body of this surface prospect.

Freiburg Mine (a.k.a. Freiberg Tungsten Prospect): (37.56.46N by -115.36.01W - #3) (Tungsten, Molybdenum, Manganese)
Coordinates are for the main entrance to this underground, past producer.

Freiberg Mining District (a.k.a. Freiburg Mining District; Freyberg Mining District, Worthington Mining District: (Silver, Lead, Zinc, Copper, Tungsten)
Description of the District:

Tingley, Joseph V.; "Mining Districts of Nevada"; Nevada Bureau of Mines and Geology, Report 47, Second Edition; 1998; Pages 93 & 94: The Freiberg Mining District was discovered in 1865 and organized as the Worthington Mining District that same year. It was later reorganized as the Freiberg Mining District about 1869. It includes the area of the Northern Worthington Mountains, with the major historic mines located in the Central part of Township 1 North, Range 57 East.
Mines Included in the District:
        Florence Prospect (Silver, Gold, Fluorite)
        Unnamed Prospect 030 (Tungsten)

<u>Garrison Mine</u>: (37.56.30N by -114.29.17W - #3)
Coordinates are for an ore body.

Gelder Mine (a.k.a. NBMG Sample Site 1431): (37.56.23N by -114.28.51W - #3) (Gold, Silver, Lead, Zinc, Copper, Antimony, Manganese, Arsenic)
Coordinates are for an ore body.
USGS MRDS Data Base Record 10046409, Released April 1, 1984: The site of the Gelder Mine is shown at 37.94163N by -114.47862W, placing it in the Pioche Mining District and in the area included on the USGS Pioche 24K and Caliente 100K and 250K maps. The Public Land Survey System locators are Section 16, Township 1 North, Range 67 East. Gold, Silver and Lead are present and are shown as primary commodities with Copper and Zinc secondary and Antimony, Manganese and Arsenic tertiary in this Polymetallic Vein Deposit (USGS Model Number 22c). Mineralization includes Tetrahedrite, Chalcopyrite, Malachite, Sphalerite and Psilomelane, with a gangue of Pyrite and Quartz, in a host of Limestone, Late Cambrian Quartzite and Shale of the Pinoche Shale Unit. The deposition of the mineralization was controlled by the intersection of a Southerly-dipping, low-angle fault and a North 60° East-trending shear zone. The ore body was developed by a series of shafts and adits, now partially caved, surface cuts, prospect pits and an old ore chute. The lower workings are in Pioche Shale and explore a South-dipping, low-angle fault, which is intersected by a North 60° East trending, 75° Southeast-dipping shear zone. Rocks are Argillically altered and stained with Iron and Manganese Oxides, with abundant Psilomelane staining. The shear separates the Prospect Mountain Quartzite, on the Northwest from the Pioche Shale on the Southeast. The shear zone is Hydrothermally altered and Gossany. At the main adit, above the lower workings, Limestone beds strike North 35° West, dip 30° Southwest and are bleached and altered, with an exposed bedding plane shear zone that is heavily stained with Iron-Manganese Oxides. Most of the dump material, at the adit, is Pioche Shale while the main ore bin is full of Quartzite and Limestone carrying minor grains of Galena and Pyrite in Quartz Veins. The adjacent shaft is caved in. At the shaft, a rib of Silicified Siltstone/Limestone, cut by vitreous Quartz Veins carrying fine-grained, Oxidized Pyrite, Chalcopyrite, Argentiferous Galena and possibly Sphalerite, is found. It is also stained with minor Malachite and Iron-Manganese minerals. Most of the rocks exhibit slickensides. Mineralization occurs in fissure-filling Quartz Veins. Most of the Pyrite found is Oxidized with Malachite staining, probably from the oxidization of the Chalcopyrite, or possibly the Tetrahedrite. Some minor yellow Oxides were also noted. The site was not active when reviewed in 1983. The geology, in the general area of the site is described as Limestone and Dolomite with locally-thick sequences of Shale and Siltstone. The Land Status, Ownership Category of this past producer, which began production in 1925, is shown as "Private".

<u>Gentry Prospect</u>: (37.40.30N by -115.21.45W - #3) (Manganese)
Coordinates are for an ore body.

Geyser Mine (a.k.a. Geyser; Lake Valley Mine): (38.40.15N by -114.42.15W - #3) (Tungsten, Gold, Silver, Fluorite)
Coordinates are for the main entrance to this underground, past producer.
USGS MRDS Data Base Record 10198453; Released June 14, 1993: The main entrance to the Geyser Mine is shown at 38.67075N by -114.70505W, placing it in the Patterson Mining District and in the area included on the USGS Mount Grafton 24K, Garrison 100K and Lund 250K maps. The location accuracy, of these coordinates, is shown as +/- 100 meters. The Public Land Survey System locators are Section 5, Township 9 North, Range 65 East. Tungsten is present and is shown as a primary commodity with Gold, Silver and Fluorite tertiary. The geology, in the area of the main entrance, is described as Limestone and

Dolomite with locally-thick sequences of Shale and Siltstone. The Land Status, Ownership Category of this underground, past producer is shown as "BLM Administrative Area".

Geyser Mining District (a.k.a. Geyser Ranch Area): (Tungsten, Silver, Gold, Zinc, Molybdenum, Lead, Manganese, Fluorite)
Description of the District:
Tingley, Joseph V.; "Mining Districts of Nevada"; Nevada Bureau of Mines and Geology, Report 47, Second Edition; 1998; Page 98: The Geyser Mining District is located on the Eastern slope of Mount Grafton in the Schell Creek Range, along the White Pine-Lincoln County line. The Southern part of the District, containing Manganese occurrences, extends into Lincoln County and is sometimes included in the Patterson Mining District.
Mines Included in the District:
       Schwartz Tunnel (Tungsten, Zinc, Gold, Silver, Molybdenum, Lead, Fluorite)

Gold 1-22 Prospect: (37.17.51N by -114.15.42W - #3) (Gold)
Coordinates are for the claim area of this surface prospect.
USGS MRDS Data Base Record 10232408; Released September 25, 1991: The Claim area of the Gold 1-22 Prospect is shown at 37.29748N by -114.26252W, placing it in the area included on the USGS Garden Spring 24K, Clover Mountains and Caliente 250K maps. The location accuracy, of these coordinates, is shown as +/- 10 meters. The Public Land Survey System locators are Section 34, Township 7 South, Range 69 East. Gold is present and is shown as a primary commodity. The geology, in the Claim area, is described as Andesite and related rocks of intermediate composition. The Land Status, Ownership Category of this surface occurrence is described as "BLM Administrative Area". Mineral Rights are held through "Located Claims".

Gold 23-31 Prospect: (37.18.32N by -114.16.32W - #3) (Gold)
Coordinates are for the claim area of this surface prospect.
USGS MRDS Data Base Record 10198306, Released September 25, 1991: The Claim area of the Gold 23-31 Prospect is shown at 37.30887N by -114.27642W, placing it in the area included on the USGS Garden Spring 24K, Clover Mountains 100K and Caliente 250K maps. The location accuracy, of these coordinates, is shown as +/- 10 meters. The Public Land Survey System locators are the Southeast ¼ of Section 28, Township 7 South, Range 69 East. Gold is present and is shown as a primary commodity. The geology, in the area of the Claim, is described as welded and non-welded Silicic, Ash-flow Tuffs. The Land Status, Ownership Category of this surface occurrence is shown as "BLM Administrative Area". Mineral Rights are held through "Located Claims".

Gold Butte Claims (a.k.a. NBMG Sample Site 3035-3037): (37.42056N by -115.802W – USGS MRDS) (Gold, Silver)
USGS MRDS Data Base Record 10198670, Released February 2, 1984: The pit area of the Gold Butte Claims is shown at 37.42056N by -115.80167W, placing it in the Groom Mining District and in the area included on the USGS Cattle Spring 24K, Pahranagat Range 100K and Caliente 250K maps. The location accuracy, of these coordinates, is shown as +/- 500 meters. The Public Land Survey System locators are Section 13, Township 6 South, Range 55 East. Gold is present and is shown as a primary commodity with Silver tertiary. Mineralization of this Tabular, Fissure-Vein, Shear-Zone controlled deposit includes Magnetite and Hematite. The geology, in the pit area, is described as Quartzite and minor amounts of Conglomerate, Phyllitic Siltstone, Limestone and Dolomite. The Land Status, Ownership Category of this surface prospect is shown as "Military Reservation".

Gold Chance Prospect: (37.15.57N by -114.21.30W - #3) (Gold)
Coordinates are for the main entrance to this underground, exploration prospect.
USGS MRDS Data Base Record 10295634; Released September 25, 1991: The main entrance to the Gold Chance Prospect is shown at 37.26578N by -114.35913W, placing it in the area included on the USGS Garden Spring 24K, Clover Mountains 100K and Caliente 250K maps. The location accuracy, of these coordinates, is shown as +/- 10 meters. The Public Land Survey System locators are the Southeast ¼ of Section 10, Township 8 South, Range 68 East. Gold is present and is shown as a primary commodity. The geology, in the area of the main entrance, is described as Cherty Limestone and sparse Dolomite, Shale and

Sandstone. The Land Status, Ownership Category of this underground prospect is shown as "BLM Administrative Area". Mineral Rights are held through "Located Claims".

Gold Chief (a.k.a. Gold Chief Mine; Chief; Silver Wedge #10): (37.41.57N by -114.30.00W - #3) (Gold, Silver, Zinc, Lead, Copper, Manganese, Barite, Iron, Arsenic)
Coordinates are for the ore body of this underground, past producer.
USGS MRDS Data Base Record 10111426, Released February 1, 1980; Updated August 1, 1984: The site of the Gold Chief Mine is shown at 37.69775N by -114.51473W, placing it about 5 miles North of Caliente and on the South side of Chief Gulch, in the Chief Mining District and in the area included on the USGS Chief Mountain 24K and Caliente 100K and 250K maps. The Public Land Survey System locators are Section 8, Township 3 South, Range 67 East. Gold and Silver are present and are shown as primary commodities with Copper, Lead and Zinc secondary and Manganese, Iron, Barite and Arsenic tertiary. Mineralization of this Polymetallic Replacement Deposit (USGS Model Code 19a) is found with a gangue of Quartz and Calcite in a host of Late Cambrian Quartzite. Three samples were taken at the site. While most of the recorded samples showed from 0.2 to 0.5 ounces of Gold per ton and minor Silver these three samples showed somewhat less.

1.) Sample 118 assayed greater than 2% Calcium, 1,500 parts per million (PPM) Manganese, 200PM Boron, 150PPM Barite, 100PPM Strontium, 50PPM Lead, 50PPM Copper and 2PPM Silver.
2.) Sample 119 assayed greater than 2% Calcium, greater than 10,000PPM Lead, greater than 10,000PPM Zinc, greater than 5,000PPM Manganese, greater than 5,000PPM Barite, 500PPM Copper, 500PPM Strontium, 200PPM Arsenic, 150PPM Boron and 50PPM Silver.
3.) Sample 120 assayed greater than 2% Calcium, greater than 5,000PPM Manganese, greater than 5,000PPM Barite, 2,000PPM Lead, 2,000PPM Boron, 1,000PPM Zinc, 1,000PPM Arsenic, 200PPM Lead, 200PPM Strontium, 50PPM Copper, 10PPM Silver and 10PPM Gold.

The ore body is described as being Tabular to Irregular, striking North 25° to 30° East, dipping 69° West at the surface, but only about 36° West in the workings and controlled by a thrust fault striking North 50° East at the mine and intersecting fault zones.
The main fault zone, which is along Quartzite on the Northwest and Limestone on the Southeast, strikes North 30° East, dips 30° to 40° Southeast and is 20 or more feet wide. An adit or incline follows a second, more steeply inclined, intersecting shear (striking East-West and dipping 55° South). All exposed rock is highly Brecciated, cut by high-angle fissures and Iron-stained. The zone contains large, recrystallized boulders of Limestone, which are Veined by Calcite, Barite and some Quartz. These minerals also occur as gangue materials in the Breccia samples. This fault zone also contains abundant Manganese, Iron and Clay. Barite-bearing Gossan was found on the dump. Filling intersects between the Barite crystals are Iron-Manganese Oxides, Hemimorphite, Mimetite and Quartz. The fault Breccia is cut by intersecting slip planes. The major ore is in the thrust Breccia between the Limestone and Quartzite. The lower adit begins in a tan-gray, recrystallized Limestone, which strikes North 50° East, dips 20° Southeast and is fractured and faulted. Quartzite outcrops 10 to 15 feet West of the caved portal. The fault contact, between the two rock types, strikes North 40° to 45° East and dips 70° Southeast. The major ore deposits are found in the thrust Breccia between the Limestone and Quartzite. The stopes trend North 25° to 30° East and the fissure flattens with depth, going from 68° West to 36° West. The Vein filling is a network of Tabular Barite crystals and scattered grains of Galena. Colloform (grape-like bunches) Chalcedonic Quartz replaces and Veins the Barite.
Workings, upslope from the lower adit, lie along this fault zone. Rocks along this zone are highly Oxidized and Brecciated. An altered Brecciated zone is exposed in a stoped exposure which extends for about 25 feet above the partially-caved portal. The stope and inclined adit lie along the main fault zone which juxtaposes Quartzite against Limestone on the Southeast. This zone strikes North 30° East, dips 30° to 40° Southeast and is about 20 feet wide, or more. The adit, or incline, follows a more steeply-inclined, intersecting shear, which strikes East-West and dips about 55° to the South. All rock exposed is highly Brecciated, Iron-stained and cut by high-angle fissures. Large, recrystallized Limestone boulders are caught up in this zone. Limestone in the zone is Veined by Calcite, Barite and minor Quartz. These minerals also occur as a gangue in the Breccia samples. A 20-ton Cyanide plant was built in 1911 and a 50-ton plant added in 1914. Between 1911 and 1917 the mine produced about $25,000 (period values) worth of ore. Some Gold ore was shipped in 1931. By 1932 all equipment and buildings had been removed and the stopes were caved at the surface. About 189 tons of ore was produced between 1937 and 1940, with the value of the 1940 production being about $32,000. The present Claims were located in 1979. There was no activity at the site

when reviewed in 1983; however, the Claims are probably active as there was evidence of recent geochemical sampling.

The geology, in the general area of the site, is described as Quartzite and minor amounts of Conglomerate, Phyllitic Siltstone, Limestone and Dolomite. The Land Status, Ownership Category of this past producer is unknown. A 1913, record lists the Operator as the Standard Leasing Company and a 1931 record shows the Owners as Lawrence, Burt and J. W. Cooke as the locators and C and C Mining and Land Company. This, however, probably doesn't mean much as the record indicated the site was relocated in 1979.

USGS MRDS Data Base Record 10173678, Released January 19, 1994: The main entrance to the Gold Chief is shown at 37.69747N by -114.51444W, placing it in the Chief Mining District. The location accuracy, of these coordinates, is shown as +/- 10 meters. The Public Land Survey System locators are the Southwest ¼ of Section 8, Township 3 South, Range 67 East. Gold is present and is shown as a primary commodity with Silver, Lead, Zinc and Manganese tertiary. The geology, in the area of the main entrance, is described as Quartzite and minor amounts of Conglomerate, Phyllitic Siltstone, Limestone and Dolomite. The Land Status, Owner ship Category of this underground, past producer, first producing in 1911, is shown as "BLM Administrative Area".

Gold Eagle Mine: (37.56.21N by -114.28.58W - #3)
Coordinates are for the ore body of this underground operation.

Gold Fever Claim: (38.57384N by -114.964W – USGS MRDS) (Gold, Silver, Zinc, Arsenic)
Coordinates are for a surface occurrence.

Gold Occurrence 001: (38.07.50N by -114.03.27W - #3) (Gold)
Coordinates are for an ore body. (Decimal Equivalents 38.130556N by -114.0575W)

Gold Occurrence 002: (37.56.05N by -114.05.25W - #3) (Gold)
Coordinates are for an ore body. (Decimal Equivalents of 37.934722N by -114.0902778W)

Gold Occurrence 003: (37.30.00N by -115.45.00W - #3) (Gold)
Coordinates are for an ore body. (Decimal Equivalents 37.5000N by -115.7500W)
USGS MRDS Data Base Record 10173780, Released January 12, 1994: The ore body of the Gold Occurrence is shown at 37.49826N by -115.73617W, placing it in the area included on the USGS Groom Range 24K, Pahranagat Range 100K and Caliente 250K maps. The location accuracy, of these coordinates, is shown as +/- 5,000 meters. The Public Land Survey System locators are Section 24, Township 5 South, Range 55 East. Gold is present and is shown as a primary commodity. The geology, in the area of the ore body, is described as Limestone and Dolomite with locally-thick sequences of Shale and Siltstone. The Land Status, Ownership Category of this surface occurrence is unknown.

Gold Occurrence 004: (37.25.23N by -115.48.08W - #3) (Gold)
Coordinates are for an ore body. (Decimal equivalents 37.4230556N by -115.80222W)
USGS MRDS Data Base Record 10198356, Released January 12, 1994: The ore body of the Gold Occurrence is shown at 37.41806N by -115.79117W, placing it in the Groom Mining District and in the area included on the USGS Cattle Spring 24K, Pahranagat Range 100K and Caliente 250K maps. The location accuracy, of these coordinates, is shown as +/- 1,000 meters. The estimated, general Public Land Survey System locators are Township 6 South, Range 55⁺ East. Gold is present and is shown as a primary commodity. The geology, in the area of the ore body, is described as Quartzite and minor amounts of Conglomerate, Phyllitic Siltstone, Limestone and Dolomite. The Land Status, Ownership Category of this surface occurrence is shown as "Military Reservation".

Gold Prospect 007: (37.53079N by -115.739W – USGS MRDS) (Gold)
Coordinates are for a surface occurrence.
USGS MRDS Data Base Record 10046489, Released June 1, 1984: The site of the Gold Prospect is shown at 37.53079N by -115.73893W, placing it about 2.7 miles North of the peak of Bald Mountain, on the Northeast flank of the Groom Range, in an area of springs, in the Don Dale Mining District, in the Groom Mining District and in the area included on the USGS Tempiute Mountain South 24K, Timpahute Range 100K and Caliente 250K maps. The location accuracy, of these coordinates, is shown as +/- 500 meters.

The Public Land Survey System locators are Section 12, Township 5 South, Range 55 East. Gold, in a host of Prospect Mountain Quartzite, associated with Basalt and Late Cambrian to Pliocene Volcanic rock, is present and is shown as a primary commodity. The nearby Basalt cone is not believed to have had any real effect on the ore deposition which is described as "spotty". Gold nuggets, up to the size of a grain of wheat, were recovered by washing Gravels below the workings, which consisted of "shallow diggings". The geology, in the general area of the site, is described as Quartzite and minor amounts of Conglomerate, Phyllitic Siltstone, Limestone and Dolomite. The Land Status, Ownership Category of this occurrence, is shown as "BLM Administrative Area".

USGS MRDS Data Base Record 10270979, Released January 26, 1994: The pit area of the Gold Prospect is shown at 37.53076N by -115.73897W, placing it in the Don Dale Mining District. The location accuracy, of these coordinates, is shown as +/- 100 meters. The ore body is described as a Placer with Disseminated Gold. The geology, in the pit area, is described as Quartzite and minor amounts of Conglomerate, Phyllitic Siltstone, Limestone and Dolomite. The Land Status, Ownership Category of this surface prospect is unknown.

Gold Prospect 008 (a.k.a. NBMG Sample Site 3054): (37.39856N by -115.795W – USGS MRDS) (Gold, Silver, Lead)
Coordinates are for a surface occurrence.
USGS MRDS Data Base Record 10222218, Released January 26, 1994: The pit area of the Gold Prospect is shown at 37.39856N by -115.79477W, placing it in the Groom Mining District and in the area included on the USGS Cattle Spring 24K, Pahranagat Range 100K and Caliente 250K maps. The location accuracy, of these coordinates, is shown as +/- 500 meters. The Public Land Survey System locators are Section 24, Township 6 South, Range 55 East. Gold is present and is shown as a primary commodity with Silver and Lead tertiary. Mineralization of this Tabular, Hydrothermal Fissure Vein deposit includes Galena. The geology, in the pit area, is described as Quartzite and minor amounts of Conglomerate, Phyllitic Siltstone, Limestone and Dolomite. The Land Status, Ownership Category of this surface prospect is shown as "Military Reservation".

Gold Prospects 005: (37.30.38N by -115.47.22W - #3) (Gold)
Coordinates are for an ore body. (Decimal Equivalents 37.510556N by -115.789444W)
USGS MRDS Data Base Record 10037345, Released February 1, 1980: The site of the Gold Prospects is shown at 37.51052N by -115.79031W, placing it about 12 miles North of the Groom Mine, in the Groom Mining District and in the area included on the USGS White Blotch Springs Southeast 24K, Timpahute Range 100K and Caliente 250K maps. The area was unsurveyed at the time of the review, but the general Public Land Survey System locators were estimated as Township 4 South, Range 55 East. Gold, in a host of Quartzite, is present and is shown as a primary commodity. The ore body is along a Breccia zone in the Quartzite. The geology, in the general area of the site, is described as Alluvial deposits. The Land Status, Ownership Category of this occurrence is shown as "Private".

Gold Prospects 006: (37.23.20N by -115.46.28W - #3) (Gold)
Coordinates are for an ore body. (Decimal Equivalents 37.38889N by -115.77444W)
USGS MRDS Data Base Record 10037347, Released February 1, 1980: The site of the Gold Prospects is shown at 37.38885N by -115.77531W, placing it about 5 miles Northwest of the Groom Mine, in the Groom Mining District and in the area included on the USGS Cattle Spring 24K, Pahranagat Range 100K Caliente 250K maps. The estimated, general Public Land Survey System locators are Township 7 South, Range 55 East. Gold, in a host of Quartzite, is present and is shown as a primary commodity. The Gold is found in along Breccia zones in the Quartzite. The geology, in the general area of the site, is described as Quartzite with minor amounts of Conglomerate, Phyllitic Siltstone, Limestone and Dolomite. The Land Status, Ownership Category of this occurrence is unknown.

Gold Prospects 009: (37.40468N by -115.79W – USGS MRDS) (Gold)
Coordinates are for an occurrence.
USGS MRDS Data Base Record 10046482, Released June 1, 1984: The site of one of the several prospects in the area is shown at 37.40468N by -115.79031W, placing it in the Groom Mining District and in the area included on the USGS Cattle Spring 24K, Pahranagat Range 100K and Caliente 250K maps. As the area was unsurveyed at the time of the review, the estimated (projected from the East) Public Land Survey

System locators are the Northeast ¼ of Section 16 and Section 21, Township 6 South, Range 55 East. Gold, in a host of Late Cambrian, Prospect Mountain Quartzite is present and is shown as a primary commodity. The Tabular ore body is controlled by a Breccia zone. The Land Status, Ownership Category of this occurrence is shown as "BLM Administrative Area".

Gold Prospects 010: (37.49856N by -115.736W – USGS MRDS) (Gold)
USGS MRDS Data Base Record 10149535, Released January 21, 1994: The ore body of the Gold Prospects is shown at 37.49856N by -115.73557W, placing it in the area included on the USGS Groom Range 24K, Pahranagat Range 100K and Caliente 250K maps. The location accuracy, of these coordinates, is shown as +/- 1,000 meters. The Public Land Survey System locators are Section 24, Township 5 South, Range 55+ East. Gold is present and is shown as a primary commodity. The geology, in the area of the ore body, is described as Limestone and Dolomite with locally thick sequences of Shale and Siltstone. The Land Status, Ownership Category is unknown.

Gold Springs Mining District (a.k.a. Eagle Valley Mining District): (Gold, Silver, Lead, Uranium, Pearlite)
Description of the District:
Tingley, Joseph V.; "Mining Districts of Nevada"; Nevada Bureau of Mines and Geology, Report 47, Second Edition; 1998; Page 79: The Eagle Valley Mining District lies along the Nevada-Utah Border and is made up of a number of small, scattered mining areas in the Mahogany Mountains. These include the Gold Springs mining area, lying mostly in Utah, East of Buck Mountain.
See the Eagle Valley Mining District entry for more information.
Mines Included in the District:
        Big Buck Mine (Silver, Gold, Lead, Copper)
        Confidence Mine (Gold, Silver)
        Iris84 09 (Gold, Silver, Copper)
        Jennie Mine (Gold, Silver, Lead, Copper)
        Mountain View Group (Gold, Silver)
        NBMG Sample Site 1500 (Gold, Silver)
        NBMG Sample Site 1723 (Gold, Silver)
        NBMG Sample Site 1724 (Gold, Silver)
        Pope Mine (Gold, Silver, Lead, Copper, Antimony, Fluorite)
        Red Eagle Mine (Gold, Silver)
        Redlite Claims (Gold, Silver)
        Snowflake Mine 002 (Gold, Silver, Copper, Iron)
        Tempa Mine (Gold, Silver)
        Thor Mine (Gold, Silver, Lead, Copper)
        Unnamed Adit 003 (Gold, Silver)
        Uvada Tunnel (Gold, Silver)

Gold Springs Wash Adit: (37.88386N by -114.061W – USGS MRDS) (Gold)
USGS MRDS Data Base Record 10046540, Released February 1, 1984: The site of the Gold Springs Wash Adit is shown at 37.88386N by -114.06054W, placing it in the Eagle Valley Mining District, on the North side of Gold Springs Wash, about one mile South of Buck Mountain, in the Gold Springs Mining District and in the area included on the USGS Deer Lodge Canyon 24K and Caliente 100K and 250K maps. The location accuracy, of these coordinates, is shown as +/- 250 meters. The Public Land Survey System locators are the Southwest ¼ of Section 4, Township 1 South, Range 71 East. Gold, with a gangue of Quartz and Limonite, in a host of Pliocene Volcanic rock, is present and is shown as a primary commodity. The ore body is Tabular, North-trending, about 6 inches thick, 35 feet long and controlled by fractures. The geology, in the general area of the site, is described as Alluvial deposits. The Land Status, Ownership Category of this occurrence is unknown.
USGS MRDS Data Base Record 10198384, Released January 26, 1994: The site of the Gold Springs Wash Adit is shown at 37.88387N by -114.06052W, placing it in the Eagle Valley Mining District. The location accuracy, of these coordinates, is shown as +/- 100 meters. The Public Land Survey System locators are the Southwest ¼ of Section 4, Township 1 South, Range 71 East. Gold is present and is shown as a primary commodity. The ore body is described as a Tabular Fissure Vein of Hydrothermal origin. The geology, in

the area of the main entrance, is described as Alluvial deposits. The Land Status, Ownership Category of this underground prospect is shown as "BLM Administrative Area".

Gold Stake (a.k.a. Gold Stake Mine): (37.41.00N by -114.31.45W - #3) (Gold, Silver, Lead, Arsenic) Coordinates are for the ore body of this surface-underground operation.
USGS MRDS Data Base Record 10037352, Released February 1, 1980; Updated August 1, 1984: The site of the Gold Stake Mine is shown at 37.69386N by -114.5239W, placing it about 70 miles North of Alamo, in the Chief Mining District and in the area included on the USGS Chief Mountain 24K and Caliente 100K and 250K maps. The Public Land Survey System locators are Section 18, Township 3 South, Range 67 East. Gold, in a host of Diorite and Quartzite, is present and is shown as a primary commodity. The ore body is Tabular and follows an altered Diorite dike, so the strike is somewhat Irregular, but generally has a strike of about South 20° West and dips from 70° East to vertically. The ore consists of zones of Brecciated Quartzite, cemented by Iron Oxide, about 4 feet wide and traceable for about 155 feet. En echelon Veins, containing crushed Quartzite and gouge, also follow the altered dike. This Diorite dike, the Brecciation and the fault gouge are considered the controls for ore emplacement. The main workings are 3 shafts, all inaccessible; 2 pits and a 285-foot tunnel dug in 1936. In 1936, ore taken from the tunnel assayed from $3 to $27 per ton, over a distance of 70 feet. Discovered in 1892, the Land Status, Ownership Category of this past producer is shown as "BLM Administrative Area".
See the Advance and Old Democrat entries for more information.

Gold Stake Tunnel (a.k.a. Gold Stake; NBMG Sample Site 126): (37.69027N by -114.518W – USGS MRDS) (Gold, Silver, Lead, Arsenic)
USGS MRDS Data Base Record 10125644, Released January 28, 1994: The main entrance to the Gold Stake Tunnel is shown at 37.69027N by -114.51774W, placing it in the Chief Mining District and in the area included on the USGS Chief Mountain 24K and Caliente 100K and 250K maps. The location accuracy, of these coordinates, is shown as +/- 250 meters. The Public Land Survey System locators are the Northeast ¼ of Section 18, Township 3 South, Range 67 East. Gold is present and is shown as a primary commodity with Silver, Lead and Arsenic tertiary. Mineralization is found in a Fissure Vein, of Hydrothermal origin, along with a gangue of Quartz, Pyrite and hydrated Iron Oxides. The geology, in the area of the main entrance, is described as Quartzite and minor amounts of Conglomerate, Phyllitic Siltstone, Limestone and Dolomite. The Land Status, Ownership Category of this underground prospect is shown as "BLM Administrative Area".
See the NBMG Sample Site 126 entry for more information.

Gold Tower Claims: (38.06.16N by -114.20.06W - #3) (Gold)
Coordinates are for the main entrance to this surface-underground, exploration prospect.
USGS MRDS Data Base Record 10270731, Released January 21, 1994: The main entrance to the Gold Tower Claims is shown at 38.10436N by -114.33643W, placing it in the area included on the USGS Pierson Summit 24K, Wilson Creek Range 100K and Lund 250K maps. The location accuracy, of these coordinates, is shown as +/- 10 meters. The Public Land Survey System locators are the Northwest ¼ of the Northwest ¼ of the Southwest ¼ of Section 23, Township 3 North, Range 68 East. Gold is present and is shown as a primary commodity. The geology, in the area of the main entrance, is shown as Rhyolitic flows and shallow intrusive rocks. The Land Status, Ownership Category of this surface-underground prospect is unknown.

Goldcup (a.k.a. April Fool); (37.27.45N by -114.45.30W - #3) (Gold, Silver, Copper, Bismuth, Antimony)
See the April Fool and Delamar Prospect 002 entries for more information.

Golden Eagle (a.k.a. Golden Eagle Mine): (37.54.32N by -114.28.27W - #3) (Silver, Zinc, Lead, Gold, Manganese, Iron)
Coordinates are for the ore body of this underground, past producer.
USGS MRDS Data Base Record 10037333, Released October 1, 1979; Updated December 1, 1984: The site of the Golden Eagle is shown at 37.9044N by -114.47584W, placing it about 2 miles Southwest of Pioche and in the area included on the USGS Pioche 24K and Caliente 100K and 250K maps. The location accuracy, of these coordinates, is shown as +/- 1,000 meters. The Public Land Survey System locators are

Section 33, Township 1 North, Range 67 East. Silver, Lead and Zinc, in a host of Limestone and Shale, associated with Late Cambrian Granite, are present and are shown as primary commodities, with Gold, Manganese and Iron secondary. The oxidized ore resembles that of the Prince and Caselton Mines and occurs as 8 layers in the lower part of the Highland Peak and Pioche Shale rocks. The area is complexly faulted and cut by a Granite Porphyry dike. The deposit has reported 63 shipments of ore, however values were not found. The geology, in the general area of the site is described as Alluvial deposits. The Land Status, Ownership Category of this past producer is shown as "Private".
USGS MRDS Data Base Record 10173566, Released January 19, 1994: The main entrance to the Golden Eagle Mine is shown at 37.90886N by -114.47474W, placing it in the Pioche Mining District. The location accuracy, of these coordinates, is shown as +/- 10 meters. The Public Land Survey System locators are the Northeast ¼ of the Northeast ¼ of the Northwest ¼ of Section 33, Township 1 North, Range 67 East. This record shows Silver present and as a primary commodity with Gold, Lead, Zinc and Iron tertiary. The geology, in the area of the main entrance, is described as Alluvial deposits. The Land Status, Ownership Category of this underground, past producer is unknown.

Golden Gate Range Mining District: (Lead, Silver)
Description of the District:
Tingley, Joseph V.; "Mining Districts of Nevada"; Nevada Bureau of Mines and Geology, Report 47, Second Edition; 1998; Page 105: The Golden Gate Range Mining District covers the Golden Gate Range about 4 miles North of the Murphy Gap.
Mines Included in the District:

Golden Rule (Bill Nye Mine): (37.56.43N by -114.04.17W - #3) (Gold, Silver)
See the Bill Nye Mine entry for more information.

Golden Star Mine: (37.26.41N by -115.46.10W - #3) (Lead, Silver, Gold)
Coordinates are for the ore body of this surface-underground, past producer.

Gourd Spring: (36.59.00N by -114.18.09W - #3) (Barite, Iron)
Coordinates are for a spring and exploration sites.

Gourd Springs Mining District: (Tungsten, Manganese, Barite, Gypsum)
Description of the District:
Tingley, Joseph V.; "Mining Districts of Nevada"; Nevada Bureau of Mines and Geology, Report 47, Second Edition; 1998; Page 108: The Gourd Springs Mining District is located about 8 miles North of the Lincoln-Clark County line and includes the Eastern flank of the East Mormon Mountains.
Mines Included in the District:

Grandview Claims: (37.24.04N by -114.18.31W - #3) (Gold)
Coordinates are for the claim area of this surface prospect.
USGS MRDS Data Base Record 1019826, Released September 25, 1991: The Claim area of the Grandview Claims is shown at 37.40107N by -114.30943W, placing it in the area included on the USGS Fife Mountain 24K, Clover Mountains 100K and Caliente 250K maps. The location accuracy, of these coordinates, is shown as +/- 10 meters. The Public Land Survey System locators are the Northeast ¼ of Section 30, Township 6 South, Range 69 East. Gold is present and is shown as a primary commodity. The geology, in the Claim area, is described as welded and non-welded Silicic Ash-flow Tuffs. The Land Status, Ownership Category of this surface occurrence is shown as "BLM Administrative Area". Mineral Rights are held via Located Claims.

Grant Deposit: (37.38.37N by -114.32.25W - #3) (Perlite)
Coordinates are for an ore body.

Great Basin (a.k.a. Great Basin Mine): (36.46.25N by -114.39.55W - #3) (Gold, Silver)
Coordinates are for a plant area.
USGS MRDS Data Base Record 10198406, Released January 21, 1994: The pit area of the Great Basin Mine is shown at 36.77778N by -114.66613W, placing it in the area included on the USGS Farrier 24K,

Overton 100K and Las Vegas 250K maps. The location accuracy, of these coordinates, is shown as +/-
1,000 meters. The Public Land Survey System locators are Section 25, Township 13 South, Range 65 East.
Gold is present and is shown as a primary commodity with Silver tertiary. The geology, in the pit area, is
described as Alluvial deposits. The Land Status, Ownership Category of this Leach plant is unknown. A
1987 record shows the Operator as Great Basin Mine, Incorporated.
Comment: The reported legal description, Public Land Survey System locators, places the mine in Clark
County; as such, I will show it in both Lincoln and Clark Counties until I get some better location data.

Great Western Claims (a.k.a. Cave Valley Mine 002): (38.38.39N by -114.47.49W - #3) (Lead, Silver,
Copper, Zinc, Gold, Vanadium, Arsenic, Clay)
See the Cave Valley Mine 002 entry for more information.

Green Spar Prospect: (38.02.30N by -115.44.45W - #3) (Fluorite)
Coordinates are for the claim area of this exploration prospect.

Greenwood Shaft: (37.55.36N by -114.27.24W - #3) (Silver, Lead, Zinc, Gold, Copper)
Coordinates are for the main entrance to this underground, past producer.
USGS MRDS Data Base Record 10246699, Released November 14, 1983: The main entrance to the
Greenwood Shaft is shown at 37.92716N by -114.45754W, placing it in the Pioche Mining District and in
the area included on the USGS Pioche 24K and Caliente 100K and 250K maps. The location accuracy, of
these coordinates, is shown as +/- 100 meters. The Public Land Survey System locators are the Northeast ¼
of the Southeast ¼ of the Southwest ¼ of Section 22, Township 1 North, Range 67 East. Lead is present
and is shown as a primary commodity with Silver, Zinc and Copper tertiary. The geology, in the area of the
main entrance, is described as Limestone and Dolomite with locally thick sequences of Shale and Siltstone.
The Land Status, Ownership Category of this underground, past producer is shown as "Private".
USGS MRDS Data Base Record 10046410, Released May 1, 1984: The site of the Greenwood Shaft is
shown at 37.92635N by -114.45778W. The location accuracy, of these coordinates, is shown as +/- 50
meters. This record shows Gold, Silver, Lead, Zinc and Copper present and all as primary commodities.
The mineralization includes Galena and Sphalerite, with a gangue of Pyrite, in a host of Late Cambrian,
Pioche Shale. The Tabular ore body is controlled by the Greenwood fissure and favorable lithology. The
mine was developed by a 350-foot shaft and at least one crosscut. Initial development began around 1910,
and in 1914 lessees developed a large body of complex-Sulfide ore on the 350-foot level and anticipated
shipping in the near future. The material assayed 13.5% Zinc, 6.5% Lead and 7 ounces of Silver and 0.03
ounces of Gold per ton. The geology, in the general area of the site, is described as Limestone and
Dolomite with locally thick sequences of Shale and Siltstone. The Land Status, Ownership Category of this
underground, past producer is shown as "Private".

**Groom (a.k.a. Groom Mine; Conception No. 1 Claim; East Side No. 1 and No. 2 Claims; June Claim;
July Claim; Maria Claim; No. 2 Patented Claim; Panorama Claim; Senior Claim; White Lake No. 2
Claim; Willow Claim)**: (37.20.45N by -115.46.03W - #3) (Silver, Lead, Zinc, Copper, Gold, Barite)
Coordinates are for the main entrance to this underground, past producer.
USGS MRDS Data Base Record 10072154, Released February 1, 1980; Updated September 1, 1984: The
site of the Groom Mine is shown at 37.34579N by -115.76865W, placing it about 72 miles West-Southwest
of Caliente, about 23 miles South-Southwest of Tem Piute, near the South end of the Groom Range, on a
U.S. Air Force gunnery range, in the Groom Mining District and in the area included on the USGS Groom
Mine 24K, Pahranagat Range 100K and Caliente 250K maps. While the area was unsurveyed at the time of
the review, the estimated Public Land Survey System locators, as projected from the East, was Sections 11
& 14, Township 7 South, Range 55 East. Silver and Lead are present and are shown as primary
commodities with Gold, Zinc and Copper secondary and Barite tertiary. Mineralization of this Polymetallic
Replacement deposit (USGS model 19a) includes Anglesite, Tetrahedrite, Sphalerite, Chalcopyrite and
Barite; with a gangue of Quartz, Pyrite and Siderite; in a host of Quartzite of the Lyndon Limestone and
Pioche Shale formations, associated with Plutonic rock. Along the Limestone – Shale contact, large masses
of pure white Quartz occurs, which are more or less connected by Quartz Veins, which are partially
Brecciated and broken. The ore body is described as being Tabular, in 3 thin Limestone beds which strike
North, dip 25° to 66° West. The full ore body is about 75 feet thick, 300 feet wide and about 2,000 feet
long, although the best ore is in an area about 250 feet long, lying between the Groom Fault and the No. 3

Thrust Fault and along the North-South fissures. Some good ore is also found in the small East-West fractures. Ore occurs along the 'Gob' Intrusion as well as out along the bedding planes of the Limestone where replacements consist of a mixture of Lead and Silver minerals, Calcite, Siderite and a little Barite. The mine was developed by a 210-foot shaft and 2 adits, with the best ore being found above the 100-foot level. Some evidence was found for deeper mineralization, below 390 feet, but this was not developed. The geology, in the general area of the site, is described as Limestone and Dolomite with locally-thick sequences of Shale and Siltstone. The Land Status, Ownership Category of this past producer, which was discovered in 1864 and produced from 1865 to 1956, is shown as "BLM Administrative Area".
USGS MRDS Data Base Record 10246411, Released January 12, 1994: The main entrance to the Groom Mine is shown at 37.34606N by -115.76837W, placing it in the Groom Mining District. The Public Land Survey System locators are Section 8, Township 7 South, Range 55+ East. Lead is present and is shown as a primary commodity with Silver, Gold, Zinc and Copper tertiary. Mineralization of this Tabular, Fissure Vein and Irregular Replacement Deposit, includes Galena, Anglesite, Cerussite, Sphalerite and Chalcopyrite. The deposit is about 30 feet thick, 250 feet long, about 100 feet underground and controlled by faulting and favorable lithology. Zinc is present is varying concentration, ranging from trace to 22%. The geology, in the area of the main entrance, is described as Limestone and Dolomite with locally thick sequences of Shale and Siltstone. The Land Status, Ownership Category of this underground, past producer is shown as "BLM Administrative Area". A 1969 record shows the Owner as Vincent D. Miller, Incorporated of Washington.

Groom Mining District: (Lead, Zinc, Silver, Gold, Copper, Barite)
Description of the District:
Tingley, Joseph V.; "Mining Districts of Nevada"; Nevada Bureau of Mines and Geology, Report 47, Second Edition; 1998; Page 110: Discovered and organized in 1869, the Groom Mining District is located around the Groom Mine, in the Southern Groom Range, in the vicinity of Township 7 South, Range 55 East. The Groom Mining District lies South of and adjoins the Tempahute Mining District.
Mines Included in the District:
 B. W. Claims (Gold)
 Chicago/Illinois/Wisconsin Claims (Gold, Silver)
 Gold Butte Claims (Gold, Silver)
 Gold Occurrence 004 (Gold)
 Gold Prospects 006 (Gold)
 Gold Prospect 008 (Gold, Silver, Lead)
 Gold Prospect 009 (Gold)
 Groom (Silver, Lead, Zinc, Copper, Gold, Barite)
 Tram Workings (Gold, Silver)
 Unnamed Gold Prospect 011 (Gold)

Gs Claims (a.k.a. Iris84 09): (37.92329N by -114.07444W - MRDS) (Gold, Silver, Copper)
See the Iris84 09 entry for more information.

Gusset Patch Claims (a.k.a. Black Metal Mine 001): (38.09635N by -114.596W – USGS MRDS)
(Silver, Manganese, Iron, Gold, Lead, Copper, Bismuth, Coal)
See the Black Metal Mine 001 entry for more information.

Gypsy: (37.53.02N by -114.37.29W - #3) (Copper, Silver, Gold, Lead, Manganese)
Coordinates are for the ore body of this past producer.
USGS MRDS Data Base Record 10198510, Released September 30, 1996: The main entrance to the Gypsy is shown at 37.95966N by -114.59254W, placing it in the Highland Mining District and in the area included on the USGS Highland Peak 24K and Caliente 100K and 250K maps. The location accuracy, of these coordinates, is shown as +/- 5,000 meters. The general Public Land Survey System locators are Township 1 South, Range 66 East. Silver is present and is shown as a primary commodity with Gold, Lead and Copper tertiary. The geology, in the area of the main entrance, is described as Limestone and Dolomite with locally thick sequences of Shale and Siltstone. The Land Status, Ownership Category of this underground, past producer, which went into production in 1921, is shown as "BLM Administrative Area".

Gypsy and Helen (a.k.a. Gypsy and Helen Groups; Bluebird; Blue Bird Claim; Interocean; Interocean Claim; Silver Star; Silver Star Claim; White Horse Claim): (37.57.03N by -114.04.35W - #3) (Gold, Silver, Copper)
Coordinates are for an ore body.
USGS MRDS Data Base Record 10037377, Released February 1, 1980; Updated August 1, 1984: The site of the Gypsy and Helen Groups is shown at 37.95079N by -114.07722W, placing it in the Eagle Valley Mining District and in the area included on the USGS Deer Lodge Canyon 24K and Caliente 100K and 250K maps. The Claims are believed to extend for about 1,000 feet, or so, around the coordinate point. The Public Land Survey System locators are Section 18, Township 1 North, Range 71 East. Gold and Silver are present and are shown as a primary commodity with Copper tertiary. Mineralization includes Cerargyrite and Native Copper with a gangue of Fluorite and Pyrite in a host of Latite. The ore body is a Vein system, extending both North and South and East and West, having a general strike of North 30° East and a dip of 40° to the Southeast. The Vein, which is crustified and fissure filling, contains Chalcedonic and Comb Quartz, yellowish Adularia and lamellar Carbonate, can be traced for about 3 miles. Production, which was found recorded, includes 17 carloads of ore, shipped in 1936 & 1937, having a period value of $36,760; 3 carloads of ore shipped from the Gypsy and Helen in 1941; and, 2 carloads shipped from the Silver Star in 1947. The geology, in the general area of the site, is described as welded and non-welded Silicic Ash-flow Tuffs. The Land Status, Ownership Category of this past producer is shown as "Private".
USGS MRDS Data Base Record 10222282, Released September 30, 1996: The main entrance to the Gypsy and Helen Groups is shown at 37.96216N by -114.07143W, placing it in the Eagle Valley Mining District. The location accuracy, of these coordinates, is shown as +/- 1,000 meters. This record shows Copper present and as a primary commodity with Gold and Silver tertiary. The geology, in the area of the main entrance, is described as welded and non-welded Silicic Ash-flow Tuffs. The Land Status, Ownership Category of this past producer is shown as "Patented".
See the White Horse Mine entry for more information.

Gypsy and May Day Mines (a.k.a. Gypsy Mine): (38.07.10N by -114.36.02W - #3)
Coordinates are for the ore body of this underground operation.

Gypsy Vein (a.k.a. Bristol-Jackrabbit Mines): (38.08107N by -114.617W – USGS MRDS) (Silver, Copper, Lead, Zinc, Gold, Manganese)
See the Bristol-Jackrabbit Mine entry for more information.

Hackberry Spring Prospect: (36.54.57N by -114.26.20W - #3) (Copper, Silver)
Coordinates are for the pit area of this surface, exploration prospect.

Half Moon: (37.55.53N by -114.29.05W - #3) (Silver, Lead, Zinc, Copper, Gold, Tungsten, Arsenic)
Coordinates are for the main entrance to this underground, past producer.

Hamburg: (37.56.35N by -114.33.33W - #3) (Lead, Silver, Gold)
Coordinates are for the ore body of this underground, past producer.

Hanus Claims (a.k.a. Chicago/Illinois/Wisconsin Claims): (37.39326N by -115.798W – USGS MRDS) (Gold, Silver)
See the Chicago/Illinois/Wisconsin Claims entry for more information.

Harney Group (a.k.a. Wide Awake and Volcano): (37.54.56N by -114.25.50W - #3) (Silver, Lead, Manganese, Zinc, Antimony, Gold, Copper, Iron, Barite, Arsenic)
See the Wide Awake and Volcano entry for more information.

Hanus (a.k.a. Hanus Shaft): (37.23.06N by -115.48.02W - #3) (Gold)
Coordinates are for the ore body of this underground, exploration prospect.

Hedman Mining Property: (37.56.02N by -114.41.30W - #3) (Silver, Gold, Tungsten, Manganese)
Coordinates are for the ore body of this underground, past producer.

Helen Group (a.k.a. Bill Nye Mine): (37.56.43N by -114.04.17W - #3) (Gold, Silver)
See the Bill Nye Mine entry for more information.

Helen Mine: (37.56.43N by -114.04.17W - #3) (Silver, Gold)
Coordinates are for the ore body of this underground, past producer.

Hidden Fissure Group (a.k.a. Cave Valley Mine 002): (38.38.39N by -114.47.49W - #3) (Lead, Silver,
Copper, Zinc, Gold, Vanadium, Arsenic, Clay)
See the Cave Valley Mine 002 entry for more information.

Highland Mary: (37.56.21N by -114.33.48W – #3) (Gold, Silver, Lead, Copper)
Coordinates are for the ore body of this underground, past producer.

**Highland Mining District (a.k.a. Highland Valley Mining District; Pioche Mining District; Stampede
Gap Mining District)**: (Gold, Silver, Lead, Zinc, Copper, Antimony, Tungsten, Manganese, Iron)
Description of the District:
*Tingley, Joseph V.; "Mining Districts of Nevada"; Nevada Bureau of Mines and Geology, Report 47,
Second Edition; 1998; Page 110*: Discovered and organized in 1869, the Highland Mining District is
located in the Northern Highland Range and the Southern Bristol Range and generally includes the area
from near Arizona Peak to North of Stampede Gap. The Highland Mining District is sometimes included
with the Pioche Mining District, which lies to the East. The Highland Mining District appears to overlap
with the Comet Mining District, lying to its South, as a number of the properties are referenced to both
Districts. In his 1962 *Directory of Southern Nevada Place Names*, W. R. Averett referred to the area about
10 miles West of Pioche, in the area of Stampede Gap as the Stampede Gap Mining District, which would
be included in the modern Highland Mining District.
*Tingley, Joseph V.; "Mining Districts of Nevada"; Nevada Bureau of Mines and Geology, Report 47,
Second Edition; 1998; Page 174*: Discovered in 1863 and organized in 1864, the Pioche Mining District is
oriented around the Pioche Hills. The Highland area to the West is sometimes included in the Pioche
Mining District, leading to it being referred to as the Highland Mining District at times.
Mines Included in the District:
        Blue Bell (Gold, Silver, Lead, Zinc)
        Florence (Silver, Lead, Gold, Copper)
        Last Chance (Gold, Silver, Lead, Copper)
        NBMG Sample Sites 1390 through 1392 (Gold, Silver, Lead, Copper)
        NBMG Sample Site 1396 (Gold, Silver, Copper, Lead)
        NBMG Sample Location 1435 (Gold, Silver, Zinc, Manganese)
        Peppers 1, 2, 3 (Manganese, Gold, Silver, Lead)
        Tara Claims (Gold, Silver, Lead, Manganese)
        Unnamed Adit 007 (Gold, Silver, Zinc, Manganese)
        Unnamed Shaft 069 (Silver, Gold, Copper, Lead)
        West Manhattan Vein Prospect (Gold, Silver, Lead, Copper)

Highland Queen: (37.56.23N by -114.33.06W - #3) (Silver, Gold, Copper, Lead)
Coordinates are for the ore body of this underground, past producer.

Hiko Mining District (a.k.a. Pahranagat Mining District): (Silver, Gold, Lead, Zinc, Copper,
Manganese)
Description of the District:
*Tingley, Joseph V.; "Mining Districts of Nevada"; Nevada Bureau of Mines and Geology, Report 47,
Second Edition; 1998; Page 166*: Alternate names for the Pahranagat Mining District include the Hiko
Mining District, referring to the nearest settlement of any significance
See the Pahranagat Mining District entry for more information.
Mines Included in the District:
        Black Prince (Silver, Gold, Lead, Zinc, Manganese)
        Gypsy (Copper, Silver, Lead, Gold, Manganese)

Hillside (a.k.a. Hillside Claim; Hillside Mine): (38.05.36N by -114.36.14W - #3) (Copper, Silver, Gold, Lead, Zinc, Manganese, Iron)
Coordinates are for the ore body of this underground, past producer.
USGS MRDS Data Base Record 10111464, Released February 1, 1985: The site of the Hillside Mine is shown at 38.08357N by -114.61028W, placing it in the Bristol-Jackrabbit Mining District and in the area included on the USGS Bristol Range SE 24K, Wilson Creek Range 100K and Lund 250K maps. The area of the mine was unsurveyed at the time of the entry, but the Public Land Survey System locators, as projected from the East, were Section 32, Township 3 North, Range 66 East. Copper and Silver are present and are shown as primary commodities with Gold and Lead secondary and Zinc, Manganese and Iron tertiary. Mineralization of this Polymetallic Replacement Deposit includes Malachite and Chrysocolla, Galena and Limonite in a host of Limestone and Late Cambrian Marble. The ore body, which is controlled by the May Day Fissure, strikes North 60° to 75° East, dips 40° to 70° South, is about 16 feet thick, about 200 feet deep and traceable for a length of about 120 feet. The ore consists primarily of Oxidized Silver-Copper material. The ore body is on the same May Day Fissure as the main Bristol orebody. It intersects with North-South fissures and intersects with at least one, steeper, but parallel fissure of the Tempest set. The dip of the fissure flattens from about 75°, at the surface, to 40° or less below 200 feet. The deposit was developed by a, now-inaccessible, 900-foot-long inclined shaft, with levels every 100 feet, and a smaller, second shaft. The Hillside was the main supplier of ore to the Bristol Wells Smelter in the late 1870s and early 1880s. Masses of this Sulfide ore assayed 72.5 ounces of Silver and 0.04 ounces of Gold per ton and about 4% Lead. The Bristol Wells Smelter closed due to small amounts of Sulphur in the ore causing the Silver and Copper to be lost in the slag. To process the ore a pan amalgamation site was built at the Toeder Mill Site and up to 10,000 tons of Hillside ore was processed there. When that mill was shut down, ore and slag from the smelter(s?) were sent to Salt Lake, Utah, processing facilities. In 1877 the Hillside Company was organized to take over A. M. G. Steel's properties, including the Hillside Mine. In 1921 the remaining ore was estimated to assay 6.7 ounces of Silver and 0.02 ounces of Gold per ton and 2.32% Lead. The geology, in the general area of the site, is described as Limestone and Dolomite with locally thick sequences of Shale and Siltstone. The Land Status, Ownership Category of this past producer is shown as "Private". A 1913 record shows the Operator as the Hillside Leasing Company.
USGS MRDS Data Base Record 10295699, Released January 21, 1994: The main entrance to the Hillside Mine is shown at 38.08326N by -114.61024W, placing it in the Bristol-Jackrabbit Mining District. The location accuracy, of these coordinates, is shown as +/- 10 meters. The Public Land Survey System locators are Section 29, Township 3 North, Range 66 East. This record shows Silver present and as a primary commodity with Copper, Gold and Lead tertiary. The geology, in the area of the main entrance, is described as Limestone and Dolomite with locally thick sequences of Shale and Siltstone. The Land Status, Ownership Category of this underground, past producer, is unknown.
See the Bristol-Jackrabbit Mine entry for more information.

Hog Pen Claim (a.k.a. Delamar Prospect 002): (37.28.07N by -114.42.57W - #3) (Gold, Silver, Copper, Iron)
USGS MRDS Data Base Record 10310400, Released January 1, 2005; Updated and Edited September 1, 2007: Most of the ore of the Delamar Prospect 002 was Oxidized and had a reddish or greenish tint. Only the Hog Pen shoot contained Free Gold.
See the Delamar Prospect 002 entry for more information.

Hollinger Perlite Deposit: (38.07.26N by -114.21.44W - #3) (Perlite)
Coordinates are for the pit area of this surface, past producer.

Home Run (a.k.a. Home Run Mine): (38.04.18N by -114.37.13W - #3) (Lead, Copper, Silver)
Coordinates are for the main entrance to this historic, underground operation.
See the Bristol-Jackrabbit Mines entry and the Prince Consolidated, *Goodwin's Weekly, November 23, 1912* article for more information.

Homestake Mine: (37.55.30N by -114.04.15W - #3) (Gold, Silver, Mercury)
Coordinates are for the main entrance to this underground, past producer.

Homestake Tunnel: (37.55.18N by -114.26.36W - #3) (Silver, Lead, Zinc)
Coordinates are for the main entrance to this underground operation.

Hope Prospect (a.k.a. Pennsylvania Mine): (37.24.37N by -114.29.31W - #3) (Copper, Gold, Silver, Lead, Zinc)
See the Pennsylvania Mine entry for more information.

Horn (a.k.a. Jumbo): (37.27.18N by -114.45.30W - #3) (Gold, Silver, Zinc, Lead, Copper, Barite)
See the Jumbo entry for more information.

Horn Silver Claims (a.k.a. Ida May): (38.05.54N by -114.36.57W - #3) (Silver, Lead, Gold, Copper, Zinc)
See the Ida May entry for more information.

Hornsilver Nos. 1-5 (a.k.a. Silver Horn): (38.09.30N by -114.41.47W - #3) (Silver, Lead, Gold, Nickel)
See the Silver Horn entry for more information.

Horseshoe Mine: (37.54.39N by -114.04.12W - #3) (Gold, Silver, Copper)
Coordinates are for the main entrance to this underground, past producer.

Hulse Mine (a.k.a. Hulse Claim; Blue Bird Mine 001; Ella Claim; Lucky Dog Claims; Minnie Claim):
(38.45523N by -114.334W – USGS MRDS) (Uranium, Silver, Gold, Copper, Lead, Arsenic)
USGS MRDS Data Base Record 10008830, Released February 1, 1980; Updated January 1, 1985; Updated and Edited June 9, 1995: The site of the Hulse Mine is shown at 38.45523N by -114.33362W, placing it 1 mile South of Atlanta, on a small hill 3,500 feet South of the Atlanta Mill, in the Atlanta Mining District, in the Silver Park Mining District, in the Silver Springs Mining District and in the area included on the USGS Atlanta 24K, Wilson Creek Range 100K and Lund 250K maps. Uranium is present and is shown as a primary commodity with Silver and Gold secondary and Copper, Lead and Arsenic tertiary. Mineralization includes Uraninite, Uranophane and Argentite with a gangue of Quartz, Pyrite and Marcasite. Chemical analysis of two samples, of unknown location, showed 0.11% and 0.67% Uranium and 0.1% and 0.3% Arsenic. One sample from the Pyrite carried 0.133% U_3O_8. One of the two initial samples was checked for precious/base metal content and assayed 0.41 Ounces of Silver per ton, no Gold and 0.2% Copper and 0.12% Lead. This Volcanogenic Uranium Deposit, USGS Model Code 25f, is hosted in Ely Springs Dolomite and Limestone and is associated with Rhyolite. Pods of Pyrite-Uraninite ore occur in Tabular Jasperoid zones along gently-dipping faults which contain 1 to 4-foot thick Silicified gouge zones. The ore body is described as Tabular to Pod-shaped, exposed to the surface, about 9 inches thick and up to 50 feet deep. Mineralization appears to have been controlled by an intrusive Breccia zone or pipe which was later cut by many minor faults striking North 35° to 55° West. The Jasperoid body consists of fragments of Dolomite and Volcanics which are completely Silicified. Open spaces in the Breccia are common rocks from the upper levels of the mine which are completely Oxidized. On the lowest mine level, abundant Pyrite is Disseminated in dark grey to black, highly Silicified Breccia. The Silicified Breccia Zone has been intruded by many altered Rhyolite dikes which strike North 70° East and dip 15° to 20° West. The Uranium mineralization appears confined to the Silicified Breccia between the dikes. Yellow, secondary Uranium Oxides occur near the surface. The Pyrite reportedly alters to Carphosiderite, a yellow, basic, Hydrous Iron Sulfate often found as crusts on other rocks. The older, underground workings include about 275 feet of drifts, crosscuts and winzes. In 1955 three Diamond drill holes were sunk to a combined depth of 660 feet. Test pits were dug by the US Bureau of Mines. In 1981 the old, wooden headframe was still there. An estimated two carloads of ore was produced by the mine. The geology, in the general area of the site, is described as welded and non-welded Silicic Ash-flow Tuffs. The Land Status, Ownership Category of this past producer is shown as "BLM Administrative Area". A 1945 (1954?) record shows the Owner as James G. Hulse of Pioche.
See the Blue Bird Mine 001 entry for more information.

Ida May (a.k.a. Ida May Mine; Bay State Mining and Leasing Company; Bertha; E and F Mine; Horn Silver Claims; Little Ford): (38.05.54N by -114.36.57W - #3) (Silver, Lead, Gold, Copper, Zinc)
Coordinates are for the ore body of this underground, past producer.

USGS MRDS Data Base Record 10103587, Released November1, 1979; Updated February 1, 1985: The site of the Ida May Mine is shown at 38.09829N by -114.60834W, placing it about 2 miles West of Highway 93, about 15 miles Northwest of Pinoche, in an unsurveyed area on the North Slope of a Ridge, in the Bristol-Jackrabbit Mining District and in the area included on the USGS Bristol Range SE 24K, Wilson Creek Range 100K and Lund 250K maps. The Public Land Survey System locators are Section 30, Township 3 North, Range 66 East. Copper, Silver, Lead and Zinc are present and shown as primary commodities with Gold secondary. This Polymetallic Replacement deposit is hosted in Limestone associated with Late Cambrian Plutonic rock. The small replacement deposits are found in several Northwest and East-West-bearing fissures which have been intersected by North-South faults, which traverse this formation. Copper Oxides and Copper Carbonates fill fissures together with a limited replacement by Limestone. It was operated as the E and F Mine in the early 1900s, and consisted of a series of adits and shafts, up to 100 feet in depth, which intersected the fissures. The mine was shut down in 1907; was again operated from 1918 to 1921, but was idle when reviewed in 1924. The only recorded production numbers were for 1908 (this is probably the last production from 1907) when ore, having a gross value of $21,300 was produced. The area geology is described as Limestone and Dolomite with locally-thick sequences of Shale and Siltstone. The Land Status, Ownership Category of this past producer is shown as "Private". A 1930 record shows the Owner as the A. C. Ellis Estate, operating as the Bay State Mining and Leasing Company.

USGS MRDS Data Base Record 10295260, Released January 19, 1994: The main entrance to the Ida May Mine is shown at 38.09826N by -114.61664W, placing it in the Bristol-Jackrabbit Mining District. The location accuracy, of these coordinates, is shown as +/- 10 meters. The Public Land Survey System locators are the Northeast ¼ of Section 30, Township 3 North, Range 66 East. This record shows Silver present and as a primary commodity with Copper, Gold, Lead and Zinc tertiary. The geology, in the area of the main entrance, is described as Limestone, Dolomite, Shale and Quartz. The Land Status, Ownership Category of this underground, past producer is unknown.

Independence: (37.53.17N by -114.23.50W - #3) (Manganese, Copper, Iron)
Coordinates are for the ore body of this underground operation.

Indian Valley Mining District (a.k.a. Atlanta Mining District): (Gold, Silver, Copper, Lead, Tungsten, Vanadium, Manganese, Uranium)
Description of the District:
Tingley, Joseph V.; "Mining Districts of Nevada"; Nevada Bureau of Mines and Geology, Report 47, Second Edition; 1998; Page 22: In 1869, the *Territorial Enterprise* cited an Indian Valley Mining District, which was located about 20 miles East of the Patterson Mining District, which was likely in the area of the modern Atlanta Mining District.
See the Atlanta Mining District entry for more information.
Mines Included in the District:

Inman Mine: (38.08.05N by -114.33.07W - #3) (Silver, Copper, Zinc, Lead, Iron)
Coordinates are for the ore body of this underground operation.

Interocean/Interocean Claim (a.k.a. Gypsy and Helen; Silver Star Mine; White Horse Mine):
(37.57.03N by -114.04.35W - #3) (Gold, Silver, Copper)
See the Gypsy and Helen, Silver Star Mine and White Horse Mine entries for more information.

Iris: (37.55.24N by -114.04.25W - #3) (Gold, Silver)
Coordinates are for the main entrance to this past producer.

Iris84 09 (a.k.a. Iris Mine; Gs Claims; NBMG Sample Site 1726): (37.92329N by -114.07444W - MRDS) (Gold, Silver, Copper)
USGS MRDS Data Base Record 10037375, Released February 1, 1980; Updated September 1, 1984: The site of the Iris84 09 is shown at the above coordinates, placing it about ½ mile South of Deer Lodge, in the Eagle Valley Mining District, in the Fay Mining District, in the Gold Springs Mining District, in the Deer Lodge Mining District and in the area included on the USGS Deer Lodge Canyon 24K and Caliente 100K and 250K maps. The Public Land Survey System locators are Section 30, Township 1 North, Range 71

East. Gold and Silver are present and are shown as primary commodities with Copper secondary. Mineralization includes various Copper ores with a gangue of Quartz, Fluorite, Pyrite and Siderite. This Comstock-type, Epithermal Vein is hosted in Andesite and associated with Latite. The Vein is a "Crustified Epithermal Quartz Vein" with Chalcedonic, Comb Quartz, yellowish Adularia and lamellar Carbonates". The controls for the ore deposition are the fractures and Brecciation. The area, and especially that of the ore body, is further described as having Cockade and Drusy Quartz encrustations around altered rock fragments. White Quartz and Siderite Veins are also common; however the Quartz Veins predominate. Quartz after Calcite texture is common. Partially Oxidized Pyrite is common in both the Veins and altered fragments.

USGS MRDS Data Base Record 10198471, Released January 19, 1994: The main entrance to the Iris Mine is shown at 37.92326N by -114.07443W, placing it in the Eagle Valley Mining District. The location accuracy, of these coordinates, is +/- 10 meters. The Public Land Survey System locators are the Northeast ¼ of the Northeast ¼ of the Northwest ¼ of Section 30, Township 1 North, Range 71 East. The geology, in the area of the main entrance, is described as Andesite and related rocks of intermediate composition. The Land Status, Ownership Category of this underground, past producer is unknown.

Irish Mountain Manganese: (37.39.55N by -115.23.55W - #3) (Manganese)
Coordinates are for an ore body.

Irish Mountain Mining District (a.k.a. Pahranagat Mining District): (Silver, Lead, Copper, Manganese)
Description of the District:
Tingley, Joseph V.; "Mining Districts of Nevada"; Nevada Bureau of Mines and Geology, Report 47, Second Edition; 1998; Page 166: Alternate names for the Pahranagat Mining District include the Irish Mountain Mining District, named after the 8,625-foot Mount Irish, located at 37.38.39N by -115.24.06W – USGS Mount Irish 24K map.
See the Pahranagat Mining District entry for more information.
Mines Included in the District:

Irmine and Postum (a.k.a. Ermine; Irvine and Bowers): (37.55.40N by -114.38.45W - #3) (Gold, Silver, Copper, Lead, Zinc, Manganese, Iron)
Coordinates are for the ore body of this past producer.
USGS MRDS Data Base Record 10037359, Released February 1, 1980: The site of the Irmine and Postum is shown at 37.92635N by -114.68556W, placing it on the West side of the Ely Springs Range and in the area included on the USGS Ely Springs 24K and Caliente 100K and 250K maps. The Public Land Survey System locators are Section 24, Township 1 North, Range 65 East. The geology, in the general area of the site, is described as Limestone and Dolomite with locally thick sequences of Shale and Siltstone. Gold is present and is shown as a primary commodity with Lead, Manganese and Iron tertiary. Galena, in a Quartz Vein up to a foot wide, is hosted in Late Cambrian Limestone. Leaf Gold is deposited along planes of fractures and foliation in the Shale layer. The Gold ore is reported to be from 12 to 18 inches thick. The mine was developed by a 50-foot inclined shaft and an 80-foot adit. The Land Status, Ownership Category of this past producer is unknown.
USGS MRDS Data Base Record 10173714, Released January 19, 1994: The main entrance to the Irmine and Postum is shown at 37.92936N by -114.63694W. The location accuracy, of these coordinates, is shown at 37.92936N by -114.63694W. The location accuracy, of these coordinates, is shown as +/- 10 meters. The Public Land Survey System locators are the Northwest ¼ of the Southwest ¼ of Section 24, Township 1 North, Range 65 East. This record shows Gold present and as a primary commodity, with Silver, Copper Lead and Zinc tertiary. The geology, in the area of the main entrance, is described as Limestone and Dolomite with locally thick sequences of Shale and Siltstone. The Land Status, Ownership Category of this underground, past producer is shown as "BLM Administrative Area".
See the Tara Claims entry for more information.
Notes: I went back to the original records and verified the longitudes of the two entries; they really are about 0.05 different (.68 vs .63); while the latitudes look fairly close (both .92). If you have better data for this mine, or can confirm which is correct, please let me know.

Iron (a.k.a. Bristol-Jackrabbit Mines): (38.08107N by -114.617W – USGS MRDS) (Silver, Copper, Lead, Zinc, Gold, Manganese)
See the Bristol-Jackrabbit Mine entry for more information.

Iron Blossom 001: (37.01.52N by -114.27.58W - #3) (Lead, Zinc)
Coordinates are for the claim area of this prospect.

Iron Blossom Prospect 002: (37.23.28N by -114.29.32W - #3) (Gold, Silver)
Coordinates are for trenching associated with this surface prospect.
USGS MRDS Data Base Record 10246714; Released September 25, 1991: Trenching associated with the Iron Blossom Prospect is shown at 37.39107N by -114.49303W, placing it in the area included on the USGS Ella Mountain 24K, Clover Mountain 100K and Caliente 250K maps. The location accuracy, of these coordinates, is shown as +/- 10 meters. The Public Land Survey System locators are Section 28, Township 6 South, Range 67 East. Gold is present and is shown as a primary commodity with Silver tertiary. The geology, in the area of the trenching, is described as Andesite and related rocks of intermediate composition. The Land Status, Ownership Category of this surface prospect, is shown as "BLM Administrative Area". Mineral rights are held through Located Claims.

Iron Mine (a.k.a. Iron Claim): (38.05.14N by -114.37.12W - #3) (Silver, Lead, Zinc, Copper, Gold, Manganese)
Coordinates are for the ore body of this underground, past producer.
USGS MRDS Data Base Record 10047173; Released February 1, 1985: The site of the Iron Mine is shown at 38.08718N by -114.62084W, placing it 1 mile Northwest of Bristol Camp, in an unsurveyed area about 2,700 feet Northwest of the Gypsy Shaft and in the area included on the USGS Bristol Range SE 24K, the Wilson Creek Range 100K and Lund 250K maps. The estimated Public Land Survey System locators are Section 30, as projected from the East, Township 3 North, Range 66 East. Silver and Lead are present and are shown as primary commodities with Gold, Copper and Zinc Secondary. Mineralization includes Anglesite, Galena, Chrysocolla and Calamine (a.k.a. Hemimorphite) with a gangue of Quartz in a host of Late Cambrian Marble and Highland Peak Limestone. Geology in the area is described as Limestone, Dolomite, Shale and Quartzite in an area broken by local faults. The ore body is a group of Irregular Lenses which strike North 12° to 15° East, dip 48° to 50° Southeast, are up to 8 feet thick and controlled by these faults and fissures. The hanging wall of the main fissure is in Limestone, with the footwall in Marble. Workings consist of 3 shafts and 2 shallow cuts located 200 yards South of the shaft, with small stopes at one end. The shafts contained 4 working levels about 90 feet apart from which the ore has been stoped to the surface. The longest drifts are on the 200-foot level and are about 165 feet long. On the Iron Fissure, the ore is soft, Iron-stained, Lead Carbonate with the lower grade ore containing significant un-replaced Limestone. A large quantity of high-grade, sorted ore is on the dump, which consists of hard, massive Cerussite. In this ore, rounder residual kernels of Galena are encased with layers of Anglesite and Cerussite. Some of the ore contains minor amounts of Copper Carbonate, and thin films of Silica have been deposited in openings and crevices of the ore. The ore was found in the hanging and footwalls of the fissure. The Land Status, Ownership Category of this past producer is shown as "Private". 1916 records show the Owner as Day-Bristol Consolidated and the Operator as J. A. Nesbit, Lessee and other Lessees in 1924. As late as 1924, shipments were being made about once a month.

Irvine & Bauers (a.k.a. Irmine & Postum; Tara Claims): (37.92913N by -114.637W – USGS MRDS) (Gold, Silver, Lead, Manganese)
See the Irmine & Postum and Tara Claims entries for more information.

Jack Rabbit Mining District/Jackrabbit Mining District (a.k.a. Bristol Mining District): (Silver, Copper, Lead, Zinc, Gold, Manganese, Montmorillonite)
Description of the District:
Tingley, Joseph V.; "Mining Districts of Nevada"; Nevada Bureau of Mines and Geology, Report 47, Second Edition; 1998; Page 38: The Bristol Mining District is located in the Northern Bristol Range about 15 miles North of Pioche. The Historic Blind Mountain Mining District (of 1871) covered the Southern part of the present Bristol Mining District. The Bristol Mining District originally only included the area around the mines on the Western slope of the Bristol Range; the Jackrabbit Mining District includes the area on the

East side of the Bristol Range. The modern Bristol Mining District includes both the old Bristol Mining District and the Jackrabbit Mining District areas and extends from the West Range, North of Bristol Pass, South to Blind Mountain Spring, in the Southern Bristol Range.

See the Bristol Mining District entry for more information.

Mines Included in the District:

Jackrabbit Mine (a.k.a. Jackrabbit; Jackrabbit Incline; Jackrabbit Tunnel; Black Metal Mine; Black Metals; Day; Day Mine; Onandaga; Onandago Claim): (38.05.40N by -114.35.52W - #3) (Silver, Manganese, Gold, Copper, Lead, Iron, Bismuth)

Coordinates are for the ore body of this surface-underground, past producer.

USGS MRDS Data Base Record 10037379; Released October 1, 1979; Updated February 1, 1985: The site of the Jackrabbit Incline is shown at 38.0944N by -114.59862W, placing it 15 miles North of Pioche, in an unsurveyed area about 2,000 feet North of the Day Shaft, in the Bristol-Jackrabbit Mining District and in the area included on the USGS Bristol Range SE 24K, Wilson Creek Range 100K and Lund 250K maps. The Public Land Survey System locators are Section 29, Township 3 North, Range 66 East. Silver and Manganese are present and are shown as primary commodities with Gold, Copper, Lead and Iron secondary and Bismuth tertiary. Mineralization of this Manganese Replacement Deposit included Wad, Cerargyrite and Copper ores with a gangue of Calcite in a host of Late Cambrian Limestone. A carload of ore in 1924 assayed 36% Lead, 6.5% Copper, 2.1% Bismuth and 0.04 ounces of Gold and 329 ounces of Silver per ton. The general assay of the ore, at that time, was 40% Calcite, 10% Manganese, 3% Iron, 0.8% Lead and 0.01 ounce of Gold and 10 ounces of Silver per ton. In 1926 a general assay of the ore gave 15% to 20% Manganese, 0.8% Lead and 10 ounces of Silver per ton. The geology, in the general area of the site, is described as Limestone and Dolomite with locally thick sequences of Shale and Siltstone. The Onandago Vein is described as Irregular to Tabular, striking North 25° East, dipping 40° West, about 3 feet thick and controlled fractures and faults. The richest ore was found at the intersection of a North-South fissure with a North 70° East-striking fissure. The ore body is further described as a vertical pipe, 25 feet thick, from which ore beds extend out laterally into the Limestone. From the center out, the ore becomes higher in Manganese and lower in Silver and Lead. The Highland Peak Limestone is shattered and Brecciated over a large area, much of it is white Dolomite Marble, but this seems to have no bearing on the occurrence of ore. The ore consists of soft, black Wad (Oxide) and Pyrolusite mixed with a Carbonate gangue. The high-grade ore has a steely luster. The surface-underground mine was developed by a 20° to 30° incline, bearing South 50° West with a crosscut at the bottom which connects the Day Shaft of the Black Metal Mine. During the latter part of 1926 shipments were made at the rate of 1,900 tons per month. The general grade ran 15% to 20% Manganese, 0.8% Lead and about 3 ounces of Silver per ton. Early ore was used as an Iron-Manganese-Calcite fluxing ore for three of the early area smelters. From 1924 to 1927 the high-grade Manganese ore (22%) was being shipped to Columbia Steel. The Land Status, Ownership Category of this past producer, discovered in 1870, is shown as "Private". A 1940 record shows the 84% Owner as the Bristol Silver Mining Company.

USGS MRDS Data Base Record 10173834, Released October 18, 1996: The main entrance to the Jackrabbit Tunnel is shown at 38.09416N by -114.59894W, placing it in the Bristol-Jackrabbit Mining District. The location accuracy, of these coordinates, is shown as +/- 10 meters. The Public Land Survey System locators are the Northeast ¼ of Section 29, Township 3 North, Range 66 East. This record shows Silver, Manganese, Gold, Lead, Zinc, Iron, Silica and Phosphates present, but only at tertiary levels. The geology, in the area of the main entrance, is described as Limestone and Dolomite with locally-thick sequences of Shale and Siltstone. This record shows the ore body striking North 25° East, dipping 30° North, under about 10 feet of overburden, about 26 feet thick, about 684 feet wide and 1,000 feet long. The Land Status, Ownership Category of this underground, past producer is shown as "Private" and "Patented". A 1976 record shows the 51% Owner as the Bristol Silver Mines of Pioche, Nevada, with the balance held by Kerr-Mc Gee Corporation.

Mohave County Mineral Our Mineral Wealth; Black Metal Mines Show Big Production; December 11, 1920, Page 4, Column 3: "The Black Metal Mining company is producing an increased tonnage of ore from the Jackrabbit Mine and an extra train will soon be run by the Pioche railroad to take care of the increased business.

The strike of Carbonate ore on the 300-foot level in the bedded Vein area last week is responding nicely to development and though as yet insufficient work has been done to determine the extent and magnitude of the ore body, the discovery has merit and the increased tonnage being mined will be welcome news to the district.

The uncertainty of the freight situation has had a deterrent effect upon operations at the mine, and shipments and development work have both been curtailed.

With definite assurances of an equitable freight rate on the low-grade ore produced and the recent strike of ore, the future of the property seems particularly promising.

John Gilmer is Superintendent of the Black Metal mine, which is operated under the management of E.H.Snyder. – Pioche Record"

See the Bristol-Jackrabbit Mine entry for more information.

Jackson Mine (a.k.a. NBMG Sample Site 3060; North Section 34 Prospect): (37.32.53N by -115.45.33W - #3) (Lead, Zinc, Silver, Copper)

Coordinates are for the ore body of this surface-underground operation.

USGS MRDS Data Base Record 10125240; Released January 27, 1994: The main entrance to the Jackson Claim is shown at 37.55886N by -115.77947W, placing it in the Don Dale Mining District and in the area included on the USGS White Bloch Springs SE 24K, Timpahute Range 100K and Caliente 250K maps. The location accuracy, of these coordinates, is shown as +/- 500 meters. The Public Land Survey System locators are Section 34, Township 4 South, Range 55 East. Silver is present and is shown as a primary commodity with Gold tertiary. The ore body is a Tabular Fissure-Vein of Hydrothermal origin. The geology, in the area of the main entrance, is described as Quartzite and minor amounts of Conglomerate, Phyllitic Siltstone, Limestone and Dolomite. The Land Status, Ownership Category of this surface-underground prospect is shown as "Military Reservation".

Jennie Mine (a.k.a. NBMG Sample Site 1718): (37.53.56N by -114.02.58W - #3) (Gold, Silver, Lead, Copper)

Coordinates are for the main entrance to this underground, past producer.

USGS MRDS Data Base Record 10046535, Released February 1, 1984: The site of the Jennie Mine is shown at 37.89858N by -114.05026W, placing it straddling the Nevada-Utah border, in the Gold Springs Mining District, in the Stateline Mining District and in the area included on the USGS Deer Lodge Canyon 24K and Caliente 100K and 250K maps. The Public Land Survey System locators are Section 32, Township 1 North, Range 71 East. Gold and Silver are present and are shown as primary commodities with Copper and Lead secondary. Mineralization of this Comstock-type, Epithermal Vein deposit includes Gold and Cerargyrite (Silver Chloride) with a gangue of Pyrite, Quartz and Calcite in a host of Andesite and associated with Pliocene Rhyolite. The ore body strikes North 10° West to North 15° West, dips 55° to 70° Northeast and is about 20 feet thick. Ore emplacement was controlled by the areas pre-mineral faulting which acted as conduits for ore-forming liquids. There is a fault, striking North 80° East, dipping 55° South which displaces the Jennie Vein North of the Shaft. The Vein is well exposed in the North wall of the lower shaft where it forms a resistant white knob 7 to 10 feet wide. The Vein has sharp, but undulating contact with the altered Andesite wall rock and indicates a slight "pinch and swell" tendency. The Iron-stained Andesite, adjacent to the Vein, is fractured and Veined parallel to the main Vein orientation. Veining in the wall rock is prevalent in both the hanging and footwalls. Exposures extend outward from the main Vein for a distance of about 5 feet. On the large dump the most abundant rock types are Quartz, Calcite Vein and Quartz Vein materials, along with a wide variety Quartz-Calcite combinations of minerals. Most of the Calcite is white, coarsely crystalline and contains little Iron. The Quartz is generally "sugary" or massive, white and occurs as radiating or prismatic and interlocking crystals in Veins and Breccia. Most Veins are open-centered and drusy Quartz fills vugs and fractures or replaces Calcite. The altered Andesite fragments contained in the Vein are highly Silicified and stained with Limonite, after Pyrite, Some of the fragments show a Stockwork of vitreous Quartz Veinlets.

The stopes and open shafts are inclined along the Vein Structure. The millsite was still intact, as of 1983, along with several of the large head frames, assay labs and old drill roads. The mine was developed on the 60-, 100-, 200-, and 300-foot levels, with drifts Northwest and Southeast along the Vein. The property appears to have been relatively inactive for a number of years (as of 1984), but possibly has some small scale activity on an intermittent basis. This was the largest Gold producer in the Gold Springs Mining District. The geology, in the general area of the site, is described as welded and non-welded Silicic ash-flow Tuffs. The Land Status, Ownership Category of this past producer is shown as "Private".

USGS MRDS Data Base Record 10125696, Released January 12, 1994: The main entrance to the Jennie Mine is shown at 37.89887N by -114.05002W, placing it in the Stateline Mining District, the Gold Mining District and in the area included on the USGS Deer Lodge Canyon 24K and Caliente 100K and 250K maps. The location accuracy, of these coordinates, is shown as +/- 10 meters. The Public Land Survey System locators are Section 32, Township 1 North, Range 71 East, but also extending into Sections 26, Township 33 South, Range 20 West in Utah (readings here come off of the Salt Lake Meridian). Gold is present and is shown as a primary commodity with Silver tertiary. The geology, in the area of the main entrance, is described as welded and non-welded Silicic ash flow Tuffs. The Land Status, Ownership Category of this underground, past producer is unknown.

Jerry Claims (a.k.a. AD Prospect): (38.37.32N by -114.43.40W - #3) (Tungsten, Zinc, Gold, Silver, Molybdenum, Lead, Fluorite)
See the AD Prospect entry for more information.

Jesse Knight/Jesse Knight Property (a.k.a. Silver Park): (38.27.37N by -114.21.13W - #3) (Silver, Gold, Copper, Lead, Zinc, Antimony, Uranium)
See the Silver Park entry for more information.

Jim Crow Claim (a.k.a. Delamar Prospect 002): (37.28.07N by -114.42.57W - #3) (Gold, Silver, Copper, Iron)
See the Delamar Prospect 002 entry for more information.

Johnnie (a.k.a. NBMG Sample Site 1737; Viola Claims): (37.13.50N by -114.22.25W - #3) (Gold, Silver, Mercury, Barite)
Coordinates are for the ore body of this underground operation.
USGS MRDS Data Base Record 10037361, Released February 1, 1980; December 1, 1984: The site of the Jonnie Mine is shown at 37.22776N by -114.36111W, placing it in an unsurveyed area Northwest of Tule Desert, 8 to 10 miles East of Meadow Valley Wash, in the Viola Mining District and in the area included on the USGS Blue Nose Peak 24K, Clover Mountains 100K and Caliente 250K maps. The Public Land Survey System locators are Section 27, Township 8 South, Range 68 East. Gold, Silver, Mercury and Barite are present and are shown as primary commodities. Mineralization is found with a gangue of Pyrite and Quartz, hosted in Volcanic Ash and associated with Miocene ash-flow Tuff. The ore body is Tabular, strikes North 50° West to East-West, dips 55° Southwest and is controlled by a Breccia Zone and a dike. It is further described as a 12-foot Quartz Vein which forms a prominent ridge on Volcanic rocks. The Vein is barren Southwest of the shaft. There are low outcrops and a float of Limey sediments in the area. A second, more detailed description includes the following: "The width of the exposed outcrop is likely over 10 feet. About 20 feet North of the shaft is a prominent resistant rib of a finely crystalline, pinkish-white, Quartz Vein and Quartz-cemented Volcanic Breccia. The outcrop underlies the East-West ridgeline and strikes North 70° West and dips 55° Southwest. Below the crest of the resistant outcrop, the Vein carries Breccia fragments of altered Rhyolitic rocks and possibly also sedimentary Conglomerate. The fragments seem to increase with depth – toward the lower contact with the Volcanics. Iron Oxides are deposited along Brecciated cracks, crevices and vugs in the Vein material. Druzy Quartz lining vugs and ghosts after Pyrite are common. Some of the outcrop contains Quartz phenocrysts, suggesting that this is actually an aplitic dike. Very minute specks of Sulfides or Iron-Manganese Oxides occur in the matrix of the Vein material. Some unusual bright red Oxides may be from Mercury materials, or possibly just hydrated Iron. Some Chalcedonic banding and fine breccia zones cut across the outcrop. Very fine-grained, Oxidized Pyrite occurs in the pink Rhyolite Breccia. This site, which was located by P. Kipfel, 1776 Lincoln Street, #810, Denver, Colorado, 80203 on November 14, 1981, was developed by a 90-foot vertical shaft. Not much appears to have been done since, other than some staking done in 1983. The geology, in the general area of the site, is described as welded and non-welded Silicic ash-flow Tuffs. The Land Status, Ownership Category of this underground prospect is shown as "BLM Administrative Area".
USGS MRDS Data Base Record 10295040, Released November 14, 1983: The main entrance to the Jonnie is shown at 37.22778N by -114.36083W, placing it in the Viola Mining District. The location accuracy, of these coordinates, is shown as +/- 10 meters. The Public Land Survey System locators are the Eastern ½ of the Northeast ¼ of Section 27, Township 8 South, Range 68 East. Gold is present and is shown as a

primary commodity. The Land Status, Ownership Category of this occurrence is shown as BLM Administrative Area.

Johnson/Johnson Mine (a.k.a. Culverwell Mine 005): 37.41775N by -114.475W – USGS MRDS) (Gold, Silver, Copper, Tungsten, Lead)
See the Culverwell Mine 005 entry for more information.

Johnson and Fitchett: (37.13.33N by -114.37.31W - #3) (Perlite)
Coordinates are for the ore body of this surface prospect.

Johnson Mine: (37.15.11N by -114.32.58W - #3)
Coordinates are for the ore body of this surface, past producer.

July Claim (a.k.a. Groom Mine): (37.20.45N by -115.46.03W - #3) (Silver, Lead, Zinc, Copper, Gold, Barite)
See the Groom entry for more information.

Jumbo (a.k.a. Jumbo Mine; Blue Jay Claims; Horn; NBMG Sample Site 1754): (37.27.18N by -114.45.30W - #3) (Gold, Silver, Zinc, Lead, Copper, Barite)
Coordinates are for the ore body of this underground, past producer.
USGS MRDS Data Base Record 10037388, Released November 1, 1979; Updated August 1, 1984: The site of the Jumbo Mine is shown at 37.45941N by -114.76223W, placing it on the South side of a wash, in the Delamar Mining District, in the Ferguson Mining District and in the area included on the USGS Delamar 24K, Clover Mountains 100K and Caliente 250K maps. The Public Land Survey System locators are Section 1, Township 6 South, Range 64 East. Gold and Silver are present and are shown as primary commodities with Copper, Lead and Zinc secondary and Barite tertiary. Mineralization includes Gold, Cerargyrite, Tetrahedrite, Chalcopyrite, Galena and Sphalerite, with a gangue of Pyrite, in a host of Quartzite, associated with Early Cambrian to Pliocene Rhyolite. The Tabular ore body strikes North 15° West, dips 68° West, is about 78 feet underground, 5 feet thick, about 6 inches wide and about 1,500 feet long. The 6-inch width is the Cherry Quartz Vein which is accompanied by numerous Quartz Stringers. The largest ore shoot in the tunnel is about 90 feet long, which then pitches to the North. The Northern part of the Vein terminates against a group of fractures containing East-West dikes. A second significant ore Vein bears North 22° East and dips 63° West. Horn Silver was found on many of the fracture surfaces.
A description, found in the notes, was, as follows: "The Vein parallels the April Fool Vein. Stopes and shafts explore the Quartz Vein in the Quartzite, which consists of Quartz-cemented, Quartzite Breccia and strikes North 20° East and dips 70° Northwest. The footwall of this Vein forms a bold, resistant outcrop, traceable for 1,000 to 1,500 feet. The shear rock face is Silicified and Iron-stained and shows Quartz Veins and Quartz-cemented Breccia zones which contain angular fragments of Quartzite. The mined portion of the Breccia zone contains significant rubble and small boulders. The Breccia zone itself appears truncated at the North end by a fault running up Delamar Canyon. The rock on the dump is mainly Quartzite and Quartz from the Vein with a little Siltstone mixed in. White Comb and Prismatic Quartz cover most of the Quartzite and Micaceous Green Siltstone fragments. The Breccia contains open (or euhedral) vugs between the fragments, most of which are filled with Quartz, although some are filled with Clay and Iron Oxides. Some of the Vein material includes Tetrahedrite, Chalcopyrite, Copper Oxides and Pyrite."
The productive Vein was explored by 3 closely spaced levels, at least one winze and a small stope. Mine development reached a depth of 110 to 115 feet and included over 460 feet of underground workings. There was no activity, however, at the site when examined in 1983. The geology, in the general area of the site, is described as Quartzite and minor amounts of Conglomerate, Phyllitic Siltstone and Dolomite. The Land Status, Ownership Category of this surface-underground, past producer, discovered in 1892, is shown as "Private". A 1930 record shows the Owner as Mrs. Agnes Horn of Delamar.
A final note on this mine is as follows: "The surface exposures and underground workings show extensive Brecciation and mineralization, and it is suggested that the Claim warrants more extensive prospecting and development than it had received in 1937."
USGS MRDS Data Base Record 10271440, Released January 19, 1994: The main entrance to the Jumbo Mine is shown at 37.45687N by -114.76334W, placing it in the Delamar Mining District and in the Ferguson Mining District. The location accuracy, of these coordinates, is shown as +/- 10 meters. The

Public Land Survey System locators are the Southeast ¼ of the Southwest ¼ of the Northeast ¼ of Section 1, Township 6 South, Range 64 East. Gold is present and is shown as a primary commodity, with Silver, Copper and Lead tertiary. The geology, in the area of the main entrance, is described as Quartzite and minor amounts of Conglomerate, Phyllitic Siltstone, Limestone and Dolomite. The Land Status, Ownership Category of this underground, past producer is shown as "Private", with mineral rights held via "Patented Claims".

Jumbo Claims (a.k.a. NBMG Sample Sites 3031 and 3032): (37.42716N by -115.79807W – USGS MRDS) (Gold, Silver)
USGS MRDS Data Base Record 10125406, Released January 26, 1994: The main entrance to the Jumbo Claims is shown at 37.42716N by 115.79807W, placing it in the Groom Mining District and in the area included on the USGS Cattle Spring 24K, Pahranagat Range 100K and Caliente 250K maps. The location accuracy, of these coordinates, is shown as +/- 500 meters. The Public Land Survey System locators are Section 12, Township 6 South, Range 55 East. Gold is present and is shown as a primary commodity with Silver tertiary. Mineralization includes Hematite, Limonite and Magnetite, with a gangue of Quartz. The ore body is a Tabular, Fissure Vein of Hydrothermal origin. The geology, in the area of the main entrance, is described as Quartzite and minor amounts of Conglomerate, Phyllitic Siltstone, Limestone and Dolomite. The Land Status, Ownership Category of this surface-underground prospect is shown as Military Reservation.

Jumbo Pit (a.k.a. Caliente Prospects): (37.61691N by -114.52W – USGS MRDS) (Gold, Silver, Copper)
See the Caliente Prospects entry for more information.

June Claim (a.k.a. Flagstaff): (37.28.20N by -114.46.35W - #3) (Gold, Manganese, Iron, Barite)
See the Flagstaff entry for more information.

June Claim (a.k.a. Groom Mine): (37.20.45N by -115.46.03W - #3) (Silver, Lead, Zinc, Copper, Gold, Barite)
See the Groom entry for more information.

Kathleen Shaft and Middle Tunnel: (37.55.41N by -115.35.58W - #3) (Silver, Gold, Zinc, Lead)
Coordinates are for the main entrance to this underground, past producer.

Kelly: (37.09.27N by -115.47.05W - #3) (Gold, Silver, Lead)
Coordinates are for the ore body of this past producer.

Keno Claims (a.k.a. Delta Claims; NBMG Sample Site 1709): (37.92056N by -114.07973W USGS MRDS) (Gold, Silver, Barite)
USGS MRDS Data Base Record 10046543, Released February 1, 1984: The site of the Keno Claims is shown at 37.92052N by -114.07972W, placing it in the Eagle Valley Mining District, the Fay Mining District and in the area included on the USGS Deer Lodge Canyon 24K and Caliente 100K and 250K maps. The Public Land Survey System locators are the Northwest ¼ of the Northwest ¼ of Section 30, Township 1 North, Range 71 East. Gold and Silver are present and are shown as primary commodities with Barite tertiary. Mineralization of this Comstock-type, Epithermal Vein deposit includes Barite, with a gangue of Fluorite, Quartz, Calcite, Pyrite and Clay, in a host of Dacite. The ore body, which strikes both North-South and East-West, dips from 65° to vertically, is about 4 feet wide, about 100 feet in length and is controlled by a vertical shear zone and Brecciated areas. Black Obsidian occurs as float in the area. The mine was developed by a double-portal adit which begins in the massive Siliceous outcrop of the Quartz-lined, Volcanic and Quartz-cemented Volcanic Breccia. The mine's two adits trend East-West and North-South, although the North-South adit later trends to the Northwest. Outcrops of rubbly, Quartz-cemented Breccia continue for at least 100 feet above the lower adit (which is NBMG Sample Location 1709). The outcrops consist of an interlocking network of Cockscomb, prismatic, banded and open-centered, sugary white Quartz Veins and Veinlets, which cement light purple Andesite-Dacite Volcanic Breccia fragments. Into this formation, lying above the adit, is driven an inclined shaft, with a raise, which connects with the East-West adit. The property was actively explored in 1983 and more recently the underground workings were sampled. The dump at the portal was bulldozed, the roads were improved and recent surface exploration

was indicated. There was, however, no activity noted across the drainage to the North or in the Northwest-trending adit. The geology, in the general area of the site, is described as Andesite and related rocks of intermediate composition. The Land Status, Ownership Category of this prospect is shown as BLM Administrative area. A 1983 record shows the Owner as D. Burgess.

USGS MRDS Data Base Record 10174028, Released January 26, 1994: The main entrance to the Keno Claims is shown at 37.92056N by -114.07973W, placing it in the Eagle Valley Mining District. The location accuracy of these coordinates is shown as +/- 100 meters. This record shows Gold present and as a primary commodity with Silver and Barite tertiary. The ore body is a Tabular Fissure Vein of Hydrothermal origin. Mineralization includes Fluorite, Quartz, Calcite, Hydrous Manganese Oxides, Pyrite, Adularia and Anauxite (a hydrous Aluminum Silicate). The geology, in the general area of the main entrance, is described as Andesite and related rocks of intermediate composition. The Land Status, Ownership Category of this surface-underground prospect is unknown. A 1983 record shows the Owner as D. Burgess.

Kismet Properties: (38.07.00N by -114.37.15W - #3) (Zinc, Lead, Copper)
Coordinates are for the ore body of this surface-underground operation.

Klondike Mining District (a.k.a. Eagle Valley Mining District): (Gold, Silver, Lead, Uranium, Pearlite)
Description of the District:
Tingley, Joseph V.; "Mining Districts of Nevada"; Nevada Bureau of Mines and Geology, Report 47, Second Edition; 1998; Page 79: In W. R. Averett's 1962 work, *Directory of Southern Nevada Place Names*, he described a mining district named Klondike, located near the historical village of Fay (37.54.29N by -114.04.12W – USGS Deer Lodge Canyon 24K map), which supposedly operated for a short time. The location described would place it in the modern Eagle Valley Mining District area.
See the Eagle Valley Mining District entry for more information.
Mines Included in the District:

Kopenite Perlite Mine: (37.33.02N by -115.00.59W - #3) (Perlite)
Coordinates are for trenching associated with this surface, past producer.

Koyen Scheelite Mine: (37.39.22N by -115.37.10W - #3) (Tungsten)
Coordinates are for the ore body of this underground, past producer.

Kyle Siding Prospect (a.k.a. Kyle Group; Cinnabar Claim; Cinnabar Group; Cinnabar No. 1 Claim; Tinledge Claim): (37.18.57N by -114.28.59W - #3) (Gold)
Coordinates are for the main entrance to this underground, exploration prospect.
USGS MRDS Data Base Record 10173932, Released January 27, 1994: The main entrance to the Kyle Siding Prospect is shown at 37.31577N by -114.48393W, placing it in the area included on the USGS Leith 24K, Clover Mountains 100K and Caliente 250K maps. The location accuracy, of these coordinates, is shown as +/- 10 meters. The Public Land Survey System locators are the Northwest ¼ of the Northwest ¼ of Section 27, Township 7 South, Range 67 East. Gold is present and is shown as a primary commodity. Mineralization of the Tabular Fissure Vein deposit includes Cinnabar. The geology, in the area of the main entrance, is described as Andesite and related rocks of intermediate composition. The Land Status, Ownership Category of this underground prospect is shown as "BLM Administrative Area".
Comment: I went back and confirmed, from the original records, that the latitude values were as shown. The older (degrees, minutes and seconds) is for a location at the top of the ridge, while the newer set of coordinates place it at the base of the ridge, indicating it may have been for an adit or tunnel.
See the Cinnabar Group entry for more information.

Lady No.1 Claim (a.k.a. Florence): (37.58.51N by -114.35.44W - #3) (Silver, Lead, Gold, Copper)
See the Florence entry for more information.

Lake Valley Mine (a.k.a. Geyser Mine): (38.40.15N by -114.42.15W - #3) (Tungsten, Gold, Silver, Fluorite)
See the Geyser Mine entry for more information.

<u>**Lanter Mine**</u>: (38.38.46N by -114.45.03W - #3) (Tungsten, Gold, Silver, Lead, Zinc)
Coordinates are for the main entrance to this underground, exploration prospect.
USGS MRDS Data Base Record 10173538, Released June 14, 1993: The main entrance to the Lanter Mine is shown at 38.64605N by -114.75165W, placing it in the area included on the USGS Parker Station 24K, Garrison 100K and Lund 250K maps. The location accuracy, of these coordinates, is shown as +/- 100 meters. The Public Land Survey System locators are the Southeast ¼ of the Southeast ¼ of the Southeast ¼ of Section 11, Township 9 North, Range 64 East. Tungsten is present and is shown as a primary commodity with Gold, Silver, Lead and Zinc tertiary. The geology, in the area of the main entrance, is described as Alluvial deposits. The Land Status, Ownership Category of this underground prospect is shown as "BLM Administrative Area".

<u>**Larson**</u>:
See the Crystal Mercury entry for more information.

<u>**Last Chance (a.k.a. Last Chance Mine)**</u>: (37.55.59N by -114.33.06W - #3) (Gold, Silver, Lead, Copper)
Coordinates are for the ore body of this past producer.
USGS MRDS Data Base Record 10046465, Released December 1, 1982: The site of the Last Chance Mine is shown at 37.93302N by -114.55251W, placing it in the Highland Mining District and in the area included on the USGS Highland Peak 24K and Caliente 100K and 250K maps. The Public Land Survey System locators are the Southwest ¼ of the Northwest ¼ of Section 23, Township 1 North, Range 66 East. Lead, as Galena, and Silver in a host of Late Cambrian Limestone, are present and are shown as primary commodities. The deposit is believed to have been developed by two shafts. The geology, in the general area of the site, is described as Limestone and Dolomite with locally thick sequences of Shale and Siltstone. The Land Status, Ownership Category of this occurrence is shown as "Private".
USGS MRDS Data Base Record 10173544, Released January 10, 1994: The main entrance to the Last Chance is shown at 37.93326N by -114.55254W, placing it in the Highland Mining District. The location accuracy, of these coordinates, is shown as +/- 10 meters. (Between 120 and 200 feet Southwest, South and Southeast of the coordinate point are three large areas of ground disturbance resembling tailings piles or old dumps.) The Public Land Survey System locators are the Southeast ¼ of the Southwest ¼ of the Northwest ¼ of Section 23, Township 1 North, Range 66 East. Gold is present and is shown as a primary commodity with Silver, Lead and Copper tertiary. The geology, in the area of the main entrance, is described as Limestone and Dolomite with locally thick sequences of Shale and Siltstone. The Land Status, Ownership Category of this underground, past producer is unknown.

<u>Lead Occurrence</u>: (37.15.00N by -114.19.10W - #3) (Lead)
Coordinates are for an ore body.

<u>Leech</u>: (38.07.29N by -114.21.43W - #3) (Perlite)
Coordinates are for an ore body.

<u>Limestone Occurrence</u>: (37.15.12N by -114.09.18W - #3) (Limestone)
Coordinates are for an ore body.

<u>Little Buck Mine</u>: (37.54.19N by -114.03.30W - #3) (Gold, Silver, Copper, Lead)
Coordinates are for the main entrance to this underground, past producer.

<u>Lincoln Mine</u>
Mineral and Water Resources of Nevada; U.S. Geological Survey and the Nevada Bureau of Mines; Senate Document No. 87, 88th Congress, 2nd Session; 1964; Mackay School of Mines, University of Nevada-Reno; Page 156: The Lincoln mine in the Tem Piute mining district,
Lincoln County has produced over 300,000 units of WO_3, from underground workings extending to a depth of over 400 feet. Scheelite bearing, Garnet-Tactite occurs in Limestone along the West side of a Granite intrusive body. The Tactite, which contains 0.2 to 1 percent WO_3, forms a 15- to 100-foot band directly at the contact and also is present as irregular masses extending up to 450 feet away from the Granite. Some higher grade ore was found in small Calcite-Fluorite-Scheelite-Sphalerite masses along minor faults in Marbleized Limestone adjoining Tactite. Powellite, some Pyrite, Chalcopyrite, and Pyrrhotite, and minor

Molybdenite and Bismuthinite also are present in the Tactite. To the North Tactite bodies also are exposed along the West side of a second Granite body but are too narrow, discontinuous, and low-grade to be economically significant.

Little Buck Claim (a.k.a. Big Buck Claim): (37.90107N by -114.058W – USGS MRDS) (Gold, Silver)
See the Big Buck Claim entry for more information.

Little Ford (a.k.a. Ida May): (38.05.54N by -114.36.57W - #3) (Silver, Lead, Gold, Copper, Zinc)
See the Ida May entry for more information.

Little Mountain Mining District (a.k.a. Cinnamon Bear Mining District): (Copper, Molybdenum, Silver)
Description of the District:
Tingley, Joseph V.; "Mining Districts of Nevada"; Nevada Bureau of Mines and Geology, Report 47, Second Edition; 1998; Page 137: The Little Mountain Mining District is located about 12 miles Southeast of Panaca in the Southwestern Cedar Range, in the area of Little Mountain, which is usually referred to as Empty Mountain today. The area on the North and South sides of Little Mountain is where the most of the mining activity took place in the District. In the April 13, 1873 issue of the *Territorial Enterprise* an article described an area, referred to as the Cinnamon Bear Mining District, that was about 20 miles Southeast of Pioche, and may have been in the area of what is today the Little Mountain Mining District.
Mines Included in the District:

Log Cabin: (37.54.06N by -114.36.34W - #3) (Lead, Zinc)
Coordinates are for the ore body of this underground operation.

Lone Mountain Mining District (a.k.a. Ely Mining District): (Gold, Silver, Lead, Zinc, Manganese)
Description of the District:
Tingley, Joseph V.; "Mining Districts of Nevada"; Nevada Bureau of Mines and Geology, Report 47, Second Edition; 1998; Page 86: The Ely Springs Mining District is located about 13 miles West of Pioche, on the West side of the Ely Springs Mountain Range. Much of the confusion surrounding the Lone Mountain Mining District stemmed from the fact that in 1912, J. M. Hill, in his *The Mining Districts of the Western United States*, referred to the area of the Ely Mining District, as the Lone Mountain Mining District. This confusion was compounded in 1932 when C. Stoddard, in his *Metal and Non-Metal Occurrences in Nevada*, also referred to the area as the Lone Mountain Mining District; likely relying on the prior Hill publication.
See the Ely Mining District entry for more information.
Mines Included in the District.
        Tara Claims (Gold, Silver, Lead, Manganese)

Long Valley Mining District (a.k.a. Viola Mining District): (Silver, Gold, Lead, Zinc, Copper, Manganese, Fluorspar)
Description of the District:
Tingley, Joseph V.; "Mining Districts of Nevada"; Nevada Bureau of Mines and Geology, Report 47, Second Edition; 1998; Page 239: The Viola Mining District is believed to be the modern equivalent of the historic Long Valley Mining District, which was identified in the March 20, 1873 edition of the *Territorial Enterprise* as being about 40 miles Southeast of Pioche. The current Viola Mining District extends along the Southern flank of the Clover Mountains, from Meadow Valley Wash, near Cottonwood Canyon, on the West, East to the Blue Nose Peak area. It was discovered sometime in the 1860s and rediscovered in 1917. It was initially organized in 1902, but was basically inactive until 1917
See the Viola Mining District entry for more information.
Mines Included in the District:

Lost Mining District (a.k.a. Panaca Mining District): (Gold, Silver, Lead, Copper, Vanadium, Titanium, Uranium)
Description of the District:

Tingley, Joseph V.; "Mining Districts of Nevada"; Nevada Bureau of Mines and Geology, Report 47, Second Edition; 1998; Page 168: On the 1880 version of the Land Office Map, there was a reference to a Lost Mining District in what would be the Eastern part of the current Panaca Mining District, but the reference was not shown in later versions.
Mines Included in the District:

Lost Treasure Mine: (37.56.10N by -114.28.20W - #3)
Coordinates are for an ore body.
Pioche Record (The); January 21, 1921; "Around the Mines"; Page 3; Column 1: "The Lost Treasure Silver Mines Company has commenced active development of its holdings in the Pahranagat Lake Mining District, near Hiko, in Lincoln County, Nevada. The Lost Treasure group produced a considerable tonnage of Silver ore in the early days of mining on Mt. Irish."

Lost Treasure Silver Mines Company: (Silver)
The Lost Treasure Silver Mines Company was active in Lincoln County in the first quarter of the 20th Century; primarily through its Ownership and Operation of the Lost Treasure Mine in the Pahranagat Lake Mining District, near Hiko. See the Lost Treasure Mine entry for more information.

Louie & Leone Claims: (38.00.26N by -115.01.53W - #3)
Coordinates are for a mineral location.

Lucky Bar Claim (a.k.a. Delamar Prospect 002): (37.28.07N by -114.42.57W - #3) (Gold, Silver, Copper, Iron)
See the Delamar Prospect 002 entry for more information.

Lucky Boy 001: (37.21.20N by -114.26.20W - #3) (Barite)
Coordinates are for an ore body.

Lucky Boy 002: (37.57.34N by -114.35.27W - #3) (Silver, Lead)
Coordinates are for the ore body of this underground operation.

Lucky Boy 003: (37.54.59N by -114.04.16W - #3) (Gold, Silver)
Coordinates are for the ore body of this underground, past producer.

Lucky Chief: (37.42.00N by -114.31.09W - #3) (Silver, Lead, Zinc, Gold, Manganese)
Coordinates are for the ore body of this underground, past producer.

Lucky Dog Claim (a.k.a. Blue Bird Mine 001; Hulse Mine): (38.45523N by -114.334W – USGS MRDS) (Uranium, Silver, Gold, Copper, Lead, Arsenic)
See the Blue Bird Mine 001 and the Hulse Mine entries for more information.

Lucky Friday: (37.51.32N by -114.35.53W - #3) (Manganese)
Coordinates are for a main entrance.

Lucky Hobo: (38.26.54N by -114.18.54W - #3) (Silver, Lead, Zinc, Gold, Antimony, Manganese Iron, Arsenic)
Coordinates are for the ore body of this underground, past producer.

Lucky Jim: (37.52.25N by -114.33.40W - #3) (Silver, Lead)
Coordinates are for an ore body.

Lucky Lead-Zinc Prospect: (37.15.00N by -114.25.45W - #3) (Zinc, Lead, Silver, Cadmium, Copper)
Coordinates are for the ore body of this surface-underground, development deposit.

Lucky Star: (38.06.31N by -114.37.21W - #3) (Manganese, Silver, Lead, Zinc, Iron, Phosphates)
Coordinate are for the main entrance to this underground, past producer.

Lucky Strike Claims (a.k.a. Lucky Strike Nos. 1-9 Claim): (38.02.05N by -115.04.43W - #3) (Uranium)
Coordinates are for the ore body of this underground, past producer.

M. K. Pit and Mill: (37.36.55N by -114.38.02W - #3) (Sand & Gravel)
Coordinates are for the ore body of this surface, past producer.

MacBruson Claims (a.k.a. Bruson Prospect; NBMG Sample Sites 1449 & 1450): (36.96165N by -114.292W – USGS MRDS) (Molybdenum, Tungsten, Gold, Silver)
USGS MRDS Data Base Record 10037368, Released February 1, 1980; Updated September 1, 1984: The site of the MacBruson Claims is shown at 36.96165N by -114.29165W, placing it about 2 miles South of Gourd Springs, on the East side of the Mormon Mountains, in the Gourd Springs Mining District and in the area included on the USGS Davidson Peak 24K, Overton 100K and Las Vegas 250K maps. Although the area was unsurveyed at the time, the projected Public Land Survey System locators were Sections 32 & 33, Township 11 South, Range 69 East and Section 4, Township 12 South, Range 69 East. The properties consist of 28 Claims, which were intermittently explored in the 1920s. Tungsten and Molybdenum are present and are shown as primary commodities with Gold and Silver secondary. Mineralization of this Tungsten Skarn Deposit includes Molybdenite, Scheelite and Powellite, with a gang of Tourmaline, Garnet, Epidote, Idocrase and Muscovite, in a host of Amphibolite and associated with Neoproterozoic Pegmatite. The Scheelite tends to be disseminated in the Amphibolite, near large Pegmatite bodies. Clots and Stringers of Scheelite and Powellite are in the Skarn. The Quartz Pegmatite also carries fine sprays and clots of Molybdenite and Oxidized Pyrite crystals. Late stage Opaline Silica coats the rocks. Garnetiferous Phyllite and/or Schist are often found in the float. Intrusive dikes, striking North 30° East and dipping 30° Northwest, are intensely fractured and crushed at the exposed base. Thin Quartz Veinlets, 6 inches to a foot wide, also carry Scheelite. A thin Tactite zone, about 200 feet long, borders the Granite Pegmatite, which also contains a small amount of Scheelite. A semi-quantitative spectrographic analysis was run on samples from the property which showed an average of over 10% Silica, Aluminum and Cobalt combined; 7% Iron; 1.5% Magnesium, Sodium and Titanium combined; 0.4% Tungsten; 0.3% Manganese; 0.15% Barite, Beryllium, Vanadium and Zirconium combined; and, 70 Parts Per Million (PPM) Bismuth, Niobium, Strontium and Yttrium combined. A sample run by the U.S. Bureau of Mines, as part of the Strategic Reserve program, showed 1.08% WO_3. The geology, in the general area of the site, is described as Metamorphic rocks. The mine was developed by numerous open cuts and prospect pits in a 200-square-foot area and a 20-foot shaft, although no underground workings were noted in 1983 emanating from it, nor was any activity noted at the site. There were some old stone cabins and haulage roads, but these did not appear to have been used in the recent past. The Land Status, Ownership Category of this occurrence is shown as "Private".
See the NBMG Sample Sites 1449 and 1450 entry for more information.

Mackie Pearlite: (37.37.12N by -115.00.00W - #3) (Perlite)
Coordinates are for the ore body of this underground producer (as of 1996).

Magnolia Mine (a.k.a. Bamberger Delamar Gold Mining Company): (37.46219N by -114.769W – USGS MRDS) (Gold, Silver)
See the Bamberger Delamar Gold Mining Company entry for more information.

Magnolia 002: (37.29.20N by -114.47.15W - #3)
Coordinates are for the ore body of this underground, past producer. (Decimal Equivalents 37.4889N by -114.7875W)

Magnolia Mine 001 (NBMG Sample Site 1747): (37.48275N by -114.776 – USGS MRDS) (Gold, Silver, Copper, Lead, Zinc, Bismuth, Arsenic)
USGS MRDS Data Base Record 10037390, Released November, 1, 1979; Updated August 1, 1984: The site of the Magnolia Mine is shown at 37.48275N by -114.7764W, placing it on a Quartzite ridge just North of Helena Wash, about 1.7 miles North of Delamar, in the Delamar Mining District, in the Ferguson Mining District and in the area included on the USGS Delamar 24K, Clover Mountains 100K and Caliente 250K maps. The Public Land Survey System locators are Sections 25 & 26, Township 5 South, Range 64 East.

Gold and Silver are present and are shown as primary commodities with Lead secondary and Zinc, Copper, Bismuth and Arsenic tertiary. Mineralization includes Pyromorphite, Tetrahedrite, Chalcopyrite, Malachite, Pyrolusite and Psilomelane, in a host of Quartzite, associated with Rhyolite and Early Cambrian to Pliocene Volcanic Breccia. The ore body is described as Tabular, striking North 18° West, dipping 80° East, about 160 feet thick, 100 feet wide and traceable for a length of over 1,100 feet. The ore, the deposition of which was controlled by a fracture zone, is found along a dike or Volcanic Breccia plug in an area of numerous Rhyolite dikes. The ore Breccia consists of Quartzite fragments cemented by Igneous material, in Lenses and Pockets. Additional ore may be found by following some of the seams that branch off from the main shoot. The mine was developed by over 4,300 feet of underground workings that attained a maximum vertical depth of 300 feet, with workings on 5 levels. Most of the stopes are inaccessible and many of the drifts are partially or completely blocked by waste filling. In 1977 records indicate the wooden framed hoist house and trestle were still standing. When visited in 1983 there was one open adit, which ran North 10° West, scattered caved and/or smaller adits, large ore dumps and building ruins. The open adit dipped 60° Southwest and followed the Quartz Vein and Quartz-cemented Breccia exposed at the portal. This Vein is from 1 to 1½ feet thick and the Quartzite wall rock is fractured and Brecciated, but shows a sharp contact with the Vein. The Quartzite is cut by Quartz Veinlets and contains numerous, Iron-stained vugs filled with prismatic Quartz. The central portion of the main Vein is made up of Quartz-cemented, Quartzite Breccia containing angular fragments of pink Quartzite, cemented by a mixture of Manganese Oxides and Chalcedonic Quartz. Outward from the Breccia are banded Comb Quartz and Chalcedonic Quartz Veins which are generally vuggy and contain Iron Oxides and dark streaks, which are believed to be fine Manganese Oxides or dispersed Sulfides. Quartz stringers fill fractures in the footwall Quartzite. These stringers parallel the orientation of the Main Vein., which is along a fault, as evidenced by Brecciation of the host rock and the central Vein and by the presence of slickensides on the footwall Quartzite. Quartz material found on the dump is banded, white to clear and Cockscomb, sugary or Chalcedonic in texture. Comb Quartz cements the Breccia fragments. Some Oxidized Pyrite was found in Iron-stained vugs. "Pyritized" dark grey, finely crystalline, Siliceous Breccia was also observed. Some Siliceous or "Jaspery" Breccia contained bands of finely crystalline Chalcopyrite and un-Oxidized Pyrite. The Siliceous Breccias show fine, late-stage Quartz Veinlets. Malachite, Tetrahedrite, Psilomelane and Pyrolusite were identified in the Vein material. Malachite-coated, Comb Quartz Vein material, on the dump, contains specks of visible Gold. Monzonite Porphyry and Rhyolitic Volcanic rocks were found on the dump, but not located in place. Analysis from smelter returns of 6 samples showed:

1. Return 1: 2.86 ounces of Gold and 27.3 ounces of Silver per ton, 3.2% Iron and 1.1% Sulfur
2. Return 2: 1.43 ounces of Gold and 18.0 ounces of Silver per ton, 0.3% Copper, 2.2% Iron and 0.9% Sulfur.
3. Return 3: 0.81 ounces of Gold and 11.3 ounces of Silver per ton, and 1.1% Lead.
4. Return 4: 1.87 ounces of Gold and 17.0 Ounces of Silver per ton, 1.8% Lead, 0.25% Copper, 2.9% Iron and 1.0% Sulfur.
5. Return 5: 1.2 ounces of Gold and 12.7 ounces of Silver per ton and 3.2% Iron.
6. Return 6: 0.88 ounces of Gold and 14.2 ounces of Silver per ton, 0.2% Copper, 2.5% Iron and 0.2% Sulfur.

Additional assay data is contained in the record for NBMG Sample 1747.

Approximately 470 tons of ore was mined and shipped prior to 1902, and small shipments were made in 1920 and 1921. The first ore was mined at Hiko. In 1931 exploration was undertaken at the Magnolia Mine and the J. L. Baird and W. L. Aiken lease produced considerable ore in 1932 & 1933. There was no evidence of activity at the time of the examination, in 1983, but there was evidence that staking and trenching had occurred within the last few years at the mouth of the canyon. The Land Status, Ownership Category of this underground, past producer is shown as "Private".

USGS MRDS Data Base Record 10270995, Released January 10, 1994: The main entrance to the Magnolia Mine is shown at 37.48247N by -114.77584W, placing it in the Delamar Mining District and in the Ferguson Mining District. The location accuracy, of these coordinates, is shown as +/- 10 meters. The Public Land Survey System locators are Section 25, Township 5 South, Range 64 East. Gold is present and is shown as a primary commodity with Silver, Copper, Manganese and Iron tertiary. The geology, in the area of the main entrance, is described as Quartzite with minor amounts of Conglomerate, Phyllitic Siltstone, Limestone and Dolomite. The Land Status, Ownership Category of this underground, past producer is unknown.

COMMENT: The Magnolia Mine lies about 2/3 of an air mile Northeast (22.8°) of the old Delamar cemetery; however by road/trail this would be about a mile and a half.

Magnolia Mine 003: (37.28.20N by -114.46.30W - #3)
Coordinates are for the ore body of this underground operation. (Decimal Equivalents of 37.47222N by -114.7750W)

Malefactor Claims: (38.05.15N by -114.34.15W - #3) (Silver, Lead, Copper)
Coordinates are for an ore body.

Manganese Occurrence 001: (37.21.45N by -115.46.31W - #3) (Manganese)
Coordinates are for the ore body of this surface, past producer.

Manganese Occurrence 002: (37.16.00N by -114.09.24W - #3) (Manganese)
Coordinates are for the ore body of this prospect.

Manganese Prospects 003: (37.36.27N by -114.46.26W - #3) (Manganese)
Coordinates are for the ore body of this surface-underground operation.

Manganese-Iron Occurrence 004: (37.18.35N by -114.05.55W - #3) (Iron, Manganese)
Coordinates are for the ore body of this prospect.

Manhattan: (37.57.34N by -114.35.31W - #3) Silver, Lead, Gold, Copper, Molybdenum, Iron)
Coordinates are for the ore body of this past producer.

Maria Claim (a.k.a. Groom Mine): (37.20.45N by -115.46.03W - #3) (Silver, Lead, Zinc, Copper, Gold, Barite)
See the Groom entry for more information.

Marion Mine: (37.56.43N by -114.28.51W - #3)
Coordinates are for an ore body.

May Day (a.k.a. Bristol-Jackrabbit Mines): (38.08107N by -114.617W – USGS MRDS) (Silver, Copper, Lead, Zinc, Gold, Manganese)
See the Bristol-Jackrabbit Mine entry for more information.

Mayday and Shendell Claims (a.k.a. Andies Mine): (37.33.35N by -115.44.31W - #3) (Mercury, Silver, Zirconium, Barite)
See the Andies Mine entry for more information.

Mazeppa Mine: (37.92524N by -114.449W – USGS MRDS) (Lead, Silver)
USGS MRDS Data Base Record 10046415, Released May 1, 1984: The site of the Mazeppa Mine is shown at 37.92524N by -114.44945W, placing it on Treasure Hill, adjacent to the Chapman Mine, in the Ely Mining District, in the Pioche Mining District and in the area included on the USGS Pioche 24K and Caliente 100K and 250K maps. The Public Land Survey System locators are the Southeast ¼ of the Southeast ¼ of Section 22, Township 1 North, Range 67 East. Lead and Silver are present and are shown as a primary commodity. Mineralization includes Galena, in a host of Prospect Mountain Quartzite, associated with Late Cambrian Plutonic rock. The ore body is a Tabular Vein which strikes East-West, dips 50° South and is controlled by the Yuba Dike and the parallel fractures in it. The ore occurs along both the hanging wall and the footwall of the Yuba Dike, as well as along a set of fractures paralleling the strike of and wholly within the Yuba Dike, known as the "Middle Vein". The ore body was developed by a shaft of unknown depth. The geology, in the general area of the site, is described as Quartzite and minor amounts of Conglomerate, Phyllitic Siltstone, Limestone and Dolomite. The Land Status, Ownership Category of this occurrence is unknown.
USGS MRDS Data Base Record 10173840, Released January 26, 1994: The main entrance to the Mazeppa Mine is shown at 37.92526N by -114.44944W, placing it in the Ely Mining District and in the Pioche

Mining District. The location accuracy, of these coordinates, is shown as +/- 100 meters. The Public Land Survey System locators are the Southeast ¼ of the Southeast ¼ of Section 22, Township 1 North, Range 67 East . Lead, as Galena, in a Tabular Fissure Vein, is present and is shown as a primary commodity with Silver tertiary. The Land Status, Ownership Category of this underground prospect is shown as "Private" with Mineral Rights held through "Patented Located Claims".

MDDS 1-15 Claims (a.k.a. Andies Mine): (37.33.35N by -115.44.31W - #3) (Mercury, Silver, Zirconium, Barite)
See the Andies Mine entry for more information.

MDM Claims (a.k.a. AD Prospect): (38.37.32N by -114.43.40W - #3) (Tungsten, Zinc, Gold, Silver, Molybdenum, Lead, Fluorite)
See the AD Prospect and Schwartz Tunnel entries for more information.

Meadow Valley Mountains Mining District: (Gold, Silver, Uranium)
Description of the District:
Tingley, Joseph V.; "Mining Districts of Nevada"; Nevada Bureau of Mines and Geology, Report 47, Second Edition; 1998; Page 146: The Meadow Valley Mountains Mining District is located East of Highway 93.
Mines Included in the District.

Meadow Valley Mining District (a.k.a. Pioche Mining District): (Gold, Silver, Lead, Zinc, Copper, Antimony)
Description of the District:
Tingley, Joseph V.; "Mining Districts of Nevada"; Nevada Bureau of Mines and Geology, Report 47, Second Edition; 1998; Page 174: Discovered in 1863 and organized in 1864, the Pioche Mining District is oriented around the Pioche Hills. When established, the Pioche Mining District was called the Meadow Valley Mining District, but the name was changed to the Ely Mining District in 1868.
See the Pioche Mining District entry for more information.
Mines Included in the District:

Meadow Valley Mines (a.k.a. Raymond & Ely Extension): (37.55.50N by -114.26.26W - #3) (Gold, Silver, Lead)
See the Raymond & Ely Extension entry for more information.

Meadow Valley Mountains Mining District: (Gold, Silver, Uranium)
Description of the District:
Tingley, Joseph V.; "Mining Districts of Nevada"; Nevada Bureau of Mines and Geology, Report 47, Second Edition; 1998; Page 146: The Meadow Valley Mountains Mining District is located East of Highway 93.
Mines Included in the District:

Meadow Valley No. 3 Mine (a.k.a. Meadow Valley No. 3 Shaft): (37.55.35N by -114.27.11W - #3) (Silver, Lead, Zinc)
Coordinates are for an ore body.

Meadow Valley No. 5 Mine: (37.55.36N by -114.27.04W - #3) (Silver, Lead, Zinc)
Coordinates are for an ore body.

Mendha: (37.56.33N by -114.33.54W - #3) (Gold, Silver, Lead, Zinc)
Coordinates are for the ore body of this underground, past producer.

Minnie Claim (a.k.a. Blue Bird Mine 001; Hulse Mine): (38.45523N by -114.334W – USGS MRDS) (Uranium, Silver, Gold, Copper, Lead, Arsenic)
See the Blue Bird Mine 001 and the Hulse Mine entries for more information.

Minto Perlite Deposit: (37.37.03N by -114.25.05W - #3) (Perlite)
Coordinates are for the ore body of this prospect.

Monarch: (38.03.10N by -114.35.45W - #3) (Silver, Lead, Copper)
Coordinates are for the ore body of this underground, past producer.

Monitor Claim (a.k.a. Delamar Prospect 002): (37.28.07N by -114.42.57W - #3) (Gold, Silver, Copper, Iron)
See the Delamar Prospect 002 entry for more information.

Monitor No. 2 Claim (a.k.a. Delamar Prospect 002): (37.28.07N by -114.42.57W - #3) (Gold, Silver, Copper, Iron)
See the Delamar Prospect 002 entry for more information.

Monkey Wrench Wash Prospect (a.k.a. Monkey Wrench Wash Diggings): (37.35.10N by -114.48.55W - #3) (Gold, Copper, Iron)
Coordinates are for the ore body of this prospect.

Mopa Venture (a.k.a. Moapa, Moapa Project): (36.52.47N by -114.40.27W - #3) (Gold, Platinum Group Metal)
Coordinates are for the ore body of this surface producer (as of 1996).
USGS MRDS Data Base Record 10046371; Released June 1, 1984: The site of the Moapa Venture is shown at 36.88998 by -114.67805, placing it in the area included on the USGS Rox 24K, Overton 100K and Las Vegas 250K maps. This appears to be an estimate, as the location accuracy is only shown as +/- 5,000 meters. The Public Land Survey System locators are Section 23, Township 12 South, Range 65 East. Gold is present as Alluvial deposits and is shown as a primary commodity. In 1982 and 1983 this mine was listed as an active open pit mine and Cyanide mill employing 4 persons. The Owner was listed as Enoch Resources, Gregory Brandt-General Manager, 1515 East Reno Avenue, Las Vegas, Nevada 84119.
USGS MRDS Data Base Record 10125179; Released December 5, 1996: The Pit area of the Moapa is shown at 36.87968 by -114.67503. This also appears to be an estimate as the location accuracy is shown as +/- 1,000 meters. This record shows Gold present and as a primary commodity with Platinum Group Elements present at tertiary levels – likely recovered from refinery slimes. As of 1996 the Ownership was shown as Louisiana Mining Company, 59%; Force Resources Limited 10% and Various Private Interests 31%. Estimates of the ore body inferred a resource of 6.26 million Metric Tonnes of ore at a cut-off for Gold of 2.37 grams/MT. As of 1996 preliminary exploration drilling was scheduled.

Monkey Wrench Wash Diggings (a.k.a. Monkey Wrench Claim): (37.49027N by -114.79524W – USGS MRDS) (Gold, Copper, Iron)
USGS MRDS Data Base Record 10046498, Released January 1, 1984: The approximate site of the Monkey Wrench Wash Diggings is shown at 37.49025N by -114.79528W, placing it about a half of a mile North of the Magnolia Mine, in the Delamar Mining District and in the area included on the USGS Delamar 24K, Clover Mountains 100K and Caliente 250K maps. The Public Land Survey System locators are Section 23, Township 5 South, Range 64 East. Gold and Copper are present and are shown as primary commodities with Iron tertiary. Mineralization includes Iron ores with a gangue of Quartz in a host of Quartzite, Shale and Limestone. The Quartz appears rusty and Irregularly replaces materials in a North-striking fault zone away from its intersection with a West-striking fault zone. Samples of this material, taken in 1891, when the deposit was discovered, ran as high as 4,000 Troy Ounces of Silver per ton. Workings are described as "a few diggings, none extensive". The geology, in the general area of the site, is described as Alluvial deposits. The Land Status, Ownership Category of this occurrence is shown as "BLM Administrative Area".
USGS MRDS Data Base Record 10222243, Released January 26, 1994: The Pit area of the Monkey Wrench Wash Diggings is shown at 37.49027N by -114.79524W, placing it in the Delamar Mining District and in the Ferguson Mining District. The location accuracy of these coordinates is shown as +/- 100 meters. *Comment*: Review of the coordinate area on a mapping program places it in the Northwest Corner of an intersection of trails, on the Western edge of an area covered with old prospect pits. The deposit is shown as two types of ore bodies, an Irregular Fissure Vein and a Hydrothermal Replacement. Gold is shown as

present and is shown as a primary commodity with Copper and Iron tertiary. The geology, in the pit area, is described as Alluvial deposits. The Land Status, Ownership Category of this surface prospect is shown as "Private", with all Claims being "Patented".

Mormon Mountains: (37.04.45N by -114.33.27W - #3) (Gold, Silver, Tellurium)
Coordinates are for an ore body.
Mohave County Miner; May 14, 1904; Rich Strike of Gold Ore; Page 3; Column 4: Prospector Dana, who passed through Caliente on route to his recently located claims at Mormon Mountain, showed assays made by Salt Lake assayers going $2,040.75 and $1,700 in Gold and Silver; Gold predominating. He also had a cube of Tellurium weighing about five or six ounces, taken from the same mine. He said that his partner and he had eight claims located, and on one had opened up a sixteen-inch Vein, at grass roots, which carried the ore assaying $2,040.75, and the lesser assay was of a black Quartz taken from an eight and a half inch vein, at the base of a fifty foot ledge, cropping out at the foot of a mountain.
Both of these claims lie about one and a half miles from Mormon Mountain, which is between twenty-five and thirty miles Southwest from Caliente and five miles from the line of the San Pedro Railway.

Mormon Mountains Deposit: (36.97308N by -114.55W – USGS MRDS) (Vermiculite)
Coordinates are for a surface prospect.

Mormon Mountains Mining District: (Copper, Silver)
Description of the District:
Tingley, Joseph V.; "Mining Districts of Nevada"; Nevada Bureau of Mines and Geology, Report 47, Second Edition; 1998; Page 153: The Mormon Mountains Mining District, discovered in 1899, includes the part of the Mormon Mountains between Mormon Peak and Moapa Peak, extending from Meadow Valley Wash to the East flank of the Mormon Mountains.
Mines Included in the District:

Mountain Lion: (37.56.23N by -114.36.32W - #3) (Silver, Lead, Zinc, Copper, Gold, Arsenic)
Coordinates are for the ore body of this underground, past producer.

Mountain View: (37.55.38N by -115.36.17W - #3) (Lead, Silver, Zinc, Gold)
Coordinates are for the main entrance to this underground, exploration prospect.

Mountain View #3: (37.55.50N by -115.36.41W - #3) (Lead, Zinc, Silver, Gold)
Coordinates are for the main entrance to this underground, exploration prospect.

Mountain View Group (a.k.a. Charley Ross Claim): (37.90719N by -114.056W – USGS MRDS) (Gold, Silver)
USGS MRDS Data Base Record 10037374, Released February 1, 1980: The site of the Mountain View Group is shown at 37.90719N by -114.0561W, placing it near the Utah-Nevada border, in the Gold Springs Mining District and in the area included on the USGS Deer Lodge Canyon 24K and Caliente 100K and 250K maps. The Public Land Survey System locators are Section 32, Township 1 North, Range 71 East. Gold and Silver, as Sylvanite in a host of Latite, are present and are shown as primary commodities. The Vein contains milling ore with very high-grade, Telluride-rich streaks, which assayed up to $3,000 per ton and had shipment returns of $2,900 per ton in 1908. This underground operation reached a depth of 175 feet. The Charley Ross Claim is on a body of Talc ore 40 feet wide. The geology, in the general area of the site, is described as Andesite and related rocks of intermediate composition. The Land Status, Ownership Category of this underground, past producer is unknown.
See the Charley Ross Mine entry for more information.

Murphy (a.k.a. Cinch Mine): (38.35.58N by -114.41.29W - #3) (Tungsten, Gold, Silver)
See the Cinch Mine entry for more information.

Murphy Prospect: (37.89274N by -114.613W – USGS MRDS) (Tungsten, Manganese, Iron, Copper)
USGS MRDS Data Base Record 10046424, Released March 1, 1984: The site of the Murphy Prospect is shown at 37.89274N by -114.61334W, placing it about 1,000 feet North of the Comet Mine, in the Comet

Mining District and in the area included on the USGS Highland Peak 24K and Caliente 100K and 250K maps. The location accuracy, of these coordinates, is shown as +/- 250 meters. The Public Land Survey System locators are Section 5, Township 1 South, Range 66 East. Tungsten and Copper are present and are shown as primary commodities with Manganese and Iron secondary. Mineralization, of this Quartz Vein deposit, includes Pyrite, Oxidized Copper minerals and Wolframite, in a host of Late Cambrian, Prospect Mountain Quartzite. The ore body strikes North 85° West, dips steeply South and is up to a foot thick. It was developed by two shafts, both now inaccessible, which were originally 120 feet and 65 feet deep. The geology, in the general area of the site, is described as Alluvial deposits. The Land Status, Ownership Category of this occurrence is unknown.

USGS MRDS Data Base Record 10198043, Released January 26, 1994: The main entrance to the Murphy Prospect is shown at 37.89276N by -114.61334W, placing it in the Comet Mining District. This record shows Copper present and as a primary commodity with Tungsten, Manganese and Iron tertiary. Mineralization of this Tabular, Fissure Vein Deposit, of Hydrothermal origin, includes Wolframite and Pyrite. The geology, in the area of the main entrance, is described as Alluvial deposits. The Land Status, Ownership Category of this underground prospect is shown as "BLM Administrative Area".

National Group: (37.57.10N by -114.34.05W - #3) (Lead, Silver)
Coordinates are for an ore body.
See the Bristol-Jackrabbit Mine entry for more information.

NBMG Sample Site 117 (a.k.a. Soa Lode Claims): (37.69887N by -114.51364W – USGS MRDS) (Lead, Gold, Silver, Arsenic, Barite)
See the Soa Lode Claims entry for more information.

NBMG Sample Location 126 (a.k.a. Gold Stake Tunnel): (37.69025N by -114.52W – USGS MRDS) (Gold, Silver, Lead, Arsenic)
USGS MRDS Data Base Record 10046439, Released January 1, 1984: The site of the NBMG Sample Location 126 is shown as 37.69025N by -114.52028W, placing it on the South side of Cobalt Canyon, in the Chief Mining District, in the Caliente Mining District and in the area included on the USGS Chief Mountain 24K and Caliente 100K and 250K maps. The Public Land Survey System locators are the Northeast ¼ of Section 18, Township 3 South, Range 67 East. Gold and Silver, with a gangue of Quartz and Pyrite, in a host of Late Cambrian, Prospect Mountain Quartzite, are present and are shown as primary commodities with Lead secondary and Arsenic tertiary. The ore body, a Vein along a bedding plane fracture, strikes North-South and dips about 30° East. The mine was developed by at least 2 South-trending adits, which are only open around the portals; some trenching, estimated to be 5 to 10 years old; and, an old, corrugated building housing an assay lab near the upper adit. The rock on the dump is mostly Quartzite with smaller amounts of a dark brown, earthy and Siliceous Gossan Quartz which is Iron-stained and contains small Quartz Veins and recrystallizations. All the rocks observed contained Iron and Manganese Oxides. There were also substantial quantities of green, yellow and bright orange Oxides, probably from Arsenic, Iron, Sulfur or Lead mineralization present. Some of the dump's Quartz Vein material contains small vugs filled with Iron-stained, prismatic Quartz and small amounts of un-Oxidized Pyrite. Although the Vein is not visible at the workings, the bedding of the Quartzite, measured at the lower portal is what was used to estimate the North-South strike and 30° East dip of the bedding planes. Most Veins in this area follow a North-South strike and probably developed along fractures in these bedding planes.
NBMG Sample 126 assayed about 10% Iron, 7,000 Parts Per Million (PPM) Arsenic, 2,000PPM Boron, 1,000PPM Strontium, 700PPM Lead, 500PPM Antimony, 500PPM Zirconium, 200PPM Zinc, 150PP Barite, 100PPM Copper and 5PPM Silver.
The Geology, in the general area of the site, is described as Quartzite and minor amounts of Conglomerate, Phyllitic Siltstone, Limestone and Dolomite. The Land Status, Ownership Category of this occurrence is shown as "BLM Administrative Area".
See the Gold Stake Tunnel entry for more information.

NBMG Sample Site 579 (a.k.a. Easter Mine; Taylor Mine): (37.30.46N by -114.37.54W - #3) (Gold, Silver, Iron)

USGS MRDS Data Base Record 10046506, Released May 1, 1984: NBMG Sample 579 assayed 1,000 Parts Per Million (PPM) Manganese, 500PPM Barite, 200PPM Strontium, 200PPM Zinc, 100PPM Copper, 100PPM Lead, 70PPM Silver, 20PPM Chromium and 10PPM Gold.
See the Easter Mine and the Taylor Mine entries for more information.

NBMG Sample Site 580 (a.k.a. Antique Prospect): (37.6258N by -114.69W – USS MRDS) (Gold, Silver)
USGS MRDS Data Base Record 10046491, Released May 1, 1984: Sample 580 contained 200 Parts Per Million (PPM), 150 PPM Boron, 100PPM Manganese, 100PPM Strontium, 15 PPM Lead.
See the Antique Prospect entry for more information.

NBMG Sample Site 788 (a.k.a. Unnamed Prospect 034): (37.35554N by -114.061W – USGS MRDS) (Gold, Barite, Lead)
USGS MRDS Data Base Record 10046366, Released March 1, 1984: The site of the NBMG Sample Site 788 is shown at 37.35554N by -114.0611W, placing it in the Vigo Mining District and in the area included on the USGS Dodge Spring 24K, Clover Mountains 100K and Caliente 250K maps. The Public Land Survey System locators are Section 12, Township 7 South, Range 71 East. Gold and Barite are present and are shown as primary commodities with Lead tertiary. Mineralization of this Epithermal Manganese-type deposit includes Barite, Psilomelane, Sericite, Calcite and Quartz. NBMG Sample 788 assayed at 500 Parts Per Million (PPM) Manganese, 200PPM Barite, 100PPM Lead, 70PPM Copper and 5PPM Silver. The ore body is Tabular, strikes North 65° East, dips vertically, is about 12 feet wide and is controlled by the fault zone Brecciation. The Hydrothermal Breccia zone is in an intrusive. The fault zone in the wall of the shaft is filled and cemented with massive, sugary Quartz and crystalline Calcite Veins, which are, in turn, Iron-stained and coated with minor Psilomelane. The intrusive on either side of the fault is intensely Brecciated and cemented with Cockscomb, Hydrothermal Quartz, which has abundant open spaces. The Quartz crystals are very fine-grained to ½ inch and radiate from central nucleation points and extend from the Breccia fragments. The Quartz is heavily Iron and Manganese stained, and from the weight of the rocks, it appears that Barite might be inter-grown. Platy, crystalline Calcite fills fractures and is also coated with Iron and Manganese stains. The intrusive is gray-green, equi-granular and strongly weathered showing Argillic alteration. Sericite occurs locally. Breccia fragments exhibit milling. Intersecting the main fault zone are sets of North 20° East, vertical shears. A very minor amount of Oxidized Pyrite and a lone grain of Galena was found in the Quartz cement. The geology, in the general area of the site, was described as Andesite and related rocks of intermediate composition. The deposit was developed by a single shallow, shaft, which was mostly caved when visited. Most of the dump had washed away, down drainage. The access road was in good condition, but this is believed to have been maintained for the benefit of hunters. The Land Status, Ownership Category of this occurrence is unknown.
See the Unnamed Prospect 034 entry for more information.

NBMG Sample Site 791 (a.k.a. Unnamed Prospect 031; Unnamed Prospect 037): (37.29581N by -114.08082W – USGS MRDS) (Gold, Silver, Manganese, Iron, Gemstones, Copper)
USGS MRDS Data Base Record 10046369, Released June 1, 1984: NBMG Sample contained 10% Iron, 20% Calcium, 2,000 Parts Per Million (PPM) Manganese, 200PPM Strontium and 150PPM Barite.
See Unnamed Prospect 031 and Unnamed Prospect 037 entries for more information.

NBMG Sample Site 799 (a.k.a. Wide Awake and Volcano): (37.54.56N by -114.25.50W - #3) (Silver, Lead, Manganese, Zinc, Antimony, Gold, Copper, Iron, Barite, Arsenic)
USGS MRDS Data Base Record 10037339, Released October 1, 1979; Updated December 1, 1984: There are a number of assays associated with this Sample Site at the Wide Awake and Volcano. The official Sample No. 799 assayed 15% Iron, 1.0% Zinc, 0.7% Lead, 0.2% Antimony, 0.1% Copper, 0.1% Barite, 100 parts per million (PPM) Silver and 100 PPM Cadmium. There was also data on returns from three smelter shipments.
Shipment #1 showed 0.045 ounces of Gold (about 1.4 grams) and 72.8 ounces of Silver per ton, 0.18% Copper, 11.55% Lead, 4.15% Zinc, 14% Iron, 39.8% Silicon and 0.35% Sulfur.
Shipment #2 showed 0.13 ounces of Gold (about 4 grams) and 151.4 ounces of Silver per ton, 0.3% Copper, 57.15% Lead, No Zinc, 3.05% Iron, 15.4% Silicon and 4.5% Sulfur.

Shipment #3 showed 0.34 ounces of Gold (about 10.5 to 10.6 grams) and 24.1 ounces of Silver per ton, No Copper, 10.7% Lead, No Zinc, 14.4% Iron, 58.1% Silicon and 0.55% Sulfur.
See the Wide Awake and Volcano entry for more information.

NBMG Sample Site 807 (a.k.a. Schwartz Tunnel): (38.37.32N by -114.43.40W - #3) (Tungsten, Zinc, Gold, Silver, Molybdenum, Lead, Fluorite)
USGS MRDS Data Base Record 10045918, Released March 1, 1982; Updated February 1, 1985: NBMG Sample 807 was taken from a Quartz Vein at the Schwartz Tunnel. The sample assayed 700 Parts Per Million (PPM) Barite, 500PPM Manganese, 500PPM Zinc, 500PPM Zirconium, 70PPM Chromium, 70PPM Lanthanum, 70PPM Vanadium, 70PPM Yttrium, 50PPM Bismuth, 50PPM Copper, 20PPM Lead, 20PPM Tin, 15PPM Beryllium, 15PPM Nickel, 15PPM Scandium, and 10PPM Molybdenum.
See the Schwartz Tunnel entry for more information.

NBMG Sample Site 808 (a.k.a. Schwartz Tunnel): (38.37.32N by -114.43.40W - #3) (Tungsten, Zinc, Gold, Silver, Molybdenum, Lead, Fluorite)
USGS MRDS Data Base Record 10045918, Released March 1, 1982; Updated February 1, 1985: NBMG Sample 808 was taken from Tactite located 300 feet North of the Schwartz Tunnel. The sample assayed 15% Calcium, 10% Iron, over 5,000Parts Per Million (PPM) Manganese, 5,000PPM Zinc, 300PPM Copper, 200PPM Tin, 150PPM Beryllium, 150PPM Strontium, 150PPM Tungsten, 100PPM Zirconium, 50PPM Cadmium, 50PPM Lanthanum, 30PPM Lead, 30PPM Yttrium, 20PPM Molybdenum, 10PPM Cobalt and 10PPM Nickel.
See the Schwartz Tunnel entry for more information.

NBMG Sample Site 809 (a.k.a. Schwartz Tunnel): (38.37.32N by -114.43.40W - #3) (Tungsten, Zinc, Gold, Silver, Molybdenum, Lead, Fluorite)
USGS MRDS Data Base Record 10045918, Released March 1, 1982; Updated February 1, 1985: This sample was incorrectly shown in the record as NBMG Sample 810, and should have been shown as NBMG Sample 809. NBMG Sample 809 was taken from the Gossany Tactite Southwest of the Schwartz Tunnel area. The sample assayed 15% Iron, over 1% Zinc, over 5,000 Parts Per Million (PPM) Manganese, 1,000PPM Copper, 700PPM Barite, 500PPM Arsenic, 300PPM Bismuth, 200PPM Cadmium, 150PPM Beryllium, 150PPM Tungsten, 70PPM Lead, 70PPM Tin, 50PPM Cobalt, 50PPM Lanthanum, 50PPM Vanadium, 50PPM Yttrium, 20PPM Nickel, 20PPM Zirconium and 10PPM Silver.
See the Schwartz Tunnel entry for more information.

NBMG Sample Sites 814W and 8145 (a.k.a. Eagle Rock): (38.37.00N by -114.38.25W - #3) (Antimony, Lead, Zinc, Copper, Tungsten, Silver, Manganese, Iron, Gold)
USGS MRDS Data Base Record 10045922, Released March 1, 1982; Updated February 1, 1985: Two NBMG Assays were recorded along with one from the US Bureau of Mines, shown under the Eagle Rock Entry. The sample for Assay 8145 contained 10% Iron, 3,000 parts per million (PPM) Barite, 2,000PPM Arsenic, 700PPM Lead, 700PPM Zinc, 500PPM Copper, 500PPM Tungsten, 500PPM Antimony, 150PPM Silver, 150PPM Manganese, 50PPM Bismuth, 20PPM Cobalt, 20PPM Zirconium, 15PPM Molybdenum and 10PPM Nickel.
Sample 814W contained 3% Iron, 2,000PPM Tungsten, 1,000PPM Copper, 1,000PPM Manganese, 500PPM Zinc, 200PPM Antimony, 150PPM Lead, 100PPM Barite, 70PPM Bismuth and 30PPM Silver.
See the Eagle Rock entry for more information.

NBMG Sample Sites 815-817 and 818a and 818b (a.k.a. Cave Valley Mine 002): (38.38.39N by -114.47.49W - #3) (Lead, Silver, Copper, Zinc, Gold, Vanadium, Arsenic, Clay)
See the Cave Valley Mine 002 entry for more information.

NBMG Sample Site 1389 (a.k.a. Blue Bell): (37.57.48N by -114.34.41W - #3) (Gold, Silver, Lead, Zinc)
USGS MRDS Data Base Record 10046459, Released December 1, 1984: Sample 1389 assayed at over 20% Iron, 2% or 20,000 parts per million (PPM) Lead, 5,000PPM Zinc, 3,000PPM Manganese, 2,000PPM Arsenic, 1,000PPM Copper, 200PPM Tin, 100PPM Antimony and 50PPM Silver. Data regarding the location of the sample was not found in the record.
See the Blue Bell entry for more information.

<u>**NBMG Sample Sites 1390 through 1392 (a.k.a. West Manhattan Vein Project)**</u>: (37.95774N by -114.59695W – USGS MRDS) (Gold, Silver, Lead, Copper)
USGS MRDS Data Base Record 10046471, Released March 1, 1984: The central point of the three samples of NBMG Sample Site 1390, 1391 and 1392, is shown at 37.95774N by -114.59695W, placing it in the Highland Mining District and in the area included on the USGS Highland Peak 24K and Caliente 100K and 250K maps. The Public Land Survey System locators are Section 8, Township 1 North, Range 66 East. Gold, Silver and Lead are present and are shown as primary commodities with Copper secondary. Mineralization includes Malachite, with a gangue of Calcite and Quartz, in a host of Lyndon Limestone and Late Cambrian Shale. The ore body runs North-South, dips vertically, is traceable for about 40 feet and is controlled by a fault contact between formations and bedding plane faults. Three samples were taken: NBMG Sample 1390 assayed over 20% Iron, over 2% Copper, 1,000 Parts Per Million Manganese, 500PPM Tungsten, 500PPM Zinc, 300PPM Arsenic, 200PPM Barite, 100PPM Molybdenum, 100PPM Lead and 1.5PPM Silver.
NBMG Sample 1391 assayed over 20% Iron, 700PPM Zinc, 300PPM Manganese, 200PPM Arsenic, 100PPM Tungsten, 70PPM Molybdenum, 50PPM Barite, 50PPM Lead, 2PPM Copper and 1.5PPM Silver.
NBMG Sample 1392 assayed over 20% Iron, 1,000PPM Tungsten, 200PPM Manganese, 50PPM Barite, 50PPM Lead, 50PPM Molybdenum and 2PPM Copper.
The site was developed by several shafts adits and old haulage roads; however, at the time of the examination in 1983 there was no activity at the site. The geology, in the general area of the site, is described as Limestone and Dolomite with locally thick sequences of Shale and Siltstone. The Land Status, Ownership Category of this past producer is shown as "BLM Administrative Area".
A note to file explaining the site more fully was found. It reads as follows: "Workings explore and possibly produced ore from a fault zone and replacement body along bedding plane faults. The ore zone probably contained primary Base Sulfides which were Hydrothermally altered to Gossan. Dense, Siliceous and stained with Iron and Manganese Oxides, it weathered to a resistant rib in the host rock. A series of workings follows the fault contact separating Cambrian Pioche Shale on the West from Cambrian Lyndon Limestone on the East. Malachite coats much of the Gossan material at the Southern-most workings. Surface factures are coated with crystalline Calcite. Farther North are Breccias cemented by white Quartz. Northward, the bedding flattens to almost horizontal and strikes North 20° East. Additional workings continue to explore the North-trending Vertical fault zone."
See the West Manhattan Vein Project entry for more information.

<u>**NBMG Sample Site 1396 (a.k.a. NBMG Sample Location 1396; Unnamed Shaft 069)**</u>: (37.95635N by -114.58278W – USGS MRDS) (Gold, Silver, Copper, Lead)
USGS MRDS Data Base Record 10046470, Released March 1, 1984: The site of the NBMG Sample Location 1396 is shown at the above locations, placing it in the Highland Mining District and in the area included on the USGS Highland Peak 24K and Caliente 100K and 250K maps. The Public Land Survey System locators are the Southern ½ of Section 9, Township 1 North, Range 66 East. Gold and Silver are present and are shown as primary commodities with Copper and Lead secondary. Mineralization of this Polymetallic Replacement deposit includes Tetrahedrite and Galena, with a gangue of Pyrite, Quartz and Calcite, in a host of Late Cambrian, Highland Peak Limestone. The deposit contains Siliceous replacement bedding deposits up to 5 feet thick which follow bedding plane faults. Near the faults the Limestone has been Silicified and erosion has exposed small Jasperoid ribs. The replacement bodies are Oxidized to Gossan and fill cavities and fractures. Cutting the Gossan are Brecciated, white, massive Quartz Veins with Calcite crystals and grains carrying Oxidized Sulfides (Chalcopyrite and Pyrite, possibly with Tetrahedrite and Galena). The exposed bedding exhibits significant faulting resulting in the variable depths of the Carbonate beds and the variance in strikes, from due West to North 20° West, and dips from none, or flat, to 30° North. A set of vertical shears, striking North 65° East, was exposed in the middle of the workings. The site was developed by 4 or 5 vertical and inclined shafts, which were partially caved at the time of the visit. These were sunk along a Westerly trend along with peripheral surface cuts and trenching. It is believed that the site was probably explored and worked in the 1860 to mid-1880 time period. Original hand-hewn timbers in the shaft collars were visible. At the time of the examination, in 1983, there was no activity at the site. The geology, in the general area of the site, is described as Alluvial deposits. The Land Status, Ownership Category of this past producer is shown as "BLM Administrative Area".
See the Unnamed Shaft 069 entry for more information.

NBMG Sample Site 1397 (a.k.a. X-Ray Adit): (37.56.53N by -114.35.12W - #3) (Gold, Silver, Lead, Antimony, Barite)
USGS MRDS Data Base Record 10098662, Released December 1, 1982: NBMG Sample 1397 assayed at over 20% Calcium, 200 Parts Per Million (PPM) Strontium, 150PPM Manganese, 50PPM Lead and 1.5 PPM Silver.
See the X-Ray Adit entry for more information.

NBMG Sample Site 1416 (a.k.a. Daly East): (37.55.05N by -114.26.08W - #3) (Gold, Silver, Arsenic)
USGS MRDS Data Base Record 10037393, Released October 1, 1979; Updated August 1, 1984: The assay for NBMG Sample 1416 showed 1,000 parts per million (PPM) Arsenic; 500PPM Zirconium, 200PPM Barite, 150PPM Lead, 100PPM Copper, 100PPM Antimony and 20PPM Silver.
See the Daly East entry for more information.

NBMG Sample Site 1417 (a.k.a. Unnamed Shaft 071): (37.91885N by -114.43806W – USGS MRDS) (Gold, Silver, Lead, Zinc)
USGS MRDS Data Base Record 10098658, Released April 1, 1984: The location of the NBMG Sample Site 1417 is shown at 37.91885N by -114.43806W, placing it in the Pioche Mining District and in the area included on the USGS Pioche 24K and Caliente 100K and 250K maps. Gold, Silver, Lead and Zinc are present and are shown as primary commodities. Mineralization of this Polymetallic Vein Deposit includes Galena, Sphalerite, and Hemimorphite with a gangue of Jarosite and Quartz, in a host of Late Cambrian Prospect Mountain Quartzite. The ore body is described as a bedding fault which strikes North 60° West and dips 30° to 50° Northeast and a shear zone striking North 20° West with a vertical dip. A grey to white, sugary to massive, vitreous, fractured Quartz Vein follows the bedding plane and is cut by the intersecting, vertical shear zone which is about 8 feet wide. The control of the ore emplacement was the intersection of the bedding plane fault and the vertical shear zone. The Quartzite is heavily Iron and Manganese stained and coated with abundant Jarosite and possibly some Sphalerite, Cerussite and Hemimorphite. The Quartz Vein also contains some finely disseminated, fresh Pyrite. Grey zones in the Quartz and the weight of the rock suggest that it may carry finely disseminated Sulfides; probably Galena. The deposit was developed by a single vertical shaft. The geology, in the general area of the site, is described as Quartzite and minor amounts of Conglomerate, Phyllitic Siltstone, Limestone and Dolomite. The Land Status, Ownership Category of this past producer is unknown.
See the Unnamed Shaft 071 entry for more information.

NBMG Sample Site 1421 (a.k.a. Treasure Hill Mine): (37.55.25N by -114.26.58W - #3) (Silver, Gold, Lead, Iron, Arsenic)
USGS MRDS Data Base Record 10037337, Released November 1, 1979; Updated December 1, 1984; Updated February 1, 1993: While I found no record on for NBMG Sample 1420, I did find NBMG Sample 1421. It assayed as follows: 10% Iron, 7,000 Parts Per Million (PPM) Lead, 1,000PPM Arsenic; 200PPM Antimony, 100PPM Barite, 70PPM Copper and 30PPM Silver.
See the Treasure Hill Mine entry for more information.

NBMG Sample Site 1425 (a.k.a. California-Pioche Shaft): (37.92107N by -114.456W – USGS MRDS) (Gold, Silver, Lead, Copper, Antimony, Manganese, Barite)
USGS MRDS Data Base Record 10046400, Released April 1, 1984: The Nevada Bureau of Mines and Geology Sample 1425 assayed over 20% Calcium, 1.0% Lead, 1,500 parts per million (PPM) Manganese, 300PPM Antimony, 300PPM Strontium, 150PPM Barite, 100PPM Zirconium and 50PPM Copper.
See the California-Pioche entry for more information.

NBMG Sample Site 1426 (a.k.a. Unnamed Prospect Pit 055): (37.91746N by -114.45528W – USGS MRDS) (Gold, Silver, Barite, Lead)
USGS MRDS Data Base Record 10095739, Released April 1, 1984: The site of the NBMG Sample Site 1426 is shown at the above coordinates, placing it in the Pioche Mining District and in the area included on the USGS Pioche 24K and Caliente 100K and 250K maps. The Public Land Survey System locators are Section 27, Township 1 North, Range 67 East. Gold, Silver and Barite are present and all are shown as primary commodities with Lead secondary. Mineralization includes Galena and Barite with a gangue of

Pyrite, Limonite and Calcite, in a host of Late Cambrian Limestone. The geology, in the general area of the site, is described as Limestone and Dolomite with locally-thick sequences of Shale and Siltstone. NBMG Sample 1426 assayed 72% Calcium, 1,000 Parts Per Million (PPM) Lead, 1,000PPM, Manganese 500PPM Strontium, 20PPM Barite and 5PPM Silver. The location from which it was taken was a Vertical Shear Zone, about 6 inches wide, in the fault contact between the Pioche Shale and the Davidson Formation, which strikes North 20° West. The site was developed by shallow exploration pits; however, there was no activity when the site was reviewed in 1983. The Land Status, Ownership Category of this occurrence is unknown.

A note, further describing the deposit was found in the file; it reads as follows: "Workings explore a fault contact between the Pioche Shale and Davidson Formation. Workings are in shattered, altered, bleached, medium grey Limestone with crystalline Calcite coating fractures and cementing Breccia. Abundant Limonite stains from Oxidized Pyrite grains are found in the Veins. The pit exposes a North 20° West trending, vertical, 6-inch wide shear zone where rocks are extensively crushed. The dump rock shows slickensides. The Limestone is partially Silicified in the vicinity of the shear and the weight of the rocks suggests that Barite or finely disseminated Galena is inter-grown with the Calcite."

See the Unnamed Prospect Pit 055 entry for more information.

NBMG Sample Sites 1429 & 1430 (a.k.a. Ely Valley Mine): (37.56.54N by -114.29.31W - #3) (Zinc, Manganese, Silver, Gold, Lead, Copper, Tungsten)
USGS MRDS Data Base Record 10037332, Released October 1, 1979; Updated December 1, 1984: NBMG Samples 1429 & 1430 were taken of Mangano-Siderite gangue and Unoxidized Pyritized Quartzite/ Pyrite-Quartz Vein material. Sample 1429 assayed 5,000 parts per million (PPM) Zinc, 500PPM Lead, 500PPM Arsenic, 200PPM Copper, 100PPM Manganese, 100PPM Cadmium, 100PPM Zirconium, 50PPM Bismuth and 5PPM Silver. Sample 1430 assayed 20,000PPM (2%) Lead, 10,000PPM (1%) Zinc, and over 5,000PPM Manganese, with 700PPM Arsenic, 200PPM Copper, 200PPM Cadmium and 10PPM Silver.
See the Ely Valley Mine entry for more information.

NBMG Sample Site 1432 (a.k.a. Prince Consolidated): (37.54.04N by -114.28.23W - #3) (Manganese, Silver, Lead, Zinc, Gold, Iron)
USGS MRDS Data Base Record 10008111, Released October 1, 1979; Updated December 1, 1984; Updated and Edited April 27. 1995: NBMG Sample 1432 was assayed and gave the following values; 15% Iron, 1% Zinc, 7,000 Parts Per Million (PPM) Lead, over 5,000PPM Manganese, 5,000PPM Arsenic, 1,500PPM Copper, 500PPM Cadmium, 100PPM Tin and 20PPM Silver.
See the Prince Consolidated Mine entry for more information.

NBMG Sample Location 1435: (37.94996N by -114.53417W – USGS MRDS) (Gold, Silver, Zinc, Manganese)
USGS MRDS Data Base Record 10046472, Released March 1, 1984: The site of the NBMG Sample Location 1435 is shown at the above coordinates, placing it in the Highland Mining District and in the area included on the USGS Highland Peak 24K and Caliente 100K and 250K maps. The Public Land Survey System locators are Section 13, Township 1 North, Range 66 East. Gold and Silver are present and are shown as primary commodities with Zinc and Manganese secondary. Mineralization includes Pyrite, Hematite and Quartz in a host of Late Cambrian, Mendha Limestone and Granite. The ore body is Tabular, dips vertically, strikes North 60° East and is controlled by the fault zone. NBMG Sample 1435 contained 15% Iron, 5,000 Parts Per Million (PPM) Manganese, 2,000PPM Zinc, 1,000PPM Arsenic, 500PPM Bismuth, 300PPM Copper, 200PPM Barite, 100PPM Antimony, 100PPM Tin, 100PPM Vanadium, 50PPM Tungsten and 5PPM Silver. The mine was developed by a single adit, about 30 feet long, with minor surface cuts. This adit follows the fault zone. The fault Breccia contains discreet, Oxidized Pyrite grains altered to Hematite which have been coated with Opaline Silica. Limestone carries Pyrite crystals, up to ¼ of an inch and Quartz Veins and Veinlets follow the bedding planes. Fault gouge on the dump is Silicified and coated with drusy Quartz on surfaces and in cavities. Doubly-terminated Quartz crystals occur in the Breccia. Breccia and Limestone are cut by massive to open-centered Vitreous Quartz Veins. The geology, in the general area of the site, is described as Limestone and Dolomite with locally thick sequences of Shale and Siltstone. The Land Status, Ownership Category of this past producer is shown as "BLM Administrative Area".
See the Unnamed Adit 007 entry for more information.

<u>NBMG Sample Site 1436 (a.k.a. Black Prince)</u>: (37.55.27N by -114.31.56W - #3) (Silver, Gold, Lead, Zinc, Manganese)
USGS MRDS Data Base Record 10103585, Released January 1, 1980, Updated September 1, 1984: The general assay for the Siliceous Manganese ore at the Black Prince 001 runs about 13% Manganese, 1% combined Lead & Zinc and about 7 ounces of Silver per ton. The maximum Lead content found was around 5%.
Sample 1436 assayed at 20%+ Calcium, 5,000+ parts per million (PPM) Manganese, 1,000 PPM Zinc, 500PPM Strontium, 200PPM Lead, 200PPM Antimony, 200PPM Barium, 100PPM Silver, 100PPM Copper and 100PPM Vanadium.
See the Black Prince entry for more information.

<u>NBMG Sample Site 1443 (a.k.a. Old Democrat)</u>: (37.41.36N by -114.31.45W - #3) (Gold, Silver, Zinc, Lead, Copper, Manganese, Cadmium, Uranium, Iron, Arsenic, Zirconium)
USGS MRDS Data Base Record 10037356, Released February 1, 1980; Updated August 1, 1984: The Nevada Bureau of Mines and Geology (NBMG) Sample 1443 assayed 20% Iron, 1.0% Lead. 1.0% Zinc, over 0.5% Manganese, 1,000 parts per million (PPM) Barium, 500PPM Cadmium, 500PPM Arsenic, 300PPM Strontium, 200PPM Copper, 100PPM Silver, 100PPM Tin and 100PPM Zirconium.
Another assay was taken at the portal of the collapsed inclined shaft, which showed; 1.5% Zinc, ½% Lead, 1.5 ounces of Silver per ton and 15% to 18% Manganese.
See the Old Democrat entry for more information.

<u>NBMG Sample Site 1445 (a.k.a. Unnamed Prospect 048)</u>: (37.93496N by -114.60667W – USGS MRDS) (Gold)
USGS MRDS Data Base Record 10046473, Released March 1, 1984: The site of the NBMG Sample Site 1445 is shown at the above coordinates, placing it in the area included on the USGS Highland Peak 24K and Caliente 100K and 250K maps. The location accuracy, of these coordinates, is shown as +/- 100 meters. The Public Land Survey System locators are the Northwest ¼ of Section 20, Township 1 North, Range 66 East. Gold is present and is shown as a primary commodity. Mineralization, which includes Pyrite, is hosted in Limestone and Late Cambrian Shale. The geology, in the general area of the site, is described as Alluvial deposits of the Mendha Overthrust Area. An assay, taken from drill samples and labeled 1445 contained 10% Iron, 1,000 Parts Per Million (PPM) Manganese, 500PPM Zinc, 500PPM Zirconium, 500PPM Barite, 300PPM Strontium, 200PPM Copper, 150PPM Lead, 100PPM Chromium, 100PPM Nickel and 2PPM Silver. It is believed that this assay came from drill chips taken from a mid-1983 drill hole on the East side of the Range Front Road. These chips contained Shale, Siltstone and Limestone and fine-to-medium crystalline, Unoxidized and partially Oxidized Pyrite distributed sparingly throughout the sample. At the time of the review Kerr-McGee, who was shown as the Owner, was doing exploratory drilling in the area. The Land Status, Ownership Category of this small prospect is shown as "BLM Administrative Area"
See the Unnamed Prospect 048 entry for more information.

<u>NBMG Sample Sites 1449 & 1450 (a.k.a. MacBruson Claims)</u>: (36.96165N by -114.292W – USGS MRDS) (Molybdenum, Tungsten, Gold, Silver)
USGS MRDS Data Base Record 10037368, Released February 1, 1980; Updated September 1, 1984:
NBMG Sample 1449 assayed 2,000 Parts Per Million (PPM) Manganese, 1,000PPM Tungsten, 700PPM Vanadium, 500PPM Strontium, 300PPM Tin, 200PPM Barite, 100PPM Boron, 100PPM Lead and 7PPM Beryllium. Although searched for, Gold, Silver, Molybdenum and Antimony were not found.
NBMG Sample 1450 assayed 1% (10,000PPM) Tungsten, 300PPM Gold, 200PPM Molybdenum, 150PPM Beryllium, 100PPM Silver, 100PPM Antimony, 100PPM Barite, 100PPM Strontium, and70PPM Lead. Although searched for, Boron, Tin and Vanadium were not found.
See the MacBruson Claims entry for more information.

<u>NBMG Sample Sites 1452 through 1454 (a.k.a. New Tempiute Mine)</u>: (37.63079N by -115.629W – USGS MRDS) (Tungsten, Silver, Zinc, Bismuth, Fluorite)
USGS MRDS Data Base Record 10046523, Released March 1, 1984: Samples 1452, 1453 and 1454 contain 15% to 20% Iron, 50 to greater than 10,000 (1%) Parts Per Million (PPM) Tungsten, 700 to greater

than 10,000PPM Zinc, 3,000 to greater than 5,000PPM Manganese, 0 to 1,000PPM Barite, 0 to 300PPM Molybdenum, 0 to 300PPM Strontium, 100 to 200PPM Copper, 0 to 200PPM Arsenic, 0 to 150PPM Cobalt, 20 to 150PPM Vanadium, 10 to 100PPM Lead, 0 to 70PPM Nickel and 0 to 1PPM Silver.
See the New Tempiute Mine entry for more information.

NBMG 1455 & 1456 (a.k.a. Schofield Mine): (37.63218N by -115.624W – USGS MRDS) (Tungsten, Molybdenum, Zinc, Fluorite)
USGS MRDS Data Base Record 10107653, Released January 1, 1980; Updated August 1, 1984; Updated and Edited June 9, 1995: Although specific assays were not found for NBMG Samples 1455 &1456, the Schofield Mine entry does contain assay data for the mine area.
See the Schofield Mine entry for more information.

NBMG Sample Site 1467 (a.k.a. Andies Mine): (37.33.35N by -115.44.31W - #3) (Mercury, Silver, Zirconium, Barite)
USGS MRDS Data Base Record 10040521, Released December 1, 1975; Updated August 1, 1984: The Nevada Bureau of Mines and Geology (NBMG) Sample 1467 assayed 20% Iron, 0.15% Barium, 200 parts per million (ppm) Zirconium and 7 ppm Silver.
See the Andies Mine entry for more information.

NBMG Sample Sites 1468 & 1469 (a.k.a. Don Dale Mine): (37.31.40N by -115.44.31W - #3) (Lead, Silver, Copper, Gold)
Coordinates are for the ore body of this underground, past producer.
USGS MRDS Data Base Record 10037343, Released February 1, 1980; Updated August 1, 1984: NBMG Sample 1468 assayed 10% Iron, 7,000 parts per million (PPM) Lead, 2,000PPM Copper, 1,000PPM Zinc, 500PPM Antimony, 500PPM Barite, 300PPM Zirconium, 200PPM Manganese and 7PPM Silver. NBMG Sample 1469 assayed 2% Iron, 300PPM Zinc, 200PPM Lead, 200PPM Manganese, 200PPM Zirconium, 200PPM Arsenic, 150PPM Barite, 30PPM Copper and 7PPM Silver.
See the Don Dale Mine entry for more information.

NBMG Sample Site 1470 (a.k.a. East Section 34 Prospect): (37.55552N by -115.773W – USGS MRDS) (Silver, Copper, Gold, Manganese)
USGS MRDS Data Base Record 10046490, Released February 1, 1984: The NBMG Sample Site 1470 is located at 37.55552N by -115.77254W, placing it about 0.35 miles North 30º East of the Don Dale Mine and in the area included on the USGS White Blotch Southeast 24K, Timpahute Range 100K and Caliente 250K maps. The Public Land Survey System locators are Section 34, Township 4 South, Range 55 East. Gold, Silver and Copper, as Malachite, in a host of Pioche Shale and Quartzite, are present, with a gangue of Pyrite and Quartz, and are shown as primary commodities with Manganese tertiary. The NBMG Sample 1470 assay contained 2,000 parts per million (PPM) Manganese, 300PPM Zinc, 200PPM Lead, 150PPM Barite and 5PPM Silver. The ore body is Tabular, strikes North 55º East, dips vertically, is about 2 feet thick and controlled by the fault separating the Shale from the overlying Quartzite. Workings include trenching and scraping along the slope, believed to be assessment work. There was no activity at the site when reviewed in 1983. The geology, in the general area of the site, is described as Quartzite and minor amounts of Conglomerate, Phyllitic Siltstone, Limestone and Dolomite. The Land Status, Ownership Category of this occurrence is shown as "BLM Administrative Area".
See the East Section 34 Prospect entry for more information.

NBMG Sample Sites 1494 & 1495 (a.k.a. Caliente Prospects): (37.61691N by -114.52W – USGS MRDS) (Gold, Silver, Copper)
See the Caliente Prospects entry for more information.

NBMG Sample Site 1499 (a.k.a. Confidence Mine): (38.11552N by -114.054W – USGS MRDS) (Gold, Silver)
See the Confidence Mine entry for more information.

NBMG Sample Site 1500 (a.k.a. NBMG Sample Location 1500; Unnamed Shaft 075): (37.94052N by -114.085W – USGS MRDS) (Gold, Silver)
USGS MRDS Data Base Record 10046538, Released June 1, 1984: The site of the NBMG Sample Location 1500 is shown at 37.94052N by -114.085W, placing it in the Eagle Valley Mining District, the Fay Mining District, the Gold Springs Mining District, the Stateline Mining District and in the area included on the USGS Deer Lodge Canyon 24K and Caliente 100K and 250K maps. The Public Land Survey System locators are Section 13, Township 1 North, Range 70 East. Gold and Silver, with a gangue of Quartz, in a host of Andesite, are present and are shown as primary commodities. The ore body is described as Tabular, striking North 35° East, dipping 40° Northwest, about 20 feet thick and controlled by a crush zone. The site was developed by an inclined shaft, now caved, an old ore bin, a house near the shaft and some new trenching. There was no activity at the time of the review, but recent sampling was evident as was the recent trenching. The geology, in the general area of the site, is described as Andesite and related rocks of intermediate composition. The Land Status, Ownership Category of this occurrence is shown as "BLM Administrative Area".
See the Unnamed Shaft 075 record for more information.

NBMG Sample Site 1563 (a.k.a. Tempa Mine): (37.56.55N by -114.04.40W - #3) (Gold, Silver)
See the Tempa Mine entry for more information.

NBMG Sample Site 1566 (a.k.a. Florence): (37.58.51N by -114.35.44W - #3) (Silver, Lead, Gold, Copper)
See the Florence entry for more information.

NBMG Sample Site 1706 (a.k.a. Culverwell Mine 005): (37.41775N by -114.475W – USGS MRDS) (Gold, Silver, Copper, Tungsten, Lead)
USGS MRDS Data Base Record 10037383, Released February 1, 1980; Updated December 1, 1984: Sample 1706 consists of Quartz Vein and Quartz-cemented Breccia with clots and crystals of Oxidized Pyrite, Chalcopyrite and surface coatings of Copper, Iron and Manganese Oxides. The Vein material has small vugs lines with Manganese-coated Quartz crystals and radiating Malachite. This, open-centered Veinlets cut more massive and sugary Vein material. The sampled Vein is dark grey, especially in areas containing crystals of Unoxidized Pyrite, indicating a high percentage of dispersed Sulfides.
Grab samples were indicated to have been taken, although the literature does not indicate if these were considered NBMG Sample 1706, or not. The grab samples assayed about 2 ounces of Gold and 15 to 25 ounces of Silver per ton. The maximum Gold assay was about 3 ounces per ton. Two channel samples were taken and these contained 3 and 5 ounces of Silver and 0.46 and 0.25 ounces of Gold per ton.
See the Culverwell Mine 005 entry for more information.

NBMG Sample Site 1707 (a.k.a. Culverwell 002): (37.25.29N by -114.30.00W - #3) (Silver, Copper, Tungsten, Gold, Iron)
See the Culverwell 002 entry for more information.

NBMG Sample Site 1708 (a.k.a. Deer Lodge Canyon Shaft): (37.92276N by -114.093W – USGS MRDS) (Gold, Copper)
USGS MRDS Data Base Record 10095744, Released February 1, 1984: The site of the NBMG Sample Site 1708 is shown at 37.92274N by -114.09277W, placing it in Deer Lodge Canyon, in the Eagle Valley Mining District, the Fay Mining District and in the area included on the USGS Deer Lodge Canyon 24K and Caliente 100K and 250K maps. The Public Land Survey System locators are the Northeast ¼ of the Northwest ¼ of Section 25, Township 1 North, Range 70 East. Gold is present and is shown as a primary commodity with Copper secondary. Mineralization is found with a gangue of Quartz, Pyrite, Sanidine [a high-temperature Potassium Feldspar – $K(AlSi_3O_8)$] and Clay, in a host of Rhyolite. Altered rock on the dump displays a porous, Clay-like, altered matrix containing altered Feldspar and fresh Biotite Phenocrysts in addition to Rhyolitic-Lattic Volcanic rock fragments. The mine was developed by one shaft, now caved, with old timbers at the collar, and a small dump.
Sample 1708 is from the dump and consists of maroon-colored Rhyolite or Latite with Sanidine and Potassium Feldspar Phenocrysts showing some effects of Silicification and/or Kaolinization. These rocks contain small vugs encrusted with Quartz and Iron Oxides. The rocks are Iron-stained and some show

Gossan coatings and vug fillings and have Quartz-filled Veinlets of cracks. There is no obvious mineralization on the dump; but, as mentioned, the Volcanic rocks show alteration effects, such as Silicification, Iron-staining and bleaching. The Iron Oxides are possibly from Oxidized Pyrite. NBMG Sample 1708 contains 300 Parts Per Million (PPM) Manganese, 150PPM Copper, 100PPM Zirconium, 50PPM Lead, 50PPM Yttrium and 2PPM Silver.
See the Deer Lodge Canyon Shaft entry for more information.

NBMG Sample Site 1709 (a.k.a. Keno Claims): (37.92056N by -114.07973W USGS MRDS) (Gold, Silver, Barite)
See the Keno Claims entry for more information.

NBMG Sample Site 1710 (a.k.a. Unnamed Shaft 066): (37.92302N by -114.0825W – USGS MRDS) (Gold, Silver, Fluorite, Barite)
USGS MRDS Data Base Record 10046507, Released February 1, 1984: The site of the NBMG Sample Site 1710 is shown at the above coordinates, placing it in the Eagle Valley Mining District, the Fay Mining District and in the area included on the USGS Deer Lodge Canyon 24K and Caliente 100K and 250K maps. The Public Land Survey System locators are the Northeast ¼ of the Northeast ¼ of Section 25, Township 1 North, Range 70 East. Gold and Silver are present and are shown as primary commodities with Fluorite and Barite secondary. The deposit is described as Tabular, striking North 30° East, dipping 75° Southeast and being about 4 feet wide. Mineralization includes Fluorite and Barite, with a gangue of Calcite and Quartz in a host of Latite. A prominent rib of banded, fissure and cockscomb Quartz, as a Vein, outcrops at the South end of a caved shaft. The entire rib is composed of several banded, Iron-stained, sub-parallel Quartz Veins which together form a total Vein outcrop width of 3 to 4 feet. Prismatic Comb Quartz forms the mid-portion of the Vein outcrop while massive to crudely banded white, Iron-stained Quartz makes up the rest of the Vein. Quartz, after Calcite laminae are common in the more massive, white Vein material. Latite host is sheared on both side of the Vein due to forcible intrusion of the Vein. Also some portions of the Vein appear Brecciated and re-cemented by Quartz. Massive to banded, prismatic to sugary, white Quartz Vein material from the dump contains Oxidized Pyrite and possibly minor Magnetite. Some clear to pink Fluorite, possibly inter-grown with Vein material or coating vugs is present. Also, some of the Vein material is heavy and may contain Barite. The area rock contains vugs and Iron-staining. NBMG Sample 1710 contained 150 Parts Per Million (PPM) Barite, 100PPM Manganese, 20PPM Lead and 7PPM Silver. The site was developed by a shaft, now caved and filled with debris to a depth of about 7 feet, and several small prospect pits in the general area. The geology, in the general area of the site, is described as Andesite and related rocks of intermediate composition. The Land Status, Ownership Category of this occurrence is unknown.
See the Unnamed Shaft 066 entry for more information.

NBMG Sample Site 1711: (37.92218N by -114.084W – USGS MRDS) (Gold Silver, Fluorite, Barite)
USGS MRDS Data Base Record 10046508, Released February 1, 1984: The site of the NBMG Sample Site 1711 is shown at 37.92218N by -114.08444W, placing it in the Eagle Valley Mining District, the Fay Mining District and in the area included on the USGS Deer Lodge Canyon 24K and Caliente 100K and 250K maps. The Public Land Survey System locators are the Northeast ¼ of the Northeast ¼ of Section 25, Township 1 North, Range 70 East. Gold and Silver in a host of Latite are present and are shown as primary commodities with Fluorite and Barite secondary. The ore body is described as a Tabular, sheeted Quartz Vein system, striking North-South, dipping 65° East and being about 10 feet thick. The Veins are composed of Comb or Prismatic Quartz and are sub-parallel in orientation and cut the host rock in a zone more than 10 feet wide. The main Vein is 1 to 3 feet wide with smaller sub-parallel Veins and Veinlets extending outward into the host. Typically the Veins are white and banded or form radiating or drusy encrustations on Silicified and bleached rock fragments. Most Veins have open centers or Iron-stained vugs. Calcite and Siderite inter-lenses compose almost half the Vein. Quartz, after Calcite pseudomorphs are very common. Several stages of Veining are evident. Some of the Vein material is Brecciated. The geology, in the general area of the site, is described as Andesite and related rocks of intermediate composition. The deposit was developed by a stope-shaft combination with several small prospects and workings. Some recent (1983) flagging has been done on the property. The Land Status, Ownership Category of this prospect is shown as "BLM Administrative Area".
See the Unnamed Shaft 067 entry for more information.

105

NBMG Sample Site 1712 (a.k.a. NBMG Sample Location 1712; Unnamed Shaft 073): (37.88247N by -114.1194W – USGS MRDS) (Gold, Silver)
USGS MRDS Data Base Record 10046509, Released February 1, 1984: The site of the NBMG Sample Location 1712 is shown at 37.88247N by -114.11944W, placing it in the Eagle Valley Mining District and in the area included on the USGS Deer Lodge Canyon 24K and Caliente 100K and 250K maps. The Public Land Survey System locators are in an unsurveyed area but are estimated as Section 2, Township 1 South, Range 70 East. Gold and Silver are present and are shown as primary commodities. Mineralization of this deposit includes Native Silver and Silver ores, Pyrite and Limonite and Quartz in a host of Rhyolite and Andesite. The deposit was developed by a single shaft, about 100 feet deep, and an old homestead on the property. NBMG Sample 1712 assayed 1,000 Parts Per Million (PPM) Strontium, 200PPM Manganese, 150PPM Barite, 50PPM Zirconium and 20PPM Lead. The geology, in the general area of the site, is described as Rhyolitic flows and shallow intrusive rocks. The Land Status, Ownership Category of this occurrence is unknown. There was no activity at the site when reviewed in 1983.
See the Unnamed Shaft 073 entry for more information.

NBMG Sample Site 1713 (a.k.a. NBMG Sample Location 1713; Tara Claims): (37.92913N by -114.637W – USGS MRDS) (Gold, Silver, Lead, Manganese)
See the Tara Claims entry for more information.

NBMG Sample Site 1718 (a.k.a. Jennie Mine): (37.53.56N by -114.02.58W - #3) (Gold, Silver, Lead, Copper)
USGS MRDS Data Base Record 10046535, Released February 1, 1984: A stope sample, taken in 1976, assayed a trace Gold and 0.2 ounces of Silver per ton. Sample 1718 contained 300 Parts Per Million (PPM) of Manganese, 200PPM Barite, 50PPM Zirconium, 30PPM Lead and 2 PPM Silver.
See the Jennie Mine entry for more information.

NBMG Sample Site 1719 (a.k.a. Thor Mine): (37.53.56N by -114.03.04W - #3) (Gold, Silver, Lead, Copper)
USGS MRDS Data Base Record 10098664, Released February 1, 1984: NBMG Sample 1719 assayed 300 Parts Per Million (PPM) Barite, 300PPM Manganese, 100PPM Strontium, 70PPM Zirconium, 50PPM Lead and 10PPM Silver.
See the Thor Mine entry for more information.

NBMG Sample Site 1720 (a.k.a. Snowflake Mine 002): (37.54.04N by -114.03.23W - #3) (Gold, Silver, Copper, Iron)
USGS MRDS Data Base Record 10037373, Released February 1, 1980; Updated September 1, 1984: NBMG Sample 1720 assayed at 500 Parts Per Million (PPM) Manganese, 200PPM Barite, 100PPM Strontium, 50PPM Lead and 10PPM Silver.
See the Snowflake Mine 002 entry for more information.

NBMG Sample Site 1721 (a.k.a. Big Buck Mine): (37.54.11N by -114.03.32W - #3) (Silver, Gold, Lead, Copper)
USGS MRDS Data Base Record 10046445, Released February 1, 1984: Sample 1721 was a 1-foot Vein sample which assayed 0.17 ounces of Gold (about 5.3 grams) and 0.3 ounces of Silver (about 9.3 grams) per ton along with 700 Parts Per Million (PPM) Barite, 300PPM Manganese, 200PPM Strontium, 200PPM Zirconium and 50PPM Lead.
See the Big Buck Mine entry for more information.

NBMG Sample Site 1723 (a.k.a. Pope Mine): (37.54.39N by -114.03.26W - #3) (Gold, Silver, Lead, Copper, Antimony, Fluorite)
USGS MRDS Data Base Record 10046512, Released February 1, 1984: The official NBMG Sample 1723 assayed 500 Parts Per Million (PPM) Manganese, 200PPM Beryllium, 100PPM Barite, 100PPM Strontium, 50PPM Lead, 50PPM Silver and 50PPM Zirconium. However, three other samples were noted in the file. These assayed 0.58, 0.27 and 0.63 ounces of Gold and 3.3, 1.1.and 1.9 ounces of Silver per ton.
See the Pope Mine entry for more information.

NBMG Sample Site 1724 (a.k.a. Redlite Claims; Redelite Claims;): (37.91025N by -114.051W – USGS MRDS) (Gold, Silver)
USGS MRDS Data Base Record 10100748, Released February 1, 1984: NBMG Sample 1724 assayed 500 Parts Per Million (PPM) Manganese, 200PPM Barite, 200PPM Strontium, 20PPM Lead and 2PPM Silver. Most other samples taken at the time showed no Silver. A sample from the second Vein back of the adit assayed 0.02 Troy Ounces of Gold per ton.
See the Redlite Claims entry for more information.

NBMG Sample Site 1725 (a.k.a. Fortuna and Helen Claims): (37.93607N by -114.087W – USGS MRDS) (Gold, Silver, Lead)
USGS MRDS Data Base Record 10046541, Released February 1, 1984: NBMG Sample assayed at 1,000 parts per million (PPM) Manganese, 200PPM Silver, 200PPM Strontium, 200PPM Barite, 100PPM Lead, 100PPM Molybdenum and 70PPM Zirconium.
See the Fortuna and Helen Claims entry for more information.

NBMG Sample Site 1726 (a.k.a. Iris84 09): (37.92329N by -114.07444W - MRDS) (Gold, Silver, Copper)
USGS MRDS Data Base Record 10037375, Released February 1, 1980; Updated September 1, 1984: Sample 1726 contains 300 Parts Per Million (PPM) Manganese, 300PPM Barite; 100PPM Strontium; 50PPM Zirconium; 20PPM Lead and 5PPM Silver.
See the Iris84 09 entry for more information.

NMBG Sample Site 1737 (a.k.a. Johnnie): (37.13.50N by -114.22.25W - #3) (Gold, Silver, Mercury, Barite)
USGS MRDS Data Base Record 10037361, Released February 1, 1980; December 1, 1984: Sample 1737 contained 500 Parts Per Million (PPM) Barite and 10PPM Silver.
See the Jonnie entry for more information.

NBMG Sample Sites 1743, 1744 (a.k.a. 100 Foot Incline): (37.30.46N by -114.47.10W - #3) (Gold, Copper, Silver, Nickel, Cobalt)
USGS MRDS Data Base Record 10037392, Released November 1, 1979; Updated August 1, 1984: Sample 1743 is interesting for the levels of Cobalt and Nickel found. It assayed over 20% Iron, 0.5% Manganese, 200 Parts Per Million (PPM), Vanadium, 100 PPM Cobalt, 100PPM Nickel, 100PPM Barite, 50PPM Copper, 20PPM Lead and no Gold or Silver.
Sample 1744 assayed 1.5% Iron, 300 PPM Lead, 100PPM Manganese, 100PPM Barite, 50PPM Vanadium, 15PPM Copper, 2PPM Silver with no Gold, Cobalt or Nickel.
See the 100 Foot Incline entry for more information.

NBMG Sample Site 1746 (a.k.a. NBMG Sample Location 1746; Unnamed Shaft 068): (37.4833N by -114.774W – USGS MRDS) (Gold, Silver, Lead, Zinc, Copper, Manganese, Barite)
USGS MRDS Data Base Record 10046501, Released January 1, 1984: The site of the NBMG Sample Location 1746 is shown at 37.4833N by -114.77362W, placing it in the Delamar Mining District and in the area included on the USGS Delamar 24K, Clover Mountains 100K and Caliente 250K maps. The Public Land Survey System locators are the Northwest ¼ of the Southwest ¼ of Section 25, Township 5 South, Range 64 East. Gold, Silver and Lead are present and are shown as primary commodities with Zinc, Copper and Manganese secondary and Barite tertiary. The ore body is described as Tabular Quartz Vein, striking North 75º East, dipping steeply Southeast and controlled by the Brecciation. Mineralization includes Pyrite, with a gangue of Quartz, in a host of Late Cambrian Pioche Shale. The site was developed by a shaft, of which the head frame has collapsed. Drill roads extend along the Northern flank of the knoll, which was occupied by the workings, into the saddle area and to the East of the prospects. Additional shafts were noted higher up the knoll. The area has been recently staked and there is evidence of surface and subsurface exploration within the last 3 or 4 years. Just North of the shaft collar, a Vein of vuggy, prismatic, Comb Quartz strikes North 75º East and dips steeply Southeast (this is identified elsewhere in the record as the ore body). This Vein is composed of several, splayed, sub-parallel, branching Veinlets, each less than 4 inches wide. However, if taken together with the intervening wall rock, the Veins comprise

a thickness of 2 to 3 feet. The Quartz Vein is vitreous and white, and, in some cases forms cockade structures around bleached, angular fragments of Shale. Some of the Shale fragments show an early stage of fine Quartz Veining which predates emplacement of the main Vein. The Shale fragments and enclosing wall rocks have responded to alteration by becoming more Micaceous and bleaching to a light tan or green color. Very fine-grained, Oxidized Pyrite is present in the Comb Quartz Vein and Quartz-cemented Shale Breccia. Manganese Oxides, including some crystalline Pyrolusite, are common as coatings of the Vein material. The Veins are vuggy and open centered. Iron Oxides, which are less abundant, are generally associated with the presence of Pyrite. NBMG Sample 1746 assayed 10,000 Parts Per Million (PPM), or 1% Lead, 5,000PPM Manganese, 2,000PPM Zinc, 500PPM Barite, 500PPM Strontium, 300PPM Silver, 200PPM Copper and 100PPM Vanadium. The geology, in the general area of the site, is described as Quartzite and minor amounts of Conglomerate, Phyllitic Siltstone, Limestone and Dolomite. The Land Status, Ownership Category of this occurrence is shown as "BLM Administrative Area".
See the Unnamed Shaft 068 entry for more information.

NBMG Sample Site 1747 (a.k.a. Magnolia Mine): (37.48275N by -114.776 – USGS MRDS) (Gold, Silver, Copper, Lead, Zinc, Bismuth, Arsenic)
USGS MRDS Data Base Record 10037390, Released November, 1, 1979; Updated August 1, 1984: NBMG Sample 1747 assayed at 3% Iron, 10,000 Parts Per Million (PPM) Lead, over 5,000 PPM Manganese, 2,000PPM Copper, 1,000PPM Zinc, 500PPM Strontium, 300PPM Silver, 200PPM Arsenic, 150PPM Vanadium, 100PPM Molybdenum and 100PPM Zirconium.
See the Magnolia Mine entry for more information.

NBMG Sample Site 1748 (a.k.a. NBMG Sample Location 1748; Unnamed Shaft 070): (37.46414N by -114.775W – USGS MRDS) (Gold, Silver, Iron)
USGS MRDS Data Base Record 10046502, Released February 1, 1984: The site of the NBMG Sample Location 1748 is shown at 37.46414N by -114.77501W, placing it in the Delamar Mining District and in the area included on the Delamar 24K, Clover Mountains 100K and Caliente 250K maps. The Public Land Survey System locators are the Southwest ¼ of the Southwest ¼ of Section 36, Township 5 South, Range 64 East. Gold and Silver are present and are shown as primary commodities with Iron tertiary in a roughly Tabular ore body controlled by the fault zone. Mineralization includes Pyrite, Sericite, Quartz and Clay associated with Rhyolite, Clay and mud. The geology, in the general area of the site, is described as Rhyolitic intrusive rocks. The intrusive rock on the dump is bleached, leached or shows slick or Argillic alteration. It contains abundant clots of Iron and "ghosts" after Pyrite. The intrusive forms knobby, white outcrops in the mine area. The deposit was developed by several shafts in an area along a dike. The shaft from which the sample was taken is about 20 feet deep. The sample 1748 (USGS Record shows it as Sample 7748) assayed at 1% Iron, 300 Parts Per Million (PPM) Manganese, 300PPM Strontium, 200PPM Barite, 150PPM Lead, 50PPM Zirconium and 5PPM Silver. There was no activity at the site when visited in 1983. The Land Status, Ownership Category of this occurrence is shown as "Private".
See the Unnamed Shaft 070 entry for more information.

NBMG Sample Sites 1751 and 1752 (a.k.a. April Fool): (37.27.45N by -114.45.30W - #3) (Gold, Silver, Copper, Bismuth, Antimony)
USGS MRDS Data Base Record 10037386, Released November 1, 1979; Updated August 1, 1984: This record was for a group of random and labeled assays. The location was shown as being on a ridge Northeast of Delamar at 37.46247N by -114.76556W. (Note: A mapping program shows these coordinates to be a tailings pile on the East side of a ridge, Northeast of the old town of Delamar.
A series of assays taken near the No. 1 Porphyry Dike generally gave values of 0.08 (about 2.5 grams) to .10 ounces of Gold and 0.4 to 5.6 ounces of Silver per ton. One assay, from the area, gave a reading of 0.55 ounces of Gold per ton.
An assay from the Goldcup workings gave 0.08 ounces of Gold (about 2.5 grams) and 11.03 ounces of Silver per ton, along with 1.16% Bismuth and 0.72% Antimony.
Some handpicked ore (or float), taken from near the surface in 1932, assayed 0.82 ounces of Gold and 2.7 ounces of Silver per ton. A similar selected surface sample, taken in 1933, assayed 2.6 ounces of Gold and 1.52 ounces of Silver per ton.

Sample NBMG 1751 assayed 2,000 parts per million (PPM) Barite, 1,000PPM, 700PPM Copper, 500PPM Lead, 300PPM Zirconium, 200PPM Arsenic, 200PPM Strontium, 100PPM Antimony, 100PPM Manganese, 50PPM Bismuth, 50PPM Molybdenum and 50PPM Silver.
Sample NBMG 1752 assayed 2,000 parts per million (PPM) Antimony, 500PPM Barite, 500PPM Copper, 200PPM Arsenic, 200PPM Bismuth, 150PPM Lead, 30PPM Silver, 20PPM Zirconium and 10PPM Gold.
See the April Fool entry for more information.

NBMG Sample Site 1753 (a.k.a. NBMG Sample Location 1753): (37.45941N by -114.765W – USGS MRDS) (Gold Silver, Copper, Lead, Antimony)
USGS MRDS Data Base Record 10097292, Released January 1, 1984: The site of the NBMG Sample Location 1753 is shown at 37.45941N by -114.76528W, placing it in the Delamar Mining District and in the area included on the USGS Delamar 24K, Clover Mountains 100K and Caliente 250K maps. The Public Land Survey System locators are Section 1, Township 6 South, Range 64 East. Gold, Silver and Copper are present and shown as primary commodities with Lead and Antimony tertiary. Mineralization includes Tetrahedrite, Pyrite, Limonite, Hematite and Quartz in a host of Late Cambrian, Prospect Mountain Quartzite. The ore body is Tabular and about 4 inches thick. The Quartzite is fractured and Veined by Quartz along a North 25° West orientation. Some Breccia was also observed. Material on the dump consists of Quartzite and Quartz-cemented Quartzite Breccia. Vuggy, open-centered Quartz Veins cut the Quartzite. Many of the Veins are about 1 inch wide and the Quartz is typically white to Vitreous grey. Vugs in the Vein are filled by Limonite and Hematite. Streaks and clots of very fine grained Sulfides occur in the Quartz. Clots of Tetrahedrite are common with rims Oxidized to Copper Oxides. Some sugary, dense Quartz Vein material contains abundant, finely-disseminated, un-Oxidized Pyrite. Chert pebble Conglomerate is seen as float on the road below the mine. The deposit was developed by several Northwest-trending adits and raises, which were found to be mostly caved upon inspection. One or some of these adits may be the lower access to the April Fool Mine. The area surrounding the old workings was drilled sometime between 1973 and 1978. This drill area connects into the drill area of the April Fool Mine. The dumps have recently (1982 or 1983) been trenched with a backhoe for 30 to 50-foot lengths and apparently sampled within the last year (1983). The geology, in the general area of the site, is described as Quartzite and minor amounts of Conglomerate, Phyllitic Siltstone, Limestone and Dolomite. The Land Status, Ownership Category of this prospect is shown as "Private".
See the Unnamed Adit Near the April Fool Mine 008 entry for more information.

NBMG Sample Site 1754 (a.k.a. Jumbo): (37.27.18N by -114.45.30W - #3) (Gold, Silver, Zinc, Lead, Copper, Barite)
See the Jumbo entry for more information.

NBMG Sample Site 1755 (a.k.a. Delamar Wash Workings): (37.27.24N by -114.46.10W - #3) (Gold, Silver, Lead, Copper)
USGS MRDS Data Base Record 10046495; Released January 1, 1984: The sample was taken from an open adit trending North 10° West; most of the rest of the workings were caved and could not be accessed.
Sample 1755 assayed 10% Iron, 500 parts per million (PPM) Antimony, 500PPM Barite, 100PPM Manganese, 100PPM Zirconium, 70PPM Vanadium, 50PPM Copper, 50PPM Lead and 2PPM Silver.
See the Delamar Wash Workings entry for more information.

NBMG Sample Sites 1756 & 1757 (a.k.a. Culverwell Mine 004): (37.47719N by -114.746W – USGS MRDS) (Gold, Silver, Copper, Zinc, Bismuth)
USGS MRDS Data Base Record 10037387, Released November 1, 1979; Updated August 1, 1984: Sample 1756 assayed 200 parts per million (PPM) Manganese. 200PPM Zinc, 150PPM Arsenic, 100PPM Zirconium, 30PPM Yttrium, 20PPM Lead and 7PPM Silver.
Sample 1757 assayed 300 parts per million (PPM) Manganese, 200PPM Zirconium, 100PPM Arsenic, 20PPM Lead, 10PPM Yttrium and 5PPM Silver.
See the Culverwell Mine 004 entry for more information.

NBMG Sample Site 1758 (a.k.a. Denton Summit Workings): (37.47691N by -114.716W – USGS MRDS) (Tungsten, Gold, Silver)
USGS MRDS Data Base Record 10046496, Released February 1, 1984: The sample was taken from the area East of a large Rhyolite outcrop. The sample assayed 20% Iron, 10% Calcium, 2,000 parts per million (PPM) Manganese, 500PPM Strontium, 200PPM Zirconium, 200PPM Barite, 100PPM Nickel, 100PPM Lead, 70PPM Yttrium, 20PPM Cobalt and 1PPM Silver. Although the sample showed no Tungsten, small flakes of, what is believed to be, Scheelite were seen when lamped.
See the Denton Summit Workings entry for more information.

NBMG Sample Site 1770 (a.k.a. Blue Bell Prospect): (39.00.28N by -115.42.05W - #3) (Fluorite, Gold)
USGS MRDS Data Base Record 10046525, Released August 1, 1983; Updated January 1, 1985: Sample 1770 was taken across the Vein and assayed detectable Gold. The Vein is within a highly Silicified, crystal-lithic Breccia that forms bold outcrops and cliffs on the West side of the Drainage. The assay of the NBMG Sample Site 1770 was not included in the record.
See the Blue Bell Prospect entry for more information.

NBMG Sample Site 1773: (38.00884N by -115.698W - USGS MRDS) (Gold)
USGS MRDS Data Base Record 10047168, Released January 1, 1985: The location of the NBMG Sample Site 1773 is shown at 38.00884N by -115.69781W, placing it ¼ mile East of the Blue Bell Prospect, as an outcrop in the middle of the road, in the Quinn Canyon Mining District and in the area included on the USGS Badger Gulch 24K, Quinn Canyon Range 100K and Lund 250K maps. The Public Land Survey System locators are the Northwest ¼ of Section 29, Township 2 North, Range 56 East. Gold, with a gangue of Quartz, in a host of Quartz Latite, is present and is shown as a primary commodity. Sample 1773 contained detectable Gold. The ore body is described as generally Tabular. A highly Silicified and Brecciated Vein strikes North 20° East, crossing the road to the Blue Bell Mine. The area surrounding the mine and road abounds in Silicified Breccia, the same material which forms prominent ridges locally. The geology, in the general area of the site, is described as welded and non-welded Silicic Ash-flow Tuffs. The Land Status, Ownership Category of this occurrence is shown as "National Forest".

NBMG Sample Site 3001 (a.k.a. April Fool Spring Trench): (37.53326N by -115.739W – USGS MRDS) (Gold)
See the April Fool Spring Trench entry for more information.

NBMG Sample Site 3014 and 3030 (a.k.a. Tram Workings): (37.40386N by -115.79697W – USGS MRDS) (Gold, Silver)
See the Tram Workings entry for more information.

NBMG Sample Site 3021 (a.k.a. Outcrop North of Radar Site): (37.54496N by -115.77197W – USGS MRDS) (Gold)
See the Outcrop North of Radar Site entry for more information.

NBMG Sample Sites 3026 and 3027 (a.k.a. B. W. Claims): (37.49356N by -115.738W – USGS MRDS) (Gold)
See the B. W. Claims entry for more information.

NBMG Sample Site 3030 and 3014 (a.k.a. Tram Workings): (37.40386N by -115.79697W – USGS MRDS) (Gold, Silver)
See the Tram Workings entry for more information.

NBMG Sample Sites 3031 and 3032 (a.k.a. Jumbo Claims): (37.42716N by -115.79807W – USGS MRDS) (Gold, Silver)
See the Jumbo Claims entry for more information.

NBMG Sample Sited 3035-3037 (a.k.a. Gold Butte Claims): (37.42056N by -115.802W – USGS MRDS) (Gold, Silver)
See the Gold Butte Claims entry for more information.

NBMG Sample Site 3048 (a.k.a. Sidewinder Prospect): (37.53856N by -115.77757W – USGS MRDS) (Gold, Silver)
See the Sidewinder Prospect entry for more information.

NBMG Sample Site 3049 (a.k.a. Blue Streak Prospect): (37.53826N by -115.778W – USGS MRDS) (Gold, Silver)
See the Blue Streak Prospect entry for more information.

NBMG Sample Site 3050 (a.k.a. Big Red Prospect Northwest): (37.53466N by -115.784W – USGS MRDS) (Gold, Silver)
See the Big Red Prospect Northwest entry for more information.

NBMG Sample Site 3051 (a.k.a. Big Red Prospect West): (37.53326N by -115.782W – USGS MRDS) (Silver, Gold)
See the Big Red Prospect West entry for more information.

NBMG Sample Site 3052 (a.k.a. Big Red Prospect): (37.53386N by -115.781W – USGS MRDS) (Gold, Silver)
See the Big Red Prospect entry for more information.

NBMG Sample Site 3054 (a.k.a. Gold Prospect 008): (37.39856N by -115.795W – USGS MRDS) (Gold, Silver, Lead)
See the Gold Prospect 008 entry for more information.

NBMG Sample Sites 3055-3057 (a.k.a. Chicago/Illinois/Wisconsin Claims): (37.39326N by -115.798W – USGS MRDS) (Gold, Silver)
See the Chicago/Illinois/Wisconsin Claims entry for more information.

NBMG Sample Site 3059 (a.k.a. Ridge Vein): (37.54716N by -115.77977W – USGS MRDS) (Gold)
See the Ridge Vein entry for more information.

NBMG Sample Sites 3060 (a.k.a. Jackson Mine): (37.32.53N by -115.45.33W - #3) (Lead, Zinc, Silver, Copper)
See the Jackson Mine entry for more information.

Nevada (a.k.a. Nevada Workings): (37.26.30N by -114.45.00W - #3) (Gold, Lead, Silver)
Coordinates are for the ore body of this underground, past producer. (Decimal Equivalents 37.441667N by -114.750W)

Nevada Des Moines: (37.56.02N by-114.26.52W - #3) (Silver, Zinc, Lead)
Coordinates are for the ore body of this underground, development deposit.

Nevada Lead (a.k.a. Fairview 002): (38.10.00N by -114.38.14W - #3) (Lead, Silver, Gold)
See the Fairview 002 entry for more information.

Nevada Rath Claims (a.k.a. Nevada Rath Claims Nos. 1-13): (38.27.15N by -114.16.26W - #3) (Uranium)
Coordinates are for the ore body of this surface operation.

Nevada Vein (a.k.a. Nevada): (37.45077N by -114.766W – USGS MRDS) (Gold, Silver, Lead)
USGS MRDS Data Base Record 10149665, Released January 10, 1994: The main entrance to the Nevada Vein is shown at 37.45077N by -114.76614W, placing it in the Delamar Mining District, Ferguson Mining District and in the area included on the USGS Delamar 24K, Clover Mountains 100K and Caliente 250K maps. The location accuracy, of these coordinates, is shown as +/- 10 meters. The Public Land Survey System locators are the Southeast ¼ of Section 1, Township 6 South, Range 64 East. Gold is present and is shown as a primary commodity with Silver and Lead tertiary. The geology, in the area of the main

entrance, is described as Quartzite and minor amounts of Conglomerate, Phyllitic Siltstone, Limestone and Dolomite. The Land Status, Ownership Category of this underground, past producer is shown as "BLM Administrative Area".

New Tempiute Mine (a.k.a. Emerson Mine; NBMG Sample Sites 1452 through 1454; Phylis Claim; Rae Ella Claim;): (37.63079N by -115.629W – USGS MRDS) (Tungsten, Silver, Zinc, Bismuth, Fluorite)
USGS MRDS Data Base Record 10046523, Released March 1, 1984: The site of the New Tempiute Mine is shown at 37.63079N by -115.62893W, placing it in the Tempiute Mining District and in the area included on the USGS Tempiute Mountain North 24K, Tempahute Range 100K and Caliente 250K maps. This mine represents the Southern-most workings of Union Carbide's property at Tempiute. The area is unsurveyed, but the projected Public Land Survey System locators are Section 6, Township 4 South, Range 57 East. Tungsten, Silver, Zinc and Fluorite are present and are shown as primary commodities with Bismuth tertiary. Mineralization of this Tungsten Skarn Deposit includes Scheelite, Sphalerite, Bismuthite, Chalcopyrite and Fluorite with a gangue of Pyrite, Siderite and other Iron minerals; Garnet, Wollastonite, Tremolite, Nontronite, Calcite and Quartz, in a host of Black Shale, Carbonate rock and Limestone and is associated with Mississippian to Pliocene age Granite. The ore body is along the Igneous contact, where there are intersecting high and low-angle faults, striking Northwest and Southwest. It is exposed on the face of the open pit, where the shearing is parallel to the bedding. The Skarn zone, of which only minor remnants remain, is exposed along 3 to 5 benches. On the East and West sides, tongues of the Granite Body extend into the Limestone unit and are Argillically altered, bleached and heavily iron-stained with Limestone-Hornfels along the contact. Skarn materials include Garnet, Pyrite, Bismuthite, Pyrrhotite, Chalcopyrite, Sphalerite, Fluorite, Calcite and Wollastonite. The Iron-rich Sulfides are altered to a greenish, Clayey material, resembling Nontronite. The Western edge of the Skarn zone is more Gossany, Limonite-stained, exhibits a greater degree of Hydrothermal alteration and contains much Slag-like material. A massive, white Quartz Vein, with abundant open spaces, carries Oxidized Pyrite grains and "ghosts", and cuts both the Skarn zone and the Limestone. Very fine Tremolite crystals are inter-grown in the Limestone. Massive Veins and Clots, up to several feet wide, of crystalline Calcite, Siderite and/or Mangano-Siderite occur in the Limestone. Locally the Limestone is Silicified near and adjacent to the Quartz Veins. Workings East of the open pit, near the saddle, include another small, rather deep and narrow open pit which excavated ore along the contact of the intrusive and the Skarn zone. Development included the above-mentioned pit, which is narrow and fairly deep, and either an adit or a cave. No production was taking place at the time of the examination in 1983, but it was apparent that development work, such as blasting, was being continued. The geology, in the pit area is described as Shale, Siltstone, Sandstone, Chert-pebble Conglomerate and Limestone. The Land Status, Ownership Category of this past producer is shown as "BLM Administrative Area".
USGS MRDS Data Base Record 10125114, Released January 27, 1994: The pit area of the New Tempiute Mine is shown at 37.63076N by -115.62897W. The location accuracy, of these coordinates, is shown as +/- 100 meters. The Public Land Survey System locators are Section 6, Township 4 South, Range 57 East, extending into, or having a second location in Section 1, Township 4 South, Range 56 East. This record shows Tungsten present and as a primary commodity with Silver, Zinc, Molybdenum, Bismuth and Fluorite tertiary. The ore body is described as a Tabular Replacement of Contact Metasomatic origin. The geology, in the pit area, is described as Shale, Siltstone, Sandstone, Chert-pebble Conglomerate and Limestone. The Land Status, Ownership Category of this surface-underground, past producer is shown as "Private", with Mineral Rights held through "Patented Claims". A 1992 record shows the Owner-Operator as the Minerals Division of the Union Carbide Corporation.
See the NBMG Sample Sites 1452 through 1454 entry for more information.

Newport Mine: (37.55.18N by -114.28.08W - #3) (Gold, Silver, Lead)
Coordinates are for the ore body of this past producer.
USGS MRDS Data Base Record 10046377, Released May 1, 1984: The site of the Newport Mine is shown at 37.92079N by -114.47084W, placing it in the Pioche Mining District and in the area included on the USGS Pioche 24K and Caliente 100K and 250K maps. The Public Land Survey System locators are the Northeast ¼ of Section 28, Township 1 North, Range 67 East. Gold, Silver and Lead are present and are shown as primary commodities. The geology, in the general area of the site, is described as Limestone and Dolomite with locally-thick sequences of Shale and Siltstone. The Land Status, Ownership Category of this occurrence is shown as "BLM Administrative Area".

USGS MRDS Data Base Record 10198085, Released January 10, 1994: The main entrance to the Newport Mine is shown at 37.92136N by -114.47024W, placing it in the Pioche Mining District. The location accuracy, of these coordinates, is shown as +/- 100 meters. The Public Land Survey System locators are the Southeast ¼ of the Northwest ¼ of the Northeast ¼ of Section 28, Township 1 North, Range 67 East. Gold is shown as present and as a primary commodity with Silver tertiary. The geology, in the area of the main entrance, is described as Limestone and Dolomite with locally-thick sequences of Shale and Siltstone. The Land Status, Ownership Category of this occurrence is shown as "Private".

Newport Nevada (a.k.a. Newport-Nevada Property): (37.54.59N by -114.04.16W - #3) (Gold, Silver)
Coordinates are for the ore body of this underground, past producer.
See the Utah Spur Mine entry for more information.

Nickel Group (a.k.a. Silver Horn): (38.09.30N by -114.41.47W - #3) (Silver, Lead, Gold, Nickel)
See the Silver Horn entry for more information.

No. 1 Mine: (37.55.20N by -114.27.47W - #3)
Coordinates are for an ore body.
See the Combined Metals No. 1 Mine entry for more information.

No. 2 Patented Claim (a.k.a. Groom Mine): (37.20.45N by -115.46.03W - #3) (Silver, Lead, Zinc, Copper, Gold, Barite)
See the Groom entry for more information.

No. 10 Mine: (37.56.25N by -114.28.21W - #3) (Gold, Silver, Lead)
Coordinates are for an ore body.

Non Pareil: (37.52.35N by -114.37.00W - #3) (Gold, Silver)
Coordinates are for an ore body.

North Extension of the Blue Mary Claim (a.k.a. Blue Mary Claim North Extension): (37.69327N by -114.522W – USGS MRDS) (Gold)
See the Blue Mary Claim North Extension entry for more information.

North Pole Tunnel: (37.55.15N by -114.26.42W - #3)
Coordinates are for the main entrance to this underground operation.

North Section 34 Prospect (a.k.a. Jackson Mine): (37.32.53N by -115.45.33W - #3) (Lead, Zinc, Silver, Copper)
See the Jackson Mine entry for more information.

North Tem Piute (a.k.a. Rae Ella; Schofield; Y-Z): (37.37.53N by -115.37.37W - #3) (Tungsten, Silver, Zinc, Lead, Molybdenum, Fluorite)
Coordinates are for the main entrance to this underground, past producer.
USGS MRDS Data Base Record 10270988, Released January 10, 1994: The main entrance to the North Tem Piute Mine is shown at 37.63416N by -115.63167W, placing it in the Tem Piute Mining District and in the area included on the USGS Tempiute Mountain North 24K, Timpahute Range 100K and Caliente 250K maps. The Public Land Survey System locators are the Northeast ¼ of Section 1, Township 4 South, Range 56 East. Tungsten is present and is shown as a primary commodity with Molybdenum, Silver, Lead, Zinc and Fluorite tertiary. First production of the mine is shown in 1941, likely in conjunction with the effort to develop critical minerals for the World War 2 effort. The geology, in the area of the main entrance, is described as Shale, Siltstone, Sandstone, Chert-pebble Conglomerate and Limestone. The Land Status, Ownership Category of this underground, past producer, which was discovered in 1928, is shown as "BLM Administrative Area".
See the Schofield Mine entry for more information.

<u>Ohio-Kentucky</u>:
See Prince Consolidated, *Goodwin's Weekly, November 23, 1912* article for more information.

<u>Old Boundary</u>:
Nevada Historical Marker #57; On U.S. Highway 93, Thirty Miles South of Alamo, Nevada: "The 37th degree North latitude is marked at this point as the dividing line between the territories of Utah and New Mexico under the provisions of the Compromise of 1850 which originally organized the land ceded by Mexico in 1848.
When the Territory of Nevada was carved from Western Utah in 1861, this line became the Southern boundary of the new Territory and continued to serve as such when the Territory and State were enlarged by extensions to the east in 1862 and 1866 respectively.
In 1867, the Nevada legislature approved the action of Congress to add that portion of the Territory of Arizona which lay to the South of this line, West of the 114 West longitude and the Colorado River, and to the East of the boundary of California. This action, taken on January 18, 1867, gave the state of Nevada the permanent boundaries as they are today."

<u>Old Democrat (a.k.a. Advance Claim; Caliente Cobalt Mining Company; Coalition Mines Company; Gold Stake Claim; NBMG Sample Site 1443)</u>: (37.41.36N by -114.31.45W - #3) (Gold, Silver, Zinc, Lead, Copper, Manganese, Cadmium, Uranium, Iron, Arsenic, Zirconium)
Coordinates are for the ore body of this underground, past producer.
USGS MRDS Data Base Record 10037356, Released February 1, 1980; Updated August 1, 1984: The site of the Old Democrat Mine is shown at 37.69386N by -114.5239W, placing it about 0.8 miles Northeast of the Comet Mine, at the mouth of Peaslee Canyon, in the Chief Mining District and in the area included on the USGS Chief Mountain 24K and Caliente 100K and 250K maps. The Public Land Survey System locators are the Northwest ¼ of the Northwest ¼ of the Southwest ¼ of Section 18, Township 3 South, Range 67 East. Silver, Lead and Zinc are present and are shown as primary commodities with Copper secondary and Antimony, Tin, Cadmium, Manganese, Zirconium and Arsenic tertiary. Mineralization of this Polymetallic Replacement Deposit (USGS Model Code 19a) includes Galena, Sphalerite, Pyrolusite, Psilomelane and Manganite, with a gangue of Pyrite, Lepidocrocite (Iron Oxide Hydroxide), Goethite and Clay, in a host of Pioche Limestone, associated with Late Cambrian Shale, Siltstone and Lamprophyre. Here muddy brown, Micaceous Siltstones and Shales overlie the Limestone beds which strike North-South and dip 8° to 15° East. There is a local fault, striking North 18° West about 400 feet from the portal. Host rocks show some Iron-Manganese Veining and bleaching effects. The ore body is described as Tabular to Irregular and strikes South 25° East, dips vertically, is exposed at the surface and is controlled by fractures and gouge zones. An exploration, incline shaft was driven North 75° West to North 82° West, although when visited in 1983, it had caved and could not be explored. Nerco was doing assessment work at the site. There were several old structures and a moderate dump also on the property. A 1932 study indicated the average grade of ore remaining to be 1.0% Lead and 0.89 ounces of Gold and 8 ounces of Silver per ton. The geology, in the general area of the site, is described as Quartzite and minor amounts of Conglomerate, Phyllitic Siltstone, Limestone and Dolomite. The Land Status, Ownership Category of this past producer is unknown. A 1983 record shows the Operator as Nerco.
USGS MRDS Data Base Record 10198165, Released January 21, 1994: The main entrance to the Old Democrat Mine is shown at 37.69187N by -114.52444W. The location accuracy, of these coordinates, is shown as +/- 10 meters. The Public Land Survey System locators are the Northwest ¼ of the Northeast ¼ of Section 18, Township 3 South, Range 67 East. Gold is present and is shown as a primary commodity with Silver, Lead, Zinc, Copper and Uranium tertiary. The geology, in the area of the main entrance, is described as Quartzite and minor amounts of Conglomerate, Phyllitic Siltstone, Limestone and Dolomite. The Land Status, Ownership Category of this underground, past producer is shown as "Private". Mineral Rights are held as "Patented, Located Claims". A 1936 record shows the 100% Owner-Operator as the Caliente Cobalt Mining Company of Nevada.
See the Advance and NBMG Sample Site 1443 entries for more information.

<u>Old Tem Piute (a.k.a. Tem Piute Mine)</u>: (37.35.58N by -115.39.01W - #3) (Lead, Silver, Antimony, Copper, Arsenic)
See the Tem Piute Mine entry for more information.

Old Timer Mine (a.k.a. Oldtimer Mine; True Racket Group): (37.56.11N by -114.29.14W - #3) (Gold, Silver, Zinc, Lead, Copper)
Coordinates are for the ore body of this past producer.
USGS MRDS Data Base Record 10046378, Released May 1, 1984: The site of the Oldtimer Mine is shown at 37.9369N by -114.48751W, placing it in the Pioche Mining District and in the area included on the USGS Pioche 24K and Caliente 100K and 250K maps. The Public Land Survey System locators are the Northeast ¼ of Section 20, Township 1 North, Range 67 East. Gold, Silver and Lead are present and are shown as primary commodities. Mineralization is primarily Galena, in a host of Late Cambrian Chisholm Shale. It is estimated that ore deposition was controlled by a bedding plane fault which trended North 40° East and dipped to the Southeast. The deposit was developed by 3 adits. The Land Status, Ownership Category of this past producer is unknown.
Note: This mine is often mixed up with the Chisolm Mine, which is about 350 yards to the South-Southeast.
USGS MRDS Data Base Record 10270851, Released January 10, 1994: The main entrance to the Old Timer Mine is shown at 37.93686N by -114.48754W, placing it in the Pioche Mining District and in the area included on the USGS Pioche 24K and Caliente 100K and 250K maps. The location accuracy, of these coordinates, is shown as +/- 10 meters. The Public Land Survey System locators are the Northern ½ of the Northeast ¼ of Section 20, Township 1 North, Range 67 East. This record shows that Gold is present and is a primary commodity with Silver, Lead, Zinc and Copper tertiary. The geology, in the area of the main entrance, is described as Limestone and Dolomite with locally thick sequences of Shale and Siltstone. The Land Status, Ownership Category of this underground, past producer is unknown.

Old Times (a.k.a. Chisholm): (37.56.02N by -114.29.08W - #3) (Lead, Silver, Gold)
See the Chisholm entry for more information.

On Winner No. 2 Patented Claim (a.k.a. Big Buck Mine): (37.54.11N by -114.03.32W - #3) (Silver, Gold, Lead, Copper)
See the Big Buck Mine entry for more information.

Ora Lovell: (37.39.27N by -115.22.33W - #3) (Silver, Lead, Copper)
Coordinates are for the ore body of this underground, past producer.

Original Cave Group (a.k.a. Cave Valley Mine 002): (38.38.39N by -114.47.49W - #3) (Lead, Silver, Copper, Zinc, Gold, Vanadium, Arsenic, Clay)
See the Cave Valley Mine 002 entry for more information.

O. S. L. Mine (a.k.a. Red Cloud Claim): (38.08302N by -114.611W – USGS MRDS) (Silver, Copper, Lead, Zinc, Tungsten, Iron)
USGS MRDS Data Base Record 10047178, Released January 1, 1985: The site of the O. S. L. Mine is shown at 38.08302N by -114.6114W, placing it at the head of a gulch, about 300 feet South 65° West and about 100 feet below the collar of the Hillside shaft, in the Bristol-Jackrabbit Mining District and in the area included on the USGS Bristol Range SE 24K, Wilson Creek Range 100K and Lund 250K maps. Silver and Copper are present and are shown as primary commodities with Iron secondary and Lead tertiary. Mineralization includes Copper minerals and Galena in a host of Late Cambrian Limestone. The Irregular ore body lies along the May Day fissure at the intersection with a strong North-South fissure, with the ore occurring as replacement bodies. The deposit was developed by a 150-foot inclined shaft with lateral stoping run from it, which produced a reported several thousand tons of ore. The geology, in the general area of the site, is described as Limestone and Dolomite with locally thick sequences of Shale and Siltstone. The Land Status, Ownership Category of this underground, past producer, is shown as "BLM Administrative Area".

Outcrop North of Radar Site (a.k.a. NBMG Sample Site 3021): (37.54496N by -11577197W – USGS MRDS) (Gold)
USGS MRDS Data Base Record 10295544, Released January 24, 1997: The ore body of the Outcrop North of the Radar Site is shown at 37.54496N by -115.77197W, placing it in the Don Dale Mining District and in the area included on the USGS White Blotch Springs SE 24K, Timpahute Range 100K and Caliente

250K maps. The location accuracy, of these coordinates, is shown as +/- 500 meters. The Public Land Survey System locators are Section 6, Township 3 South, Range 55+ East. Gold is present in a deposit of Hydrated, Iron Oxides. The ore body is a Tabular, Fissure Vein of Hydrothermal Origin. The geology, in the area of the ore body, is described as Quartzite and minor amounts of Conglomerate, Phyllitic Siltstone, Limestone and Dolomite. The Land Status, Ownership Category of this surface occurrence is shown as "Military Reservation".

Our Boys In Blue Claims (a.k.a. 100 Foot Incline): (37.30.46N by -114.47.10W - #3) (Gold, Copper, Silver)
See the 100 Foot Incline entry for more information.

Pacific Tunnel: (37.55.31N by -114.26.36W – #3) (Gold, Silver, Lead, Zinc, Copper)
Coordinates are for the main entrance to this underground, past producer.
USGS MRDS Data Base Record 10046379, Released May 1, 1974: The site of the Pacific Tunnel is shown at 37.92524N by -114.44417W, placing it in the Pioche Mining District and in the area included on the USGS Pioche 24K and Caliente 100K and 250K maps. The Public Land Survey System locators are the Southwest ¼ of the Southwest ¼ of Section 23, Township 1 North, Range 67 East. Gold, Silver and Lead are shown as present and all as primary commodities. Mineralization of this Tabular deposit, which is up to 20 feet wide, includes Galena with a gangue of Quartz in a host of Prospect Mountain Quartzite, associated with Late Cambrian Plutonic rock. This ore body, which is controlled by the Yuba Dike, assayed 50% Lead and 200 to 300 ounces of Silver per ton and $20 to $30 in Gold, at then-current prices. The Yuba Dike was intersected and crosscut. A 4-foot to 5-foot shoot of milling ore was found. The East end of the drift on the dike is at the 150-foot station of the shaft of the Mascot Silver Mining Company, the successor of the Boston-Pioche Mining Company. In this part of the dike it was reported that an ore shoot was found that was 100 feet long and 2 to 3 feet thick. It contained ore that ran 57% Lead, 157 Troy Ounces of Silver and about $10 per ton in Gold (1932 period values). This ore was found by following a Quartzite fissure Vein into the Porphyry. The geology, in the general area of the site, is described as Quartzite and minor amounts of Conglomerate, Phyllitic Siltstone, Limestone and Dolomite. The Land Status, Ownership Category of this underground, past producer, with about 1,200 linear feet of horizontal underground workings, is shown as "Private".
USGS MRDS Data Base Record 10149829, Released January 10, 1994: The main entrance to the Pacific Tunnel is shown at 37.92526N by -114.44414W, placing it in the Pioche Mining District. The location accuracy, of these coordinates, is shown as +/- 10 meters. This record shows Gold present and as a primary commodity with Silver, Lead, Zinc and Copper tertiary. The geology, in the area of the main entrance, is described as Quartzite and minor amounts of Conglomerate, Phyllitic Siltstone, Limestone and Dolomite. The Land Status, Ownership Category of this underground, past producer is shown as "Private".

Pahranagat Mining District (a.k.a. Pahranagat Lake Mining District; Boomerang Mining District; Crescent Mining District; Hiko Mining District; Irish Mountain Mining District): (Silver, Lead, Copper, Manganese)
Description of the District:
Tingley, Joseph V.; "Mining Districts of Nevada"; Nevada Bureau of Mines and Geology, Report 47, Second Edition; 1998; Page 166: Discovered and organized in 1865, the Pahranagat Mining District is located in the Mount Irish Mountain Range, about 10 miles Northwest of Hiko, in the Silver Canyon area. As established, the District had the Pahranagat (only) name; however, it is also widely referred to as the Pahranagat Lake Mining District. Alternate names include the Hiko Mining District, referring to the nearest settlement of any significance or the Irish Mountain Mining District after the 8,625-foot Mount Irish, located at 37.38.39N by -115.24.06W – USGS Mount Irish 24K map. In 1871 there was also a Crescent Spring Mining District around Crescent Spring, which had been cut out of the Pahranagat Mining District. The Crescent Spring District only lasted a short time and was reabsorbed into the Pahranagat Mining District. A final alternate name, which has come up in history, is the Boomerang Mining District. This came from an article in the September 15, 1902, *Nevada Miner*, that mentioned a Boomerang Mining District in the area of Crescent Spring. This would have put it, by default, in the area later reverting to the Pahranagat Mining District.
Mines Included in the District:
        Crescent 001 (Gold, Silver, Lead)

Lost Treasure Mine (Silver)

Pahranagat Valley:
Nevada Historical Marker #38; On U.S. Highway 93 at Alamo Junction: "The rolling stones of
Pahranagat," a hoax article on magnetic currents written in 1862 by Dan De Quille of the Territorial
Enterprise made this valley world famous. Three local springs fill its lakes and irrigate its fields.
The Crystal Spring area, used as a watering spot and campsite, was a principal stopover on the Mormon
trail alternate route. In the late 1850s, this area was a haven for outlaws who pastured hundreds of head of
stolen cattle in its meadows. Although named as the provisional county seat in 1866, no significant town
was built here.
Ore was discovered in 1865 on Mount Irish, and Logan City sprang briefly into existence. A stamp mill
was established at Hiko in 1866 to crush the ore, and it became the center of activity for the valley when it
became the county seat in 1867. It was the largest community in Lincoln County until local mining
declined and Pioche claimed the county seat in 1871.
Alamo, established in 1900 is the valley's largest present-day settlement. The area now includes several
ranches and the Pahranagat Valley National Wildlife Refuge."

Pan American Mine: (37.52.16N by -114.36.19W - #3) (Zinc, Lead, Silver, Gold, Copper, Manganese,
Iron, Barite)
Coordinates are for the main entrance to this underground, past producer.

Panaca (town):
Nevada Historical Marker #39; On State Route 319 at Panaca Firehouse: Southern Nevada's first
permanent settlement was settled as a Mormon colony by Francis C. Lee and others in 1864. Poor in
resources, but rich in people, Panaca has changed little through the years. Although mining at nearby
Bullionville and Pioche has had its effect, Panaca remains an agricultural community.
The post office was established in 1867, moved to Bullionville in 1874, and returned in 1879. During the
1870s coke ovens produced charcoal here for the smelters at Bullionville.
Originally located in Washington County, Utah, Panaca became part of Nevada by an act of Congress,
dated May 5, 1866. As the boundary was not then surveyed, a dispute arose over taxes levied by Lincoln
County, Nevada. The matter settled in favor of the Panaca citizenry on December 4, 1871, after a long
period of bitter litigation."

Panaca Diatomaceous Earth: (37.48.05N by -114.21.40W - #3) (Diatomite)
Coordinates are for the ore body of this underground, past producer.

Panaca Ilmenite Placers: 37.47.22N by -114.3000W - #3) (Titanium)
Coordinates are for a placer ore body.

Panaca Mining District (a.k.a. Chief Mining District; Lost Mining District): (Gold, Silver, Lead,
Copper, Vanadium, Titanium, Uranium)
Description of the District:
*Tingley, Joseph V.; "Mining Districts of Nevada"; Nevada Bureau of Mines and Geology, Report 47,
Second Edition; 1998; Page 54*: In his 1962 *Directory of Southern Nevada Place Names,* W. R. Averett
indicated the Cobalt Mining District and the Panaca Mining District as alternate names for the Chief
Mining District, although where these names came from was not indicated.
*Tingley, Joseph V.; "Mining Districts of Nevada"; Nevada Bureau of Mines and Geology, Report 47,
Second Edition; 1998; Page 168*: The Panaca Mining District was established to include the scattered
Uranium occurrences which lie to the East and Southeast of Panaca. On the 1880 version of the Land
Office Map, there was a reference to a Lost Mining District in what would be the Eastern part of the current
Panaca Mining District, but the reference was not shown in later versions.
See the Chief Mining District entry for more information:
Mines Included in the District:

Panaglass Nos. 1-18 Claims; (37.50.54N by -114.25.47W - #3)
Coordinates are for the claim area of this surface prospect.

Panorama Claim (a.k.a. Groom Mine): (37.20.45N by -115.46.03W - #3) (Silver, Lead, Zinc, Copper, Gold, Barite)
See the Groom entry for more information.

Papoose Mining District (a.k.a. Papoose Mining Area): (Lead, Silver, Gold, Copper)
Description of the District:
Tingley, Joseph V.; "Mining Districts of Nevada"; Nevada Bureau of Mines and Geology, Report 47, Second Edition; 1998; Page 169: Discovered in 1909 and active from 1916 to about 1937, The Papoose Mining District includes the entire Papoose Mountain Range between Papoose Lake at the South end of Emigrant Valley and Groom Lake, or Area 51, which lies on the Northeastern side of the Papoose Mountains. Approximately the Southern 2/3 of the Papoose Range is in the Desert Wildlife Refuge.
Mines Included in the District

Patterson Mining District (a.k.a. Patterson Pass Mining District; Cave Valley Mining District): (Gold, Silver, Lead, Copper, Vanadium, Zinc, Tungsten, Molybdenum, Manganese, Fluorite)
Description of the District:
Tingley, Joseph V.; "Mining Districts of Nevada"; Nevada Bureau of Mines and Geology, Report 47, Second Edition; 1998; Page 51: The Cave Valley Mining District is often included with the Patterson Mining District, which borders it on the East.
See the Cave Valley Mining District entry for more information.
Mines Included in the District:
        AD Prospect (Tungsten, Zinc, Gold, Silver, Molybdenum, Lead, Fluorite)
        Cave Valley Mine 002 (Lead, Silver, Copper, Zinc, Gold, Vanadium, Arsenic, Clay)
        Cinch Mine (Tungsten, Gold, Silver)
        Eagle Rock (Antimony, Lead, Zinc, Copper, Tungsten, Silver, Manganese, Iron, Gold)
        Geyser Mine (Tungsten, Gold, Silver, Fluorite)
        Pip (Tungsten, Gold, Silver)
        Schwartz Tunnel (Tungsten, Zinc, Gold, Silver, Molybdenum, Lead, Fluorite)

Patterson Pass Prospect: (38.35.48N by -114.43.50W - #3) (Silver, Lead, Tungsten)
Coordinates are for the main entrance to this surface-underground, exploration prospect.
USGS MRDS Data Base Record 10149679, Released June 14, 1993: The main entrance to the Patterson Pass Prospect is shown at 38.59665N by -114.73145W, placing it in the area included on the USGS Milk Ranch Spring 24K, Garrison 100K and Lund 250K maps. The Public Land Survey System locators are the Western ½ of Section 31, Township 9 North, Range 65 East. Silver is present and is shown as a primary commodity with Tungsten and Lead tertiary. The geology, in the area of the main entrance, is described as Limestone and Dolomite with locally thick sequences of Shale and Siltstone. The Land Status, Ownership Category of this surface-underground prospect is shown as "BLM Administrative Area".

Pay Zone Claim: (37.47.30N by -114.22.45W - #3) (Uranium)
Coordinates are for an ore body.

Peak Claims (Nos. 1-12): (37.57.46N by -114.03.00W - #3) (Uranium)
Coordinates are for the ore body of this prospect.

Peggy Lee: (37.31.55N by -114.47.00W - #3) (Zinc)
Coordinates are for the ore body of this prospect.

Pennsylvania Mine (a.k.a. Pennsylvania Copper Mine; Caliente Prospect; Hope Prospect):
(37.24.37N by -114.29.31W - #3) (Copper, Gold, Silver, Lead, Zinc)
Coordinates are for the pit area of this surface-underground, past producer.
USGS MRDS Data Base Record 10149684, Released March 28, 1997: The pit area of the Pennsylvania Mine is shown at 37.41027N by -114.49273W, placing it in the Pennsylvania Mining District and in the area included on the USGS Ella Mountain 24K, Clover Mountain 100K and Caliente 250K maps. The Public Land Survey System locators are Section 22, Township 6 South, Range 67 East. Copper is present

and is shown as a primary commodity with Gold, Silver, Lead and Zinc tertiary. The geology, in the Pit area, is described as Andesite and related rocks of intermediate composition. The Land Status, Ownership Category of this surface-underground, past producer is shown as "BLM Administrative Area". See the Caliente Prospects entry for more information.

Pennsylvania Mining District: (Gold, Silver, Copper, Tungsten, Iron)
Description of the District:
Tingley, Joseph V.; "Mining Districts of Nevada"; Nevada Bureau of Mines and Geology, Report 47, Second Edition; 1998; Page 171: The Pennsylvania Mining District, discovered in 1867, is near the head of Pennsylvania Canyon on the Southwestern Flank of the Clover Mountains. The Clover Mountains are the range of mountains between Meadow Valley and Clover Valley.
Mines Included in the District:
       Culverwell 002 (Silver, Copper, Tungsten, Gold, Iron)
       Culverwell Mine 005 (Gold, Silver, Copper, Tungsten, Lead)
       Pennsylvania Mine (Copper, Gold, Silver, Lead, Zinc)

Peppers 1, 2, 3: (37.55.42N by -114.32.10W - #3) (Manganese, Gold, Silver, Lead)
Coordinates are for an ore body.
USGS MRDS Data Base Record 10125340, Released March 20, 1985: The estimated location of the ore body of the Peppers 1, 2, 3, is shown at 37.93326N by -114.54664W, placing it about 10 miles out of Pioche, about 1½ miles from Wheeler Ranch, in the Highland Mining District and in the Highland Peak 24K and Caliente 100K and 250K maps. The location accuracy, of these coordinates, is shown as +/- 5,000 meters. The Public Land Survey System locators are Township 1 North, Range 66 East. Manganese is present and is shown as a primary commodity with Gold, Silver and Lead tertiary. The geology, in the area of the ore body, is described as Limestone and Dolomite with locally-thick sequences of Shale and Siltstone. The Land Status, Ownership Category of this surface prospect is unknown.

Perkins Barite Prospect: (36.58.20N by -114.17.57W - #3) (Barite)
Coordinates are for the main entrance to this underground, exploration prospect.

Perlite Deposit 001: (38.32.27N by -114.43.13W - #3) (Perlite)
Coordinates are for a deposit area.

Perlite Deposit 002: (38.07.15N by -114.23.00W - #3) (Perlite)
Coordinates are for a deposit area.

Perlite Deposit 003: (37.37.46N by -114.06.30W - #3) (Perlite)
Coordinates are for a deposit area.

Perlite Deposit 004: (37.30.55N by -114.13.27W - #3) (Perlite)
Coordinates are for a deposit area.

Perlite Deposit 005: (37.31.00N by -114.12.13W - #3) (Perlite)
Coordinates are for a deposit area.

Perlite Deposit 006: (37.26.27N by -114.38.30W - #3) (Perlite)
Coordinates are for a deposit area.

Phylis (a.k.a. Schofield Mine): (37.63218N by -115.624W – USGS MRDS) (Tungsten, Molybdenum, Zinc, Fluorite)
USGS MRDS Data Base Record 10107653, Released January 1, 1980; Updated August 1, 1984; Updated and Edited June 9, 1995: This was an alternate name for the Schofield Mine.
See the New Tempiute and Schofield Mine entries for more information.

Pike's Diggings Mining District (a.k.a. Eagle Valley Mining District): (Gold, Silver, Lead, Uranium, Pearlite)
Description of the District:
Tingley, Joseph V.; "Mining Districts of Nevada"; Nevada Bureau of Mines and Geology, Report 47, Second Edition; 1998; Page 79: Near the village of Fay (37.54.29N by -114.04.12W – USGS Deer Lodge Canyon 24K map) was the Pike's Diggings Mining District, which was in operation from 1898 to about 1905.The location described would place it in the modern Eagle Valley Mining District area.
See the Eagle Valley Mining District entry for more information.
Mines Included in the District:

Pink Hills Alunite: (37.45.00N by -114.30.00W - #3) (Aluminum)
Coordinates are for an ore body.

Pioche (town):
Deseret Evening News (Great Salt Lake City, Utah); December 31, 1910; "History and Geology Of Pioche District – Interesting Matter Given in Booklet Issued by Brokerage House – Future Looks Bright"; Page 8; Column 2: "A short Interesting history and geological conditions of Pioche in a brief concise manner are given in a pamphlet issued by the brokerage house of Dern & Thomas on the Eastern Prince Gold & Silver Mining company. In part the statement says: When the Indians in Lincoln County, Nevada in the early 60s led Hamblin, a Mormon missionary to a rich outcrop of ore in Meadow Valley where later the famous old camp of Pioche sprung up, none of them knew that they were lifting the lid to one of the greatest treasure boxes in the world. Hamblin located the first claims. It was not until 1868 that that famous old Frenchman and Argonaut, F.L.A. Pioche of California, who sailed the Horn in search of treasure with the forty-niners, purchased those claims on the recommendation of his engineer Charles E Hoffman and formed the great Meadow Valley Mining Company the first to start mining in the famous camp.
The great bodies of rich Chlorides and Bromides of Silver attracted the world. From 1870 to 1876 the great camp boomed, money was as free as water and things rolled on untamed and unchecked, violent deaths were as common as from natural causes and the District was then 200 miles from a railroad. About Pioche were 10,000 people, a daily paper with the Associated Press reports, daily stage lines, fast mule freight lines with a penalty for not making a certain distance a day, livery stables and 30 hoists puffing over shafts. During that period no less than $20,000,000 were taken out, so the records show, but it was probably much more.
Then, from 1883 to 1893 was the smelter era, under W. S. Godbe and his sons. Mills run and smelters glowed until the Panic of 1893 put a quiet on the District. During that period, more than $10,000,000 more was taken from the great garner house of riches.
Pioche of Today:
A new era was started in Pioche in 1908 with the finishing of the branch of the Salt Lake Route into the camp. Since then thousands of dollars of work has been performed and millions of tons of ore has been blocked out. At no time in the history of the camp has there been so much ore in sight or the District better understood than it is today. The camp is now on the eve of a great merger, which will again put the District in the Lime-light as a great shipper, dividend payer and produce; and, in a way that has never been known before.
Only the richest Oxidized ore was extracted in the early days, mining and extraction were the crudest. The Sulphides of the camp are probably far richer that anything ever taken out and are untouched. There is still a world of Oxides left, and it is safe to say that many a million more will be taken out in the rich Carbonates, Bromides and Chlorides.
During this period the great Prince Mine was developed, a mile and a half to the Southeast of Pioche.
Geology of Pioche:
The buried treasure of the Pioche Camp was found along a rather low-appearing range of mountains which run in a Northwest and Southeast direction. On the North side of this range is the town of Pioche, nestling up close to the noted old producers of the early days. Along each side of this range there is a system of fissuring that makes the big mines. On the Pioche side is the famous Yuba dike, an intrusive porphyry, bearing millions of dollars in Sulphides, paralleled by a rich fissure of Oxidized ore known as the Raymond and Ely Fissure, from which millions were taken. On this side the surface has been eroded to the Quartzite in which rich values were found.

Across the range, a mile and a half Southwest of Pioche, is the great Prince mine, in which there has already been blocked out $8,500,000 worth of ores. Here the Lime and Shale have not been eroded, but stand about 550 feet above the Quartzite. Rich, continuous and large bedded ore planes and fissures form in the Lime and Shale at the Prince Mine. The fissures are found to be continuous into the underlying Quartzite, and engineers are of the opinion that with depth should be found even greater and richer ore bodies.

Similar Distributor:

A similar mineral distributor to the Yuba dike has affected the Prince side of the camp. A glance at the map will show that the Gladstone claim adjoins the Helen claim of the Eastern Prince. Striking Northwest and Southeast through the Gladstone claim is a porphyry dike through which the solutions have undoubtedly come from below and replaced the beds of Lime in the Shale with a heavy Sulphide ore. Later, these beds of ore were Oxidized by descending waters and wherever a portion of the bed is found that is in an unaltered condition, the ore is of a very high grade, running over 50 percent Lead and 1,000 ounces Silver. Work on the Eastern Prince is being pushed under the management of Murray C. Godbe. The new hoist has been erected at the shaft and no time is being lost in sinking. The management believes that the mineralization of the Eastern Prince side of the dike is as great as on the Prince Consolidated side and it is to prove this theory that the shaft is being pushed."

Nevada Historical Marker #5; On U.S. Highway 93 Alternate in Pioche, Nevada: "Silver ore was discovered in this range of mountains in 1864, but no important development took place until 1869 when mines were opened and the town of Pioche was founded. Pioche soon became the scene of a wild rush of prospectors and fortune seekers. It gained a reputation in the 1870s for tough gunmen and bitter lawsuits. Miners had retrieved over five million dollars in ore by 1872, but by 1900, Pioche was nearly a ghost town. Designated as the seat of Lincoln County in 1871, Pioche survived hard times as a supply and government center for a vast area. Beginning in 1937, Pioche enjoyed two decades of profitable lead-zinc mining.

Pioche Bristol Mine: (38.06.09N by -114.36.11W - #3) (Silver, Lead, Copper)
Coordinates are for the ore body of this surface-underground, past producer.

Pioche Demijohn (a.k.a. Demijohn): (37.55.52N by -114.29.38W - #3) (Lead, Silver, Manganese, Gold)
Coordinates are for the ore body of this past producer.
See the Demijohn entry for more information.

Pioche King Mine: (37.54.16N by -114.28.23W - #3) (Silver, Lead, Zinc)
Coordinates are for the main entrance to this underground, exploration prospect.

Pioche Metals Mine: (37.57.11N by -114.30.36W - #3) (Gold, Silver, Lead, Zinc, Copper, Manganese)
Coordinates are for an ore body.

Pioche Mill: (37.56.51N by -114.26.38W - #3) (Silver)
Coordinates are for a past-producing, processing plant.

Pioche Mining District (a.k.a. Ely Mining District; Highland Mining District; Meadow Valley Mining District): (Gold, Silver, Lead, Zinc, Copper, Antimony, Tungsten, Manganese, Iron, Barite, Arsenic)
Description of the District:
Tingley, Joseph V.; "Mining Districts of Nevada"; Nevada Bureau of Mines and Geology, Report 47, Second Edition; 1998; Page 174: Discovered in 1863 and organized in 1864, the Pioche Mining District is oriented around the Pioche Hills. When established, the Pioche Mining District was called the Meadow Valley Mining District, but the name was changed to the Ely Mining District in 1868. The Highland area, to the West, is sometimes included in the Pioche Mining District, leading to it being referred to as the Highland Mining District at times.
Mines Included in the District:
        Abe Lincoln Mine (Lead, Silver, Gold, Zinc, Manganese, Iron)
        Alps (Gold, Silver, Lead, Zinc, Copper, Antimony)
        Bumagin Shaft (Gold, Silver, Zinc, Lead, Copper)
        California-Pioche Shaft (Gold, Silver, Lead, Copper, Antimony, Manganese, Barite)
        Centennial Shaft (Lead, Silver, Manganese, Zinc, Copper, Gold)

Chisholm (Lead, Silver, Gold)
Combined Metals No. 1 Mine (Silver, Zinc, Lead, Gold)
Daly East (Gold, Silver, Arsenic)
Davidson Shaft (Silver, Lead, Zinc, Gold, Manganese)
Demijohn (Lead, Silver, Manganese, Gold)
Eastern Prince (Manganese, Iron, Silver, Gold, Lead, Zinc)
Ely Valley Mine (Zinc, Manganese, Silver, Gold, Lead, Copper, Tungsten)
Mazeppa Mine (Lead, Silver)
NBMG Sample Site 1417 (Gold, Silver, Lead, Zinc)
NBMG Sample Sites 1420 & 1421 (Silver, Gold, Lead, Iron, Arsenic)
NBMG Sample Site 1426 (Gold, Silver, Lead, Barite)
Newport Mine (Gold, Silver, Lead)
Old Timer Mine (Gold, Silver, Lead, Zinc, Copper)
Pacific Tunnel (Gold Silver, Lead, Zinc, Copper)
Prince Mine (Manganese, Silver, Lead, Zinc, Gold, Iron)
Raymond & Ely Extension (Gold, Silver, Lead)
Salt Lake Pioche Mining Company Mines (Gold, Silver, Lead, Zinc, Copper)
Treasure Hill Mine (Silver, Gold, Lead, Iron, Arsenic)
Unnamed Prospect Pit 055 (Gold, Silver, Barite, Lead)
Unnamed Shaft 071 (Gold, Silver, Lead, Zinc)
Washington and Creole Mine (Silver, Lead, Zinc)
West End Group (Gold, Silver, Lead)
Wide Awake Mine and Volcano (Silver, Lead, Manganese, Zinc, Antimony, Gold, Copper, Iron, Barite, Arsenic)

Pioche Plant: (37.56.32N by -114.27.35W - #3) (Sand & Gravel)
Coordinates are for the pit area of this surface, past producer.

Pioche-Xray Mining and Milling Company Property (a.k.a. Easter 001; Taylor Mine): (37.25.40N by -114.36.20W - #3) (Gold, Lead, Silver, Copper)
See the Easter 001 and Taylor Mine entries for more information.

Pip (a.k.a. Pip Claim): (38.36.04N by -114.42.35W - #3) (Tungsten, Gold, Silver)
Coordinates are for the main entrance to this underground, exploration prospect.
USGS MRDS Data Base Record 10042640, Released February 1, 1980; Updated February 1, 1985: The site of the Pip Claim is shown at 38.35939N by -114.70029W, placing it just East of Patterson Pass, in the Patterson Pass Mining District, in the Patterson Mining District, in the Cave Valley Mining District and in the area included on the USGS Grassy Mountain 24K, Wilson Creek Range 100K and Lund 250K maps. The Public Land Survey System locators are Section 32, Township 9 North, Range 65 East. Tungsten and Silver are present and are shown as primary commodities. Mineralization of this Tabular ore body includes Scheelite, with a gangue of Quartz, in a host of Late Cambrian Limestone. The geology, in the general area of the site, is described as Shale, Siltstone, Sandstone, Chert-pebble Conglomerate and Limestone. The deposit was developed by pits. The Land Status, Ownership Category of this occurrence is shown as "Private".
USGS MRDS Data Base Record 10246931, Released June 14, 1993: The main entrance to the Pip is shown at 38.60105N by -114.71055W, placing it in the area included on the USGS Milk Ranch Spring 24K, Garrison 100K and Lund 250K maps. The location accuracy, of these coordinates, is shown as +/- 100 meters. The Public Land Survey System locators are Section 32, Township 9 North, Range 65 East. Tungsten is present and is shown as a primary commodity with Silver and Gold tertiary. The geology, in the area of the main entrance, is described as Limestone and Dolomite with locally thick sequences of Shale and Siltstone. The Land Status, Ownership Category of this underground prospect is shown as "BLM Administrative Area".
See the Cinch Mine entry for more information.
Note: The latitude in the older record may be in question as the other records consistently show the latitude to be in the range of 38.6, not 38.359; the three may be an accidental typo in Record 10042640. I double checked the 38.35939 to the USGS Record 10042640 and confirmed that is what it showed. The older

USGS Record places the site about 17.2 miles South of the coordinate point for Record 10246931. The coordinate point for Record 10246931 lies about 1¼ miles East (or Northeast) of Patterson Pass.

Pittsburg Mining District (a.k.a. Viola Mining District): (Silver, Gold, Lead, Zinc, Copper, Manganese, Fluorspar)
Description of the District:
Tingley, Joseph V.; "Mining Districts of Nevada"; Nevada Bureau of Mines and Geology, Report 47, Second Edition; 1998; Page 239: The Pittsburg Mining District was shown by Tingley as an alternate name for the Viola Mining District, but it is not clear where the reference originated, unless it was the Pittsburg Silver and Copper mine in the area.
See the Viola Mining District entry for more information.
Mines Included in the District:

Pittsburg: (37.13.21N by -114.18.57W - #3) (Silver, Copper)
Coordinates are for an ore body.

Piute Group (a.k.a. Blue Bell Prospect): (39.00.28N by -115.42.05W - #3) (Fluorite, Gold)
See the Blue Bell Prospect entry for more information.

Poorman Mine: (37.55.23N by -114.26.02W - #3) (Silver, Lead, Zinc, Gold, Copper)
Coordinates are for trenching associated with this surface, past producer.

Pope Mine (a.k.a. NBMG Sample Site 1723; Winner Mine): (37.54.39N by -114.03.26W - #3) (Gold, Silver, Lead, Copper, Antimony, Fluorite)
Coordinates are for the main entrance to this underground, past producer.
USGS MRDS Data Base Record 10046512, Released February 1, 1984: The site of the Pope Mine is shown at 37.9108N by -114.05804W, placing it in the Eagle Valley Mining District, the Gold Springs Mining District and in the area included on the USGS Deer Lodge Canyon 24K and Caliente 100K and 250K maps. The Public Land Survey System locators are the Southwest ¼ of Section 29, Township 1 North, Range 71 East. Gold and Silver are present and are shown as primary commodities with Lead and Copper secondary and Antimony and Fluorite tertiary. Mineralization of this Comstock-type, Epithermal Vein deposit is included with a gangue of Pyrite, Limonite and Quartz, in a host of Rhyolite. The ore body strikes North 60° East to North 65° East, dips steeply Southeast, is from 2 to 6 inches thick, traceable for about 1,200 feet and controlled by the zone of fracturing or shearing. It contains "sugary" to Chalcedonic, light green to white banded, open-centered Quartz Veins which cut the Argillized, pink, flow-banded Rhyolite Tuff. Fissure-type Quartz Veins average 1 to 2 inches wide. Veins often have light green or purple coloration, possibly due to Fluorite or Tourmaline, which has been reported in the area. Fine grained, Oxidized Pyrite occurs in the Vein and host rock. Also found was a silver-grey, needle-like mineral which is thought to be Stibnite or some Silver mineral. The Sulfides appear to be concentrated along the drusy Iron and Manganese-stained vugs in the Quartz Vein. Numerous banded Chalcedonic Veins were also found. The Vein is only 2 to 6 inches wide, but is marked by a wider zone of fracturing or shearing and Argillic alteration. The main working is a vertical shaft, but a number of shallow stopes, open cuts and prospect pits are on the Vein structure to the Northeast and Southwest of the main shaft. A number of old buildings are also present and some recent drill roads have been cut both West and North of the shaft. At the time of the examination, in 1983, there was no activity at the site. The geology, in the general area of the site, is described as Andesite and related rocks of intermediate composition. The Land Status, Ownership Category of this surface-underground, past producer is unknown.
USGS MRDS Data Base Record 10208519, Released January 10, 1994: The main entrance to the Pope Mine is shown at 37.91077N by -114.05772W, placing it in the Eagle Valley Mining District. The location accuracy, of these coordinates, is shown as +/- 10 meters. This record shows Gold present and as a primary commodity with Silver, Lead and Copper tertiary. The geology, in the area of the main entrance, is shown as Andesite and related rocks of intermediate composition. The Land Status, Ownership Category of this underground, past producer is unknown.
See the NBMG Sample Site 1723 entry for more information.

Prince Consolidated (a.k.a. Prince Mine; NBMG Sample Site 1432; Virginia Louise): (37.54.04N by -114.28.23W - #3) (Manganese, Silver, Lead, Zinc, Gold, Iron)
Coordinates are for the main entrance to this underground, past producer.

USGS MRDS Data Base Record 10008111, Released October 1, 1979; Updated December 1, 1984; Updated and Edited April 27, 1995: The site of the Prince Mine is shown at 37.90107N by -114.4739W, placing it about 2¼ miles Southwest of Pioche, on the Southwest side of the Ely Range, in the Pioche Mining District and in the area included on the USGS Pioche 24K and Caliente 100K and 250K maps. The Public Land Survey System locators are Section 33, Township 1 North, Range 67 East. Manganese, Silver and Lead are present and are shown as primary commodities, with Zinc, Copper, Vanadium and Arsenic at tertiary levels. Mineralization of this Polymetallic Replacement Deposit includes Pyrolusite, Braunite [$Mn^2Mn^3_6(O_8\text{-}SiO_4)$], Galena (PbS), Anglesite (PbSO₄), Plumbojarosite (a hydrated Lead-Iron Sulfate), and Calamine, with a gangue of Pyrite, Sericite, Limonite, Goethite, Apatite, Calcite and Quartz, in a host of Shale. The ore body is described as Irregular to Discontinuous, striking North 20° West, dipping 5° to 20° South-Southwest, about 120 feet thick, 500 feet wide and 1,500 feet long. The ore deposition was along bedding surfaces, especially in areas along fractures and shears where they intersected with favorable host rock. The ore deposits are further identified as being Irregular Replacement bodies in layers, in a stratigraphic interval of over 1,200 feet. The deposits are primarily Manganiferous fluxing ores. High-grade Lead-Silver ore was mined from 2 Quartz Veins and an Irregular Siliceous Replacement body. At the Pioche Shale-Prospect Mountain Quartzite contact, Siliceous ore was encountered that ran 10% Zinc. Two underground, Fissure Veins, which contain Siliceous ore, are present in the Prince Mine. The ore in one of the Veins is completely Oxidized while the other carries some Sulfide ore. The ore concentration in these Veins, however, is somewhat erratic. The Vein with the Sulfide ore carries 10% to 25% Lead and about 35 ounces of Silver per ton. The deepest workings on the Fissure Veins contain Oxidized ore, but with spotty metal content; although, in some areas, it runs up to 100 ounces of Silver per ton. Here the host rocks strike North-South and dip 15° East.

The Prince Mine includes 4 Patented Claims, 1 Patented Fractional Claim and 14 Unpatented Claims, which, in total cover 386 acres. The workings consisted of two vertical shafts and a 60° inclined shaft with 6 working levels, crosscuts and raises. The Prince and Virginia Louise Mines were connected; the 3rd level of the Prince Mine was connected to the 2nd level of the Virginia Louise Mine at a depth of 286 feet. Underground workings totaled about 3,000 linear feet with a maximum depth of about 853 feet attained. Mine development also included a "Glory Hole", a number of shallower shafts, a mill and smelter. During the 1983 review it was noted that the townsite still had people living in it and many of the old mine buildings were being used for storage.

Prince Consolidated Mining was formed in 1907 by J. L. Hackett of Kentucky and the Godbe Brothers of Salt Lake City. In 1912 the Godbe Brothers built a railroad from the mine to Pioche and from 1912 to 1921 they also built large ore bins at the mine so a major ore body could be developed. The first mining was done by "caving", but later a "shrinkage" system was adopted. In the early years the ore was in high demand as a fluxing ore due to its high Iron-Manganese content. Most of the shallow-bedded ore came from the Big Red and Twenty-Foot Beds. By 1920 most of this ore was depleted and the bulk of shipments came from the Davidson ore body, which had been taken over in 1918. From 1920 to 1923 the mine found itself in financial trouble and was sold to the Owners of the adjacent Virginia Louise Mine. The Prince Mine was dewatered after the take over and the construction of the Caselton Mill was undertaken so that Sulfide ore from the bottom 835-foot level of thee mine could be mined and shipped. This allowed the extension of the Prince into what was called the "Sulphide Ore Body"; which was developed and mined until 1926. Today, much of the Oxidized ore remains unmined and the Fissure Veins at the 835-foot level were never fully prospected.

The geology, in the general area of the site, is described as Alluvial deposits. The Land Status, Ownership Category of this surface-underground, past producer is shown as "Private". A 1932 record shows the Owner as the Prince Consolidated Mining Company.

USGS MRDS Data Base Record 10295752, Released July 20, 1988: The main entrance to the Prince Mine is shown at 37.90106N by -114.47394W, placing it in the Pioche Mining District. The location accuracy, of these coordinates, is shown as +/- 10 meters. The Public Land Survey System locators are the Northern ½ of the Northern ½ of the Southern ½ of Section 33, Township 1 North, Range 67 East. Zinc is present and is shown as a primary commodity with Gold, Silver and Lead secondary and Manganese and Iron tertiary. This record shows mineralization to include Cerussite and Hemimorphite, Anglesite, Pyrolusite, Braunite, Limonite, Goethite, Hematite, Calcite and Quartz. This record described the ore body in two parts, a

Tabular Fissure Vein and a Replacement Deposit, both of which strike North 20° West, dip15° East, at a depth of about 790 feet; which are about 42 feet thick and about 1,250 feet in length. Historical production of the mine was 1,112,000 tons of ore grading an average of 102.8 grams per ton Silver, 1.03 grams per ton Gold, 3% Lead, 4% Zinc and 12% Manganese. The mine has not produced since 1949. The geology, in the general area of the site, is described as Alluvial Deposits. The Land Status, Ownership Category of this underground, past producer, discovered in 1869 and put into production the following year, is shown as "Mixed" with some "Patented Located Claims". A 1983 record shows the 100% Owner as Prince Consolidated Mining Company of Utah.

Goodwin's Weekly, November 23, 1912, Mining and Financial; page 7; Columns 2 & 3: The statements from Pioche are of special interest to Salt Lake traders. They show that the Prince Consolidated in the quarter preceding September 30, shipped 8,846 tons of crude ore with a gross value of $72,525; and 11,464 tons of tailings from Bullionville, with a value of $152,576; the Day-Bristol shipped 2,027 tons worth $44,889; the Mendha-Nevada, 993 tons worth $9,803; the Home Run Copper, 57¼ tons, worth $2,431; J.A. Nesbett, tailings from Condor canyon, 2,852 tons worth $39,971; Patrick Sheahan, ore from Raymond & Ely dump, 64 tons worth $2,553.

Multiplying the certified output of the Prince for the quarter by the number of quarters in the year, we find that the gross receipts annually should be $610,304. In the next year the production of crude ore will undoubtedly increase, but at the same time the income from the Bullionville tailings will diminish through the exhaustion of the dumps, so that the figures for the last quarter are a pretty good basis for estimating the future earnings, subject, of course, to possible changes in the market value of the metals. The Prince, more than any other mine at Pioche, is dependent for its position in the stock market on its actual performances as a shipper. The Godbe brothers, who have long been in charge of the property, may accept as a compliment the slight effect on the price of the stock of the announcement that Charles E. Knox and other Eastern capitalists had completed payments which gave them absolute control of the Prince. The change of management was regarded in mining circles as of no great moment and such additional strength as may have come to the stock from anticipation of the change is accounted for fully by the impression that the new ownership might give the shares better standing in the eastern stock markets. As for the Godbes it may be safely predicted that the sale of a part of their interests in the Prince will extend rather than circumscribe their activities at Pioche. They are identified, whether individually or collectively with the Centennial-Pioche, the Virginia-Louise, the Ohio-Kentucky, the Home Run and the Eastern Prince. Some, if not all of the properties named, will receive some of the attention which has been given to the Prince.

One effect of the Prince Consolidated sale, of purely local interest, is the transfer of the business management from Salt Lake to Pioche. This city will continue to be headquarters for the transfer of stock certificates, but supplies will be purchased, contracts let and operations directed from the Nevada office.

Notes: The term Calamine is no longer considered a valid mineral term. What was believed to be a specific mineral in the early 1800s, called Calamine, was later found to be either of two, or a combination thereof, Smithsonite (Zinc Carbonate – $ZnCO_3$) and/or Hemimorphite [Zinc Silicate – $Zn_4Si_2O_7(OH)_2$-H_2O]. A second item, that may be of interest, especially to mineral sample collectors, is the presence of Phosgenite; a relatively rare Lead Chloro-Carbonate [$(PbCl)_2CO_3$]; good samples of which can command some fairly high prices.

Prince Divide: (37.54.59N by -114.04.16W - #3) (Gold, Silver)
Coordinates are for the ore body of this underground, past producer.
USGS MRDS Data Base Record 10149813, Released January 21, 1994: The main entrance to the Prince Divide is shown at 37.91667N by -114.07163W, placing it about 15 miles Northwest of Modena, Utah, in the Eagle Valley Mining District and in the area included on the USGS Deer Lodge Canyon 24K and Caliente 100K and 250K maps. The location accuracy of these coordinates is shown as +/- 1,000 meters. The Public Land Survey System locators are Section 30, Township 1 North, Range 71 East. Gold is shown as present and as a primary commodity with Silver tertiary. The geology, in the area of the main entrance, is described as Andesite and related rocks of intermediate composition. The Land Status, Ownership Category of this underground past producer, which first produced in 1927, is unknown. A 1927 record shows the Owner-Operator as E. N. Lovelace of California.

Prince Group of Claims (a.k.a. Eagle Rock): (38.37.00N by -114.38.25W - #3) (Antimony, Lead, Zinc, Copper, Tungsten, Silver, Manganese, Iron, Gold)
See the Eagle Rock entry for more information.

Prospect 001: (37.04.35N by -114.53.54W - #3)
Coordinates are for the ore body of this prospect.
Google Earth Review; 2013-02-18: A review of the coordinates shows a large area of ground disturbance at
37.36.59N by -114.42.42W, about 850 feet North of US Highway 93, also called The Great Basin
Highway. The old quarried area appears to lie just North of this location.

Quarry: (37.37.00N by -114.42.31W - #3)
Coordinates are for the deposit area of this surface operation.

Quartzite Quarry: (37.38.00N by -114.31.40W - #3) (Stone)
Coordinates are for the ore body of this surface operation.

Quinn Canyon Mining District (a.k.a. Willow Creek Mining District): (Gold, Tungsten, Fluorite,
Beryllium)
Description of the District:
*Tingley, Joseph V.; "Mining Districts of Nevada"; Nevada Bureau of Mines and Geology, Report 47,
Second Edition; 1998; Page 180*: The Quinn Canyon Mining District is primarily a Fluorite mining district
located in the Center and on the Southeastern side of the Quinn Canyon Range in Nye County, extending
into Lincoln County. In his 1951 publication, *Mineral Resources of Nye County, Nevada,* V. E. Kral
included the primarily Fluorite, Quin Canyon Mining District, the Sharp Mining District (Nye County) and
the Willow Creek area (Nye County) in a large Willow Creek Mining District which covered much of the
Southern Quin Canyon Mountain Range. This was reinforced by a similar reference in F. J. Kleinhampl and
J. I. Ziony's *Mineral Resources of Northern Nye County*, released in 1984. The modern Quinn Canyon
Mining District is somewhat reduced in size, but includes areas in both Lincoln and Nye Counties.
Mines Included in the District:
      Blue Bell Prospect (Lincoln County)
      Horseshoe Mine (Nye County)
      Nyco Mine (Nye County)
      Rainbow Mine (Nye County)

Rae Ella/Rae Ella Nos. 2 and 3 Claims (a.k.a. North, Tem Piute; Schofield Mine): (37.63218N by -
115.624W – USGS MRDS) (Tungsten, Molybdenum, Zinc, Fluorite)
*USGS MRDS Data Base Record 10107653, Released January 1, 1980; Updated August 1, 1984; Updated
and Edited June 9, 1995*: This was an alternate name for the North Tem Piute and Schofield Mines.
See the new Tempiute Mine, the North Tem Piute and the Schofield Mine entries for more information.

Rattlesnake (a.k.a. Silver Park): (38.27.37N by -114.21.13W - #3) (Silver, Gold, Copper, Lead, Zinc,
Antimony, Uranium)
See the Silver Park entry for more information.

Raymond & Ely Extension (a.k.a. Meadow Valley Mines): (37.55.50N by -114.26.26W - #3) (Gold,
Silver, Lead)
Coordinates are for the ore body of this underground operation.
USGS MRDS Data Base Record 10046532, Released December 1, 1982: The site of the Raymond & Ely
Extension is shown at 37.93052N by -114.44112W, placing it in the Pioche Mining District and in the area
included on the USGS Pioche 24K and Caliente 100K and 250K maps. The Public Land Survey System
locators are Section 23, Township 1 North, Range 67 East. Gold, Silver and Lead, in a host of Quartzite,
associated with Late Cambrian Plutonic rock, are present and all are shown as primary commodities. The
ore body is a zone of black, Zinc-Lead-Iron Sulfide ore, several feet wide, along the Quartzite footwall. The
ore was locally referred to as the "Black Lead" and early miners did not find it profitable to mine and
process. The best ore was located below the 1,200-foot level. The Meadow Valley No. 3 shaft was sunk to
a depth of 1,374 feet, on an incline, before water was reached; so sinking was stopped at 1,375 feet.
Considerable low-grade ore was later discovered below the water level, with grade increasing with depth.
In 1868, F. L. A. Pioche had their agent, Charles Hoffman, purchase the Claims, which were later
transferred or sold to the Meadow Valley Mining Company which he had organized and which did much of

the shaft-sinking and underground development work. The Yuba Leasing Company, who was active on the property in 1914, found a good ore shoot on the 900-foot level. Notes indicate that the main ore shoot was covered by 100 feet of Shale and the only surface exposure was thin seams in Shale. The geology, in the general area of the site, is described as Limestone and Dolomite with locally-thick sequences of Shale and Siltstone. The Land Status, Ownership Category of this occurrence is shown as "Private".
See the Snowflake Mine 002 entry for more information.

Red Cloud Claim (a.k.a. O. S. L. Mine): (38.08302N by -114.611W – USGS MRDS) (Silver, Copper, Lead, Zinc, Tungsten, Iron)
See the O. S. L. Mine entry for more information.

Red Eagle Mine (a.k.a. Snowflake No. 2 Claim): (37.53.49N by -114.03.15W - #3) (Gold, Silver)
Coordinates are for the main entrance to this underground operation.
USGS MRDS Data Base Record 10046513, Released February 1, 1984; Updated October 1, 1990: The site of the Red Eagle Mine is shown at 37.89691N by -114.05499W, placing it on the Southeast slope of Buck Mountain at an elevation of 2,103 feet, about ¼ of a mile Southwest of the Jennie Mine, about 1,000 feet from the Nevada-Utah State Line, in the Eagle Valley Mining District, in the Gold Springs Mining District and in the area included on the USGS Deer Lodge Canyon 24K and Caliente 100K and 250K. The Public Land Survey System locators are the Southeast ¼ of the Southwest ¼ of Section 32, Township 1 North, Range 71 East. Gold and Silver are present and are shown as primary commodities. Mineralization includes Hematite, Calcite, Clay and Quartz in a host of Andesite. The ore body is thought to be about 20 feet thick and controlled by the Brecciation in the fault zone. The deposit is further described as bladed Calcite with much Quartz and Hematite. There is also a fault zone containing Clay and Hematite on the hanging wall of which there is a zone of massive Calcite with some Quartz. The Calcite is Brecciated along the fault and has been re-cemented with Calcite. Some stoping has taken place in the Calcite on the hanging wall. The deposit was developed by an adit driven into Buck Mountain to intersect the Snowflake Mine Vein. The adit goes South 70° West for 70 feet at a depth of 10 feet. Workings follow the Calcite zone South 30° West for 45 feet, with some stoping. At 45 feet from the portal a drift is driven South 45° West for about 90 feet, cross-cutting and intersecting a fault where there is some stoping. Also present are some prospect pits. The geology of the general area is described as welded and non-welded Silicic Ash-flow Tuffs. The Land Status, Ownership Category of this surface-underground, past producer is shown as "Private".

Red Racer Tungsten Group: (37.36.07N by -114.55.45W - #3) (Tungsten)
Coordinates are for the ore body of this prospect.
USGS MRDS Data Base Record 10222082, Released January 10, 1994: The ore body of the Red Racer Tungsten Group is shown at 37.59996N by -114.92865W, placing it in the area included on the USGS Pahroc Summit Pass 24K and Caliente 100K and 250K maps. The location accuracy, of these coordinates, is shown as +/- 10,000 meters. The general Public Land Survey System locators are Township 4 South, Range 63 East. Tungsten is present and is shown as a primary commodity. The geology, in the area of the ore body, is described as Alluvial deposits. The Land Status, Ownership Category of this surface occurrence is shown as "BLM Administrative Area".

Red Star Mine: (37.54.59N by -114.04.16W - #3) (Silver, Gold, Lead)
Coordinates are for the ore body of this underground, past producer.

Redlite Claims (a.k.a. Redelite Claims; NBMG Sample Site 1724): (37.91025N by -114.051W – USGS MRDS) (Gold, Silver)
USGS MRDS Data Base Record 10100748, Released February 1, 1984: The site of the Redlite Claims is shown at 37.91025N by -114.05082W, placing it about 1,200 feet West of the Pope Mine, in the bottom of a gully, in the Eagle Valley Mining District, in the Gold Springs Mining District and in the area included on the Deer Lodge Canyon 24K and Caliente 100K and 250K maps. The Public Land Survey System locators are the Southwest ¼ of the Southwest ¼ of Section 29, Township 1 North, Range 71 East. Gold and Silver, with a gangue of Pyrite, Siderite, Calcite and Quartz, in a host of Andesite and Pliocene Argillite, are present in this 3-foot-thick, Comstock-type, epithermal Vein deposit, and both are shown as primary commodities. A further description shows the deposit to be composed of a series of Quartz Veins, 1 to 3 inches wide, consisting of vug-filled, open-centered, banded Quartz and Calcite, Limonitic boxworks and

Manganese Oxide staining. The deposit is controlled by a fracture zone in the Andesite which strikes South 70° East. This fracture zone is followed by an adit which crosses several Southeast-dipping faults and zones of Argillic alteration. Additionally, two, fault-bounded, Calcite-Limonite Veins were found. This adit, located on the East side of the gully, has about 300 feet of workings; a second adit on the Northwest side of the gully has about 210 feet of workings. The area has been recently (as of 1983) been flagged and worked and bulldozer work at the site was also noted. It is believed that this bulldozer work was done at the same time as the construction of a new bulldozer road through the canyon. Geology, in the general area of the site, is described as welded and non-welded Silicic Ash-flow Tuffs. The Land Status, Ownership Category of this producer is unknown.

USGS MRDS Data Base Record 10173972, Released January 27, 1994: The main entrance to the Redlites Claims is shown at 37.91027N by -114.05082W, placing it in the Eagle Valley Mining District. The location accuracy, of these coordinates, is shown as +/- 100 meters. The Public Land Survey System locators are the Southwest ¼ of the Southwest ¼ of Section 29, Township 1 North, Range 71 East. Gold is present and is shown as a primary commodity with Silver tertiary. The ore body is a Tabular Fisher Vein and a Shear Zone deposit; both of Hydrothermal origin which contain Pyrite, Limonite, Siderite, Calcite and Quartz. The geology, in the area of the main entrance, is described as welded and non-welded Silicic Ash-flow Tuffs. The Land Status, Ownership Category of this underground prospect is shown as "BLM Administrative Area".

Republic (a.k.a. Republic Mine): (37.41.15N by -114.31.15W - #3) (Lead, Gold, Silver, Zinc, Copper, Vanadium)
Coordinates are for the ore body of this surface-underground, past producer.
USGS MRDS Data Base Record 10008112, Released February 1, 1980; Updated August 1, 1984; Updated and Edited April 27, 1995: The site of the Republic Mine is shown at 37.69386N by -114.5239W, placing it about 70 miles North of Alamo, at the head of Chief Canyon, in the Chief Mining District and in the area included on the USGS Chief Mountain 24K and Caliente 100K and 250K maps. The Public Land Survey System locators are Section 18, Township 3 South, Range 67 East. Gold, Silver and Lead are present and are shown as primary commodities with Copper and Zinc secondary and Vanadium tertiary. Mineralization includes Galena in a host of Late Cambrian, Prospect Mountain Quartzite. The ore body is described as Tabular to Pipe-like, in altered Quartzite, striking North 5° West and dipping nearly vertically. The ore body is controlled by fracture intersections and the altered Quartzite. A second ore shoot occurs at the intersection of the Northeast and Northwest-trending fractures. The ore body was developed by two shafts and some pits. The deeper shaft is about 180 feet deep, the upper 25 feet being inclined 73° while the rest is nearly vertical. Near the bottom of this shaft is an 18-foot drift. A 1925 smelter assay of the ore ran 0.08 to 0.39 ounces of Gold and 2 to 8.4 ounces of Silver per ton, along with 10.7% to 17.4% Lead, 0.1% to 6% Zinc and 2.3% to 4.2% Sulfur. The geology, in the general area of the site, is described as Quartzite and minor amounts of Conglomerate, Phyllitic Siltstone, Limestone and Dolomite. The Land Status, Ownership Category of this past producer is shown as "BLM Administrative Area".
USGS MRDS Data Base Record 10198277, Released January 19, 1994: The main entrance to the Republic Mine is shown at 37.69027N by -114.52254W, placing it in the Chief Mining District. The location accuracy, of these coordinates, is shown as +/- 10 meters. The Public Land Survey System locators are the Northeast ¼ of Section 18, Township 3 South, Range 67 East. Lead is present and is shown as a primary commodity with Gold, Silver, Zinc, Copper and Iron tertiary. The geology, in the area of the main entrance, is described as Quartzite and minor amounts of Conglomerate, Phyllitic Siltstone, Limestone and Dolomite. The Land Status, Ownership category of this surface-underground, past producer is unknown.

Ridge Vein (a.k.a. NBMG Sample Site 3059): (37.54716N by -115.77977W – USGS MRDS) (Gold)
USGS MRDS Data Base Record 10222453, Released January 24, 1994: The ore body of the Ridge Vein is shown at the above coordinates, placing it in the Don Dale Mining District and in the area included on the USGS White Blotch Springs SE 24K, Timpahute Range 100K and Caliente 250K maps. The location accuracy, of these coordinates, is shown as +/- 500 meters. The Public Land Survey System locators are Section 6, Township 3 South, Range 55⁺ East. Gold, with a gangue of Quartz and Hydrous Manganese Oxides is present and is shown as a primary commodity. The ore body is described as a Tabular Fissure Vein in a shear zone of Hydrothermal origin. The geology, in the area of the ore body, is described as Quartzite and minor amounts of Conglomerate, Phyllitic Siltstone, Limestone and Dolomite. The Land Status, Ownership Category of this surface occurrence is shown as "Military Reservation".

Roadside Property: (37.55.38N by -115.34.47W - #3) (Lead, Zinc, Silver, Gold)
Coordinates are for the main entrance to this underground, past producer.

Robb 001: (37.03.00N by -114.35.21W - #3) (Perlite)
Coordinates are for the ore body of this surface prospect.

Robb 002: (37.23.50N by -114.43.05W - #3) (Gypsum)
Coordinates are for an ore body.

Robinson Mine (a.k.a. Fairview 002): (38.10.00N by -114.38.14W - #3) (Lead, Silver, Gold)
See the Fairview 002 entry for more information.

Roeder Claims (a.k.a. Blue Bell): (37.57.48N by -114.34.41W - #3) (Gold, Silver, Lead, Zinc)
See the Blue Bell entry for more information.

Rosario Arcurio: (37.37.45N by -115.25.00W - #3) (Silver, Gold, Lead, Copper)
Coordinates are for an ore body of this past producer.

Rose and Pleides Group of Claims (a.k.a. Bamberger Delamar Gold Mining Company): (37.46219N by -114.769W – USGS MRDS) (Gold, Silver)
See the Bamberger Delamar Gold Mining Company entry for more information.

Ryan (a.k.a. Tem Piute Mine): (37.35.58N by -115.39.01W - #3) (Lead, Silver, Antimony, Copper, Arsenic)
See the Tem Piute Mine entry for more information.

Salt Lake Pioche Mining Company Mines (a.k.a. Apex; Apex Claim; Bumagin Claim; Bowery Vein; Financier Claim): (37.92306N by -114.437W – USGS MRDS) (Gold, Silver, Lead, Zinc, Copper)
USGS MRDS Data Base Record 10246455, Released January 12, 1994: The main entrance to the Salt Lake Pioche Mining Company Mines is shown at 37.92306N by -114.43694W, placing it in the Pioche Mining District and in the area included on the USGS Pioche 24K and Caliente 100K and 250K maps. The location accuracy, of these coordinates, is shown as +/- 10 meters. The Public Land Survey System locators are the Center of the Northern ½ of the Northern ½ of Section 26, Township 1 North, Range 67 East. Gold is present and is shown as a primary commodity with Silver, Lead, Zinc and Copper tertiary. The geology, in the area of the main entrance, is described as Quartzite and minor amounts of Conglomerate, Phyllitic Siltstone, Limestone and Dolomite. The Land Status, Ownership Category of this underground, past producer is shown as "Private", with Mineral Rights being held through "Patented Claims".

Sand Springs 001: (38.17.40N by -114.16.23W - #3) (Geothermal)
Coordinates are for a well.

Sand Springs 002: (37.44.25N by -115.45.10W - #3) (Geothermal)
Coordinates are for a well.

Schode: (37.52.49N by -114.35.52W - #3) (Silver, Lead)
Coordinates are for the ore body of this underground, past producer.

Schofield Mine (NBMG Sample Sites 1455 & 1456; North Tem Piute; Phylis; Rae Ella; Rae Ella Nos. 2 and 3 Claims; Y-Z Claims): (37.63218N by -115.624W – USGS MRDS) (Tungsten, Molybdenum, Zinc, Fluorite)
USGS MRDS Data Base Record 10107653, Released January 1, 1980; Updated August 1, 1984; Updated and Edited June 9, 1995: The site of the Schofield Mine is shown at 37.63218N by -115.62393W, placing it about 85 miles West of Caliente, in the Tem Piute Mining District and in the area included on the USGS Monte Mountain 24K, Timpahute Range 100K and Caliente 250K maps. These 40 to 53 claims adjoin the Lincoln Mine on the South. The Public Land Survey System locators are Section 1, Township 4 South,

Range 56 East. Tungsten is present and is shown as a primary commodity with Molybdenum, Zinc and Fluorite secondary. Mineralization, of this Tungsten Skarn Deposit includes Scheelite and Powellite, Molybdenite, Sphalerite and Fluorite, with a gangue of Pyrite, Limonite, Hematite, Pyrrhotite, Epidote, Diopside, Actinolite, Clinozoisite, Gypsum, Calcite and Quartz, in a host of Pilot Limestone. The ore body, which is a Tactite zone along the contact between Igneous rock and Limestone, containing minor joints, fractures and faults of small displacement, plunges 45° to 50° South. The Southern half of the Moody ore zone is on the property, with 4 ore shoots, 16 to 200 feet long and 4 to 9 feet thick, which probably extend to a depth of about 400 feet. These ore shoots occur in a single band of Tactite that is 20 to 110 feet thick along the West contact with the Granite. A narrower band is along the East contact. A number of sample assays were found in the notes. They are, as follows:

1.) The Moody ore shoots ran 0.3% to 0.7% WO_3; with the Tactite between the ore shoots running about 0.2% WO_3;
2.) A sample of the gouge ran 1.8% WO_3;
3.) An ore sample ran 1.2% WO_3; and,
4.) A sample from the trenching done on the Moody Ore Shoots ran 2.2% WO_3, with the Tactite between the ore shoots running 0.2% WO_3.

Production, from the mine, has been sporadic. The North Tempiute Mining and Development Company was organized in 1937 by the Schofield brothers of Hiko. The mine was operating in 1938 with a 50-ton mill under construction, which began operations in 1940 or 1941. The US Bureau of Mines reviewed and explored this property, along with the Lincoln property in 1942, as part of the WW2 effort to identify domestic sources of critical war materials. In 1946 the property was leased to Atolina Mining Company. The Union Carbide Company now operates the mine intermittently through its Emerson Mine Operations. From 1954 through 1955 the property was leased to the Y-Z Company. An estimate of remaining Tungsten content of the ore is 35,600 tons of WO_3. The geology, in the general area of the site, is described as Shale, Siltstone, Sandstone, Chert-pebble Conglomerate and Limestone. The Land Status, Ownership Category of this past producer, discovered in 1928, is shown as "BLM Administrative Area". A 1983 shows the Owner-Operator as Union Carbide.
See the North Tem Piute entry for more information.

Schwartz Tunnel (a.k.a. Swartz; AD Prospect; Mdm Claims; NBMG Sample Sites 807 through 809):
(38.37.32N by -114.43.40W - #3) (Tungsten, Zinc, Gold, Silver, Molybdenum, Lead, Fluorite)
USGS MRDS Data Base Record 10045918, Released March 1, 1982; Updated February 1, 1985: The site of the Schwartz Tunnel is shown at 38.62467N by -114.72946W, placing it about 50 miles North of Pioche, 45 miles South of Ely, near the crest of the Shell Creek Range, about 2 miles North of Patterson Pass, in the Cave Valley Mining District, in the Geyser Mining District, in the Patterson Mining District, in the Patterson Pass Mining District and in the Milk Ranch Spring 24K, Garrison 100K and Lund 250K maps. The Public Land Survey System locators are Section 19, Township 9 North, Range 64 East. Tungsten, Zinc, Silver and Copper are present and are shown as primary commodities with Molybdenum and Fluorite secondary. Mineralization of this Irregular, Tungsten Skarn Deposit includes Scheelite, Sphalerite, Chalcopyrite, Molybdenite and Fluorite with a gangue of Pyrite, Diopside, Epidote, Tremolite, Calcite and Quartz, in a host of Limestone, Shale and Late Cambrian, Prospect Mountain Quartzite. Some of the Vein material on the dump, from the adit above the tunnel, looks Pegmatic with coarse, white Mica and coarse terminated Quartz crystals in vugs. Below the adit dump is Pioche Shale. The adit above the tunnel displays a replacement horizon in one of the basal Limestone units of Pioche Shale. The Limestone is silicified and now displays a typical Tactite mineral assemblage of Diopside, Calcite and Epidote with some Fluorite, Calcite, Chalcopyrite and Sphalerite throughout. The altered horizon at the mouth of the adit is reddish-brown, Silicified Limestone with a polka-dot appearance due to the presence of Algal Girvanella (fossilized algae). This horizon is capped by Gossan, which can be followed for 100 feet or more to the Southwest. At the ridge crest, Southwest of the Schwartz workings, is an old shaft and several bulldozer trenches. The replaced horizon recurs here. A coarse, bladed, greenish-white mineral – possibly Wollastonite or Tremolite occurs on the Vein selvages (Vein edge areas of decreasing mineralization). The mine was developed by 2 adits, 2 shafts and several bulldozer trenches. In 1916 one of the tunnels ran 300 feet North 25° West. Although a Silver prospect in 1918, the most recent locations and staking were for Copper in 1979, by Eugene Hodges. The geology, in the general area of the site, is described as Quartzite and minor amounts of Conglomerate, Phyllitic Siltstone, Limestone and Dolomite. The Land Status, Ownership Category of this occurrence is shown as "BLM Administrative Area".

See the AD Prospect, NBMG Sample Site 807, NBMG Sample Site 808 and NBMG Sample Site 809 entries for more information.

Senior Claim (a.k.a. Groom Mine): (37.20.45N by -115.46.03W - #3) (Silver, Lead, Zinc, Copper, Gold, Barite)
See the Groom entry for more information.

Shamrock Claim:
See the Cherokee Mine entry for more information.

Sidewinder Prospect (a.k.a. NBMG Sample Site 3048): (37.53856N by -115.77757W – USGS MRDS) (Gold, Silver)
USGS MRDS Data Base Record 10295290, Released January 27, 1994: The Pit area of the Sidewinder Prospect is shown at the above coordinates, placing it in the Don Dale Mining District and in the area included on the USGS White Blotch Springs SE 24K, Timpahute Range 100K and Caliente 250K maps. The location accuracy, of these coordinates, is shown as +/- 500 meters. The Public Land Survey System locators are Section 6, Township 5 South, Range 55$^+$ East. Gold is present and is shown as a primary commodity with Silver tertiary. The geology, in the Pit area, is described as Quartzite and minor amounts of Conglomerate, Phyllitic Siltstone, Limestone and Dolomite. The Land Status, Ownership Category of this surface prospect is shown as "Military Reservation".

Sierra Chemical (Dorla #1 Mine): (37.49.56N by -114.32.34W - #3) (Limestone)
Coordinates are for the ore body of this surface producer (as of 1996).

Sierra Chemical Castleton Mill Lime: (37.54.48N by -114.29.15W - #3)
Coordinates are for a past producing, processing plant.

Sierra Chemical Kiln: (37.55.04N by -114.29.28W - #3) (Calcium)
Coordinates are for a past producing, processing plant.

Silver Comet Mines (a.k.a. Comet): (37.53.25N by -114.36.47W - #3) (Lead, Zinc, Tungsten, Silver, Gold, Copper, Manganese, Barite)
See the Comet entry for more information.

Silver Dale: (38.09.00N by -114.41.27W - #3) (Silver)
Coordinates are for the ore body of this past producer.
See the Silver Horn entry for more information.

Silver Horn (a.k.a. Silver Horn Mine; Silverhorn Mine; Silver Dale Nos. 1-4 Claims; Hornsilver Nos. 1, 5 Claims; Nickel Group): (38.09.30N by -114.41.47W - #3) (Silver, Lead, Gold, Nickel)
Coordinates are for the ore body of this past producer.
USGS MRDS Data Base Record 10047179, Released January 1, 1983: The site of the Silverhorn Mine is shown at 38.15524N by -114.69585W, placing it in the Silverhorn area of the Bristol-Jackrabbit Mining District and in the area included on the USGS Fairview Peak 24K, Wilson Creek Range 100K and Lund 250K maps. The Public Land Survey System locators are projected as Section 4, Township 3 North, Range 65 East. This is an unsurveyed area. The coordinates are for the main shaft of the Silverhorn Mine. Silver and Lead are present and are shown as primary commodities with Gold secondary and Nickel Tertiary. Mineralization included Native Silver and Argentite with a gangue of Quartz. The Quartz was part of a massive replacement of the Limestone, which, in places, is up to 100 feet thick. The ore ran from 1 to 180 ounces of Silver per ton and, in places, from 4% to 12% Nickel. The mineralization is hosted in Limestone. Shale, Clastic Sedimentary rock and Quartzite and is associated with Andesite, Rhyolite and old Limestone (of Mississippian age). The ore body is described as Tabular to Irregular, up to 100 feet thick, 200 feet wide, traceable for about 4,000 feet and exposed at the surface. The outcrop of the deposit is faulted away to the Southeast. Primary ore controls are the faults and fault Breccias. The Jasperoid is 80 feet thick and extends to a depth of more than 200 feet. The mine was developed by shafts, adits, crosscuts, trenches, long tunnels and inclines. The best values were found where cross-fracturing of the Silicified outcrop occurred.

An overall depth of about 285 feet was reached in the workings. The geology, in the general area of the site, is described as Shale, Siltstone, Sandstone, Chert-Pebble Conglomerate and Limestone. Large Jasperoid outcrops form conspicuous dull brown masses forming ridge tops. The seams that traverse the Jasperoid are splotched with films of Horn Silver. It was the high assays from these areas that drove interest in the area. The area boomed in 1920 after a series of newspaper articles touting the area. These continued through the end of 1920 and into early 1921, but interest fizzled out in the last half of 1921 when the overall, expected level of discoveries in the area was not realized and little mineable ore was found. Discovered in 1882 and put into production during the "boom" in 1921, the Land Status, Ownership Category of this past producer is shown as "Private". A 1921 record shows the Owner as the Silver Horn Mining Company and the Silver Dale Mining Company.

USGS MRDS Data Base Record 10198551, Released January 21, 1994: The pit area of the Silver Horn Mine is shown at 38.15776N by -114.69475W, placing it in the Silverhorn Mining District. The location accuracy, of these coordinates, is shown as +/- 10 meters. The Public Land Survey System locators are reported to be Section 4, Township 3 North, Range 65 East. The locators, based on the USGS Fairview Peak 24K map, are Section 33, Township 4 North, Range 65 East. This record shows Silver present and as a primary commodity. The geology, in the pit area, is described as Shale, Siltstone, Sandstone, Chert-Pebble Conglomerate and Limestone. The Land Status, Ownership Category of this surface-underground, past producer is shown as "BLM Administrative Area". A 1979 record shows the Operator as the Silver Horn Operating Company of Utah.

Silver King Mine (a.k.a. Whipple Silver King): (38.17.29N by -114.52.37W - #3) (Gold, Silver, Lead, Arsenic)

USGS MRDS Data Base Record 10037341, Released February 1, 1980: (Record same as USGS 10109802)

USGS MRDS Data Base Record 10109802; Released February 1, 1980; Updated June 1, 1985: The site of the Silver King Mine is shown at 38.29162N by -114.87724W, placing it at the Southern end of Cave Valley, in the Silver King Mining District, in the Sunnyside Mining District and in the area included on the USGS Silver King Well 24K, Wilson Creek Range 100K and Lund 250K maps. While the area was unsurveyed at the time of the estimate, the Public Land Survey System locators, as projected from the North, are Sections 14 & 15, Township 5 North, Range 63 East. This record shows Lead and Silver present and as primary commodities with Arsenic tertiary. Mineralization includes Galena, with a gangue of Limonite, in a host of Guilmette Limestone associated with Late Devonian Diorite. The ore body is described as Tabular, open to the surface, striking North 55° West, dipping vertically and controlled by a fault zone along an Igneous contact. The ore body, or ore bodies, is/are indicated to occur near the contact of the Limestone and Quartz Diorite Porphyry, both as small replacement bodies and as Veins. A 7-inch Stringer, rich with Lead-Silver-Arsenic Sulfides was exposed for 12 feet in the Vein. The rock around the shaft collar and on the dump is a dark Limestone with maroon clots. The fracture zone is apparent at the shaft with a ¼ inch Calcite surface Vein visible. The fracture can be traced along the outcrop East of the Shaft and stopes have caved along this zone. The upper, or Eastern, area of the workings explore replacement lenses in the Limestone along the North 55° West strike structure. Old dumps, along the hill slope lie along this structure. The lowest workings expose a Kaolinized dike in the portal area. The Limestone contact trends North 20° West and dips 60° to 65° to the Southwest. Development included at least 3 adits, one vertical shaft and a number of stopes extending to the surface, totaling in excess of 500 linear feet of underground development. In 1981 the property was drilled by Anaconda, with evidence of several deep holes having been completed. A notice, tacked to the old headframe and dated February, 1980, indicated the property had been located by Hill & Hendrix. Records indicate at least 8 to 10 carloads of Silver-Lead ore were produced and shipped. The geology, in the General area of the site, is described as Dolomite, Limestone and minor amounts of Sandstone and Quartzite. The Land Status, Ownership Category of this surface-underground, past producer is shown as "BLM Administrative Area". A 1980 record (above mentioned location posting) shows the Owner as Hill & Hendrix with a 1981 record showing Anaconda Company as the Operator.

See the Whipple Silver King entry for more information.

Silver King Mining District: (Gold, Silver, Lead, Arsenic)

Description of the District:

USGS MRDS Data Base Record 10109802; Released February 1, 1980; Updated June 1, 1985: This record cites the District as including several prospects in the area, but being unorganized.

Mines Included in the District:
> Silver King Mine (Gold, Silver, Lead, Arsenic)

<u>Silver Occurrence 001 (a.k.a. NBMG Sample Site 3002)</u>: (37.40826N by -115.71147W – USGS MRDS)
(Silver, Gold)
USGS MRDS Data Base Record 10271223, Released January 27, 1994: The ore body of the Silver
Occurrence 001 is shown at 37.40826N by -115.71147W, placing it in the Groom Mining District and in
the area included on the USGS Groom Range 24K, Pahranagat Range 100K and Caliente 250K maps. The
location accuracy, of these coordinates, is shown as +/- 500 meters. The Public Land Survey System
locators are Section 20, Township 6 South, Range 56 East. Silver is present and is shown as a primary
Commodity with Gold tertiary. The geology, in the area of the ore body, is described as welded and non-
welded Silicic Ash-flow Tuffs. The Land Status, Ownership Category of this surface occurrence is shown
as "Military Reservation".

<u>Silver Occurrence 002</u>: (37.62356N by -115.395 – USGS MRDS) (Silver)
Coordinates are for a surface prospect.

<u>Silver Occurrence 003</u>: (37.54.30N by -114.41.21W - #3) (Silver)
Coordinates are for an ore body.
Decimal Equivalents are 37.90833333N by -114.689166667W

<u>Silver Occurrence 004</u>: (37.38.26N by -115.23.50W - #3) (Silver)
Coordinates are for an ore body.
Decimal Equivalents are 37.64055556N by -115.3972222W.

<u>Silver Occurrence 005</u>: (37.34.23N by -115.46.56W - #3) (Silver)
Coordinates are for an ore body.
Decimal Equivalents are 37.57305556N by -115.782222W.

<u>Silver Occurrence 006</u>: (37.35.58N by -115.37.58W - #3) (Silver)
Coordinates are for an ore body.
Decimal Equivalents are 37.5994444N by -115.6327778W.

<u>Silver Occurrence 007</u>: (37.37.30N by -115.24.05W - #3) (Silver)
Coordinates are for an ore body.
Decimal Equivalents are 37.625N by -115.4013889W.

<u>Silver Park (a.k.a. Silver Park Mine; Jesse Knight; Jesse Knight Property; Rattlesnake)</u>: (38.27.37N
by -114.21.13W - #3) (Silver, Gold, Copper, Lead, Zinc, Antimony, Uranium)
Coordinates are for the ore body of this underground, past producer.
USGS MRDS Data Base Record 10037372, Released February 1, 1980; Updated January 1, 1985: The
Silver Park Mine is shown at 38.46023N by -114.35751W, placing it about 1½ miles West of Atlanta, in
the Atlanta Mining District, in the Silver Park Mining District, in the Silver Springs Mining District and in
the area included on the USGS Atlanta 24K, Wilson Creek Range 100K and Lund 250K maps. The Public
Land Survey System locators are Section 16, Township 7 North, Range 68 East. Silver and Gold are shown
as present and as primary commodities with Copper, Lead, Zinc, Antimony and Uranium tertiary.
Mineralization of this Polymetallic Replacement Deposit includes Cerargyrite (AgCl), Pyrargyrite
(Ag_3SbS_3), Copper minerals, Galena and Native Lead, with a gangue of Limonite, Calcite and Quartz, in a
host of Ely Springs Limestone and Dolomite, associated with Late Ordovician to Pliocene Rhyolite. The
ore body is Tabular, about 7 feet thick and controlled by fractures, bedding planes and joints at favorable
stratigraphic horizons. Siliceous Replacement Veins striking Northeast and North are mineralized. The
dumps and areas near the old workings are slightly more radioactive than the surrounding unaltered rocks.
A semi-quantitative spectrographic analysis, run by the USGS, gave an estimate of 0.7% Copper, 0.3%
Barite, 0.15% Silver and Antimony combined and 0.03% Lead and Zinc combined. Development included
a main shaft, which is now caved at 50 feet; other shafts, at least 2 of which are over 100 feet deep; small,
Irregular inclined drifts and stopes which follow drainage channels; adits, prospect pits and 2 mills (active

133

in 1872). Developments reached a maximum depth of about 300 feet. Most of the early production of the District came from this mine, which was discovered in 1869 and went into production in 1871. In 1975 a large amount of shallow, rotary drilling was being done by Combined Enterprises, Incorporated, in the Silver Park Area. A small zone of mineralization, called the Loren ore body, was located and a test pit mined. The effort was dropped as being uneconomical. The geology, in the general area of the site, is described as Dolomite, Limestone and minor amounts of Sandstone and Quartzite. The Land Status, Ownership Category of this surface-underground, past producer is shown as "BLM Administrative Area". *USGS MRDS Data Base Record 10173709, Released January 19, 1994*: The main entrance to the Silver Park Mine is shown at 38.46025N by -114.35304W, placing it in the Silver Park Mining District. The location accuracy, of these coordinates, is shown as +/- 10 meters. The Public Land Survey System locators are the Northwest ¼ of Section 21, Township 7 North, Range 68 East. Gold is present and is shown as a primary commodity with Silver, Copper, Lead and Uranium tertiary. The geology, in the area of the main entrance, is described as Dolomite, Limestone and minor amounts of Sandstone and Quartzite. The Land Status, Ownership Category of this underground, past producer is unknown.

Silver Park Mining District (a.k.a. Atlanta Mining District): (Gold, Silver, Copper, Lead, Tungsten, Vanadium, Manganese, Uranium)
Description of the District:
Tingley, Joseph V.; "Mining Districts of Nevada"; Nevada Bureau of Mines and Geology, Report 47, Second Edition; 1998; Page 22: In 1871, A. F. White, in the *"Report of the Mineralogist of the State of Nevada for the Years 1869 and 1870"*, referred to the modern Atlanta Mining District as Silver Peak, and located it in a low range of mountains about 35 miles Southeast of the Patterson Mining District. However, by 1873, the name Silver Park was being used for the area. However, in 1881, M. Angel, in his *History of Nevada,* gave the location of the Silver Park Mining District as the Southeastern corner of White Pine County, which was incorrect and created considerable confusion.
See the Atlanta Mining District entry for more information.
Mines Included in the District:
 Bradshaw (Gold, Silver, Copper, Uranium)
 Hulse Mine (Uranium, Silver, Gold, Copper, Lead, Arsenic)
 Silver Park (Silver, Gold, Copper, Lead, Zinc, Antimony, Uranium)
 Solo Joker (Gold, Silver, Barite)

Silver Peak Mining District (a.k.a. Atlanta Mining District): (Gold, Silver, Copper, Lead, Tungsten, Vanadium, Manganese, Uranium)
Description of the District:
Tingley, Joseph V.; "Mining Districts of Nevada"; Nevada Bureau of Mines and Geology, Report 47, Second Edition; 1998; Page 22: In 1871, A. F. White, in the *"Report of the Mineralogist of the State of Nevada for the Years 1869 and 1870"*, referred to the modern Atlanta Mining District as Silver Peak, and located it in a low range of mountains about 35 miles Southeast of the Patterson Mining District. By 1873, the name Silver Park was being used for the area. However, in 1881, M. Angel, in his *History of Nevada,* gave the location of the Silver Park Mining District as the Southeastern corner of White Pine County, which was incorrect and created considerable confusion.
See the Atlanta Mining District entry for more information.
Mines Included in the District:

Silver Springs Mining District (a.k.a. Atlanta Mining District): (Gold, Silver, Copper, Lead, Tungsten, Vanadium, Manganese, Uranium)
Description of the District:
Tingley, Joseph V.; "Mining Districts of Nevada"; Nevada Bureau of Mines and Geology, Report 47, Second Edition; 1998; Page 22: In 1871, A. F. White, in the *"Report of the Mineralogist of the State of Nevada for the Years 1869 and 1870"*, referred to the modern Atlanta Mining District as Silver Peak, and located it in a low range of mountains about 35 miles Southeast of the Patterson Mining District. By 1873, the name Silver Park was being used for the area. However, in 1881, M. Angel, in his *History of Nevada,* gave the location of the Silver Park Mining District as the Southeastern corner of White Pine County, which was incorrect and created considerable confusion. Angel further described a Silver Springs Mining District as being in the "Northeastern corner of the County, in the Snake Range Mountains", which was

probably the area of the modern Atlanta Mining District, if the County being referred to was Lincoln, which it most likely was.
See the Atlanta Mining District entry for more information.
Mines Included in the District:
        Bradshaw (Gold, Silver, Copper, Uranium)
        Hulse Mine (Uranium, Silver, Gold, Copper, Lead, Arsenic)
        Silver Park (Silver, Gold, Copper, Lead, Zinc, Antimony, Uranium)
        Solo Joker (Gold, Silver, Barite)

Silver Star/Silver Star Claim (a.k.a. Gypsy and Helen): (37.57.03N by -114.04.35W - #3) (Gold, Silver, Copper)
See the Gypsy and Helen entry for more information.

Silver Star Lode (a.k.a. Tempa Mine): (37.56.55N by -114.04.40W - #3) (Gold, Silver)
See the Tempa Mine entry for more information.

Silver Star Mine (a.k.a. Silver Star Claim; Blue Bird Claim; Gypsy & Helen Groups; Interocean Claim; White Horse Claim; White Horse Mine): (37.56.43N by -114.04.17W - #3) (Silver, Gold)
Coordinates are for the ore body of this underground, past producer.
USGS MRDS Data Base Record 10173762, Released November 14, 1983: The Main Entrance to the Silver Star Mine is located at 37.94606N by -114.08163W, placing it in the Eagle Valley Mining District and in the area included on the Deer Lodge Canyon 24K and Caliente 100K and 250K maps. The Public Land Survey System locators are Section 18, Township 1 North, Range 71 East. Silver is present and is shown as a primary commodity with Gold tertiary. The geology, in the area of the main entrance, is described as Andesite and related rocks of intermediate composition. The Land Status, Ownership Category of this underground, past producer, is unknown.
See the Gypsy & Helen Groups and White Horse Mine entries for more information.

Silver Wedge #10 (a.k.a. Gold Chief): (37.41.57N by -114.30.00W - #3) (Gold, Silver, Zinc, Lead, Copper, Manganese, Barite, Iron, Arsenic)
See the Gold Chief entry for more information.

Silverhorn Mining District (a.k.a. Fairview Mining District): (Silver, Lead, Gold, Nickel, Perlite)
Description of the District:
Tingley, Joseph V.; "Mining Districts of Nevada"; Nevada Bureau of Mines and Geology, Report 47, Second Edition; 1998; Page 212: The Silverhorn Mining District, discovered in 1882, is located on the Southeast side of the Fairview Range, Northwest of Bristol Pass. The Eastern part of the District, on the Southeast side of the Range, is sometimes referred to as the Fairview Mining District.
Comment: Some cross references would indicate the Silverhorn Mining District to be, at least partially, in the area of the Bristol Mining District; see the Bristol Mining District entry for more information.
Mines Included in the District:
        Fairview 002 (Lead, Silver, Gold)
        Silver Horn (Silver, Lead, Gold, Nickel)

Smelter Shaft: (37.55.23N by -115.34.54W - #3)
Coordinates are for the main entrance to this underground, past producer.

Smith and Dobbins: (37.03.40N by -114.55.50W - #3) (Manganese)
Coordinates are for an ore body.

Snow Perlite: (37.55.52N by -114.06.28W - #3) (Perlite)
Coordinates are for an ore body.

Snowflake Group (a.k.a. Big Buck Mine): (37.54.11N by -114.03.32W - #3) (Silver, Gold, Lead, Copper)
See the Big Buck Mine entry for more information.

Snowflake 001: (37.15.00N by -114.21.07W - #3) (Gypsum)
Coordinates are for an ore body.

Snowflake Mine 002 (a.k.a. Snowflake Quarry; Big Buck Claims; NBMG Sample Site 1720):
(37.54.04N by -114.03.23W - #3) (Gold, Silver, Copper, Iron)
Coordinates are for the main entrance to this surface-underground, past producer.
USGS MRDS Data Base Record 10037373, Released February 1, 1980; Updated September 1, 1984: The
site of the Snowflake Mine is shown at 37.9008N by -114.05749W, placing it near the Utah-Nevada
border, in the Eagle Valley Mining District, in the Fay Mining District, in the Gold Springs Mining District,
in the Stateline Mining District and in the area included on the USGS Deer Lodge Canyon 24K and
Caliente 100K and 250K maps. The Public Land Survey System locators are Section 32, Township 1
North, Range 71 East. Gold and Silver are present and are shown as primary commodities with Copper and
Iron tertiary. Mineralization of this Comstock-type, Epithermal Vein deposit includes Copper ores, Pyrite,
Limonite, Hematite, Calcite and Quartz in a host of Latite. The Tabular Snowflake Vein strikes North and
South for more than 6,000 feet, dips 60° to 70° East, has a maximum width of 100 feet and is controlled by
fractures. It is the largest Vein system in the area. It forms a bold, white, resistant outcrop and is composed
of several sub-parallel Veins of mainly Quartz, massive and vuggy in appearance, with intra-lenses of
Calcite and Quartz after Calcite. A portion of the Vein is heavily Stockwork Quartz wall rock with Veinlets
generally less than 1 inch wide, but occasionally greater than 6 inches. These tend to crosscut each other
and also crosscut the main Vein trend. Banded Veins of Quartz, after Calcite and/or Siderite crosscut the
main Vein at a high angle. Other Quartz Veins in the wall rock are truncated by the main Vein. Altered
Andesite fragments in the Vein show a fine Stockwork of Quartz. In addition to massive and prismatic
Quartz Veins and Veinlets are banded Chalcedonic and Opaline Quartz Veins cutting the wall rocks. Vein
material, sampled from the "Glory Hole", consists of heavily Iron and Manganese-stained massive
cockscomb to sugary white Quartz with open drusy centers and abundant, ripped-up fragments of bleached,
Argillized and Silicified Andesite-Latite fragments and Vein material containing Pyrite, partially Oxidized
to Hematite or pseudo morphed to Limonite. Wallrocks are fractured or sheared due to the forceful
intrusion of the Vein. Also, the Main Vein appears to have been subjected to an episode of shearing or
cross-faulting, possibly during or following emplacement. The best ore was found where the cross-
structures cause the Vein to swell.
The deposit was developed by at least three (3) shafts, the above-mentioned 100-foot by 30-foot by 25 to
30 feet deep pit or "Glory Hole" and several adits driven to intersect the Vein at depth. The Vein has been
heavily prospected and drilled (at 10-foot intervals) both North and South of the "Glory Hole", with recent
(2 to 4 years old) excavations and new drill roads surrounding the "Glory Hole". There was no activity at
the time of the review in 1983, but the area was clearly staked and likely to be active on an intermittent
basis.
The production prior to 1903 is estimated to be at least $31,000 (period values). It is estimated that the ore
averaged $10 to $15 (period values) per ton, although that from the shaft assayed up to $660 per ton.
The geology, in the general area of the site, is described as Andesite and related rocks of intermediate
composition. The Land Status, Ownership Category of this surface-underground, producer is shown as
"Private".
See the Big Buck Claim and the Red Eagle Mine entries for more information.

Snowhite Prospect: (36.57.53N by -114.12.32W - #3) (Gypsum)
Coordinates are for the pit area of this surface, exploration prospect.

Snyder Shaft (a.k.a. Bristol-Jackrabbit Mines): (38.08107N by -114.617W – USGS MRDS) (Silver,
Copper, Lead, Zinc, Gold, Manganese)
See the Bristol-Jackrabbit Mine entry for more information.

Soa Lode Claims (a.k.a. NBMG Sample Site 117): (37.69887N by -114.51364W – USGS MRDS) (Lead,
Gold, Silver, Arsenic, Barite)
USGS MRDS Data Base Record 10222743, Released January 27, 1994: The main entrance to the Soa Lode
Claims is shown at 37.69887N by -114.51364W, placing it in the Chief Mining District and in the area
included on the USGS Chief Mountain 24K and Caliente 100K and 250K maps. The location accuracy, of
these coordinates, is shown as +/- 100 meters. The Public Land Survey System locators are Section 8,

Township 3 South, Range 67 East. Lead is present and is shown as a primary commodity with Gold, Silver, Arsenic and Barite tertiary. Mineralization of this Tabular Vein and Fissure Vein deposit includes Galena, Pyrite, Limonite, Hematite, Quartz and Calcite. The geology, in the area of the main entrance, is described as Quartzite and minor amounts of Conglomerate, Phyllitic Siltstone, Limestone and Dolomite. The Land Status, Ownership Category of this surface-underground prospect is shown as "BLM Administrative Area".

Solo Joker (a.k.a. Solo Joker Claim): (38.27.26N by -114.20.47W - #3) (Gold, Silver, Barite)
Coordinates are for an ore body.
USGS MRDS Data Base Record 10097044, Released February 1, 1980; Updated January 1, 1985: The site of the Solo Joker Claim is shown at 38.45134N by -114.35945W, placing it about ½ mile South of the Silver Park Mine, on the North side of a gulley, on a small hill about ¾ of a mile West of the Hulse Mine, in the Atlanta Mining District, in the Silver Park Mining District, in the Silver Springs Mining District and in the area included on the USGS Atlanta 24K, Wilson Creek Range 100K and Lund 250K maps. The Public Land Survey System locators are Section 16, Township 7 North, Range 68 East. Gold and Silver are present and are shown as primary commodities with Barite tertiary. Mineralization of this Comstock-type, Epithermal Vein Deposit includes Barite, with a gangue of Pyrolusite, Limonite, Hematite and Quartz, in a host of Limestone and Rhyolite of the Ely Springs Dolomite Formation. The ore body is described as being in a Silicified Breccia of Rhyolite Tuff, Limestone and Jasper, about 10 to 15 feet thick. It is Wedge shaped, exposed at the surface, about 15 feet thick, plunging North 35° West and controlled by shear zones and fractures. The deposit was developed by 2 shallow shafts and a few prospect pits. The geology, in the general area of the site, is described as welded and non-welded, Silicic Ash-flow Tuffs. The Land Status, Ownership Category of this prospect is shown as "BLM Administrative Area".
USGS MRDS Data Base Record 10174120, Released January 19, 1994: The ore body of the Solo Joker Claim is shown at 38.45275N by -114.35774W, placing it about 1 mile West of the Atlanta Mine and in the Atlanta Mining District. The location accuracy, of these coordinates, is shown as +/- 500 meters. The Public Land Survey System locators are Section 21, Township 7 North, Range 68 East. This record shows Silver present and as a primary commodity with Gold tertiary. The geology, in the area of the ore body, is described as welded and non-welded Silicic Ash-flow Tuffs.

Southpaw Mine: (37.40.40N by -115.22.30W - #3) (Silver, Manganese, Iron, Aluminum, Silica, Phosphate)
Coordinates are for the ore body of this underground, past producer.

Spring Valley Mine: (38.35.55N by -114.24.30W - #3)
Coordinates are for an ore body.

Springtime Tunnel: (37.55.19N by -114.26.50W - #3) (Silver, Lead, Copper, Antimony, Arsenic)
Coordinates are for the main entrance to this underground operation.

Stampede Gap Mining District (a.k.a. Highland Mining District): (Gold, Silver, Lead, Zinc, Copper, Antimony, Tungsten, Manganese, Iron)
Description of the District:
Tingley, Joseph V.; "Mining Districts of Nevada"; Nevada Bureau of Mines and Geology, Report 47, Second Edition; 1998; Page 110: In his 1962 *Directory of Southern Nevada Place Names*, W. R. Averett referred to the area about 10 miles West of Pioche, in the area of Stampede Gap, as the Stampede Gap Mining District, which would be included in the area of the modern Highland Mining District.
See the Highland Mining District entry for more information.
Mines Included in the District:

Stateline District: (38.07.05N by -114.03.26W - #3)
Coordinates are for the ore body of this past producer.

Stateline Mining District (a.k.a. Eagle Valley Mining District): (Gold, Silver, Lead, Uranium, Pearlite)
Description of the District:
Tingley, Joseph V.; "Mining Districts of Nevada"; Nevada Bureau of Mines and Geology, Report 47, Second Edition; 1998; Page 79: The Eagle Valley Mining District lies along the Nevada-Utah Border and

is made up of a number of small, scattered mining areas in the Mahogany Mountains. These include the Stateline mining area, which is mostly in Utah, and about 5 miles North of Deer Lodge Canyon. See the Eagle Valley Mining District entry for more information.
Mines Included in the District:
        Confidence Mine (Gold, Silver) (Nevada)
        Jennie Mine (Gold, Silver, Lead, Copper) (Nevada)
        NBMG Sample Site 1500 (Gold, Silver) (Nevada)
        Snowflake Mine 002 (Gold, Silver, Copper, Iron) (Nevada)
        Thor Mine (Gold, Silver, Lead, Copper) (Nevada)
        Utah Spur Mine (Silver, Gold, Fluorite) (Utah & Nevada)

Steele (a.k.a. Blue Bell Prospect): (39.00.28N by -115.42.05W - #3) (Fluorite, Gold)
See the Blue Bell Prospect entry for more information.

Sterling Mine (a.k.a. Tem Piute Mine): (37.35.58N by -115.39.01W - #3) (Lead, Silver, Antimony, Copper, Arsenic)
See the Tem Piute Mine entry for more information.

Stewart Quarry: (37.57.00N by -115.49.51W - #3) (Volcanics)
Coordinates are for the ore body of this surface, past producer.

Stindt and Donohue Lease (a.k.a. Wide Awake and Volcano): (37.54.56N by -114.25.50W - #3) (Silver, Lead, Manganese, Zinc, Antimony, Gold, Copper, Iron, Barite, Arsenic)
See the Wide Awake and Volcano entry for more information.

Streator: (38.40.00N by -114.48.56W - #3) (Silver, Lead, Copper)
Coordinates are for an ore body.

Subterranean Group (a.k.a. Cave Valley Mine 002): (38.38.39N by -114.47.49W - #3) (Lead, Silver, Copper, Zinc, Gold, Vanadium, Arsenic, Clay)
See the Cave Valley Mine 002 entry for more information.

Sunnyside Mining District: (Gold, Silver, Lead, Arsenic)
Description of the District:
USGS MRDS Data Base Record 10109802; Released February 1, 1980; Updated June 1, 1985: This record cites the District as including several prospects in the area, but being unorganized.
Mines Included in the District:
        Silver King Mine (Gold, Silver, Lead, Arsenic)

Sunshine Prospect: (37.14.42N by -114.36.43W - #3)
Coordinates are for trenching associated with this surface prospect.

Susan Duster: (37.55.22N by -114.27.15W - #3) (Silver, Lead, Zinc, Manganese)
Coordinates are for the ore body of this underground, past producer.

Swartz Canyon Head Tactite (a.k.a. AD Prospect): (38.37.32N by -114.43.40W - #3) (Tungsten, Zinc, Gold, Silver, Molybdenum, Lead, Fluorite)
See the AD Prospect entry for more information.

Swifter Claims (a.k.a. April Fool); (37.27.45N by -114.45.30W - #3) (Gold, Silver, Copper, Bismuth, Antimony)
See the April Fool entry for more information.

T. C. Johnson Claims (a.k.a. Culverwell Mine 005): (37.41775N by -114.475W – USGS MRDS) (Gold, Silver, Copper, Tungsten, Lead)
See the Culverwell Mine 005 entry for more information.

Talisman (a.k.a. Thor Mine): (37.53.56N by -114.03.04W - #3) (Gold, Silver, Lead, Copper)
See the Thor Mine entry for more information.

Tara Claims (a.k.a. Irmine & Postum; Irvine & Bauers; NBMG Sample Location 1713): (37.92913N
by -114.637W – USGS MRDS) (Gold, Silver, Lead, Manganese)
USGS MRDS Data Base Record 10046485, Released June 1, 1984: The site of the Tara Claims is shown at
37.92913N by -114.63695W, placing it in the Ely Springs Mining District, in the Highland Mining District,
in the Lone Mountain Mining District and in the area included on the USGS Ely Springs 24K and Caliente
100K and 250K maps. The Public Land Survey System locators are Section 24, Township 1 North, Range
65 East. Gold, Silver and Lead are present and are shown as primary commodities with Manganese
secondary. Mineralization of this Polymetallic Replacement Deposit includes Gold and Galena, with a
gangue of Calcite, in a host of Quartzite and Aphanitic Volcanic rock. The ore body is described as being
Tabular Lenses and Pods which strike North 20° East, dip 20° to 25° Northwest, are about 5 feet thick, can
be traced for at least 60 feet and are controlled by the fault conduit, the bedding and favorable host rock.
Here a fault truncates the bedding at the Southwest end of the zone which strikes North 25° East and dips
70° Northwest.
A further description of the deposit was found in the notes, and reads, as follows: Oxidized Replacement
Deposit parallel to the bedding, but also includes fractured or Brecciated materials indicating the presence
of a bedding plane fault. Slickensides are visible along the zone and cross-faulting occurs such as a
prominent fault which truncates the bedding at the Southwest end of the zone (see above). This fault may
have served as a conduit for mineralizing fluids which spread out along the bedding of the host rock. The
zone of replacement is marked by numerous Lenses and Pods of Iron and Manganese Oxides and shows
Silicification, recrystallization, oxidizing and bleaching of the Limestone host rocks adjacent to the
replaced horizon. Dense Pods of massive Manganese and Iron Oxides were sampled from the dump. Leaf
Gold and Gold ore described as being in this locality may refer to the deposit explored by the adit to the
Southeast. Here Leaf Gold is deposited along planes of fracture in the Shale layer in the Mendha
Formation. Gold ore in the 50-foot inclined shaft is reported to be 12 to 18 inches thick. A 10-foot
Limestone structure has been replaced by Iron and Manganese Oxides. The Quartz-Galena Vein in the
Limestone is up to 1 foot thick and strikes North 65° West, dips 65° Northeast and is developed by an 80-
foot adit.
Development is further described as several short shafts and prospects inclined 25° to the Northwest along
the strata-bound Replacement deposit. Prospecting along the zone continued along strike for about 60 feet.
The ore was treated on a small scale near the homestead below the mine site. The adit to the Southeast was
not visited during the review, in 1983, as no sign of recent activity was noted in the vicinity of the adit. The
property was staked however, and probably worked intermittently on a small scale.
The geology, in the general area of the site, is described as Limestone and Dolomite with locally thick
sequences of Shale and Siltstone. The Land Status, Ownership Category of this producer is shown as
"BLM Administrative Area". A 1980 record shows the Owner as Eugene Elledge, 1209 Stout Way, Las
Vegas, Nevada 89101.

**Taylor Mine (a.k.a. Easter N. Mine; NBMG Sample Site 579; Pioche-Xray Mining & Milling
Company Property)**: (37.30.46N by -114.37.54W - #3) (Gold, Silver, Iron)
Coordinates are for the main entrance to this underground operation.
USGS MRDS Data Base Record 10046506, Released May 1, 1984: The site of the Taylor Mine is shown at
37.51275N by -114.63251W, placing it in the Delamar Mining District and in the area included on the
USGS Chokecherry Mountain 24K and Caliente 100K and 250K maps. The general Public Land Survey
System locators are Township 5 South, Range 66 East. The access is via a poor jeep/4X4 trail from
Meadow Valley Wash. Gold, Silver and Iron, with a gangue of Quartz, in a host of Rhyolite, are present
and all metallics are indicated as primary commodities. The ore body, described as Tabular, striking North
80° East, dipping about 50° Northwest and up to 15 feet wide. The ore body is covered by 4 full Claims
(located in 1912) along the strike of the Vein, for a distance of 6,750 feet. Ore deposition is thought to have
been controlled by a Brecciated shear zone along a normal fault which curves from the Northwest to nearly
East-West. The footwall of the fault zone is exposed for a vertical height of 300 feet, or more, and covered
with hard Quartz where Silicification has occurred along the fault. Brecciated and re-cemented Vein Quartz
along the fault zone cuts Silicified Rhyolite. The wall rock is laced with banded Chalcedonic Quartz. Rock

walls of the structure are green from propylitic alteration and Breccia fragments in the Vein are Silicified in a matrix of Chalcedonic Quartz. Open spaces are coated in needle-like Quartz crystals. Sole Lamellar Quartz, after Calcite, is present. Some of the Quartz may have replaced the original Adularia crystals. Traces of Iron Oxides and Manganese staining are found. The zone is exposed for about 1,000 feet along the strike. An Iron Oxide-stained zone in the immediate footwall of the structure has been stoped in one area. The richest ore, however, was found farther East. Development included a shaft, several adits and prospect pits and the above-mentioned stope. In 1912 the property also had three tunnels, 130, 48 and 25 feet long, respectively. The adits were driven perpendicular to the Vein and all crosscut the structure while the shaft was sunk down-dip. The water level is just a few feet below the adit level. The stream flows along the North side of the Vein; with the sloping Vein surface forming a steep South wall of the canyon. Drill-hole collars and core drilling sites on the property appear to be fairly recent (as of 1984). The property, primarily the Phil Dolan Lease, shipped 5 lots of ore to the Garfield Plant in Salt Lake City between 1933 and 1935. This material assayed 0.93 to 0.97 Ounces of Gold and 3.8 to 413 ounces of Silver per ton. The Iron content ranged from 0% to 2.8%. Geology, in the general area of the site, is described as welded and non-welded Silicic Ash-flow Tuffs. The Land Status, Ownership Category of this past producer is shown as "BLM Administrative Area". In 1933 the main Owner was Mr. E. C. D. Marriage and the Operator was Phil Dolan, Lessee.
See the Easter Mine entry for more information.

Tem Piute Mine (a.k.a. Tem Piute Silver Mine; Old Tem Piute; Ryan; Sterling Mine): (37.35.58N by -115.39.01W - #3) (Lead, Silver, Antimony, Copper, Arsenic)
Coordinates are for the ore body of this surface-underground, past producer.
USGS MRDS Data Base Record 10105796; Released January 1, 1980; Updated, August 1, 1984: The Tem Piute Silver Mine is shown at 37.61246N by -115.64254W, placing it 85 miles West of Caliente, in the Tem Piute Mining District and in the area included on the USGS Tempiute Mountain South 24K, Timpahute Range 100K and Caliente 250K maps. The Public Land Survey System locators are Section 11, Township 4 South, Range 56 East. Silver, Antimony, Copper and Arsenic are present in the Polymetallic Vein Deposit, hosted in Dolomite and Late Devonian Limestone, and all are shown as primary commodities. The ores, which were Oxidized and ran 13 to 81 Troy Ounces per ton came from Siliceous Veins and Replacement deposits along the Breccia zones. Production was about 65 carloads of ore worth $65,600, mainly from the Sterling Claim. The Land Status, Ownership Category of this small, past producer, discovered in 1868 and in production from 1869 to 1935, is shown as "BLM Administrative Area".
USGS MRDS Data Base Record 10149423, Released January 10, 1994: The main entrance to the Tem Piute Mine is shown at 37.61716N by -115.64307W, placing it in the Tem Piute Mining District. The location accuracy, of these coordinates, is shown as +/- 10 meters. The mine is made up of a number of named claims, including the Colchis Claim; Colonel Head Claim, Kinsey Claim, Legal Tender Claim, Old Abraham Claim, Old Tem Piute, Rattler Mine, South End Claim, Standard Claim, Sterling Claim, Sterling Mine, Syandot Claim, and the Thompson Claim. The Public Land Survey System locators are the Southeast ¼ of the Northeast ¼ of Section 11, Township 4 South, Range 56 East. Lead is present and is shown as a primary commodity with Gold, Silver, Zinc and Copper tertiary. The geology, in the area of the main entrance, is described as Dolomite, Limestone and minor amounts of Sandstone and Quartzite. The Land Status, Ownership Category of this surface-underground, past producer discovered and put into production in 1874, is shown as "Private", with Mineral Rights held through "Patented Claims".

Tem Piute Mining District (Don Dale Mining District; Temphute Mining District): (Gold, Silver, Copper, Lead, Mercury)
Description of the District:
Tingley, Joseph V.; "Mining Districts of Nevada"; Nevada Bureau of Mines and Geology, Report 47, Second Edition; 1998; Page 76: In his 1872 work *Preliminary Report Concerning Explorations and Surveys Principally in Nevada and Arizona*, G. M. Wheeler included the area of the Don Dale Mining District as the Southwestern part of a large Tempahute Mining District. Today the Northeastern part of the old Tempahute Mining District is the modern Tem Piute Mining District.
See the Don Dale Mining District and the Tempahute Mining District entries for more information.
Mines Included in the District.
       Tem Piute Mine (Lead, Gold, Silver, Zinc, Copper)

Tempa Mine (a.k.a. NBMG Sample Site 1563; Silver Star Lode): (37.56.55N by -114.04.40W - #3)
(Gold, Silver)
Coordinates are for the main entrance to this underground operation.
USGS MRDS Data Base Record 10046516, Released February 1, 1984: The site of the Tempa Mine is
shown 37.94857N by -114.07861W, placing it in the Eagle Valley Mining District, the Fay Mining District,
in the Gold Springs Mining District and in the area included on the USGS Deer Lodge Canyon 24K and
Caliente 100K and 250K maps. The Public Land Survey System locators are the Northwest ¼ of Section
18, Township 1 North, Range 71 East. It was noted that the mine has good accessibility, lying only about
1½ miles down a trail, West of Hackett's Ranch Road. Gold and Silver, in a gangue of Calcite and Quartz,
hosted in Andesite, are present and both are shown as primary commodities. The ore body is described as
Tabular, striking North 55° East, dipping 85° Northwest and controlled by a Brecciated zone along a North
35° East structural trend. The mine was developed along this zone in an area of pale tan Andesite. White
Quartz and white Calcite Veinlets lace the Brecciated zone. Acicular (needlelike) Quartz crystals fill vugs
and streaks and films of a black, metallic mineral occur in the Veins. A prominent outcrop East of the
headframe shows many fracture surfaces parallel to the strike of the main Breccia zone and is laced with
white Quartz Stringers. The wall rock is a highly Silicified Andesite Breccia. The geology, in the general
area of the site is described as Andesite and related rocks of intermediate composition. The Land Status,
Ownership Category of this occurrence is unknown.

Tempest Mine (a.k.a. Tempest Claim): (38.06.12N by -114.35.10W - #3) (Gold, Silver, Copper,
Bismuth, Iron, Lead)
Coordinates are for the ore body of this underground operation.
USGS MRDS Data Base Record 10104126, Released February 1, 1985; Updated September 1, 1991: The
site of the Tempest Mine is shown at 38.08246N by -114.61195W, placing it in the Bristol-Jackrabbit
Mining District and in the area included on the USGS Bristol Range SE 24K, Wilson Creek Range 100K
and Lund 250K maps. While the area was unsurveyed at the time of the initial entry, as projected from the
East, the Public Land Survey System locators are estimated as Section 32, Township 3 North, Range 66
East. Gold, Silver and Copper are present and are shown as primary commodities with Bismuth and Iron
secondary and Lead tertiary. Notes to file state that the Gold values here are considerably higher than usual
for Bristol ores. The ore body strikes North 80° to 85° East, variably dips from 70° South to 65° to 80°
Southeast and is controlled by fractures, faults, the Tempest Fissure (which strikes North 70° East and dips
60° Southeast) and a North 20° West-trending, vertical fracture zone. The ore is an Oxidized Silver-Copper
material which occurs at the intersection of two fissures. The bulk of the ore taken from the Tempest Mine
is typical of the May Day-Tempest Fissure ores, being an Iron-Silver-Copper product. The Lead ore is
found at the intersection of the North and South mineralizing fissure with the Tempest Fissure, as well as
on the North and South fissure away from the intersection. Ores carrying the highest Lead values were
found at the intersection of the North and South Vein with the East and West Vein. Stopes are mainly on
the Tempest Vein, but in part on the on the North-South fissures near their intersection with the Tempest
Vein. The fissure is filled with crushed Limestone and gouge. Irregular bodies of Oxidized Copper ore
occurred in the hanging wall. At the 150-foot level a body of ocher-colored ore, 4 to 6 feet wide, carried
small amounts of Copper Carbonate. The deposit was developed by a 350-foot-long, inclined shaft, having
4 working levels, stopes, short drifts at the 60, 150 and 200-foot levels and a 350-foot-long drift on the 300-
foot level. On the 300-foot level the ore assayed 40 ounces of Silver per ton and 5% Copper. A number of
assays were also recorded from the Tempest Fissure. One of these showed high levels of Bismuth, ranging
as high as 22%, but only averaging 1% to 2%. On April 7, 1924, an assay showed 0.1 ounces of Gold and
70 ounces of Silver per ton along with 2% Bismuth, 1% Lead, 1% Copper and 42% Iron. Another, undated,
analysis showed 0.025 ounce of Gold and 17 ounces of Silver per ton with 3.5% Copper (8.0% Copper
Oxides), 2% Manganese, 1.5% Zinc, 1% Lead and 28% Iron. Ore from 1914 is said to have averaged 0.025
ounces of Gold and 8.23ounces of Silver per ton along with 10.92% Lead. In 1918 assays showed 0.04
ounces of Gold and 18.13 ounces of Silver per ton. The geology, in the general area of the site is described
as Limestone and Dolomite with locally thick sequences of Shale and Siltstone. The Land Status,
Ownership Category of this past producer is shown as "Private". A 1916 record showed the Operator as the
lessees Nesbit and Bolling.
USGS MRDS Data Base Record 10125251, Released November 14, 1983: The main entrance to the
Tempest Mine is shown at 38.08276N by -114.61114W, placing it in the Bristol-Jackrabbit Mining District.

The location accuracy, of these coordinates, is shown as +/- 10 meters. The Public Land Survey System locators are Section 31, Township 3 North, Range 66 East. Copper is present and is shown as a primary commodity with Silver tertiary. The geology, in the area of the main entrance, is described as Limestone and Dolomite with locally thick sequences of Shale and Siltstone. The Land Status, Ownership Category of this underground prospect is shown as "Private", with Mineral Rights held via "Patented Claims". See the Bristol-Jackrabbit Mine entry for more information.

Temphute Mine and Mill: (37.37.40N by -115.42.17W - #3) (Tungsten)
Coordinates are for a past-producing, processing plant.

Tempahute Mining District (a.k.a. Don Dale Mining District; Tem Piute Mining District): (Gold, Silver, Copper, Lead, Mercury)
Description of the District:
Tingley, Joseph V.; "Mining Districts of Nevada"; Nevada Bureau of Mines and Geology, Report 47, Second Edition; 1998; Page 76: In his 1872 work *Preliminary Report Concerning Explorations and Surveys Principally in Nevada and Arizona*, G. M. Wheeler included the area of the Don Dale Mining District as the Southwestern part of a large Tempahute Mining District. Today the Northeastern part of the old Tempahute Mining District is the modern Tem Piute Mining District.
See the Don Dale Mining District and the Tem Piute Mining District entries for more information.
Mines Included in the District.
    Lincoln Mine
    New Tempiute Mine (Tungsten, Silver, Zinc, Bismuth, Fluorite)
    North Tem Piute Mine (Tungsten, Molybdenum, Silver, Lead, Zinc, Fluorite)
    Schofield Mine (Tungsten, Molybdenum, Zinc, Fluorite)

Tenacity Perlite Mine & Mill: (37.503N by -115.016W - #7) (Perlite)
2009 USGS Active Mines in the US: As of 2009 this Perlite mine and mill was operated by Wilkins Mining and Trucking Co.; the USGS Record IDs were 3543 & 3544.

Thor Mine (a.k.a. Thor Crosscut; NBMG Sample Site 1719; Talisman): (37.53.56N by -114.03.04W - #3) (Gold, Silver, Lead, Copper)
Coordinates are for the main entrance to this underground, exploration prospect.
USGS MRDS Data Base Record 10098664, Released February 1, 1984: The site of the Thor Mine is shown at 37.89858N by -114.05249W, placing it 775 feet West of the Nevada-Utah State Line, about 600 feet West of the Jennie Mine, in the Stateline Mining District, in the Gold Springs Mining District, in the Eagle Valley Mining District and in the area included on the USGS Deer Lodge Canyon 24K and Caliente 100K and 250K maps. The Public Land Survey System locators are the Southeast ¼ of Section 32, Township 1 North, Range 71 East. Gold and Silver, with a gangue of Limonite, Calcite and Quartz are present and are shown as primary commodities. This Comstock-type, Epithermal Vein Deposit is hosted in Andesite. The ore body, the Thor Vein, which is cut off at both ends by post-mineralization faults, is described as Tabular, striking North 20° West to North 15° East, dips 55° East, is about 20 feet thick and traceable for a distance of about 1,000 feet. The mine was developed by 2 open cuts and 2 adits. The Thor Adit, driven East for 240 feet, crosscuts the Thor Vein 65 feet from the portal. At this point, a drift follows the Vein South for 140 feet. At 120 feet from the portal, another drift to the South was driven along a small Calcite fissure. Another adit was driven to cut the Vein South of the Thor Adit. The remains of 3 cabins and the remains of an inclined track from the open cuts to the ore bins were still in existence at the time of the review. Also at the time of the review, in 1983, a truck-supported drill rig was operating near the road junction just North of the mine and there appeared to have been recent bulldozing of dump material and of the outcrop area above and below the workings. The geology, in the general area of the site, is described as welded and non-welded Silicic, Ash-flow Tuffs. The Land Status, Ownership Category of this surface-underground, past producer is shown as "Private".
A detailed description of the ore body was found in the notes; and it reads as follows: "Fragments of Silicified, Iron-replaced Andesite which show fine, vitreous Quartz Veinlets pre-dating Brecciation are contained in massive to prismatic, white Vein Quartz on the dump. Veins have open centers and are typically banded white to clear in appearance. They are typically Iron stained and contain Iron-stained, Quartz-encrusted vugs. Although the Veins contain scarce crystals of fine-grained Pyrite, it is less than

observed in similar Vein material at the Jennie Mine. Dark streaks and lenses in Vein material are likely dispersed Sulfides or possibly Silver-bearing material. Clots of Limonite and Manganese Oxides are found, but not in abundance. Quartz, after Calcite, textures are common. The typical Vein width is 1 to 3 inches with subparallel Veins forming widths up to 1 to 2 feet. A Quartz Vein, observed cutting the Andesite at the portal, strikes North 50° East and dips 80° Northwest. It is typical of the secondary Veins noted throughout the District, which are probably un-mineralized. It is 3 inches wide, vuggy and Iron-stained."
USGS MRDS Data Base Record 10246909, Released January 10, 1994: The main entrance to the Thor Mine is shown at 37.89827N by -114.05192W, placing it in the Stateline Mining District and the Gold Springs Mining District. The location accuracy, of these coordinates, is shown as +/- 10 meters. Gold is present and is shown as a primary commodity with Copper, Silver and Lead tertiary. The geology, in the area of the main entrance, is described as welded and non-welded Silicic, Ash-flow Tuffs. The Land Status, Ownership Category of this surface-underground, past producer is shown as "BLM Administrative Area".

Tim Claims: (37.59.32N by -115.08.46W - #3) (Silver)
Coordinates are for trenching associated with this surface, exploration prospect.

Tinledge Claim (a.k.a. Cinnabar Group; Kyle Siding Prospect): (37.3158N by -114.484W – USGS MRDS) (Gold, Mercury, Manganese)
See the Cinnabar Group and the Kyle Siding Prospect entries for more information.

Tom and Jerry Mine (a.k.a. Culverwell Mine 005): 37.41775N by -114.475W – USGS MRDS) (Gold, Silver, Copper, Tungsten, Lead)
See the Culverwell Mine 005 entry for more information.

Tom Johnson Property (a.k.a. Culverwell 002): (37.25.29N by -114.30.00W - #3) (Silver, Copper, Tungsten, Gold, Iron)
See the Culverwell 002 entry for more information.

Tom Steele: (38.00.45N by -115.41.00W - #3)
Coordinates are for an ore body.

Treasure Hill Mine (a.k.a. Treasure Hill Mines – North End; NBMG Sample Sites 1420 & 1421): (37.55.25N by -114.26.58W - #3) (Silver, Gold, Lead, Iron, Arsenic)
Coordinates are for an ore body.
USGS MRDS Data Base Record 10037337, Released November 1, 1979; Updated December 1, 1984; Updated February 1, 1993: This record refers to a number of mines, scattered along the North side of Treasure Hill, in the area of the Prospect Mountain Quartzite Veins, without individual write-ups. This would include such mines as the Boston-Pinoche, Burke Poorman, Chapman, Ely Mazeppa, Meadow Valley or Meadow Valley Alps, Newark, Washington and Creole, Yuba. The site of the Treasure Hill Mines – North End is shown at 37.92357N by -114.45028W, placing it about ¾ of a mile South of Pioche, in the Pioche Mining District and in the area included on the USGS Pioche 24K and Caliente 100K and 250K maps. The Public Land Survey System locators are Sections 22 & 23 and 26 & 27, Township 1 North, Range 67 East. Silver, Lead and Gold are present and are shown as primary commodities with Zinc secondary and Iron and Arsenic tertiary. Mineralization of this Polymetallic Vein Deposit includes Galena, Sphalerite, Limonite and Jarosite, with a gangue of Quartz, in a host of plutonic rock and Prospect Mountain Quartzite, associated with Cambrian Pioche Shale. The general ore body strikes North 40° to 65° East and dips almost vertically to the Northwest. The Raymond and Ely, Meadow Valley and Burke Veins strike roughly East and West and dip 50° South. The Oxidized Silver ore in the Quartzite decreased in grade Eastward and with depth. The Meadow Valley Vein was mined continuously for 2,000 feet and to a depth of about 1,200 feet. The average thickness of the ore was from 2 to 3 feet. Galena and Sphalerite were increasingly abundant with depth. High-grade Silver-Lead ore was taken from the Yuba dike area. Three, or more, Cross-Veins strike Northeast at a 45° angle to the principal Veins. The "Quartzite Fissures" are filled with a loose ruble of angular Quartzite fragments to Breccia cemented by Lead Carbonate, Limonite and Jarosite. The Quartzite beds strike generally North 15° to 20° West. The workings in the area explore a series of faults and shears at the North end of the Yuba Dike, which appears to have been the principal contributor to the mineralization of the area. Most of the fault Breccia shows milling texture with

Jarosite and Iron and Manganese Oxides coating exposed surfaces. The Quartzite ranges from a white to a rose-gray color with prominent banding. Pods of very-fine-grained, Argentous material, along with Galena and other Sulfides, are distributed throughout the Breccia. Yellow Oxides are also common on exposed surfaces. Abundant Sericite is also present. Locally the Breccia zones are Silicified and abundant Gossan occurs where ore minerals have weathered. Late Opaline Silica is deposited on fracture surfaces and Iron Sulfides have altered to Specular Hematite. Euhedral Quartz crystals line many of the cavities. The Quartz Vein material, which fills fault fissures, is Brecciated and re-cemented with Silica. This material is banded by layers of finely-disseminated grey Sulfides. This area was developed by shafts, adits, trenches, open cuts and prospect pits, but most of the old workings were caved when reviewed in 1983. Total production from the Raymond and Ely Mining Company and the Meadow Valley Mining Company is estimated at $16,049,000 (period values). In 1872 the Mining District shipped $5,151,200 in fine Silver bullion, $127,200 in base bullion and $42,600 in Gold. The geology, in the general area of the site, is described as Limestone and Dolomite with locally thick sequences of Shale and Siltstone. The Land Status, Ownership Category of these surface-underground, past producers is shown as "Private".
USGS MRDS Data Base Record 10271324, Released November 14, 1983: The site of the Treasure Hill Mine (which, it is noted, "may be a collective name for a gaggle of mines on this hill in the Pioche Mining District".) is shown at 37.92356N by -114.45024W, placing it in the Pioche Mining District. The location accuracy, of these coordinates, is shown as +/- 10 meters. The Public Land Survey System locators are the Northwest ¼ of the Northeast ¼ of the Northeast ¼ of Section 27, Township 1 North, Range 67 East. Silver is present and is shown as a primary commodity with Gold and Lead tertiary. The geology, in the area of the main entrance, is described as Limestone and Dolomite with locally thick sequences of Shale and Siltstone. The Land Status, Ownership Category of this underground prospect is unknown.

Tram Workings (a.k.a. NBMG Sample Sites 3014 and 3030) (37.40386N by -115.79697W – USGS MRDS) (Gold, Silver)
USGS MRDS Data Base Record 10125448, Released January 24, 1994: The site of the Tram Workings is shown at the above coordinates placing it in the Groom Mining District and in the area included on the USGS Cattle Spring 24K, Pahranagat Range 100K and Caliente 250K maps. The location accuracy, of these coordinates, is shown as +/- 500 meters. The Public Land Survey System locators are Section 24, Township 6 South, Range 55 East. Gold is present and is shown as a primary commodity with Silver tertiary. Mineralization of this Tabular, Fissure Vein deposit of Hydrothermal origin, includes Hydrated Iron Oxides and Quartz. The geology, in the area of the main entrance, is described as Quartzite and minor amounts of Conglomerate, Phyllitic Siltstone, Limestone and Dolomite. The Land Status, Ownership Category of this Surface-Underground, past producer is shown as "Military Reservation".

True Racket Group (a.k.a. Old Timer Mine): (37.56.11N by -114.29.14W - #3) (Gold, Silver, Zinc, Lead, Copper)
See the Old Timer Mine entry for more information.

Tule Valley: (37.01.40N by -114.12.30W - #3) (Gypsum)
Coordinates are for an ore body.

Tungsten Comet Mines (a.k.a. Comet): (37.53.25N by -114.36.47W - #3) (Lead, Zinc, Tungsten, Silver, Gold, Copper, Manganese, Barite)
See the Comet entry for more information.

Tungsten Prospect: (37.56.27N by -115.34.39W - #3) (Tungsten)
Coordinates are for an ore body.

Unnamed Adit 003: (37.90386N by -114.055W – USGS MRDS) (Gold, Silver)
USGS MRDS Data Base Record 10046517, Released February 1, 1984: The site of the Unnamed Adit 003 is shown at 37.90386N by -114.05471W, placing it 1,000 feet South of the Charley Ross Mine, in the bottom of a gully, in the Eagle Valley Mining District, the Gold Springs Mining District and in the area included on the USGS Deer Lodge Canyon 24K and Caliente 100K and 250K maps. The Public Land Survey System locators are Section 32, Township 1 North, Range 71 East. Gold and Silver are present and are shown as primary commodities. The ore body is described as Tabular, striking North and South,

dipping steeply West, being about 7 feet wide and controlled by the fracturing. Mineralization includes Limonite with a gangue of Calcite and Quartz in a host of Pliocene Volcanic rock. Development includes an adit driven to the West, with 200 feet of workings, which follows the Vein to the South for 70 feet and then turns sharply Northwest for 20 feet. From the partially caved portal, the workings extend 95 feet West. These workings crosscut the main 7-foot Vein, in the portal, as well as 4 smaller Veins which contain Limonite, Calcite and Quartz. The geology, in the general area of the site, is described as Andesite and related rocks of intermediate composition. The Land Status, Ownership Category of this occurrence is unknown.
See the Unnamed Adit 005 entry for more information.

Unnamed Adit 005: (37.90387N by -114.055W – USGS MRDS) (Gold, Silver)
USGS MRDS Data Base Record 10125744, Released January 27, 1994: The main entrance to the Unnamed Adit 005 is shown at 37.90387N by -114.05472W, placing it 1,000 feet South of the Charley Ross Mine, in the bottom of a gully, in the Eagle Valley Mining District and in the area included on the USGS Deer Lodge Canyon 24K and Caliente 100K and 250K maps. The Public Land Survey System locators are Section 32, Township 1 North, Range 71 East. Gold is present and is shown as a primary commodity with Silver tertiary. The ore body is described as a Tabular, Fissure Vein of Hydrothermal origin. Mineralization includes Limonite, Calcite and Quartz. The geology, in the area of the main entrance, is described as Andesite and related rocks of intermediate composition. The Land Status, Ownership Category of this underground prospect is shown as "BLM Administrative Area".
See the Unnamed Adit 003 entry for more information.

Unnamed Adit 007 (a.k.a. NBMG Sample Site 1435): (37.94966N by -114.53414W – USGS MRDS) (Gold, Silver, Zinc, Manganese)
USGS MRDS Data Base Record 10295437, Released January 26, 1994: The main entrance to the Unnamed Adit is shown at the above coordinates, placing it in the Highland Mining District and in the area included on the USGS Highland Peak 24K and Caliente 100K and 250K maps. The location accuracy, of these coordinates, is shown as +/- 100 meters. The Public Land Survey System locators are Section 13, Township 1 North, Range 66 East. Gold is present and is shown as a primary commodity with Silver, Zinc and Manganese tertiary. Mineralization of this Tabular, Fissure Vein deposit of Hydrothermal origin includes Pyrite, Hematite and Hydrated Iron Oxides, Hydrous Manganese Oxides and Quartz. The geology, in the area of the main entrance, is described as Limestone and Dolomite with locally thick sequences of Shale and Siltstone. The Land Status, Ownership Category of this underground prospect is shown as "BLM Administrative Area".
See the NBMG Sample Site 1435 entry for more information.

Unnamed Adit Near the April Fool Mine 008 (a.k.a. NBMG Sample Site 1753): (37.45937N by -114.765W – USGS MRDS) (Gold, Silver, Lead, Copper, Arsenic)
USGS MRDS Data Base Record 10222638, Released January 26, 1994: The main entrance to the Unnamed Adit Near the April Fool Mine 008 is shown at 37.45937N by -114.76524W, placing it in the Delamar Mining District, the Ferguson Mining District and in the area included on the USGS Delamar 24K, Clover Mountains 100K and Caliente 250K maps. The Public Land Survey System locators are Section 1, Township 6 South, Range 64 East. Gold is present and is shown as a primary commodity with Silver, Lead, Copper and Arsenic tertiary. The ore body is a Tabular, Fissure Vein deposit of Hydrothermal origin. Mineralization includes Tetrahedrite, Pyrite, Limonite, Hematite and Quartz. The geology, in the area of the main entrance, is described as Quartzite and minor amounts of Conglomerate, Phyllitic Siltstone, Limestone and Dolomite. The Land Status, Ownership Category of this underground prospect is shown as "Private".
See NBMG Sample Site 1783 entry for more information.

Unnamed Gold Prospect 011: (37.38526N by -115.798W – USGS MRDS) (Gold)
USGS MRDS Data Base Record 1019322, Released January 12, 1994: The main entrance to the Unnamed Gold Prospect is shown at 37.38526N by -115.79807W, placing it in the Groom Mining District and in the area included on the USGS Cattle Spring 24K, Pahranagat Range 100K and Caliente 250K maps. The location accuracy, of these coordinates, is shown as +/- 10 meters. The Public Land Survey System locators are Section 18, Township 6 South, Range 55⁺ East. Gold is present and is shown as a primary commodity.

The geology, in the area of the main entrance, is described as Quartzite and minor amounts of Conglomerate, Phyllitic Siltstone, Limestone and Dolomite. The Land Status, Ownership Category of this underground prospect is shown as "Military Reservation".

Unnamed Gold Prospect 012: (37.92666N by -114.081W – USGS MRDS) (Gold)
USGS MRDS Data Base Record 10246644, Released January 12, 1994: The main entrance to the Unnamed Gold Prospect 012 is shown at 37.92666N by -114.08113W, placing it in the area included on the USGS Deer Lodge Canyon 24K and Caliente 100K and 250K maps. The location accuracy, of these coordinates, is shown as +/- 10 meters. The Public Land Survey System locators are the Southwest ¼ of Section 19, Township 1 North, Range 71 East. Gold is present and is shown as a primary commodity. The geology, in the area of the main entrance, is described as Andesite and related rocks of intermediate composition. The Land Status, Ownership Category of this underground prospect is unknown.

Unnamed Mine 016: (38.12826N by -114.057W – USGS MRDS) (Gold)
USGS MRDS Data Base Record 10198062, Released January 21, 1994: The main entrance to the Unnamed Mine 016 is shown at 38.12826N by -114.05663W, placing it in the area included on the USGS White Rock Peak 24K, Wilson Creek Range 100K and Lund 250K maps. The Public Land Survey System locators are the Southern ½ of Section 8, Township 3 North, Range 71 East. Gold is present and is shown as a primary commodity. The geology, in the area of the main entrance, is described as welded and non-welded Silicic Ash-flow Tuffs. The Land Status, Ownership Category of this underground prospect is shown as "BLM Administrative Area".

Unnamed Perlite Deposit 020: (38.08.44N by -114.20.54W – #3) (Perlite)
Coordinates are for the deposit area of this surface operation.
Decimal Coordinates are 38.14555556N by -114.3483333W.

Unnamed Perlite Deposit 024: (38.08.34N by -114.21.35W – #3) (Perlite)
Coordinates are for the deposit area of this surface operation.
Decimal Coordinates are 38.14277778N by -114.35972222W.

Unnamed Perlite Deposit 026: (38.05.24N by -114.18.36W – #3) (Perlite)
Coordinates are for the deposit area of this surface operation.
Decimal coordinates are 38.090000N by -114.31000W.

Unnamed Perlite Prospect 028: (38.05.23N by -114.20.38W – #3) (Perlite)
Coordinates are for the pit area of this surface, exploration prospect.
Decimal Coordinates are 38.0897222N by -114.34388889W.

Unnamed Perlite Prospect 029: (38.05.24N by -114.20.08W – #3) (Perlite)
Coordinates are for the pit area of this surface, exploration prospect.
Decimal Coordinates are 38.090000N by -114.33555556W.

Unnamed Prospect 030: (37.94078N by -115.578W – USGS MRDS) (Tungsten)
USGS MRDS Data Base Record 10042575, Released February 1, 1980: The site of the Unnamed Prospect 030 is shown at 37.94078N by -115.57837W, placing it near the Western flank of the Timpahute Range, in the Freiberg Mining District, in the Worthington Mining District and in the area included on the USGS Worthington Peak 24K, Timpahute Range 100K and Caliente 250K maps. An approximation of the Public Land Survey System locators is Township 1 North, Range 57 East. Tungsten, as Scheelite and Wolframite, at levels of less than 0.4% WO_3, is present in this Tungsten Skarn Deposit and is shown as a primary commodity. The mineralization is disseminated through a light green Tactite and hosted in the Tactite Skarn which is associated with Granite. The geology, in the general area of the site, is described as Alluvial deposits. The deposit was prospected by a short adit and a shallow shaft; however, a considerable area of Tactite, favorable for Scheelite, remains to be explored. The Land Status, Ownership Category of this occurrence is shown as "Private".

<u>Unnamed Prospect 031 (a.k.a. NBMG Sample Site 791)</u>: (37.29581N by -114.08082W – USGS MRDS)
(Gold, Silver, Manganese, Iron, Gemstones, Copper)
USGS MRDS Data Base Record 10046369, Released June 1, 1984: The site of the Unnamed Prospect 031
is shown at the above coordinates, placing it in the area included on the USGS Dodge Spring 24K, Clover
Mountains 100K and Caliente 250K maps. The mine is not in a Mining District, but the Virgo Mining
District is the nearest. The Public Land Survey System locators are Section 32, Township 7 South, Range
71 East. Gold, Silver, Manganese and Iron are present and all are shown as primary commodities with
Gemstones (Jasper) secondary and Copper tertiary. Mineralization includes the Copper Carbonate
Malachite and Jasper with a gangue of Calcite in a host of Late Triassic Moenkopi Dolomite. The mine was
developed by several, shallow bulldozer cuts which explore an exposed rib of heavily, Iron-stained Jasper
or Jasperoid filling fissures between bedding planes in the Carbonate. Other Stringers and Veinlets of
Jasper or Jasperoid were observed paralleling the bedding West of the main rib. This appears to be Jasper
infilling bedding plane faults rather than a rib of Jasperoid. Carbonates carry pods of crystalline Calcite and
paralleling the beds are "sugary" Calcite Veinlets carrying Oxidized grains of Iron-stained Silica. The main
rib of Jasper is massive to Brecciated and heavily Iron-Oxide stained. The Brecciated Jasper is cemented by
Chalcedonic Silica, white to dark blue, and carries a very fine-grained metallic mineral. Cutting the Jasper
are yellowish-brown, Siliceous Veinlets. Pale green surface coatings, believed to be Malachite, occur on
exposed surfaces. Very minor Manganese Oxide spots the surfaces. This may have been the basis for the
consideration of the site as a Manganese prospect, but this was discounted in 1983. North of the Sample
Site, Rhyolitic Volcanics outcrop, which are strongly bleached and Argillically altered. The geology, in the
general area of the site, is described as welded and non-welded Silicic Ash-flow Tuffs. The Land Status,
Ownership Category of this occurrence is unknown.
See NBMG Sample Site 791 and Unnamed Prospect 037 entries for more information.

<u>Unnamed Prospect 034 (a.k.a. NBMG Sample Site 788)</u>: (37.35558N by -114.061W – USGS MRDS)
(Gold, Lead, Barite)
USGS MRDS Data Base Record 10125160, Released January 26, 1994: The main entrance to the Unnamed
Prospect 034 is shown at 37.35558N by -114.06112W, placing it in the Vigo Mining District and in the
area included on the USGS Dodge Spring 24K, Clover Mountains 100K and Caliente 250K maps. The
location accuracy, of these coordinates, is shown as +/- 100 meters. The Public Land Survey System
locators are Section 9, Township 7 South, Range 71 East. Gold is present and is shown as a primary
commodity with Lead and Barite tertiary. The ore body is a Tabular, Breccia Fill deposit of Hydrothermal
origin. Mineralization includes Galena, Barite, Psilomelane, Sericite and Hydrated Iron Oxides, Calcite and
Quartz. The geology, in the area of the main entrance, is described as Andesite and related rocks of
intermediate composition. The Land Status, Ownership Category of this underground prospect is shown as
"BLM Administrative Area".
See the NBMG Sample Site 788 entry for more information.

<u>Unnamed Prospect 037 (a.k.a. NBMG Sample Site 791)</u>: (37.29578N by -114.08082W – USGS MRDS)
(Gold, Silver, Hafnium, Manganese, Iron)
USGS MRDS Data Base Record 10125533, Released January 26, 1994: Trenching associated with
Unnamed Prospect 037 is shown at the above coordinates, placing it in the area included on the USGS
Dodge Spring 24K, Clover Mountains 100K and Caliente 250K maps. The location accuracy, of these
coordinates, is shown as +/- 100 meters. The Public Land Survey System locators are Section 32, Township
7 South, Range 71 East. Gold is present and is shown as a primary commodity with Silver, Hafnium,
Manganese and Iron tertiary. Mineralization of this Tabular, Replacement deposit of Hydrothermal origin
includes Hydrated Iron Oxides, Calcite and Quartz. The geology, in the area of the trenching, is described
as welded and non-welded Silicic Ash-flow Tuffs. The Land Status, Ownership Category of this surface
prospect is shown as "BLM Administrative Area".
See NBMG Sample Site 791 and Unnamed Prospect 031 entries for more information.

<u>Unnamed Prospect 040</u>: (37.59.25N by -115.07.37W - #3) (Silver)
Coordinates are for the pit area of this surface, exploration prospect.
Decimal Coordinates are 37.99027778N by -115.12694444W.

147

Unnamed Prospect 041: (38.37.00N by -114.44.11W - #3) (Copper)
Coordinates are for the main entrance to this surface-underground, exploration prospect.
Decimal Coordinates are 38.61694444N by -114.73638889W
USGS MRDS Data Base Record 10149450, Released June 14, 1993: The main entrance to the Unnamed
Prospect 041 is shown at 38.61665N by -114.73725W, placing it in the area included on the USGS Milk
Ranch Spring 24K, Garrison 100K and Lund 250K maps. The location accuracy, of these coordinates, is
shown as +/- 100 meters. The Public Land Survey System locators are the Southwest ¼ of the Southeast ¼
of the Southeast ¼ of Section 24, Township 9 North, Range 64 East. Copper is present and is shown as a
primary commodity with Silver, Lead, Zinc and Tungsten tertiary. The geology, in the area of the main
entrance, is described as Limestone and Dolomite with locally thick sequences of Shale and Siltstone. The
Land Status, Ownership Category of this surface-underground, prospect is shown as "BLM Administrative
Area".

Unnamed Prospect 044: (37.99026N by -115.12776W – USGS MRDS) (Gold, Silver)
USGS MRDS Data Base Record 10198028, Released June 17, 1993: The Pit area of the Unnamed Prospect
is shown at the above coordinates, placing it in the area included on the USGS Oreana Spring 24K,
Timpahute Range 100K and Caliente 250K maps. The location accuracy, of these coordinates, is shown as
+/- 100 meters. The Public Land Survey System locators are the Southeast ¼ of Section 33, Township 2
North, Range 61 East. Gold is present and is shown as a primary commodity with Silver tertiary. The
geology, in the Pit area, is described as welded and non-welded Silicic Ash-flow Tuffs. The Land Status,
Ownership Category of this surface prospect is shown as "BLM Administrative Area".

Unnamed Prospect 045: (38.02.38N by -115.07.19W - #3) (Silver)
Coordinates are for the pit area of this surface, exploration prospect.
Decimal Coordinates are 38.04388889N by -115.12194444W.

Unnamed Prospect 048 (a.k.a. NBMG Sample Site 1445): (37.93496N by -114.60664W – USGS
MRDS) (Gold)
USGS MRDS Data Base Record 10222036; Released January 26, 1994: The ore body of the Unnamed
Prospect is shown at the above coordinates, placing it in the Highland Mining District and in the area
included on the USGS Highland Peak 24K and Caliente 100K and 250K maps. The location accuracy, of
these coordinates is shown as +/- 100 meters. The Public Land Survey System locators are the Northwest ¼
of Section 20, Township 1 North, Range 66 East. Gold is present and is shown as a primary commodity.
The geology, in the area of the ore body, is described as Alluvial deposits. The Land Status, Ownership
Category of this surface prospect is shown as "BLM Administrative Area". A 1983 record shows Kerr-
McGee of Oklahoma as holding as interest in the property.
See the NBMG Sample Site 1445 entry for more information.

Unnamed Prospect 050: (37.59.55N by -115.07.40W - #3) (Silver)
Coordinates are for the pit area of this surface, exploration prospect.
Decimal Coordinates are 37.99861111N by -115.12777778W.

Unnamed Prospect 051: (38.02.52N by -115.03.57W - #3) (Calcium)
Coordinates are for the pit area of this surface, exploration prospect.
Decimal Coordinates are 38.04777778N by -115.06027778W.

Unnamed Prospect 052: (38.00.25N by -115.07.18W - #3) (Silver)
Coordinates are for the pit area of this surface, exploration prospect.
Decimal Coordinates are 38.00694444N by -115.12166667W.

Unnamed Prospect Pit 055 (a.k.a. NBMG Sample Site 1426): (37.91746N by -114.45524W – USGS
MRDS) (Gold, Silver, Lead, Barite)
USGS MRDS Data Base Record 10295658, Released January 26, 1994: The pit area of the Unnamed
Prospect Pit is shown at the above coordinates, placing it in the Pioche Mining District and in the area
included on the USGS Pioche 24K and Caliente 100K and 250K maps. The location accuracy, of these
coordinates, is shown as +/- 100 meters. The Public Land Survey System locators are Section 27, Township

1 North, Range 67 East. Gold is present and is shown as a primary commodity with Silver, Lead and Barite tertiary. Mineralization of this Tabular, Breccia Fill deposit of Hydrothermal origin includes Galena, Pyrite, Limonite, Barite and Calcite. The geology, in the pit area, is described as Limestone and Dolomite with locally-thick sequences of Shale and Siltstone. The Land Status, Ownership Category of this surface prospect is shown as "Private" with Mineral Rights held through "Patented Located Claims". See the NBMG Sample Site 1426 entry for more information.

Unnamed Prospects 060: (38.35.45N by -114.43.22W - #3) (Copper, Tungsten, Antimony, Lead)
Coordinates are for the pit area of this surface, exploration prospect.
Decimal Coordinates are 38.59583333N by -114.72277778W.
USGS MRDS Data Base Record 10149301; Released June 29, 1993: The Pit area of the Unnamed Prospects 060 is shown at 38.59575N by -114.72365W, placing it in the area included on the USGS Milk Ranch Spring 24K, Garrison 100K and Lund 250K maps. The location accuracy, of these coordinates, is shown as +/- 100 meters. The Public Land Survey System locators are Section 31, Township 9 North, Range 65 East. Copper is present and is shown as a primary commodity with Tungsten, Lead and Antimony tertiary. The geology, in the Pit area, is described as Limestone and Dolomite with locally thick sequences of Shale and Siltstone. The Land Status, Ownership Category of this surface prospect is unknown.

Unnamed Prospects 061: (38.36.37N by -114.44.23W - #3) (Silver)
Coordinates are for the main entrance to this surface-underground, exploration prospect.
Decimal Coordinates are 38.61027778N by -114.73972222W.

Unnamed Shaft 066 (a.k.a. NBMG Sample Site 1710): (37.92306N by -114.08253W – USGS MRDS) (Gold, Silver, Fluorite, Barite)
USGS MRDS Data Base Record 10149708, Released January 26, 1994: The main entrance to the Unnamed Shaft is shown at the above coordinates, placing it in the Eagle Valley Mining District and in the area included on the USGS Deer Lodge Canyon 24K and Caliente 100K and 250K maps. The Public Land Survey System locators are the Northeast ¼ of the Northeast ¼ of Section 25, Township 1 North, Range 70 East. Gold is present and is shown as a primary commodity with Silver, Fluorite and Barite tertiary. The ore body is a Tabular Fissure Vein of Hydrothermal origin containing Hydrated Iron Oxides, Fluorite, Barite, Calcite and Quartz. The geology, in the area of the main entrance, is described as Andesite and related rocks of intermediate composition. The Land Status, Ownership Category of this underground prospect is shown as "Private", with Mineral Rights held through "Patented Located Claims".

Unnamed Shaft 067 (a.k.a. NBMG Sample Site 1711): (37.92216N by -114.084W – USGS MRDS) (Gold, Silver, Fluorite, Barite)
USGS MRDS Data Base Record 10173588, Released January 26, 1994: The main entrance to the Unnamed Shaft 67 is shown at 37.92216N by -114.08443W, placing it in the Eagle Valley Mining District and in the area included on the USGS Deer Lodge Canyon 24K and Caliente 100K and 250K maps. The location accuracy, of these coordinates, is +/- 100 meters. The Public Land Survey System locators are the Northeast ¼ of the Northeast ¼ of Section 25, Township 1 North, Range 70 East. Gold is present and is shown as a primary commodity with Silver, Fluorite and Barite tertiary. The ore body is a Tabular Fissure Vein of Hydrothermal origin, cemented with Quartz. The geology, in the area of the main entrance, is described as Andesite and related rocks of intermediate composition. The Land Status, Ownership Category of this underground prospect is shown as "Private", with Mineral Rights held as "Patented Located Claims".
See the NBMG Sample Site 1711 entry for more information.

Unnamed Shaft 068 (a.k.a. NBMG Sample Site 1746): (37.48327N by -114.774W – USGS MRDS) (Gold, Silver, Zinc, Lead, Copper, Manganese, Barite)
USGS MRDS Data Base Record 10173594, Released January 26, 1994: The main entrance to the Unnamed Shaft 068 is shown at 37.48327N by -114.77364W, placing it in the Delamar Mining District, the Ferguson Mining District and in the area included on the USGS Delamar 24K, Clover Mountains 100K and Caliente 250K maps. The Public Land Survey System locators are the Northwest ¼ of the Southwest ¼ of Section 25, Township 5 South, Range 64 East. Gold is present and is shown as a primary commodity with Silver,

Zinc, Lead, Copper, Manganese and Barite tertiary. The ore body is described as a Tabular Fissure Vein deposit of Hydrothermal origin. Mineralization includes Pyrites and Hydrated Iron Oxides, Hydrous Manganese Oxides and Quartz. The geology, in the area of the main entrance, is described as Quartzite and minor amounts of Conglomerate, Phyllitic Siltstone, Limestone and Dolomite. The Land Status, Ownership Category of this underground prospect is shown as "BLM Administrative Area".
See the NBMG Sample Site 1746 for more information.

Unnamed Shaft 069 (a.k.a. NBMG Sample Site 1396): (37.95636N by -114.58274W – USGS MRDS) (Silver, Gold, Copper, Lead)
USGS MRDS Data Base Record 10198100, Released February 2, 1994: The main entrance to the Unnamed Shaft is shown at 37.95636N by -114.58274W, placing it in the Highland Mining District and in the area included on the USGS Highland Peak 24K and Caliente 100K and 250K maps. The location accuracy, of these coordinates, is shown as +/- 100 meters. The Public Land Survey System locators are the Southern ½ of Section 9, Township 1 North, Range 66 East. Silver is present and is shown as a primary commodity with Gold, Copper and Lead tertiary. The ore body is really in two parts, a Tabular Fissure Vein and a Tabular Replacement deposit, both of Hydrothermal origin. Mineralization includes Tetrahedrite, Chalcopyrite, Galena, Pyrite, Calcite and Quartz. The geology, in the general area of the site, is described as Alluvial deposits. The Land Status, Ownership Category of this surface-underground prospect is shown as "BLM Administrative Area".

Unnamed Shaft 070 (a.k.a. NBMG Sample Site 1748): (37.46417N by -114.775W – USGS MRDS) (Gold, Silver, Iron)
USGS MRDS Data Base Record 10222071, Released January 26, 1994: The main entrance to the Unnamed Shaft 070 is shown at 37.46417N by -114.77504W, placing it in the Delamar Mining District, the Ferguson Mining District and in the area included on the USGS Delamar 24K, Clover Mountains 100K and Caliente 250K maps. The Public Land Survey System locators are the Southwest ¼ of the Southwest ¼ of Section 36, Township 5 South, Range 64 East. Gold is present and is shown as a primary commodity with Silver and Iron tertiary. Mineralization includes Pyrite, Sericite and Hydrated Iron Oxides along with Quartz and Clay. The ore body is described as a Tabular Shear Zone of Contact Metasomatic origin. The geology, in the area of the main entrance, is described as Rhyolitic intrusive rocks. The Land Status, Ownership Category of this underground prospect is shown as "Private".

Unnamed Shaft 071 (a.k.a. NBMG Sample Site 1417): (37.91886N by -114.438W – USGS MRDS) (Gold, Silver, Lead, Zinc)
USGS MRDS Data Base Record 10222125, Released January 24, 1994: The main entrance to the Unnamed Shaft 071 is shown at 37.91886N by -114.43804W, placing it in the Pioche Mining District and in the area included on the USGS Pioche 24K and Caliente 100K and 250K maps. The Public Land Survey System locators are Section 26, Township 1 North, Range 67 East. Gold is present and is shown as a primary commodity with Silver, Lead and Zinc tertiary. Mineralization includes Galena and Cerussite, Sphalerite and Hemimorphite, Hydrated Iron Oxides and Jarosite, Hydrated Manganese Oxides and Quartz. The ore body is described as a Tabular Fissure Vein of Hydrothermal origin. The geology, in the area of the main entrance, is described as Quartzite with minor amounts of Conglomerate, Phyllitic Siltstone, Limestone and Dolomite. The Land Status, Ownership Category of this underground prospect is shown as "Private", with Mineral Rights held via "Patented Located Claims".
See the NBMG Sample Site 1417 entry for more information.

Unnamed Shaft 073 (a.k.a. NBMG Sample Site 1712): (37.88247N by -114.119W – USGS MRDS) (Gold, Silver)
USGS MRDS Data Base Record 10246393, Released January 26, 1994: The main entrance to the Unnamed Shaft 073 is shown at 37.88247N by -114.11943W, placing it in the Eagle Valley Mining District and in the area included on the USGS Deer Lodge Canyon 24K and Caliente 100K and 250K maps. The location accuracy, of these coordinates, is shown as +/- 100 meters. The Public Land Survey System locators are Section 2, Township 1 South, Range 70 East. Gold is present and is shown as a primary commodity with Silver tertiary. Mineralization of this Tabular, Fissure Vein Deposit, of Hydrothermal origin, includes Pyrite and Limonite, Hydrous Manganese Oxides and Quartz. The geology, in the area of the main

entrance, is described as Rhyolitic flows and shallow intrusive rocks. The Land Status, Ownership Category of this underground prospect is shown as "BLM Administrative Area".
See the NBMG Sample Site 1712 entry for more information.

Unnamed Shaft 075 (a.k.a. NBMG Sample Site 1500): (37.94056N by -114.085W – USGS MRDS) (Gold, Silver)
USGS MRDS Data Base Record 10270878, Released January 27, 1994: The main entrance to the Unnamed Shaft 075 is shown at 37.94056N by -114.08503W, placing it in the Eagle Valley Mining District and in the area included on the USGS Deer Lodge Canyon 24K and Caliente 100K and 250K maps. The location accuracy, of these coordinates, is shown as +/- 100 meters. The Public Land Survey System locators are Section 13, Township 1 North, Range 70 East. Gold is present and is shown as a primary commodity with Silver tertiary. The ore body is a Tabular Fissure Vein of Hydrothermal origin containing Calcite and Quartz. The geology, in the area of the main entrance, is described as Andesite and related rocks of intermediate composition. The Land Status, Ownership Category of this underground prospect is shown as "BLM Administrative Area".
See the NBMG Sample Site 1500 entry for more information.

Unnamed Tungsten Prospects 080: (37.57.29N by -115.36.29W - #3) (Tungsten)
Coordinates are for the main entrance to this underground, exploration prospect.
Decimal Coordinates are 37.95805556N by -115.60805556W.
USGS MRDS Data Base Record 10222046, Released June 14, 1993: The main entrance to the Unnamed Tungsten Prospects is shown at 37.95805N by -115.60897W, placing it in the area included on the USGS Worthington Peak 24K, Timpahute Range 100K and Caliente 250K maps. The location accuracy, of these coordinates, is shown as +/- 100 meters. The Public Land Survey System locators are the Southwest ¼ of the Southeast ¼ of Section 7, Township 1 North, Range 57 East. Tungsten is present and is shown as a primary commodity. The site was developed by a shaft and an adit. The geology, in the area of the main entrance, is described as Limestone, Dolomite, Shale and Quartzite. The Land Status, Ownership Category of this underground prospect is unknown.

Unnamed Prospect 081: (38.02.17N by -115.07.09W - #3)
Coordinates are for the pit area of this surface, exploration prospect.
Decimal Coordinates are 38.03805556N by -115.11916667W.

Unnamed Prospect 082: (38.01.06N by -115.06.53W - #3)
Coordinates are for the pit area of this surface, exploration prospect.
Decimal Coordinates are 38.01833333N by -115.11472222W.

Unnamed Prospect 083: (38.00.58N by -115.07.07W - #3)
Coordinates are for the pit area of this surface, exploration prospect.
Decimal Coordinates are 38.01611111N by -115.11861111W.

Unnamed Prospect 084: (37.59.51N by -115.07.39W - #3)
Coordinates are for the pit area of this surface, exploration prospect.
Decimal Coordinates are 38.00694444N by -115.12166667W.

Upper and Lower Independence Adits (a.k.a. Culverwell 002): (37.25.29N by -114.30.00W - #3) (Silver, Copper, Tungsten, Gold, Iron)
See the Culverwell 002 entry for more information.

Utah Spur Mine (a.k.a. Utah Spur and Rhode Island Queen Claims; Newport-Nevada Property):
(38.00829N by -114.051W – USGS MRDS) (Silver, Gold, Fluorite)
USGS MRDS Data Base Record 10046519, Released February 1, 1984: The site of the Utah Spur Mine is shown at 38.00829N by -114.05139W, placing it straddling the Utah-Nevada border (although most of the property lies in Utah), 2 to 3 miles from the town of Stateline, in the Eagle Valley Mining District, in the State Line Mining District and in the area included on the USGS Rice Mountain 24K, Wilson Creek Range 100K and Lund 250K maps. The Public Land Survey System locators are Section 29, Township 2 North,

Range 71 East. Gold and Silver are present and are shown as primary commodities. Two picked samples were assayed; one showed 82.4 ounces of Silver and 0.44 ounces of Gold per ton and the second 13.34 ounces of Silver and 0.06 ounces of Gold per ton; both having a gangue of Fluorite and Quartz. This Comstock-type, Epithermal Vein deposit is hosted in Tertiary to Miocene Andesite and Rhyolite. The Andesite is on the hanging wall side of the Vein, but the contact is not well-defined except where there is evidence of faulting. The Deposit is described as Tabular, striking Northwest to Southeast, dips 70° to 80° Northeast, is about 50 feet thick and traceable for about 1,000 feet. This Vein has a bold, strong outcrop and consists of both Quartz and Silicified Rhyolite and/or Andesite. Most of the Vein is barren, with 2 mineralized locations identified. At one of these an open cut exposed a small body of high-grade Silver ore; the Silver occurring as specks and bands of black Sulfide (believed to be Argentite) in the Quartz. The deposit was developed by an open cut, a 75-foot vertical shaft located several hundred feet Southeast of the open cut, a second 75-foot vertical shaft and a 200-foot long crosscut tunnel (now caved). Most of the workings are on the Utah side. The geology, in the general area of the site is described as welded and non-welded Silicic Ash-flow Tuffs. The Land Status, Ownership Category of this past producer discovered in 1896 is shown as "Private. A 1921 record shows the Owner as Mrs. Jesse Knight of Los Angeles, California.

Uvada Tunnel: (37.90108N by -114.052W – USGS MRDS) (Gold, Silver)
USGS MRDS Data Base Record 10046518, Released February 1, 1984: The site of the Uvada Tunnel is shown at 37.90108N by -114.05165W, placing it in the Eagle Valley Mining District, in the Gold Springs Mining District and in the area included on the USGS Deer Lodge Canyon 24K and Caliente 100K and 250K maps. The location accuracy, of these coordinates, is shown as +/- 250 meters. The Public Land Survey System locators are the Eastern ½ of Section 32, Township 1 North, Range 71 East. Gold and Silver are present and are shown as primary commodities. Mineralization, of this Tabular ore body, with a gangue of Hematite and Calcite, is hosted in Pliocene Andesite. This area of massive Calcite (25 feet wide at 50 feet from the face) may correlate with the Spar Vein in the Jennie Mine. The Uvada tunnel was driven to crosscut the Thor and Jennie Veins. A Calcite Vein containing Manganese Oxides, which is believed to be the Jennie Vein, was intersected 520 feet from the portal and a drift was driven along the Vein 170 feet to the North. Of 3 Vein samples only one showed Gold and Silver; it assayed 0.065 ounces of Gold and 0.1 ounces of Silver per ton. The geology, in the general area of the site, is described as welded and non-welded Silicic Ash-flow Tuffs. The Land Status, Ownership Category of this underground occurrence is shown as "BLM Administrative Area".
USGS MRDS Data Base Record 10198243, Released January 27, 1994: The main entrance to the Uvada Tunnel is shown at 37.90107N by -114.05162W, placing it in the Eagle Valley Mining District. The location accuracy, of these coordinates, is shown as +/- 250 meters. This record shows Gold present and as a primary commodity with Silver tertiary. Mineralization of this Tabular, Fissure Vein deposit of Hydrothermal origin includes Hematite, Hydrous Manganese Oxides and Calcite. The geology, in the area of the main entrance, is described as welded and non-welded Silicic Ash-flow Tuffs. The Land Status, Ownership Category of this underground occurrence continues to be shown as "BLM Administrative Area".

Valley View Property: (38.02.15N by -115.41.07W - #3) (Uranium)
Coordinates are for an ore body.

Vermiculite Deposit: (36.58.15N by -114.20.13W - #3) (Vermiculite)
Coordinates are for an ore body.

Vesuvius (a.k.a. Bristol-Jackrabbit Mines): (38.08107N by -114.617W – USGS MRDS) (Silver, Copper, Lead, Zinc, Gold, Manganese)
See the Bristol-Jackrabbit Mine entry for more information.

Vesuvius Mine: (38.08163N by -114.615W – USGS MRDS) (Silver, Gold, Lead, Zinc, Copper, Iron)
USGS MRDS Data Base Record 10047180, Released February 1, 1985: The site of the Vesuvius Mine is shown at 38.08163N by -114.61501W, placing it a short distance Northeast of the National Mine, on the South side of Tramway Hill, about midway between the Inman and Gypsy Shafts, in the Bristol-Jackrabbit Mining District and in the area included on the USGS Bristol Range SE 24K, Wilson Creek Range 100K

and Lund 250K maps. While the area is unsurveyed, if projected from the East, the Public Land Survey System locators are estimated to be Sections 31 & 32, Township 3 North, Range 66 East. Silver and Gold are present and are shown as primary commodities with Lead, Zinc, Copper and Iron tertiary. Mineralization of this Polymetallic Replacement Deposit included Malachite and Chrysocolla, with a gangue of Calcite, in a host of Late Cambrian Limestone. The ore body, which was controlled by the intersection of fissures in favorable host rock, is described as Tabular to Irregular, striking 5° North and being about 3 feet thick. The ore was the result of the replacement of Limestone at the intersection of an East-West fissure and several North 25° East-striking fissures along which a 200-foot tunnel was driven. This tunnel included a 50-foot vertical winze, driven in 1924, about 75 feet of drifting at its bottom and a large inclined stope on and above the tunnel level. Crossing the stope is a strong, vertical North 5° West fissure on which the winze was sunk. Replacement occurs South of a North 60° East fissure which dips 45° South and is exposed in the back of the lower, flat, room-like stope. The largest ore body was West of a North 16° West vertical fracture on the East side of the stopes. Two bedded deposits, about 50 feet apart, are exposed in the workings. The lower of the two consist of Lead and Zinc Carbonates replacing the dark Limestone in an area 2 to 3 feet thick with a regular floor but irregular roof, in an area that is about 50 by 100 feet in size. The upper bed, which is 18 to 24 inches thick, carries much more Copper Carbonate than does the lower bed, and also contains both Lead and Zinc Carbonates. It occurs above and South of the North 60° East fissure and West of the vertical North-South break. Both of these deposits occur in nearly pure Limestone, above beds of very dense, Siliceous, Shaley Limestone. A 1914 assay of the ore produced shows 9.76 Ounces of Silver and 0.02 Ounces of Gold per ton, 7% Copper, 7.5% Zinc and 4.95% Lead. The property is shown as idle in 1924. The geology, in the general area of the site, is described as Limestone and Dolomite with locally thick sequences of Shale and Siltstone. The Land Status, Ownership Category of this past producer is shown as "Private".

Vigo Area/Vigo Mining District (a.k.a. Bull Valley Mining District; Tule Springs Mining District):
(Manganese, Gold, Lead, Barite)
Description of the District:
Tingley, Joseph V.; "Mining Districts of Nevada"; Nevada Bureau of Mines and Geology, Report 47, Second Edition; 1998; Page 238: The Vigo Mining District includes Bull Valley Wash, in the area between Lime Mountain and the Utah State Line. The Vigo Mining District was formerly known as the Bull Valley Mining District. The Vigo Mining District is sometimes extended Southward to include the Tule Springs Hills, although the Southern part of the Tule Springs Mining District is sometimes included in the Gourd Springs Mining District."
Mines Included in the District:
      NBMG Sample Site 788 (Gold, Barite, Lead)
      Unnamed Prospect 034 (Gold, Lead, Barite)

Viola Claim/Viola No.1 Claim (a.k.a. Viola Claims; Johnnie): (37.23637N by -114.313W – USGS MRDS) (Silver, Zinc, Lead, Copper, Molybdenum, Antimony, Strontium, Manganese, Fluorite, Barite) See the Cherokee Mine and Jonnie entries for more information.

Viola Mining District (a.k.a. Bradshaw Mining District; Carp Mining District; Cherokee Mining District; Long Valley Mining District; Pittsburg Mining District): (Silver, Gold, Lead, Zinc, Copper, Manganese, Mercury, Fluorspar, Barite)
Description of the District:
Tingley, Joseph V.; "Mining Districts of Nevada"; Nevada Bureau of Mines and Geology, Report 47, Second Edition; 1998; Page 239: The Viola Mining District is believed to be the modern equivalent of the historic Long Valley Mining District, which was identified in the March 20, 1873 edition of the *Territorial Enterprise* as being about 40 miles Southeast of Pioche. The current Viola Mining District extends along the Southern flank of the Clover Mountains, from Meadow Valley Wash, near Cottonwood Canyon, on the West, East to the Blue Nose Peak area. It was discovered sometime in the 1860s and rediscovered in 1917. It was initially organized in 1902, but was basically inactive until 1917. In 1995, Walter R. Averett, in his book *Through the Rainbow Canyon*, described a Mining District, which he called the Bradshaw, which he indicated was discovered in 1928 and was located it about 19 miles Northeast of Carp. What he identified would have been in the Eastern part of the modern Viola Mining District.
Mines Included in the District:

Cinnabar Group (Mercury, Manganese)
Johnnie (Gold, Silver, Mercury, Barite)

<u>Virginia-Louise (a.k.a. Virginia Louise Mine)</u>: (37.54.03N by -114.28.18W - #3) (Silver, Lead, Manganese, Gold, Zinc)
Coordinates are for the ore body of this underground, past producer.
See Prince Consolidated entry and *Goodwin's Weekly, November 23, 1912,* article for more information.

Walker (a.k.a. Cinch Mine): (38.35.58N by -114.41.29W - #3) (Tungsten, Gold, Silver)
See the Cinch Mine entry for more information.

<u>Walker Tungsten</u>: (37.07.30N by -114.42.55W - #3)
Coordinates are for an ore body.

<u>Walker Unit Claims</u>: (38.03.40N by -114.28.15W - #3) (Uranium)
Coordinates are for the ore body of this surface, exploration prospect.

<u>Wall Street Prospect</u>: (37.16.27N by -114.23.30W - #3) (Lead, Zinc)
Coordinates are for the main entrance to this underground, exploration prospect.

Washington and Creole Mine (a.k.a. Washington and Creole): (37.92357N by -114.448W – USGS MRDS) (Silver, Zinc, Lead)
USGS MRDS Data Base Record 10046449, Released April 1, 1984: The site of the Washington and Creole is shown at 37.92357N by -114.44834W, placing it on Treasure Hill, in the Pioche Mining District and in the area included on the USGS Pioche 24K and Caliente 100K and 250K maps. The location accuracy, of these coordinates, is shown as +/- 50 meters. The general Public Land Survey System locators are Township 001 North, Range 67 East. Silver, Lead and Zinc are present and all are shown as primary commodities. Mineralization includes Galena and Sphalerite in a host of Prospect Mountain Quartzite. The ore body strikes East-West and dips 50° South. The geology, in the general area of the site, is described as Quartzite and minor amounts of Conglomerate, Phyllitic Siltstone, Limestone and Dolomite. The Land Status, Ownership Category of this past producer is shown as "Private".
USGS MRDS Data Base Record 10174187, Released January 27, 1994: The main entrance to the Washington and Creole Mine is shown at 37.92356N by -114.44834W, placing it in the Pioche Mining District. The location accuracy, of these coordinates, is shown as +/- 100 meters. This record shows the Public Land Survey System locators as Section 27, Township 1 North. Range 67 East. Silver is present and is shown as a primary commodity with Lead and Zinc tertiary. Mineralization of this Hydrothermal, Fissure-Vein deposit includes Galena and Sphalerite. The Land Status, Ownership Category of this surface-underground, past producer, which first produced in 1872, is shown as "Private". Mineral Rights are held through "Patented, Located Claims".

West End Group (a.k.a. West End Mine; West End Group No. 10): (37.56.33N by -114.28.52W - #3) (Gold, Silver, Lead)
Coordinates are for the ore body of this past producer.
USGS MRDS Data Base Record 10046450, Released December 1, 1982: The site of the West End Group is shown at 37.9419N by -114.48251W, placing it in the Pioche Mining District and in the area included on the USGS Pioche 24K and Caliente 100K and 250K maps. The Public Land Survey System locators are Section 16, Township 1 North, Range 67 East. Gold, Silver and Lead, with a gangue of Quartz, in a host of Late Cambrian, Pioche Shale, are present and are shown as primary commodities. The ore body is described as a Tabular, 6-inch-wide, banded Quartz Vein, controlled by a bedding plane. An assay done on 200 tons of ore yielded the following; $6.00 in Gold (period values) and 7 ounces of Silver per ton along with 6% Lead. The geology, in the general area of the site, is described as Limestone and Dolomite with locally thick sequences of Shale and Siltstone. The Land Status, Ownership Category of this past producer is shown as "Private". A 1932 record shows the Owner as Pioche Mines Company.
USGS MRDS Data Base Record 10270799, Released January 10, 1994: The main entrance to the West End Mine is shown at 37.94306N by -114.48194W, placing it in the Pioche Mining District. The location accuracy, of these coordinates, is shown as +/- 100 meters. The Public Land Survey System locators are the

Southwest ¼ of the Northwest ¼ of the Southwest ¼ of Section 16, Township 1 North, Range 67 East. This record shows Gold present and as a primary commodity with Silver and Lead tertiary. The geology, in the area of the main entrance, is described as Quartzite along with minor amounts of Conglomerate, Phyllitic Siltstone, Limestone and Dolomite. The Land Status, Ownership Category of this underground, past producer is unknown.

West Manhattan Vein Prospect (a.k.a. NBMG Sample Sites 1390 through 1392): (37.95776N by -114.597W – USGS MRDS) (Gold, Silver, Lead, Copper)
USGS MRDS Data Base Record 10149434, Released January 26, 1994: The main entrance to the West Manhattan Vein Prospect is shown at 37.95776N by -114.59694W, placing it in the Highland Mining District and in the area included on the USGS Highland Peak 24K and Caliente 100K and 250K maps. The location accuracy, of these coordinates, is shown as +/- 100 meters. The Public Land Survey System locators are Section 8, Township 1 North, Range 66 East. Gold is present and is shown as a primary commodity with Silver, Lead and Copper tertiary. Mineralization of this Tabular, Replacement deposit of Hydrothermal origin includes Malachite, Hydrated Manganese and Iron Oxides, Calcite and Quartz. The geology, in the area of the main entrance, is described as Limestone and Dolomite with locally thick sequences of Shale and Siltstone. The Land Status, Ownership Category of this underground prospect is shown as "BLM Administrative Area".
See the NBMG Sample Sites 1390 through 1392 entries for more information.

Western Mine: (37.25.05N by -115.38.25W - #3) (Antimony)
Coordinates are for an ore body.

Whale (a.k.a. Chisholm): (37.56.02N by -114.29.08W - #3) (Lead, Silver, Gold)
See the Chisholm entry for more information.

Wheeler: (37.59.30N by -114.22.15W - #3) (Manganese)
Coordinates are for an ore body.

Whipple Silver King (a.k.a. Silver King Mine): (38.17.29N by -114.52.37W - #3) (Gold, Silver, Lead)
Coordinates are for the ore body of this underground, past producer.
USGS MRDS Data Base Record 10246890, Released January 19. 1994: The main entrance to the Whipple Silver King is shown at 38.29135N by -114.87775W, placing it in the area included on the USGS Silver King Well 24K, Wilson Creek Range 100K and Lund 250K maps. The Public Land Survey System locators are the Northwest ¼ of Section 14, Township 5 North, Range 63 East. Gold is present and is shown as a primary commodity with Silver and Lead tertiary. The geology, in the area of the main entrance, is described as Dolomite, Limestone and minor amounts of Sandstone and Quartzite. The Land Status, Ownership Category of this underground, past producer is shown as "BLM Administrative Area".
See the Silver King Mine entry for more information.

Whiskey Barrel Mine: (37.55.55N by -114.29.43W - #3) (Lead, Gold, Silver, Copper)
Coordinates are for the ore body of this past producer.

White Cloud Uranium (a.k.a. White Cloud Prospect): (37.48.07N by -114.22.05W - #3) (Uranium)
Coordinates are for the ore body of this development deposit.

White Horse Claim (a.k.a. Gypsy and Helen): (37.57.03N by -114.04.35W - #3) (Gold, Silver, Copper)
See the Gypsy and Helen entry for more information.

White Horse Mine (a.k.a. Blue Bird Claim; Gypsy & Helen Groups; Interocean Claim; Silver Star Claim; Silver Star Mine): (37.56.43N by -114.04.17W - #3) (Gold, Silver)
Coordinates are for the ore body of this underground, past producer.
USGS MRDS Data Base Record 10295457, Released November 14, 1983: The main entrance to the White Horse Mine is shown at 37.94576N by -114.08143W, placing it in the Eagle Valley Mining District and in the area included on the USGS Deer Lodge Canyon 24K and Caliente 100K and 250K maps. The location accuracy, of these coordinates, is shown as +/- 500 meters. The Public Land Survey System locators are

Section 18, Township 1 North, Range 71 East. Gold is present and is shown as a primary commodity with Silver tertiary. The geology, in the area of the main entrance, is described as Andesite and related rocks of intermediate composition. The Land Status, Ownership Category of this underground, past producer is shown as "BLM Administrative Area".
See the Gypsy & Helen Groups and the Silver Star Mine entries for more information.

White Lake No. 2 Claim (a.k.a. Groom Mine): (37.20.45N by -115.46.03W - #3) (Silver, Lead, Zinc, Copper, Gold, Barite)
See the Groom entry for more information.

White Light Claim: (37.53.55N by -114.21.40W - #3) (Iron, Manganese, Uranium)
Coordinates are for the ore body of this underground, exploration prospect.

White Light No. 9 Claim: (37.53.55N by -114.22.50W - #3) (Uranium)
Coordinates are for the ore body of this surface, exploration prospect.

White Sands Placer: (37.50.39N by -114.25.19W - #3) (Pumice)
Coordinates are for trenching associated with this surface, past producer.

Whitmore Mine 001: (36.54.40N by -114.27.37W - #3) (Copper, Lead, Silver)
Coordinates are for an ore body.

Whitmore Mine 002: (36.55.40N by -114.27.55W - #3) (Copper, Silver)
Coordinates are for the main entrance to this surface-underground operation.

Wide Awake and Volcano (a.k.a. Wide Awake Mine; Harney Group; NBMG Sample Site 799; Stindt and Donohue Lease): (37.54.56N by -114.25.50W - #3) (Silver, Lead, Manganese, Zinc, Antimony, Gold, Copper, Iron, Barite, Arsenic)
Coordinates are for the ore body of this underground, past producer.
USGS MRDS Data Base Record 10037339, Released October 1, 1979; Updated December 1, 1984: The site of the Wide Awake Mine is shown at 37.91552N by -114.43112W, placing it 1½ miles South of Pioche, in the Pioche Mining District and in the area included on the USGS Pioche 24K and Caliente 100K and 250K maps. The Public Land Survey System locators are Section 26, Township 1 North, Range 67 East. Silver, Lead and Manganese are present and are shown as primary commodities with Gold, Copper, Zinc, Antimony, Iron, Arsenic and Barite tertiary. Mineralization of this Polymetallic Vein Deposit (Model No. 85) includes Galena and Chalcopyrite, with a gangue of Quartz, Pyrite and Jarosite, in a host of Shale and Late Cambrian, Prospect Mountain Quartzite. The ore body strikes North 10° to 30° West, dips 20° Southeast and is up to 9 feet wide and 18 inches thick. The ore is further described as Thrust Breccia, made up mostly of Argentiferous Lead Carbonate. The mine was developed by over 1,000 feet of workings, which included a 402-foot-deep, 81° inclined shaft, striking Northwest, with a covered headframe and housing and 5 working levels. From the bottom level a 196-foot winze was sunk from a point under the DuPont Shaft. In 1919 about 2,000 tons of ore was shipped which had a value of about $120,000 (at period prices). From the bottom of the winze a drift was run, in the 1920s, which cut the Yuba Dike. In addition to the underground work, a number of peripheral prospect pits and open cuts were developed. Between 1937 and 1944 about 15,000 tons of ore was shipped which had a value of $415,000, although some of this ore came from the nearby Volcano Mine. The majority of the output occurred during the Stindt and Donahue lease. In 1981 the mine was listed as an active Silver-Lead mine, employing 2 people. At the time of the review in 1983, there was no activity at the mine. The geology, in the general area of the site, is described as Quartzite and minor amounts of Conglomerate, Phyllitic Siltstone, Limestone and Dolomite. The ore on the dump consists of Euhedral to Subhedral Pyrite crystals and grains disseminated in massive Sacchoridal Quartz Vein material along with minor Chalcopyrite and Copper Oxide-Stained sheared material. The Quartzite on the dumps also carries very fine-grained, Disseminated Sulfides, as does a green Phyllitic Shale unit found on the dump. Well-formed crystals of Jarosite coat fracture surfaces and Sericite is abundant. Minor Gossan was noted. Quartzite Breccia is cemented with Opaline Silica and is stained with Iron and Manganese Oxides. Late-stage Silica "coats" are exposed on surfaces. Maps show a series of parallel, North 10° to 30° West-striking faults, which are indirectly confirmed by faulting upslope from the

workings. Local sediments have been partially Silicified. Discovered in 1937, the Land Status, Ownership Category of this producer (at the time of the review) was shown as "Private". A 1981 record shows the Owner as Iron Triangle Mines, David I. Witts, President, 5353 1st International Building, Dallas, Texas 75270.
USGS MRDS Data Base Record 10295091, Released January 10, 1994: The main entrance to the Wide Awake Mine is shown at 37.91576N by -114.43024W, placing it in the Pioche Mining District. The location accuracy, of these coordinates, is shown as +/- 10 meters. The Public Land Survey System locators are the Northwest ¼ of the Northeast ¼ of the Southeast ¼ of Section 26, Township 1 North, Range 67 East. Silver is present and is shown as a primary commodity with Gold, Copper, Lead and Manganese tertiary. The geology, in the area of the main entrance, is described as Quartzite and minor amounts of Conglomerate, Phyllitic Siltstone, Limestone and Dolomite. The Land Status, Ownership Category of this underground, past producer is unknown.
See the NBMG Sample Site 799 entry for more information.

Wilkin Popping Plant: (37.36.2N by -114.31.31W - #3)
Coordinates are for a processing plant.

Willow Claim (a.k.a. Groom Mine): (37.20.45N by -115.46.03W - #3) (Silver, Lead, Zinc, Copper, Gold, Barite)
See the Groom entry for more information.

Willow Creek Mining District (a.k.a. Quinn Canyon Mining District): (Fluorite)
Description of the District:
Tingley, Joseph V.; "Mining Districts of Nevada"; Nevada Bureau of Mines and Geology, Report 47, Second Edition; 1998; Page 180: In his 1951 publication, *Mineral Resources of Nye County, Nevada,* V. E. Kral included the primarily Fluorite, Quin Canyon Mining District, the Sharp Mining District (Nye County) and the Willow Creek area (Nye County) in a large Willow Creek Mining District which covered much of the Southern Quin Canyon Mountain Range. This was reinforced by a similar reference in F. J. Kleinhampl and J. I. Ziony's *Mineral Resources of Northern Nye County*, released in 1984. The modern Quinn Canyon Mining District is somewhat reduced in size, but includes areas in both Lincoln and Nye Counties.
See the Quinn Canyon Mining District entry for more information.
Mines Included in the District:

Winner Mine (a.k.a. Pope Mine): (37.54.39N by -114.03.26W - #3) (Gold, Silver, Lead, Copper, Antimony, Fluorite)
See the Pope Mine entry for more information.

Wm and Uc Fractions (a.k.a. Andies Mine): (37.33.35N by -115.44.31W - #3) (Mercury, Silver, Zirconium, Barite)
See the Andies Mine entry for more information.

Wonder Rock Quarry: (37.06.46N by -114.43.38W - #3) (Flagstone)
Coordinates are for the pit area of this surface, past producer.

Woodbutcher (a.k.a. Woodbutcher Mine): (38.02.14N by -114.37.53W - #3) (Gold, Silver, Lead, Copper)
Coordinates are for the ore body of this past producer.
USGS MRDS Data Base Record 10098680, Released February 1, 1985: The site of the Woodbutcher Mine is shown at 38.03274N by -114.63167W, placing it in the Bristol-Jackrabbit Mining District and in the area included on the USGS Bristol Well 24K, Wilson Creek Range 100K and Lund 250K maps. The Public Land Survey System locators are the Southeast ¼ of Section 13, Township 2 North, Range 65 East. Gold and Silver are present and are shown as primary commodities with Lead secondary. Mineralization of this Tabular to Irregular deposit includes Gold and Galena ore, with a gangue of Quartz; of which 62 tons were mined and shipped in 1939. It is noted that high-grade Silver-Lead pockets were found in the Quartz Vein. The geology, in the general area of the site, is described as Limestone and Dolomite with locally thick

sequences of Shale and Siltstone. The Land Status, Ownership Category of this past producer is shown as "Private".

USGS MRDS Data Base Record 10270912, Released January 19, 1994: The main entrance to the Woodbutcher is shown at 38.03276N by -114.63164W. The location accuracy, of these coordinates, is shown as +/- 10 meters. The Public Land Survey System locators are the Northwest ¼ of the Northeast ¼ of the Southeast ¼ of Section 13, Township 2 North, Range 65 East. Silver is present and is shown as a primary commodity with Lead, Gold and Copper tertiary. The geology, in the area of the main entrance, is described as Limestone and Dolomite with locally thick sequences of Shale and Siltstone. The Land Status, Ownership Category of this underground, past producer, which went into production in 1939, is shown as "BLM Administrative Area".

Worthington Mining District (a.k.a. Freiberg Mining District): (Silver, Lead, Zinc, Copper, Tungsten)
Description of the District:
Tingley, Joseph V.; "Mining Districts of Nevada"; Nevada Bureau of Mines and Geology, Report 47, Second Edition; 1998; Pages 93 & 94: The Freiberg Mining District was discovered in 1865 and organized as the Worthington Mining District that same year. It was later reorganized as the Freiberg Mining District about 1869.
See the Freiberg Mining District entry for more information.
Mines Included in the District:
  Unnamed Prospect 030 (Tungsten)

X-Ray Adit (a.k.a. NBMG Sample Site 1397): (37.56.53N by -114.35.12W - #3) (Gold, Silver, Lead, Antimony, Barite)
Coordinates are for the ore body of this underground activity.
USGS MRDS Data Base Record 10098662, Released December 1, 1982: The site of the X-Ray Adit is shown at 37.94802N by -114.58751W, placing it in the Highland Mining District and in the area included on the USGS Highland Peak 24K and Caliente 100K and 250K maps. The Public Land Survey System locators are Section 16, Township 1 North, Range 66 East. Gold, Silver and Lead are present and are shown as primary commodities with Antimony and Barite tertiary. Mineralization includes Galena, Stibnite and Barite with a gangue of Pyrite, Limonite, Hematite, Calcite and Quartz in a host of Late Cambrian Clastic Sedimentary rock and Highland Peak Limestone. The mine was developed by an adit on the Vein, which is now caved, but was at least 500 feet long. Also, there is evidence of an old rail system on the property. The geology, in the general area of the site, is described as Limestone and Dolomite with locally thick sequences of Shale and Siltstone. Discovered in 1925, the Land Status, Ownership Category of this past producer is shown as "Private".
See the NBMG Sample Site 1397 entry for more information.

Yankee Boy: (37.54.03N by -114.36.13W - #3) (Silver, Gold, Lead)
Coordinates are for the ore body of this past producer.

Yon Claims: (37.18.19N by -114.21.04W - #3) (Molybdenum)
Coordinates are for the claim area of this surface prospect.

Yuba Dike Mine: (37.55.27N by-114.26.52W - #3) (Lead, Zinc, Silver, Gold, Copper)
Coordinates are for the ore body of this underground, past producer.

Y-Z Claims (a.k.a. North Tem Piute; Schofield Mine): (37.63218N by -115.624W – USGS MRDS) (Tungsten, Molybdenum, Zinc, Fluorite)
USGS MRDS Data Base Record 10107653, Released January 1, 1980; Updated August 1, 1984; Updated and Edited June 9, 1995: In 1954 & 1955 the Y-Z Company operated the Schofield Mine, under lease, and was the logical source of this reference to the property.
See the North Tem Piute and the Schofield Mine entries for more information.

Zero Tunnel: (37.55.08N by -114.27.03W - #3) (Manganese)
Coordinates are for the ore body of this underground, past producer.

<u>Zinc Occurrence</u>: (37.14.22N by -114.13.30W - #3) (Zinc)
Coordinates are for the ore body of this underground operation.

BIBLIOGRAPHY – LINCOLN COUNTY, NEVADA

1.) *Annual Mining Review and Stock Ledger, 1876, San Francisco, Published by Verdenal, Harrison, Murphy & Company; 76 Pages*:

2.) *Deseret Evening News (Great Salt Lake City, Utah); December 31, 1910; "History and Geology Of Pioche District – Interesting Matter Given in Booklet Issued by Brokerage House – Future Looks Bright"; Page 8; Column 2*:

3.) *Mineral and Water Resources of Nevada; U.S. Geological Survey and the Nevada Bureau of Mines; Senate Document No. 87, 88th Congress, 2nd Session; 1964; Mackay School of Mines, University of Nevada-Reno; 330 Pages*:

4.) *Mohave County Miner; May 14, 1904; Rich Strike of Gold Ore; Page 3; Column 4*:

5.) *Mohave County Mineral Our Mineral Wealth; Black Metal Mines Show Big Production; December 11, 1920, Page 4, Column 3*:

6.) *Nevada Historical Marker #5; On U.S. Highway 93 Alternate in Pioche, Nevada*:

7.) *Nevada Historical Marker #38; On U.S. Highway 93 at Alamo Junction*:

8.) *Nevada Historical Marker #39; On State Route 319 at Panaca Firehouse*:

9.) *Nevada Historical Marker #55; On U.S. Highway 93 in Caliente, Nevada*

10.) *Nevada Historical Marker #57; On U.S. Highway 93, Thirty Miles South of Alamo, Nevada*:

11.) *Pioche Record (The); January 21, 1921; "Around the Mines"; Page 3; Column 1*:

12.) *Tingley, Joseph V.; "Mining Districts of Nevada"; Nevada Bureau of Mines and Geology, Report 47, Second Edition; 1998; 329 Pages*:

13.) *USGS: Geographic Names Information System; US Department of the Interior, US Geological Survey, 12201 Sunrise Valley Drive, Reston, VA, 20192 (Cited through the identification of the associated USGS 250K or 24K, or both, Quad maps)*

14.) *USGS Mineral Resource Data System Database Records (flat file); Produced by the U.S. Geological Survey, as of December 4, 2013; (Reference cited as #3)*:

15.) *USGS Mineral Resources, Online Spatial Data, Material Resource Data System database*:

EPILOG:

I hope you found the book interesting and possibly useful. It seems that many of these mines refer to potential treasurers, which, though highly unlikely to be discovered with 19th century methods, are real possibilities for discovery with 21st century tools. However, always get permission to hunt before proceeding no matter where you are. You never know if you might be trespassing on a claim or in a restricted area. Do your homework first on the area to be hunted and it will make things more pleasant for all involved. Good luck and good hunting!

<u>CORRECTIONS, ADDITIONS and/or COMMENTS</u>

Please understand, at this point the book is a "work in progress" and will be updated relatively frequently so I may not have everything, or even most things loaded yet. Publishing an "in-progress" work is a bit of an experiment for me, but if you have a correction or an addition, please follow the guidelines below. Thank you.

Please forward corrections, recommendations, additions and/or comments, for inclusion in future updates, to the author at:

Ivan L. Herring
202 East Houstonia
Royal Oak, MI 48073

For additions and/or corrections, please include the following:

1.) A reference to the book and specific article,
2.) Recommended additions or corrections;
3.) Any historical information you deem appropriate to support the additions or corrections;
4.) If personal research, please so indicate;
5.) GPS Coordinates for the property (generally the center) or reference points, if you have them;
6.) Written authorization to use and publish the data;
7.) An original signature pledging the accuracy of the data and authorizing use.

Please advise if I can include your name and/or your company's name as a reference and/or by-line.

I am sorry for the "Snail Mail" requirement, but right now an original signature is required (for "legal reasons") to allow the data's publication.